W9-BTI-422

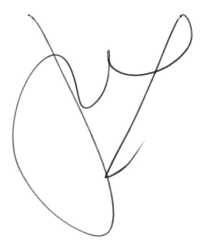

CURRENT ISSUES
IN ECONOMIC DEVELOPMENT
An Asian Perspective

CURRENT ISSUES
IN ECONOMIC DEVELOPMENT
An Asian Perspective

EDITED BY

M. G. QUIBRIA AND J. MALCOLM DOWLING

Published for the Asian Development Bank
by Oxford University Press

HONG KONG
OXFORD UNIVERSITY PRESS
OXFORD   NEW YORK
1996

3 2280 00741 0061

Oxford University Press

Oxford New York
Athens Auckland Bangkok Bogota Bombay
Buenos Aires Calcutta Cape Town Dar es Salaam
Delhi Florence Hong Kong Istanbul Karachi
Kuala Lumpur Madras Madrid Melbourne
Mexico City Nairobi Paris Singapore
Taipei Tokyo Toronto

and associated companies in
Berlin Ibadan

Oxford is a trademark of Oxford University Press

First published 1996
This impression (lowest digit)
1 3 5 7 9 10 8 6 4 2

© *Asian Development Bank 1996*

All rights reserved. No part of this publication may be reproduced, stored in
a retrieval system, or transmitted, in any form or by any means, without the
prior permission in writing of the Asian Development Bank.
Exceptions are allowed in respect of any fair dealing for the purpose
of research or private study, or criticism or review.
Enquiries concerning reproductions
should be sent to the Asian Development Bank.

This book is sold subject to the condition that it shall not, by way
of trade or otherwise, be lent, re-sold, hired out or otherwise circulated
without the publisher's prior consent in any form of binding or cover
other than that in which it is published and without a similar condition
including this condition being imposed on the subsequent purchaser.

Published for the Asian Development Bank by
Oxford University Press

British Library Cataloguing in Publication Data
available

Library of Congress Cataloging-in-Publication Data
Current issues in economic development / edited by M.G. Quibria and
J.M. Dowling, Jr.
    p.   cm.
    "The outcome of the Third Asian Development Bank Conference on
Development Economics held in Manila on 23-24 November 1994"—Pref.
    Includes bibliographical references and index.
    ISBN 0 19 587759-4
    1. Asia—Economic policy—Congresses.   2. Economic development—
Congresses.   3. Political corruption—Asia—Congresses.
I. Quibria, M.G. (Muhammad Ghulam)   II. Dowling, J. Malcolm (John
Malcolm)   III. Asian Development Bank.   IV. Asian Development Bank
Conference on Development Economics (3rd: 1994: Manila, Philippines)
HC412.C87 1996   96-9745
338.95—dc20   CIP

Printed in Hong Kong
Published by Oxford University Press (China) Ltd
18/F Warwick House, Taikoo Place, 979 King's Road,
Quarry Bay, Hong Kong

Contents

Contents

Contents

List of Tables

List of Figures

Foreword

Development economics is an active area of economic research. In recent years, the discipline has made significant intellectual advances that have deep ramifications for economic policies.

In 1992, the Bank initiated a series of conferences on development economics—the Asian Development Bank Conference on Development Economics—to discuss recent advances in the field and their empirical significance and policy implications for developing Asia.

This volume represents the proceedings of the Third Conference held in 1994. The authors discuss a wide range of important development issues facing Asian developing economies. It is hoped that these papers will contribute to a deeper understanding of the issues involved and the means to their resolution.

The views and opinions expressed in this volume are those of the authors and do not necessarily reflect the views and policies of the Asian Development Bank.

Vishvanath V. Desai
Director and Chief Economist
Economics and Development Resource Center
Asian Development Bank

Preface

This volume is the outcome of the Third Asian Development Bank Conference on Development Economics, held in Manila on 23-24 November 1994.

The conference, attended by a diverse group of participants including academic economists, policymakers from developing countries, staff of the Asian Development Bank, and representatives of other international organizations, was inaugurated by Bank President Mitsuo Sato. A number of senior officials of the Bank, namely, Vishvanath V. Desai, K. F. Jalal, John D. Taylor, Eiichi Watanabe, and Yang Weimin, chaired the various sessions of the conference.

The success of the conference owes in large part to the efforts and encouragement of Vishvanath V. Desai, Director and Chief Economist of the Economics and Development Resource Center, and the help and cooperation of a large number of senior Bank officials, including A. I. Aminul Islam, Jungsoo Lee, and Maurice Bauche. The economists of the Economics and Development Resource Center and its supporting staff, particularly Zenaida M. Acacio, Anita P. Angeles, Lutgarda T. Labios, and Ellen J. Reyes, provided indispensable assistance in organizing the logistics of the conference.

The papers presented in this volume address a number of basic themes relating governance, democracy, corruption, and ethics; regulation, privatization, the trading environment, and economic development; and population, the environment, and agricultural development. They highlight important analytical and policy issues that have come to occupy the center stage of current development debate not only in Asia but also in other parts of the world.

Given the diverse backgrounds of the participants, the essays presented at the conference were kept nontechnical. The level of technicality prescribed for the papers was equivalent to that of a typical paper in the *Journal of Economic Perspectives*, which addresses nonspecialized economists. It is therefore hoped that the present volume will be accessible to a wide readership interested in the issues of economic development.

This book has benefited from the comments and suggestions of many individuals. Those who served as designated discussants at the conference include Mohamed Ariff, J. Malcolm Dowling Jr., Peter

Drysdale, Fan Gang, Naved Hamid, Frank Harrigan, Alejandro N. Herrin, Tobias Hoschka, Morimitsu Inaba, Nurul Islam, Yoshihiro Iwasaki, Hun Kim, Rahul Khullar, Jeffrey Liang, C. S. Liu, Linda Low, Srinivas Madhur, Elisabetta Marmolo, Dilip Mookherjee, Cayetano Paderanga, Ernesto M. Pernia, M. G. Quibria, Sarfraz Khan Qureshi, Narhari Rao, Salim Rashid, Rei Shiratori, Ammar Siamwalla, Byung-Nak Song, R. Swaminathan, and Chiang Yeong-Yuh. The cooperation and conscientiousness of the authors in promptly meeting the deadlines and addressing the comments of the reviewers and the editors are also gratefully acknowledged.

The following individuals deserve special thanks for their cooperation and dedication to work. Katherine Elizabeth Kirk, the editorial consultant, did a superb job of editing the book on a tight schedule, and assisted in the preparation of the subject index. Additional editorial assistance was provided by Cherry Lynn T. Zafaralla, who also undertook the responsibility of coordinating the production of this volume. Elizabeth E. Leuterio provided valuable research assistance, along with Ma. Luisa Sinco who also prepared the author index. A team of expert secretaries, including Anita Angeles, Helen Buencamino, and Eva Olanda worked conscientiously on successive drafts of the book.

M. G. Quibria and J. Malcolm Dowling
Asian Development Bank

List of Contributors

ABHIJIT BANERJEE
Professor of Economics
Massachusetts Institute of Technology

ROBERT J. BARRO
Professor of Economics
Harvard University

J. MALCOLM DOWLING
Assistant Chief Economist
Asian Development Bank

RODNEY E. FALVEY
Professor and Head,
Department of Economics
Australian National University

MOTOSHIGE ITOH
Professor of Economics
The University of Tokyo

BASANT KAPUR
Professor and Chairman,
Department of Economics and Statistics
National University of Singapore

M. ALI KHAN
Abram G. Hutzler Professor of Economics
Johns Hopkins University

JEAN-JACQUES LAFFONT
Professor of Economics
Universite des Sciences Sociales de Toulouse

MARC L. NERLOVE
Professor of Agricultural and Resource Economics
University of Maryland

M. G. QUIBRIA
Senior Economist
Asian Development Bank

T. N. SRINIVASAN
Samuel C. Park, Jr. Professor of Economics
Yale University

PAUL STREETEN
Emeritus Professor of Economics
Boston University

Terms and Abbreviations

ADE	Asian developing economy
AFTA	ASEAN Free Trade Area
APEC	Asia-Pacific Economic Cooperation Forum
ASEAN	Association of Southeast Asian Nations
CCII	Cross-country intra-industry
EER	Effective exchange rate
EU	European Union
FAO	Food and Agriculture Organization
FTA	Free trade areas
GATS	General Agreement on Trade in Services
GATT	General Agreement on Tariffs and Trade
GDP	Gross domestic product
GNP	Gross national product
GNS	Group of Negotiations on Service
GSP	Generalized System of Preferences
HYV	High-yielding varieties
ILO	International Labour Organisation
IMF	International Monetary Fund
MFA	Multifibre Arrangement
MFN	Most favored nation
NAFTA	North American Free TradeAgreement
NIE	Newly industrializing economy
NGO	Nongovernmental organization
OECD	Organisation for Economic Co-operation and Development
PTA	Preferential trading agreement
R&D	Research and development
TFP	Total factor productivity
TRIMS	Trade-related aspects of investment measures
TRIPS	Trade-related aspects of intellectual property rights
UNCTAD	United Nations Conference on Trade and Development
UNDP	United Nations Development Programme
UNICEF	United Nations Children's Fund
WTO	World Trade Organization

Note: References to Taipei,China are to the island of Taiwan.

Chapter 1

An Overview

M.G. Quibria and J. Malcolm Dowling

A sian developing countries are at various stages of economic, political, and social development. While these countries include some of the most dynamic economies of the world, they also include some of the poorest. South Asia, with per capita incomes varying between $160 and $820,[1] has the highest incidence of poverty compared to any other region of the world.[2] On the other hand, the newly industrializing economies (NIEs) of Asia, whose per capita incomes have increased nearly sixteenfold in the past 40 years, are the world's most dynamic economies. With per capita incomes varying between $7,670 and $19,310, NIEs have virtually eliminated the scourge of poverty. Asian developing countries also diverge widely in terms of social indicators of development. The NIEs have achieved almost universal literacy[3] (the adult literacy rates in the Republic of Korea; Taipei,China; Hong Kong; and Singapore are 97, 91, 91, and 90 percent, respectively), and the other Southeast Asian countries are not far behind (Philippines 94, Thailand 94, Viet Nam 92, Indonesia 83, and Malaysia 82 percent). In contrast, South Asia (with the exception of Sri Lanka) is still struggling with a massive illiteracy problem (the adult literacy rates in India, Pakistan, Bangladesh, and Nepal are 50, 36, 36, and 26 percent, respectively). The overall educational attainments, defined in terms of expected years of schooling for various Asian developing countries, show a pattern similar to those for literacy rates.[4] The NIEs and Southeast Asian countries have generally the highest educational attainments (13 years for a citizen in Taipei,China; 14 years for the Republic of Korea; 12 years for Singapore; and 11 years for Hong Kong), followed by the Southeast Asian economies (11 years for the Philippines, 10 years for Indonesia, 9 years for Thailand). Once again, South Asian countries lie on the lower rungs of the educational ladder. The higher levels of social development of the NIEs and the Southeast Asian countries, as compared with South Asia, are also reflected in higher life expectancies, lower infant mortality rates, and better nutritional status.

1

The Asian developing countries diverge widely in terms of size and natural resource endowments. Some of these countries are continental in size, such as the People's Republic of China (PRC) and India, and some are no more than city states, such as Hong Kong and Singapore. The fastest growing NIEs are essentially resource-poor, while there are others such as Malaysia, Philippines, and Thailand that are relatively well endowed with natural resources. In terms of population size, the two most populous economies of the world are located in developing Asia, e.g., PRC and India, while Bangladesh has the highest population density (with 768 persons per square kilometer). Despite the large population, developing Asia is by and large self-sufficient in food. Indeed, some of the countries, such as Thailand and Viet Nam, are net exporters of food, particularly rice.

The Asian developing countries, which are at different stages of economic development, have followed a variety of policy regimes. The NIEs, having successfully exploited the dynamism that is inherent in the private enterprise and competitive market-based system, achieved full-fledged industrialization in the shortest time in human history. (Incomes per capita in these countries grew from below $500 in 1965 to as high as $19,310 in 1993). On the other hand, a number of countries, such as Cambodia, PRC, Lao People's Democratic Republic, and Viet Nam, have experimented with socialist economic systems, only to find that socialism is relatively inefficient at generating rapid growth and bringing about economic development. These economies are now at various stages in dismantling the socialistic economic apparatus and replacing it with the market system. Similarly, many market economies in Asia, particularly those in South Asia, had, and continue to have, large public sectors. These public sectors include not only those activities that provide public goods, but also other infrastructural activities (the so-called "commanding heights" of the economy), i.e., banks, insurance companies, public utilities, and transportation. Both the transitional economies and the public sector-dominated market economies have adopted an active program of privatization, that is, transfer of public-owned companies to the private sector. Different countries have followed different speeds and strategies for privatization and have achieved different degrees of success. While there are lessons to be learned from the experiences of different countries, one should also keep in mind that policies in different societies are subject to various degrees of autonomy. This degree of autonomy is determined by history, polity, and society, and does not afford the same degree of manipulation in every society at a particular point in time.

While the economies differ in terms of their domestic economic policies, they also differ in terms of their policies to the external sector (with a concomitant impact on industrialization). Many economies, especially those in South Asia, have pursued, and persisted with, a policy of import substitution. This policy, which discriminates against exports, created a protectionist umbrella for import-substituting industries and, in conjunction with other restrictive policies, largely deterred any foreign investment in South Asia. On the other hand, the NIEs, which have pursued a policy of nondiscrimination against exports, succeeded in creating an environment that has attracted a good deal of foreign investments. (However, much of the foreign investment that has flowed to Southeast Asian economies was induced by considerations of geographical proximity: relocation of labor-intensive industries from high-wage, capital-surplus NIEs to neighboring low-wage, capital-poor developing economies.)

The economic success of the Asian developing economies, in particular the NIEs and other rapidly growing Southeast Asian countries, is attributed largely to their success in exploiting the opportunities provided by the open international trading environment and their persistence with outward-oriented policies. The conclusion of the Uruguay Round of Multilateral Trading Agreements has deep ramifications for the future of Asian developing economies. The Agreements open up further opportunities as well as challenges for these economies. If the NIEs and other Southeast Asian countries can remain as competitive as before, they will be able to achieve equally strong economic performance in the future. Similarly, if South Asian countries and the transitional economies can improve their international competitiveness, by deepening their economic reforms and liberalizing their economies, they will also no doubt be able to benefit from the Agreements and improve on their past economic performance.

The Asian developing economies have undertaken different degrees of trade liberalization to open up their economies, either unilaterally or at the prodding of various multilateral development agencies. In any case, these economies are substantially more open than those of other regions. The NIEs have taken the lead in this matter, followed by the dynamic Southeast Asian economies. In recent years, the traditionally inward-looking South Asian economies have adopted wide-ranging economic measures aimed at trade liberalization, including liberalization of the current account (i.e., free convertibility of their currencies). The People's Republic of China is not far behind in this respect: it has undertaken a wide array of reforms to open up its economy, including some measure of convertibility of its currency.

Reforms in Asian developing economies are not confined to economic policies, they also encompass political and social dimensions. In developing Asia, as in the rest of the world, there are ongoing debates as to the proper role of government, and how to improve its performance. In many Asian countries, reforms to improve the efficiency of the public sector and the quality of the civil service are either being implemented or being contemplated. As a result, areas that have previously been in the exclusive domain of the government now belong to the private sector, many public sector industries have undergone managerial reforms, and the role of the civil service has been significantly reduced.

Most Asian developing countries, many of which were under autocratic rule until recently, are presently under democracy, although the quality and content of these democracies differ. While the trend toward democracy is unambiguous, whether democracy can be strengthened in any individual country is difficult to predict, as it will be largely determined by its success in delivering economic and social development. As experiences of Asian developing countries illustrate, the relationship between democracy and development is a complex one. It is well known that the successful economic efforts of the NIEs have not always been accompanied by democratic political regimes; it is equally well known that democratic India has had relatively lackluster economic success compared not only to the NIEs but also to PRC, which has had an autocratic political system throughout. However, at a lower stage of economic development, it is possible that democracy with a free press is more successful in ensuring the welfare of the masses—particularly in averting famines or mass starvation—than an autocratic regime as the experiences of India and PRC indicate (Sen 1983).

While it is assumed that democracy with its transparency and accountability will be prone to less corruption than autocracy with its lack of transparency and public accountability, the proposition is far from established. Similarly, it is widely assumed that corruption is a serious drag on economic development, but this hypothesis is not necessarily empirically well supported. The high-performing economies of Asia that have mesmerized the world are also characterized by high degrees of corruption. A recent survey of corruption in 41 countries, compiled by Transparency International and University of Goettingen (1995), indicates that the high-performing economies of Asia, with the exception of Singapore, also rank high in the corruption list, with Indonesia and PRC being in first and second positions, respectively. These types of surveys, which are essentially based on subjective evaluations by business executives, suffer from numerous methodological deficiencies. While one should not take the ordinal rankings in these surveys too seriously, one can nonetheless conclude safely that those economies which rank high in the list are clearly by any imagination not paragons of virtue. The superstar of the world economy, PRC, which has registered double-digit growth for the last

two decades, has also been the subject of a good deal of discussion in relation to corruption. In PRC now,

> Corruption is more than a poison afflicting Chinese busi-
> ness life. It is pervasive bureaucracy; traditions of family,
> clan, and local loyalty; the huge profits to be made in an eco-
> nomy growing at 13% a year—all contribute to a culture of
> gifts, kickbacks, and *guanxi* (connections) (*Economist* 1994).

While the interrelationship between corruption and development is complex, it is widely acknowledged that unbridled and pervasive corruption
can pose a serious constraint to economic development when scarce economic resources are diverted from productive to unproductive pursuits.[5]

Finally, it is suggested that, in a broader context, ethics, values,
and cultural norms have an important bearing on economic development.
(From this perspective, corruption is essentially an aberration from normative societal values and ethics.) In recent years, much has been made
of Asian values as the basis of its economic dynamism, which are assumed to be more communitarian, more family-oriented, less individualistic, and less self-centered. Some have emphasized the Confucian dimension of the East Asian culture as the source of its economic strength.
However, it may be noted that there is no homogenous East Asian culture
by any criterion. There are some common elements across societies
(many of which may very well run beyond the Asian borders), but there
are also many diverse elements. While Confucian values prevail to various
degrees in various Southeast and East Asian countries, there are Islamic,
Buddhist, Hindu, and Christian cultural values in these societies as well.
Predominantly Islamic countries such as Malaysia and Indonesia have
also achieved considerable success in economic development. Also, if
Confucian values are the critical element for the economic development of
East Asia, the question remains, Why did these societies remain economically underdeveloped for hundreds of years? Notwithstanding these questions, the interrelationship between ethics, values, and culture on the one
hand and economic development on the other is an important issue, and
the Asian experience may shed significant light on this subject.

The essays presented in this volume deal with a diverse set of developmental issues ranging from governance, democracy, corruption, and
ethics, to population, natural resources, and the environment; from policy
issues dealing with deregulation and privatization to trade liberalization
and the impact of the Uruguay Round. While the essays were prepared
largely from the perspective of Asian developing economies, the issues

addressed and the policies discussed have wider developmental ramifications. These essays should therefore appeal to a much wider audience of
development experts and policy makers. The following provides a brief
review and summary of the papers presented in this volume.

Governance, Democracy, Corruption, and Ethics

Economists have extended their range of interests to many new
fields in the last two decades. Areas that were traditionally earmarked for
political scientists, sociologists, and other social scientists, are now rou-
tinely being explored by economists, a tendency appropriately labeled as "the
imperialism of economics" by Stigler (1984).[6] These explorations by economists with their distinctive analytical approach have led to fruitful new
insights and the papers discussed in this section bear testimony to that.

In Chapter 2, Paul Streeten considers some select aspects of political economy relating to governance.[7] His approach is broad, and the
paper provides a quick review of various levels of governance, from global
at the international level to nongovernmental organizations at the local
level. The thesis that pervades Streeten's various arguments is that there
is a definite role for a strong state in order to make markets work. This
role includes providing a legal framework, maintaining law and order
(including the enforcement of contracts), ensuring macroeconomic stability, and encouraging competition in the economy. In addition to the above
set of functions, the role of the government includes "the construction of
physical and human infrastructure, universal health care, environmental
protection, promotion, and dissemination of basic research, promotion of
racial justice, public schooling, the rehabilitation of cities, the rehabilitation of the homeless, the provision of jobs and so on".

The provision of social services by the state, according to Streeten,
is required not only because of the contribution such services make toward human capital formation and thereby higher production, but also
because of the contribution they make toward advancing human welfare.[8]
However, state provisions of such services are often limited by fiscal constraints. Streeten contends that the limits are often due not to lack of resources but to lack of political support in favor of such expenditures (due
to the constraints of the political economy). Reallocation of resources from
military expenditures and large prestige projects, reduction of big losses
of public enterprises, and checking capital flight, some or all these in combination should generate enough resources for social sector investment.

In this connection, it may be noted that the issue of the optimal
size of the government and the public sector is perhaps difficult to resolve
on a priori theoretical grounds. It is largely a function of the political, so-

cial, and economic structures of the economy. Moreover, there is a real tradeoff between "expanded" and "effective" government, and the threshold for this tradeoff is reached at an earlier stage in developing countries because of the paucity of administrative resources in these countries. As inadequate financial resources constitute a critical constraint, most governments of developing countries need to prioritize their social services to determine which ones to provide and which ones to leave for the private sector.[9]

Streeten then turns to the issue of the interrelationship between democracy and development, a topic that Robert Barro also addresses in Chapter 3 but from a more quantitative perspective. While his review of the literature suggests that democracy is incompatible with rapid growth at low levels of development, Streeten stops short of drawing such a conclusion. Rather, he concludes by quoting Hirschman that "political and economic progress are not tied together in any easy, straightforward, functional way".

Streeten touches on a number of other aspects of governance, sometimes briefly but always with insight. With respect to transition economies, he concludes that "phased gradual reforms on wide fronts are to be preferred in many situations to shock therapy, in spite of the risks; that economic liberalization should precede political liberalization; that institutional liberalization should precede stabilization, and stabilization precede the freeing of markets, including foreign trade liberalization". This conclusion is immensely sensible if countries have the political and social flexibility to undertake the required range of reforms and to determine their timing. But most countries are devoid of the luxury of such options. The imperatives of the political economy often compel them to take decisions one way or the other, thereby making the observed choice the optimal choice in the revealed preference sense.

Streeten's paper concludes with a section on the politics of foreign aid—in which he argues for humanitarian programs and expresses skepticism on the policy conditionality that accompanies foreign aid—followed by a summary of theories of the state. In the latter, he contrasts the state as the platonic guardian, implicit in the writings of Pigou, Tinbergen, Meade, and others, with the state as the predator, explicit in the writings of the Chicago economists and economists belonging to the public choice school.[10] However, Streeten concludes that both these extreme views are wrong: "The state does not optimize anything, neither public welfare nor self-interest. It compromises, attempts to resolve conflicts, manages bargain between groups, and occasionally leads."

While Streeten explores the issue of governance and development from a general qualitative perspective, Barro focuses on the interrelationship between democracy and development from a quantitative econometric perspective. He uses the extended neoclassical growth model, in which the long-run level of per capita output depends on an array of choice and environmental variables, as a framework for his empirical analysis. Private choice variables in Barro's analysis include fertility and saving rates, while government chooses tax rates, extent of distortion of the market, maintenance of the rule of law and property rights, and degree of political freedom. The model implies the possibility of convergence in the level of economic development among countries due to diminishing rates of return and technology diffusion. However, this convergence is conditional, and since countries are likely to be poor because the underlying determinants of their steady states are unfavorable, the model does not predict a strong inverse correlation between growth rates and starting positions. The author contrasts Africa with East Asia, where convergence has failed to materialize in one and has taken place in the other.

Barro distinguishes political freedom from economic freedom and, using econometric analysis, shows that the latter is more beneficial to economic growth. He concludes that maintenance of the rule of law, small government consumption, free markets, and developed human capital enhance economic growth. However, once these variables are held constant, the contribution of democracy to growth becomes less obvious. The author challenges the widespread Western view that political and economic freedom are mutually reinforcing. His analysis suggests a nonlinear relationship between democracy and economic growth: relaxation of the political regime to some degree can enhance growth, but beyond a certain point there is a weak negative correlation between growth and democracy. Barro derives the conclusion that the middle level of democracy is most favorable to growth. The surprising result is that the lowest level comes as second best for economic growth, and the highest comes only as third.

Barro tests the "Lipset hypothesis" that prosperity tends to inspire democracy, and finds strong support for the hypothesis. His analysis shows that an improvement in the standard of living, measured in terms of real per capita gross domestic product, life expectancy, and education, increases considerably the probability of political institutions becoming increasingly democratic over time. This leads the author to characterize political freedom as a luxury good. The author, citing the examples of sub-Saharan African countries, argues that political freedom is not sustainable in less-developed countries. Barro also uses his analysis to predict political developments in selected countries over time. His predictions include the potential for an increase in the level of democracy in Taipei,China and Indonesia due to their remarkable success in economic growth, and for a decrease in the level of democracy in Bangladesh and Pakistan due to their sluggish economic performance.

Barro draws two important policy implications from his analysis: first, increased democracy is not the key to economic development; and second, political freedom is hard to sustain if it is not commensurate with the level of economic development of the country. From these, the author draws a more general conclusion that industrialized countries would contribute more to the economic growth in developing countries by promoting economic freedoms, such as enhanced property rights and free markets, rather than exporting their democratic political systems. However, Barro is careful not to draw strong causational inferences and stops short of recommending the authoritarian type of regime as a way of enhancing economic growth, being aware that dictatorships represent a rather "risky investment".

While the econometric analysis of Barro is interesting and provocative, it is not based on a well-specified theoretical model. How far this lack of a well-specified model reduces the importance of the results reported in the paper as well as their policy significance is subject to controversy.[11] In this context, in his review of the empirics of so-called new growth theory, Srinivasan (1994, 61) notes, "Cross-country regressions testing some version or the other of the convergence hypothesis relating to *aggregate* growth, whatever other insights they have yielded about the growth process, by their very nature have little to say about the microeconomic forces that together generate the aggregate outcome." Leaving aside the technical issues, on a more general level, it has been argued that the emphasis on the tradeoff between democracy and economic growth, as analyzed by Barro, is somewhat misplaced.[12] The really important policy issue from the perspective of developing countries is whether there is a tradeoff between democracy and economic welfare. It is argued that if democracy leads to a more egalitarian income distribution and a better standard of living for the majority, this outcome is preferable to one with an inequitable income distribution and a lower standard of living, even if that entails a sacrifice in terms of economic growth. Similarly, an issue of practical policy interest to many developing countries is how to enhance economic growth and welfare without sacrificing the level of democracy and political freedom already attained.

As democracy represents an important dimension of governance, corruption in the economy reflects another. In Chapter 4, Abhijit Banerjee attempts to evaluate different options for reforms to eliminate or reduce corruption. He starts with identifying the costs of corruption, which include revenue losses from tax collection, inefficient allocation of publicly provided private goods, distortions in private agents' incentives, and direct misappropriation of funds by government agents. The author considers options for eliminating or reducing corruption such as an increase in the pay of bureaucrats,[13] better technologies for record keeping, more careful procedures for selecting bureaucrats, and limiting bureaucratic discretion, but concludes that all these options have shortcomings that limit their scope.

However, the core of the paper is addressed to combating corruption in tax collection, wherein Banerjee presents a radical and controversial proposal to replace the current system of tax collection in developing countries with private tax collection, which legalizes profit making by government bureaucrats. Without suggesting that legalization of profit making is a panacea for the problem of collection, Banerjee believes that this option merits serious consideration. The proposal itself consists of the government auctioning the right to collect taxes to private individuals. Any disagreement between the tax collector and the taxpayer gets adjudicated by a tax court, which evaluates the taxpayer's claims and awards him compensation if he is proved correct. Banerjee argues that, as the tax collector does not benefit from forcing taxpayers to go to court, he is better off giving them at least the level of utility they would get by going to court and consequently no one suffers from private tax collection. Banerjee further argues that the success of this mechanism does not depend on all courts being noncorrupt: it works as long as a fraction, however small, of the courts remain noncorrupt. The reason, as Banerjee explains, is that it is always possible to compensate the taxpayer for the possibility that some courts are corrupt by paying a larger compensation when he ends up in a noncorrupt court. Banerjee argues that this kind of scheme does not require a large number of courts or other administrative institutions for its success, as people are not expected to go to court in equilibrium. This scheme will yield the government as much revenue as it would receive if it had honest collectors on its payroll, and the taxpayers would receive the same level of utility as well.[14] The author suggests that, under certain conditions, the government would be able to raise an amount equal to the revenue the tax collectors are expected to collect, less the cost of the tax collectors' time and effort. Alternatively, the government would receive as much revenue as it would if it had honest collectors on its payroll.

Banerjee rightly notes that not all kinds of corruption can be eliminated through privatization, and even if it can be eliminated or significantly reduced,[15, 16] it will not necessarily ensure the social welfare-maximizing outcome. He cites in particular the examples of noneconomic crimes and publicly-provided private goods. Finally, the author discusses the political economy of corruption and underlines the importance of the design of reforms to eliminate corruption. He seems to favor rapid and sweeping reforms, as they have certain advantages over the gradual approach. Since attempts to get rid of corruption are bound to hurt corrupt bureaucrats, they will resist such attempts at reform. However, if the welfare-improving effect of reduced corruption exceeds the amount of bribes being retained under the current system, it may be beneficial to pay off the corrupt segment of the bureaucracy. The author concludes that the real constraint to anticorruption reform is not the economist's ability to come up with a better system, but rather the political economist's ability to design a process that is socially and politically sustainable.

The author analyzes the historical experience with "tax farming" in Europe and concludes that the main reason for its eventual failure was the absence of adequate protection for taxpayers from possible extortion by tax collectors. Given the putative efficiency as well as equity of privatized tax collection, one wonders why is tax farming not more pervasive in modern times? First, the developing countries in general suffer from poorly functioning legal systems and, therefore, one doubts whether a practical system of judicial appeals that will deliver the correct outside option utility levels to citizens can be designed. It is likely that the lack of administrative resources and institutions which makes public tax collection inefficient will also make private collection inefficient. Second, there are possible constitutional and/or moral problems with the abrogation of the right of coercive collection to private enforcers, rather than elected government.[17]

The functioning of a democracy or the functioning of an economic system, including the incidence of corruption, all depends to a large extent on the ethical and value system prevailing in a particular society. But, despite the primordial importance of the ethical and value system to a society, mainstream economists have largely eschewed discussing this issue.[18] In Chapter 5, Basant Kapur deplores this omission, although he notes that there is an emerging literature on the topic.

Kapur notes that the neoclassical economic theory is based on the assumption that economic agents are motivated exclusively by the pursuit of self-interest. He argues that such an assumption is descriptively inaccurate (all economic dealings are not motivated by self-interest), predictively insufficient (many predictions have turned out to be wrong), and prescriptively misleading (in policy matters it relies exclusively on economic measures as opposed to noneconomic measures, such as moral suasion). Kapur argues that there is a strong normative prescription for nonself-interested behavior in "the great religions and cultural traditions of the world", and individuals are influenced to varying degrees by such normative prescriptions. Drawing on the writings of Robert Frank, Kapur argues that individuals are not totally driven by self-interest and rationality, but are often led by emotions. He argues that the exclusive pursuit of self-interest leads to suboptimal economic outcomes on account of the "self-control" problem. The latter also leads individuals to display a bias toward short-term rewards.

Kapur concludes that an extreme focus on material self-interest can result in an inefficient economy compared to one with a more altruistic focus. He argues that the promotion of the "me-first" mentality in the United States has eroded the competitiveness of American high-tech industries, reduced intergenerational savings, and contributed to the weakening of the family. The author states that, in a highly interdependent society, individual actions have manifold consequences that are difficult to predict, and argues that cooperative behavior leads to more efficient outcomes compared to a society that is less coordinated.

Kapur extends his argument on the role of values to the issues of economic development and calls for "balancing of the rationalism (of the West) with the spiritualism (of the East)". Contrasting what he calls the "political economy approach", which views political actors as self-interested, with the (post-war) "Japanese approach," in which "state and society are reinforcing parts of the whole" and where communitarian values are widely prevalent, Kapur thinks that the latter approach is more beneficial to economic development.[19]

The issues raised in the paper are important and deserve serious attention from social scientists. However, these issues are difficult to incorporate and analyze in the context of existing economic analytical frameworks. While economic analysis will be enriched by the incorporation of these concerns, it may also open up the possibility of diluting the present scientific rigor of economics. Without suggesting that concepts such as "ethics" and "values" are without scientific content, Becker (1976) notes that, "they can be tempting materials, for ad hoc explanation of behavior".

Regulation, Privatization, the Trading Environment, and Economic Development

With the collapse of the Soviet empire and the unimpressive performance of public enterprises in the mixed economies, developing countries are increasing efforts to deregulate their economies and have embarked on widespread privatization programs. In Chapter 6, Jean-Jacques Laffont considers the arguments advanced in favor of regulations, and privatization of natural monopolies. While it is widely agreed that some form of public intervention is required in the case of natural

monopolies,[20] there is no universal agreement on the nature of the intervention or the real domain of natural monopolies.

In addressing the issue of the design of regulatory rules and privatization programs for natural monopolies, Laffont notes a number of
specific characteristics of developing countries. These include the high
costs of public funds (the social price of raising one unit of money in a
less developed country [LDC] is much higher than in developing countries); the high cost of auditing (most developing countries lack a properly
functioning auditing system); weak constitutional control (the government
is often more easily captured by special interest groups); difficulties in
committing to long-term contracts (government and regulatory agencies
cannot make credible commitments to long-term policies); and, finally,
poorly developed credit markets (this makes limited liability constraints
more binding).

In the light of the new theories of regulation, which incorporate
asymmetric information and the principal-agent framework,[21] Laffont argues that the characteristics of developing countries suggest that regulations with low-powered incentives be favored, except in the case of a bad
auditing mechanism. The paper suggests a three-stage procedure: in the
first stage, incentive schemes should be strong, as the auditing technology is weak; in the second stage, once auditing is improved, incentive
schemes should be weak; and in the third stage, there should be stronger
incentive schemes. The paper then goes on to review the arguments in
favor of privatization and concludes that the success of privatization of
natural monopolies in developing countries depends crucially on the ability of these countries to establish a credible and stable set of regulatory
rules that can safeguard against future political interference and therefore provide a new incentive structure. The paper argues that setting up
good regulatory institutions is the key to industrial development in developing countries—and even to successful future privatizations.

However, in most LDCs, public utility businesses are owned and
operated by public enterprises in which information asymmetry may not
be a major problem because regulators have easy access to all the necessary information regarding natural monopoly. The major problems facing
public enterprises are: first, their productive efficiency is low, partly reflecting the lack of an appropriate incentive mechanism; second, the
budgetary constraints of the governments preclude provision of subsidies
to balance the budgets of public enterprises; third, the process of determination of tariffs is politicized; fourth, the regulators are "captured" by
their political principals and not by regulated firms; and finally, most
LDCs do not have a well-developed regulatory system or the capacity to

regulate natural monopolies.[22] While the above features of LDCs may give one some additional reasons to pause before trying to implement the three-stage regulatory procedure of Laffont, his fundamental insight that "efforts should be first devoted to setting up good regulatory institutions before envisioning privatization" remains valid.

Finally, as has become increasingly obvious from theoretical and empirical studies, privatization can contribute little to help consumers in the absence of measures to increase competition. Privatization should therefore be viewed as one element of a strategy to introduce greater competition into an industry. It is not an objective that can be justified on a stand-alone basis.[23]

Rodney Falvey, in Chapter 7, provides a comprehensive survey of the literature, both theoretical and empirical, on the relationship between trade liberalization and growth. While the beneficial resource allocation effects of trade liberalization are generally accepted, empirical estimates of those beneficial resource allocation effects were found to be relatively modest. Trade liberalization does more than shift an economy to a more efficient point in the production possibility curve—it influences the range of products produced and traded, the speed with which new products are introduced into the economy, the characteristics of the products traded, the degree of domestic competition, and the extent of rent-seeking in the economy. Falvey notes that recent developments in theory have made it possible to incorporate a wide range of potential resource allocation gains from trade liberalization and opened up the possibility of exploring the dynamic implications of trade reform. In this respect, Falvey notes that the trade policy implications of recent research on growth theory are potentially significant. This theory has developed a number of major explanations for growth, which include externalities associated with capital formation, learning by doing, human resource development, and research and development, all of which can generate dynamic gains (or losses) from trade.

As these theories are based on some form of externality, it is to be presumed that the market outcome will not yield the socially optimum growth. Though trade policy instruments are only second best for dealing with such externalities, Falvey notes that trade policy instruments may be one of the few instruments available to developing countries. Though government action in support of growth-promoting policies is inevitable, until the propositions on growth are adequately verified empirically, Falvey argues that the basic role of trade policy should be to keep open the international channels through which growth-promoting externalities might flow.

In this connection, it may be noted that the impact of trade policy on economic growth depends on the configuration of other policies in effect, and to what extent they complement or offset each other. Thus, the stimulative growth impact of a liberal trade policy may be neutralized by inappropriate macroeconomic policies that entail a high budget deficit, high interest rates, overvalued exchange rates, and inflationary pressure. Similarly, trade and investment policies are often interlinked in a complex way. While trade and investment are substitutes in the case of tariff-jumping foreign investment, they complement each other in a mutually reinforcing manner, as in the case of Asian fast growing economies. The intermingling of the trade and investment booms often makes it impossible to infer which caused what.[24] Indeed, in a recent paper, Rodrik (1994) went so far as to argue that it was not the export orientation that led to the rapid growth of Taipei,China and the Republic of Korea, but the investment boom which took place in these countries that led to their export orientation. He explains that these economies had an extremely well-educated labor force relative to the physical capital stock in the early 1960s, which rendered a high rate of return for physical capital. By substituting and coordinating investment decisions, Rodrik argues, governments managed to maintain a high private rate of return to capital, and that in turn led to an export orientation which enabled a steady increase in the demand for imported capital goods.

T. N. Srinivasan, in Chapter 8, analyzes the possible impact of the implementation of the Uruguay Round of multilateral trade negotiations on Asian developing economies. In particular, the paper summarizes the findings of several studies on the liberalization of international trade in sectors and commodities of special interest to the Asian developing economics, i.e., agriculture, textiles, and apparel. In agriculture, the most important aspect of the agriculture agreement is the replacement of non-tariff barriers by tariff barriers followed by the gradual reduction of the tariffs to a more modest level. However, developing countries are given special and differential treatment which offers them virtual exemption from the commitment to liberalize with respect to a predominant staple in their traditional diet. Srinivasan notes that, while the agreed-upon liberalization is substantial, fairly long implementation periods, special exemptions, and the continuation of many trade-distorting policies make it difficult to infer the short-run and medium-run impact of liberalization. A review of the studies estimating the effects of liberalizing agricultural trade leads Srinivasan to conclude that once "dirty tariffication and exemptions are taken into account, the extent of liberalization is modest. Although there are some changes in sign across models of the effects on particular countries or regions, almost all the estimates for Africa are negative, though not large." In the case of textiles and clothing, trade is essentially regulated by the Multifibre Arrangement (MFA), a system of bilaterally agreed quotas, which will be phased out in three phases over a period of ten years from 1 January 1995. The quantitative estimates from different models which trace the consequences of the MFA phase-out surveyed by Srinivasan indicate that there will be substantial gains for the United States and the European Union (EU) in the developed world, and for PRC and South Asia in the developing world, while Africa and Latin America are likely to lose, according to all estimates. However, Srinivasan cautions that the dismantling of the existing quotas under the MFA will lead to an extremely competitive export market, where poorer Asian exporters may lose out if they cannot compete in cost as well as quality.

The paper also discusses the pros and cons of possible preferential trading arrangements in South and East Asia. Srinivasan's review of the existing trend of "new regionalism" leads him to conclude that this new regionalism covers many more issues than the earlier ones, but that is not in itself a strong argument in its favor. However, given the strong preference for regional arrangements among policy makers, Srinivasan questions whether preferential trading arrangements in South Asia or East Asia, or even the whole of Asia, make sense. Srinivasan, based on his empirical study (coauthored with Canonero) reaches a number of conclusions, which include: unilateral trade liberalization by South Asian countries promises substantial gains; there are substantial gains from intraregional South Asian trade—although the gains are much larger for smaller countries than for bigger ones; and South Asia gains the most by tying up with the EU vis-a-vis other trading blocks, but a strategic tie-up with East Asia may be more beneficial given its growth potential and today's realpolitik. However, Srinivasan emphasizes that, despite considerable benefit from regional integration, the Asian developing countries will benefit the most from unilateral liberalization on a most favored nation basis.

The paper takes a critical look at two areas—the use of trade policy measures to achieve environmental goals, and the linking of market access to performance on nontrade-related objectives, such as labor standards and human rights. Future decisions by the World Trade Organization (WTO) on these issues will have serious implications for Asian developing economies. Srinivasan succinctly states the problem in this regard:

> The demand for linkages between trading rights and observance of standards with respect to environment and labor would seem to arise largely from protectionist motives. If ceded and incorporated into the charter of the WTO, it can only disrupt the healthy growth in international trade along the lines of competitive advantage, retard the development of poor countries and thereby their progress to-

ward better life of their workers and families. Monitoring
the observance of standards could lead to managed trade
and intrusion into the domestic political processes of other
countries (p. 264).

Despite the problems noted by Srinivasan, the clamor for imposing labor
and environmental standards will not die away soon. While urging developing countries to resist attempts by developed countries to use trade
policy "to achieve objectives that do not involve trade", Srinivasan rightly
suggests that the Asian developing countries can increase the credibility
of their ongoing economic reform process "by foregoing special and differential treatment, binding their own tariffs, entering into other commitments on an equal basis with other participants, and by eliminating restrictive regulations that have outlived their utility".

Motoshige Itoh and Jun Shibata, in their paper in Chapter 9, investigate how the pattern of intraregional trade and investment has been
shaped by the domestic economic structure of Japan. They note that
much of the intraregional trade reflects intrafirm trade of intermediate
goods in multinational firms across countries, development imports by
retailers in importing countries, and export of goods by subsidiaries in
host countries to the home country. They use two important products,
electronics and textiles and apparel, where Japan has extensive links with
other East Asian countries, to illustrate their arguments. They note that
the rapid appreciation of the yen prompted the shift of production locations from Japan to East Asian countries, which in turn increased, quite
unexpectedly, the domestic demand in the host countries as well as in
Japan. With the growth of Asian prosperity, third countries also became
important markets for the products of subsidiaries. In sum, Itoh and Shibata conclude that the increasing share of intra-Asian trade in electronics
largely reflects the location strategy of Japan and other industrial countries. Similarly, in the case of textiles and apparel, while Japan did follow
the quota-based MFA system, the pace of imports for textiles and apparel
was rather slow because of the structure of the traditional distribution
system consisting of numerous retailers who deal in small volumes and
large varieties. However, recent deregulation has changed the distribution
system significantly and it now includes a large number of chain stores.
As a consequence, there has been a considerable increase in the share of
imports, as well as in the kind of cross-border division of labor.

The increasing intraregional trade and investment that occurred
in East Asia in the last decade or so was propelled by economic compul-
sions and voluntary actions of these countries, and not by formal free

trade arrangements. Itoh and Shibata consider briefly the implications of regional trading arrangements, which have become increasingly popular in recent years. They note that, given the coverage of Asia Pacific Economic Cooperation (APEC) and the widely divergent economic structures of the participating countries, it is difficult to arrive at an acceptable regional framework for trade liberalization (this has led some countries to pursue unilateral trade liberalization). However, Itoh and Shibata contend that there are positive aspects of having such a framework: the liberalization process may be accelerated within such a framework; concerted liberalization with a formal framework may carry more political credibility; and a regional arrangement may lead to competition for liberalization among countries. There are, on the other hand, a number of valid concerns regarding the desirability of such a regional trading block, as raised by Srinivasan in Chapter 8 as well as by many others.[25] Being fully aware of such concerns, Itoh and Shibata are somewhat circumspect in their conclusion regarding the desirability of such a regional arrangement.

Population, the Environment, and Agricultural Development

Many environmental problems are intergenerational in the sense that they affect primarily the future generations. These problems often derive from the use of modern agricultural technology, the extension of agriculture into environmentally fragile areas to augment food supply, rapid urbanization and industrialization, and the indiscriminate exploitation of exhaustible energy and other natural resources. In Chapter 10, Marc Nerlove explores the interrelationships among population growth, agricultural development, and the quality of environment.

The critical relationship in Nerlove's analysis is between the environment and fertility. Below some threshold level of environmental degradation, the optimal utility-maximizing level of fertility for rational parents is a decreasing function of the probability of child survival. Low survival rates induce high fertility, and the survival rate is a decreasing function of environmental degradation. As long as the elasticity of births with respect to survival is less than minus unity, environmental degradation leads to population growth. But as the environmental degradation continues, this elasticity of birth with respect to survival must itself tend to zero (from below), if only because there are physical limitations on the number of children that a woman can bear. Accordingly, beyond some level of environmental degradation, population growth will begin to decline and degradation will result in a falling population, and continued environmental degradation will lead to greater increases in mortality and morbidity, thereby further reducing the population. This endogenous fertility relationship, in conjunction with the twin assumptions that a larger population degrades the environment and that the environment is not priced, leads to a number of possibilities. First, there is the pathological possibility of no equilibrium between population and environmental quality, which is akin to a catastrophe. Second, if equilibrium exists, there may be several equilibria, some of which are stable. Third, in the case of multiple equilibria, there are two distinct types, one characterized by high environmental quality and low population, and the other by high population and low environmental quality. The depressing conclusion that emerges from the analysis of Nerlove is that the economy will gravitate toward an equilibrium of high population and low environmental quality.

The pessimistic prognosis of Nerlove is based on a model in which there is no technical change or investment. Once these variables are introduced, some scope for optimism emerges. Nerlove argues that the changes associated with agricultural modernization and industrialization are likely to alter the incentives structure for parents in ways that reward investing in the quality of children rather than investing in quantity. As rising nutrition levels and incomes increase life expectancy, returns from investing in children rise. This brings about a fall in fertility, since the cost of having an additional child also rises.

Nerlove concludes that agricultural development is essential to support a growing level of world population at a tolerable level of economic development. Population growth is expected to occur at a diminishing rate over the next five generations before it stabilizes. While stability requires human fertility to decline in response to environmental changes associated with agricultural development, Nerlove argues that fertility may increase, rather than decline in the face of environmental deterioration, and therefore the prospects for stabilization of population at favorable levels of environmental quality are not bright in the absence of social intervention. Nerlove goes on to state:

> Agricultural development and modernization is essential both to the occurrence of the demographic transition and its pace and to the final outcome, that is, to the process by which population stability is finally achieved and to the state of the world and quality of life. Current complacency should not blind us either to the severe distributional problems, short-term, nor to the long-term need for investment in agricultural research and infrastructure to support essential intensification, extension and modernization (p. 339).

While the emphasis of Nerlove on agricultural development is correct, this does not mean that industrialization and urbanization do not have important implications for demographic transition. Nerlove assumes that urbanization and industrialization are largely a benign and stabilizing influence, an assumption that needs to be further explored.[26] Finally, while it is possible to argue about the basic analytical framework of Nerlove—its a priori theoretical plausibility and empirical soundness—it is difficult to argue about the fundamental conclusion of his paper, which underscores the need for controlling population growth.

M. Ali Khan, in Chapter 11, provides an integrated view of the debates under the broad rubric of population and economic development in the past half-century. Khan notes that a concept that has played a key role in the relationship between population and economic development is the demographic transition. The canonical version of this concept, devised in the 1940s, envisions a three-stage growth, from pre-industrial, to transitional, to incipient decline (when modernization has its full impact). An important ramification of industrialization is to bring about a demographic transition. The orthodox version, devised in the 1950s, envisions economic development as the dependent variable and is largely dependent on the success of population control. While the canonical version is more positive, the orthodox version is more normative, emphasizing proactive, contractive technologies. According to the author, the most important distinction between the two versions is that the canonical version emphasizes society while the orthodox form emphasizes the individual. Furthermore, two forms of theory also differ in terms of:

> ...dependent versus independent variables, demand versus supply, first order versus second order variables, positive versus normative criteria, understanding versus control, history versus prediction, and social versus individual categorizations (p. 356).

The second version of the theory received fuller articulation in the neoclassical theory of Becker and his disciples, who provided a micro-foundation for the propositions underlying the demographic transition theory. The neoclassical theory was fully complemented in the work of Easterlin and his collaborators, who combined the demand-side analysis of neoclassical economists with the supply-side analysis of demographers.

Khan notes that Amartya Sen has recently classified the literature along two lines: apocalyptic pessimism and dismissive smugness. The former views population as the cause of much of the poverty and destitution that exists, while the latter views population as largely unrelated to poverty: it is concerned neither with the stock of population nor the speed with which it is growing. According to Sen, as cited by Khan, there are two policy approaches to dealing with population—namely, collaborative versus override. While the former views economic and social development as the solution to the population problem, the latter emphasizes legal and economic pressures to reduce the birth rate. This distinction, as Khan notes, parallels the debate highlighted in the two versions of the demographic transition theory. In matters of policies, Khan is rather circumspect:

> ...(there is) no one win-win tale for the guidance of government and international organizations interested in population planning and policy. Problems of population and economic development come wrapped together; the solutions need balance and judgment; and for maximal efficiency, and sustainability, ought to emerge from within the societies for which they are prescribed (p. 383).

While the above statement is sensible, it provides precious little in terms of concrete policies. However, the conspicuous reticence of Khan to draw concrete policy conclusions highlights his belief that there is no universally effective approach to population control—every country needs to devise its own policies, based on its history, polity, and society. This simple lesson, which is often forgotten in our zeal to derive universal prescriptions for all societies at all stages of economic development, is applicable not only to population issues but also to all dimensions of economic policy making.

This volume presents a set of essays on current development issues that confront the developing economies of Asia. While it is difficult to summarize the policy lessons derived from a collection of essays addressing a disparate set of issues, one general theme that emerges in many of the essays is that institutions—economic, political, and social—do matter and policies need to take full cognizance of the institutional realities, including the stage of economic development of the particular country. If institutions are interpreted in the broadest sense of the term, including international institutions (defining rules of international transactions), the conclusion becomes even more compelling. Countries that adopted appropriate domestic policies to take full advantage of the international institutional realities, encapsulated in the global trading regime, have reaped high economic dividends, and those that failed paid an equally high economic costs in terms of growth, equity, and human welfare.

Acknowledgment

The authors are grateful to Abhijit Banerjee, Robert Barro, Rod Falvey, Frank Harrigan, Motoshige Itoh, Basant Kapur, M. Ali Khan, Jean-Jacques Laffont, Marc Nerlove, Salim Rashid, T. N. Srinivasan, Paul Streeten, and M. A. Taslim for helpful comments on an earlier draft of this paper. However, none of the above are implicated either in the viewpoints or in the remaining shortcomings of the paper.

Notes

1. These figures as well as other per capita income figures below refer to 1993, the latest year for which such data are available. These data are derived from Asian Development Bank (1995).

2. As a region, the incidence of poverty in South Asia fares worse than sub-Saharan Africa. In terms of numbers of people, the magnitude of poverty in South Asia far exceeds those of sub-Saharan Africa and Latin America combined (Chen et al. 1994).

3. The data on literacy are also taken from Asian Development Bank (1995).

4. The following data on expected years of schooling were estimated based on 1992 data on percentage of age group enrolled in education per level for three levels (primary, secondary, and tertiary). Data were based on *World Development Report 1995* (World Bank 1995), *Statistical Yearbook 1993* (UNESCO 1993a), and *World Education Report 1993* (UNESCO 1993b).

5. It is contended that all corruptions are not malign. Becker (1994) contends that corruption can often serve a social purpose by preventing "policies that would cause considerable social harm or promote policies that make an economy more efficient. For example, if all the detailed regulations regarding construction in the status and codes of most US municipalities were followed to the letter, construction would virtually cease because of the cost of compliance" (p. 18).

6. The imperialism of economics is meant to imply the tendency of economics to invade and colonize the usually sacrosanct territories of political science through public choice theory and the economic theory of voting behavior. It may be noted that Stigler himself has made an important contribution to the colonization process.

7. The term governance has been defined in many different ways. These different connotations include democracy or the lack of it; the institutional capacities of government; the role of government in setting universal rules and providing institutions for their enforcement; the culture in the design of political and administrative organizations; and the degree of human rights and the level of military expenditure.

8. As noted by Streeten elsewhere (1994), this viewpoint can be found in the writings of Aristotle to Immanuel Kant, who wrote, "So act as to treat humanity, whether in thine own person or in that of any other, in every case as an end, never as means only." This viewpoint presumably provides the

basis for the human development index of the UNDP's *Human Development Report*.

9. These comments are owed to C. Paderanga.

10.　It is interesting that the Marxist conclusion regarding the state parallels that of the public choice theory, which views the government as "the executive committee of the ruling class".

11. The methodological, conceptual, and statistical problems asso-ciated with cross-country growth empirics have been the subject of a good deal of recent studies. This critique is presented, among others, in Levine and Renelt (1991, 1992); Levine and Zervos (1993a, b); and Srinivasan (1994), who also reviews the problems with data used in these types of exercises.

12. We owe this remark to R. Shiratori.

13. The idea that an increase in the pay of bureaucrats can lead to more honest behavior and less corruption has a long historical antecedent. For example, Lord Clive, as early as 1765 understood the importance of this idea. As cited by Milgrom and Roberts (1992, 252), Thomas Macaulay, describing the efforts of Lord Clive to control corruption among English civil servants employed by the East India company, wrote "Clive saw clearly that it was absurd to give men power and to require them to live in penury. He just concluded that no reform could be effectual which should not be coupled with a plan for liberally remunerating the civil servants of the company."

14. Technically speaking, Banerjee has posed the tax collection problem within the context of a principal-agent problem, where there is a difference in the objectives of an enforcement official (personal revenue collection) and a welfarist government (welfare of citizens). The basic theoretical insight of the paper is that the problem faced by the enforcement official is mathematically dual to that faced by the welfarist government. In other words, if the outside options of the citizens are set right in the privatized regime, then the enforcement official's optimization problem is identical to that of the government. Privatization of tax collection entails no welfare loss at all, relative to the ideal solution desired by the government. Whether privatization can be made to work depends crucially on the appeal and redress mechanisms available to citizens, which help define outside options. This observation is due to D. Mookherjee.

15. While it has been implicitly assumed that all corruptions are malign, perhaps some corruptions are more malign than others. From a policy perspective, it is important to distinguish between different types of corruption. Shleifer and Vishny (1993) note that the case where there are many bribe-seekers with monopoly power with complementary services (land permit, foreign exchange permit, import certificates, etc.) is less preferred to the case where all these services are provided by a single bribe-seeker. The former case, it may be noted here, is equivalent to the problem of double marginalization in industrial organization theory, where monopoly distortions are magnified by the number of monopolists involved in the process. If there is one monopolist in the form of a high-ranking official who can internalize these distortions, the efficiency loss to society would be minimal.

16.　The impact of corruption on economic development has been the subject of a lively debate. Casual empiricism of the fast growing economies of

Asia as well as the writings of such authors as Leff (1964) and Huntington (1968) suggest that corruption may not necessarily impede growth. On the other hand, some recent writings, for example, Mauro (1995), argue that corruption necessarily reduces growth. The cross-country regression results of Mauro (1995) indicate that "corruption lowers private investment, thereby reducing economic growth". He goes on to argue that "if Bangladesh were to improve the integrity and efficiency of its bureaucracy to the level of Uruguay, its investment rate would rise by almost five percentage points and its GDP growth rate would rise by over half a percentage point" (p. 683). Cross-country growth regressions have many problems as indicated earlier. However, in this context, there is an additional data reliability problem, as figures on investment and growth might be underreported because much of the corruption money is often devoted to activities which are either not at all covered or covered inadequately by usual national income statistics.

17. In Italy, the experience with privatized tax collection was less than happy. Driven partly by the perception that the Mafia had infiltrated the tax collection process and partly by the reluctance of private financial institutions to shoulder the image of evictors and sellers of properties of delinquent taxpayers, the practice of private tax collection was discontinued. This information is due to D. Mookherjee.

18. This was succinctly expressed by S. Rashid in his written comments on the paper. On capitalism, he wrote that "the system works by weeding out the inefficient. This is the engine of the system and until mankind is differently constituted, we have no options but to base ourselves on self-interest. Whether or not capitalism as a system is viewed as just depends very much on whether there are active social mechanisms which soften the blows of the market ... . The paradox of capitalism is that a system that is ostensibly immoral and unjust requires as a prerequisite ethical and value systems, that look beyond self-interest as well as individuals who are imbued with a morality that looks beyond self-interest."

19. It is interesting but not surprising that those who have delved into the issue of culture and values and their interrelationship to economic development differ widely in terms of taxonomy of countries. Lodge and Vogel (1987), brought to our attention by Byung-Nak Song, classified countries as mixtures of two extreme types—individualism and communitarianism, with the US being the most representative individualistic country and Japan being the most communitarian country. However, Fukuyama (1995), the famous author of *The End of History and the Last Man*, has recently argued that economic success depends on a supporting culture of trust or "spontaneous sociability". According to Fukuyama, America and Japan both rank high in spontaneous sociability, which accounts for their economic dynamism. In his scheme of countries, People's Republic of China is classified as a low-trust country yet achieved the most rapid growth in recent years among all countries. As is obvious, classification of countries on the basis of culture and values is yet to achieve the status of an exact science.

20. When a firm reaches a monopoly position as a result of increasing returns to scale, it is said to be a natural monopoly. A more formal definition is provided by Baumol et al. (1977, 350): "an industry whose cost function is such that no combination of several firms can produce an industry output

vector as cheaply as it can be provided by a single supplier". Whether an industry is a natural monopoly or not depends on underlying technology and demand factors.

21.   The recent models assume that there is asymmetric information between the regulators and the regulated firms, which have private information that the regulators do not possess. As a result, the new theoretical paradigm of the principal-agent relationship becomes the more appropriate framework for analyzing incentive schemes for managers of the regulated firms.

22. We owe these comments to M. Inaba.

23. We owe these remarks to T. Hoschka.

24. We are indebted to M. Ariff for this observation.

25.   There is a burgeoning literature on regionalism. For a review of the recent literature, see De Melo and Panagariya (1993) and Frankel and Wei (1995).

26. We owe this observation to F. Harrigan.

References

Asian Development Bank, 1995.   *Key Indicators of Developing Asian and Pacific Countries 1995.* Hong Kong: Oxford University Press for the Asian Development Bank.

Baumol, W., E. Bailey, and R. Willig, 1977. "Weak Invisible Hand Theorems on the Sustainability of Multiproduct Natural Monopoly." *American Economic Review* 67(3):350-65.

Becker, G., 1976. *The Economic Approach to Human Behavior.* Chicago and London: University of Chicago Press.

―――, 1994. "To Root Out Corruption, Boot Out Big Government." *Business Week*, 31 January, p.18.

Chen, S., G. Dutt, and M. Ravallion, 1994. "Is Poverty Increasing in the Developing World?" *The Review of Income and Wealth* 40(4):359-76.

De Melo, J., and A. Panagariya, 1993. *The New Dimensions in Regional Integration.* Cambridge, New York and Melbourne: Cambridge University Press.

Economist, 1994. "The Trouble with Caesar's Wife/Corruption in Hong Kong." Vol. 330, 29 January.

Frankel, J.A., and S.J. Wei, 1995. "The New Regionalism and Asia: Impact and Options." Paper presented at the Asian Development Bank Conference on The Emerging Global Trading Environment and Developing Asia, 29-30 May 1995, Manila. Mimeo.

Fukuyama, F., 1995. *Trust: The Social Virtues and the Creation of Prosperity.* New York: The Free Press.

Huntington, S., 1968. *Political Order in Changing Societies.* New Haven: Yale University Press.

Leff, N., 1964. "Economic Development Through Bureaucratic Corruption." *American Behavioral Scientist* 8-14.

Levine, R., and D. Renelt, 1991. "Cross-Country Studies of Growth and Policy: Methodological, Conceptual and Statistical Problems." Working Paper WPS 608. World Bank, Washington, D.C. Processed.

———, 1992. "A Sensitivity Analysis of Cross-Country Growth Regression." *American Economic Review* 82: 942-63.

Levine, R., and S. Zervos, 1993a. "Looking At the Facts: What We Know About Policy and Growth from Cross-Country Regressions." Working Paper WPS 1115. World Bank, Washington, D.C.

———, 1993b. "What We Have Learned About Policy and Growth from Cross-Country Regressions?" *American Economic Review* 83(2): 426-30.

Lodge, G.C., and Vogel, E.F. 1987. *Ideology and National Competitiveness: An Analysis of Nine Countries.* Massachusetts: Harvard Business School.

Mauro, P., 1995. "Corruption and Growth." *Quarterly Journal of Economics* 110(3): 681-712.

Milgrom, P., and J. Roberts, 1992. *Economics, Organization and Management.* New Jersey: Prentice Hall.

Rodrik, D., 1994. "Getting Interventions Right: How South Korea and Taiwan Grew Rich." Working Paper No.4964. National Bureau of Economic Research, Cambridge, Massachusetts.

Sen, A. K., 1983. "Development: Which Way Now?" *Economic Journal* 93(372):742-62.

Shleifer, A., and Vishny, R. 1993. "Corruption." *Quarterly Journal of Economics* 109:599-617.

Srinivasan, T. N., 1994. "Long-Run Growth Theories and Empires: Anything New?" In T. Itoh and A. Krueger, eds., *Lessons from East Asian Growth.* Chicago: University of Chicago Press.

Stigler, G., 1984. "Economics—The Imperial Science?" *Scandinavian Journal of Economics* 86(3):301-13.

Streeten, P., 1994. "Human Development: Means and End." *American Economic Review* 84(2):232-37.

Transparency International and University of Goettingen, 1995. "The Internet Corruption Ranking."

United Nations Educational, Scientific and Cultural Organization (UNESCO), 1993a. *Statistical Yearbook 1993.* Paris: UNESCO Publishing.

———, 1993b. *World Education Report 1993.* Paris: UNESCO Publishing.

World Bank, 1995. *World Development Report 1995.* New York: Oxford University Press.

Chapter 2

Governance

Paul Streeten

66 "G lobal governance" and "the international community" are words that can be used to conceal rather than reveal meanings.[1] Many sins are committed in the name of "global governance" and the "international community". They are part of diplomacy by language, used to "dignify the sordid processes of international politics" (Orwell 1946, as cited in Ohlin 1994). We read of the business community, the black community, the gay community, and, of course, of the international community. Once upon a time community was a word with a meaning. As *The Economist* (1992b) has pointed out, we spoke of Anabaptists, or Mormons, or Benedictine monks, or Oneida as communities. Now it is a tetrasyllabic mouthful attached to everything and signifying nothing. Perhaps the most pernicious community of all is the international one. Regularly invoked, constantly cited, endlessly expected to sort out or to "address" every mess in every country, you might think that such a thing as the international community actually exists. It doesn't. There is something called the United Nations and numberless other bodies that try, for better or worse, to promote economic development, settle refugees, heal the sick, feed the hungry, and count the dead. But a community? You might as well put your trust in fairies.

Similarly, governance. It was politically difficult to complain about corruption, mismanagement, and the abuses of authoritarian regimes, especially in Africa, without giving offense. So a new term was invented whose meaning in relation to the more old-fashioned "government" is not clear. The American Heritage Dictionary defines governance as "the act, process or power of governing; government," the Oxford English Dictionary as "the act or manner of governing, of exercising control or authority over the actions of subjects; a system of regulations". The International Encyclopedia of the Social Sciences has no entry for "governance", nor does the term appear in its index.

Lateef (1992, 295) says that the World Bank defines governance as "the manner in which power is exercised in the management of a country's economic and social resources for development", while Boeninger defines governance as "the good government of society" (Lateef 1992, 295). Landell-Mills and Serageldin (1992, 304) define it as "denoting how people are ruled, and how the affairs of a state are administered and regulated. It refers to a nation's system of politics and how this functions in relation to public administration and law. Thus the concept of governance includes a political dimension." A World Bank (1989, 60) report on Africa defined governance as the "exercise of political power to manage a nation's affairs". Addressing a joint meeting of bankers and business associations in Manila on 18 October 1994, Michel Camdessus defined good governance, the fifth of his conditions "for achieving high-quality growth", as "government that serves the whole of society rather than sectional interests" (IMF 1994). Nelson (1992) distinguishes between three elements of governance: democracy, good government, and development. Perhaps the widest definition of governance is given in the Report of the Commission on Global Governance, *Our Global Neighbourhood* (1995). "Governance is the sum of the many ways individuals and institutions, public and private, manage their common affairs. It is a continuing process through which conflicting or diverse interests may be accommodated and co-operative action may be taken. It includes formal institutions and regimes empowered to enforce compliance, as well as informal arrangements that people and institutions either have agreed to or perceive to be in their interest."

Ohlin (1994) writes in the context of international cooperation, "what some may have in mind is a vague notion of something less than government but more than chaos—regimes of the kind that already exist for many purposes." But one could also interpret it as meaning more than government: including not only global, central, provincial (or, in a federation, state) and local government, but also relations with the civil society, the private profit-seeking sector, market, family, and individual citizen, in so far as these relations bear on governing a society. That civil society and civic culture (as it has evolved through a hundred years) are particularly important for good governance is shown for Italy by Robert D. Putnam's excellent book *Making Democracy Work* (Putnam with Leonardi and Nanetti 1993). He shows that what he calls civic "norms and networks of social engagement" facilitate the working of democracy. The social capital of trust and reciprocity that is invested in norms and networks of civic life is seen as a vital factor of effective government and economic progress. That the market is an important institution of governance does not need stressing nowadays.

Cultural factors, too, determine, as well as are determined by, governance. The Commission on Global Governance defines governance as "the sum of the many ways in which individuals and institutions, both public and private, manage their common affairs" (1994). I shall interpret governance in this wider sense and begin with some remarks on participation in global government, and then proceed downward to national government, including a discussion of the links between democracy and capitalism and the problems of transition, to decentralization to local government, and to the civil society. Next I shall return to the international aspects of governance and finally discuss briefly various theories of the state, selecting one as the most realistic.

Global Participation

There is an important international civil society that cuts across national boundaries: nongovernmental organizations (NGOs), churches, professional organizations, international trade unions, interest groups, citizens' groups, grassroots organizations, action groups, etc. Although they do not wield ultimate authority, they, too, can commit their members. There are also the multinational corporations and international banks. How can the United Nations (UN) agencies and other international and regional organizations become more responsive to the demands and needs of the global civil society and be more participatory? We hear a lot about the need for greater participation, but the international organizations preaching this gospel have not been outstanding in practising what they preach. It has something to do with the blind spot of auto-professionalism, a subject on which I keep a secret file. It contains facts and reflections about dentists' children having bad teeth, marriage guidance counselors suffering from broken marriages, management experts being unable to manage their own affairs, evaluators never evaluating their own activities, and the auditors of the Royal Economic Society having to refuse to audit its books. The International Labour Organisation (ILO) is unique in the United Nations family in that it already contains the germs of participation. It is not, like many others, just an intergovernmental body, but its tripartite structure consists of the representatives of workers and employers as well.

We have also heard a lot recently about the need to decentralize government (about which more below) and to draw more on participatory organizations in the political arena. The world has found unworkable and has rejected the process of centralized decision making in centrally planned economies. But the very same process governs the relations between management and labor within both capitalist and public-sector firms. We know that people under regimentation do not give their best. Democracy and participation should be introduced not only in politics but also in the private sector; and not only in government and in profit-seeking firms, but also in private voluntary societies and nongovernment organizations such as trade unions and churches; even in some families there is a need for greater participation, or at least better access to those in power, particularly by women and in some areas by children. This might be called vertical participation: to make the membership of these agencies more responsive to the needs of all its members through a higher degree of participation and access to power. Horizontal participation would mean the inclusion of some representatives of the civil society in the international organizations.

With the end of the Cold War, the role of the United Nations and its agencies can once again become what it was intended to be at its foundation, but adapted to the new power constellations of the present world. Japan and Germany must be given bigger roles. They should be encouraged to take positive initiatives in raising resources, and in the many activities surrounding various aspects of human security. Peacekeeping and peacemaking apply to military and territorial security; President Clinton talks of personal security and health security; food security is the mandate of the Food and Agriculture Organization (FAO); financial security that of the International Monetary Fund (IMF), the World Bank, and the regional development banks; environmental security that of the United Nations Environmental Program; and job and income security that of the ILO. The creation of productive, remunerative, secure, satisfying, freely chosen jobs should be a top priority for policy makers. The regional development banks have an important role in this effort.

The Role of the State: Markets and Governance

If we call the doctrine that the "correct" prices and markets have an important role to play in allocating resources efficiently and equitably, in promoting choices, in enlarging freedom, and in decentralizing power as "pricism", and the doctrine that efficiency, equity, and liberty call for minimum state intervention "state minimalism"[2] or laissez-faire, the currently prevailing view is that the two go together: get the government off our backs and let there be markets! The thesis of this paper is the opposite: that for the proper working of markets, strong, and in many cases expanded, state intervention (of the right kind, in the right areas) is necessary. It is possible to favor a strong state, with a limited agenda that would confine itself to ensuring that individuals, and the social groups in which they associate, can pursue their own purposes with a minimum of frustration. This is not the message of this paper. It argues for a strong state, with an expanded agenda, though a different one, differently implemented, from that which the state has commonly adopted in many developing countries.

The expression "getting prices right" has undergone a curious transformation. In the 1960s, it was intended to point to the calculation of correct shadow or accounting prices in the face of "distorted" market or actual prices. Because market prices reflected all sorts of "distortions,"[3] including those caused by the existing and, from an ethical point of view, arbitrary income and asset distribution, it was the task of government to intervene and allocate resources according to the "right" shadow prices. The purpose of government intervention was to correct the distortions caused by the free play of market forces. More recently the recommendation has been reversed. It now is that developing countries should get rid of state interventions in order to permit market prices to reflect the correct opportunity costs and benefits. Distortions are now regarded as caused mainly (or only) by governments.

The World Bank (1991) has promulgated the need for market-friendly government interventions. But free markets are neutral institutions that can work for good or ill. Whatever may be said for their efficiency, they are not tenderhearted toward their victims. As Robinson said, the Invisible Hand can work by strangulation. The question (asked in the spirit of President Clinton's "putting people first") should be, under what conditions are markets people-friendly? Certain conditions have to be met to make markets work efficiently, and to make them work for the benefit of people.

It is often said that administrative and managerial resources are scarce in developing countries other than the East Asian economies, and that the former therefore should not try to imitate the latter but should deregulate and privatize, and leave it all to the market. But a more sensible conclusion is that they should try to train, educate, and build an efficient, competent bureaucracy that resists the pressures of special interest groups.

There are several ways in which government intervention can contribute to a more efficient functioning of markets. It is generally agreed that government should provide a legal framework and maintain law and order, including the enforcement of contracts, property rights, etc., and pursue the correct macroeconomic policies with respect to exchange rates, interest rates, wage rates, and trade policy in order to ensure high levels of employment without inflation, and economic growth. It must also encourage competition by antimonopoly and antirestrictive practices legislation, or by setting up competitive enterprises in the public sector, or by trade liberalization or taking over natural monopolies. There is nothing in the nature of free markets that either establishes or maintains competition. On the contrary, free markets make for conspiracies against the public, as Adam Smith knew. Yet, the virtue of markets depends on the existence of competition.[4]

In addition to safeguarding competition, the government can intervene in the process of price formation, production, and finance in ways that make markets work better for all. It can encourage the introduction of private markets for insurance. The government can make banks buy private insurance. The biggest risk-takers would then pay the highest premiums. It can tax activities it wishes to discourage, e.g., pollution (by issuing tradable permits to pollute below certain levels); traffic congestion; certain types of short-term stock exchange speculation (for instance, putting a high capital gains tax on assets held for less than three months); or the consumption of cigarettes or drugs or gasoline, and can subsidize those activities it wishes to encourage, e.g., the use of public transport, or education and health. It can intervene in preventing the growth of extreme regional inequalities and in town planning.

The functions of government include the construction of physical and human infrastructure, universal health care, environmental protection, promotion and dissemination of basic research, promotion of racial justice, public schools, rehabilitation of cities, rehabilitation of the homeless, provision of jobs, and so on.

Government has a special role in promoting the development of human resources. It can improve the skills of farmers through agricultural extension services. By providing unemployment assistance and retraining facilities, it can help workers to accept more readily new labor-saving technologies. By providing information and conducting research, it can help to reduce monopolistic practices. By investing in physical infrastructure (such as irrigation to raise agricultural price elasticities of supply, rural feeder roads to bring products to markets, harbors, and communications), government can provide the conditions for price incentives (such as devaluation) to work, and stimulate private investment. It has been widely documented that, by raising profitability, public investment can "crowd in" private investment. By assisting in the design and strengthening of institutions (for land reform, information, credit, or marketing), it can contribute to the effectiveness of price policy, and so on. Some of these activities will be accepted by even quite extreme marketeers. The two questions are, (1) whether a shift from present, often very inefficient, state activities to these efficient ones can be achieved by a minimalistic state, and (2) what the functions of the state should be after this transition, once markets are working.

Perhaps the area of largest controversy is the state's involvement in social services (education, health, family planning) and its fiscal implications, and in changing the income distribution brought about by free markets. The problem here is not one of the failure of markets, but of their success, responding to the signals of unequal income and asset distributions. The neo-liberals' view is that in any government's war on poverty, it is always poverty that wins. If we are concerned only with the need for government action to strengthen both the allocative and the creative functions of markets, such involvement would have to be justified not on grounds of social justice or human needs, but on grounds of human capital formation, reducing barriers to income earning opportunities, and promoting social stability. But the need for public action can also be justified on the grounds of human needs, and this justification reinforces in a virtuous circle the instrumental justification: better education and health, both ends in themselves, also contribute to higher production which, in turn, makes more resources available for better education and health, and so on.

Progressive taxes and social services are often said to be limited by fiscal constraints. The limits are not, however, lack of resources. Military expenditures (often large in some of the poorest countries), large prestige projects, the big losses of public enterprises, capital flight, and reallocation within the social sectors from low priority to high priority areas (primary and secondary education and preventive rural health services in low-income countries) can provide ample resources. The constraints are neither technical nor economic but political.

It is important to distinguish between public and private production, provision, and finance. Various combinations of private and public can be applied to these notions. Education or health services can be privately provided and publicly financed, through vouchers for private schools or hospitals, or subsidies. Charging for the cost of publicly provided services (such as university education, but not water, health, and education for the poor) means public provision and private finance. The production of some of the components of the service can be subcontracted by the government to a private producer. The optimum combination of producing, providing, and financing depends on the particular circumstances of each case.

The proposition that pricism and state minimalism are incompatible is open to two quite different interpretations. According to the strong interpretation, liberal markets require authoritarian regimes that prevent trade unions from pushing up wages, jeopardizing exports and foreign investment, and causing inflation, and special interest groups from grasping rents. "A courageous, ruthless and perhaps undemocratic government is required to ride roughshod over these newly created special interest groups" (Lal 1983, 33; see also Wade 1990).[5] This interpretation points to the East Asian economies (and perhaps Pinochet's Chile) as the great success stories. But it is questionable whether these regimes are truly liberal in the economic sphere. Their dirigisme is to some extent, and with important exceptions, market-oriented or market-friendly. But if there is evidence of an invisible hand, it is surely guided by a strong visible arm.

According to the milder, and more realistic, interpretation, democracies and free markets can go together, although the ruthless efficiency of markets will then be tempered by the compassion of social provisions, as exemplified by the Scandinavian countries.[6] The current debate about the effects of the welfare state on incentives to work and save, on the swollen welfare bureaucracy, and on inflation is, of course, provoked by this experience. But if we are concerned only with the conditions of efficient markets, the focus is not on the state's welfare provisions but on its interventions in the areas of antimonopoly legislation, research and development, information, marketing, physical and social infrastructure, and human resource development, all of which are conditions for the efficient functioning of markets.

The state minimalists are prone to argue asymmetrically. They have said, correctly, that, market failure is not automatically an argument for state intervention, for this may produce even worse results. But they forget that government or bureaucratic or state failures are not necessarily arguments for private markets, at least not until much more empirical evidence is produced that the outcomes of government action in a particular case are necessarily worse than those of markets.

Shapiro and Taylor (1990, 867) have pointed to a peculiar asymmetry in these models, "whereby individuals coalesce to force a political redistribution, but do not do the same in the marketplace. The political arena is depicted full of lobbyists and cartel builders, while the economy is presented as being more or less subject to competition."[7]

A related asymmetry is that rent-seeking has been indicted almost exclusively as resulting from public action (Krueger 1974). It is, however, equally common in the private sector. Private allocation of contracts to subcontractors gives rise to rents in exactly the same way as important quotas. Adam Smith recognized businessmen's "conspiracy against the public" and "contrivance to raise prices", and landlords' and others' love "to reap where they never sowed". We would expect these observations by the father of market economics to encourage us to design strategies of state intervention to counteract these private rent-seeking activities. Instead, we are served today with two ideas: first, that rent-seeking is an entirely political phenomenon, and second, that the only way to reduce rent-seeking is to limit government. Both are wrong, or at least unproven without considerably more empirical evidence.

Private and public action often have to go together. Prices have their impact on demand and supply only if complementary action is taken by the government. A factory may depend on a road, which is normally constructed by the government. Increases in agricultural output in response to higher prices may depend on irrigation or research into new varieties. The ability to make use of high profit opportunities may depend on the availability of information about inputs and markets, provided by the government. When the IMF recommended that Tanzania devalue the shilling, no attention was paid to the fact that the transport system had broken down and, however attractive the prices for farmers after devaluation, their produce could not have been transported to the ports. In South Africa, the "black" taxi trade is often upheld as a splendid example of the spirit of free enterprise. And so it is, if we accept the absence of an efficient and safe public transport system for the blacks. But with roads full of potholes and without public safety regulations, the accident rate is one of the highest in the world.

In Europe there is talk of deregulating trucking. Now trucks are prohibited from picking up return loads and often have to return empty. Two opposite tendencies will be at work. On the one hand, truck traffic may be reduced, because a given amount of traffic can be carried out by fewer journeys. On the other hand, the lower costs will make it pay to increase road transport. If the net outcome were to lead to more road traffic, safety and the health of the drivers would suffer. There would be more road congestion, and reduced loads and higher losses for the underutilized railways (see Streeck 1989).

One example of the complementarity or symbiosis between public and private sectors is the "crowding-in" effect (in contrast to the normally assumed crowding-out effect, resulting from higher interest rates), according to which public investment, often in infrastructure, stimulates private investment. Various authors have estimated these crowding-in coefficients to lie between one and two (Blejer and Khan 1984, Chakravarti 1987, Ortiz and Noriega 1988, Barro 1989). The fact of crowding-in is now well established. The task of government is to raise the productivity of the investment in both the public and the private sector. There are many other nonprice, nonmarket measures, such as research, information, or the establishment of appropriate institutions, that the government must take in order to make the incentives of prices bite.

Some might say that, while the combination of price and nonprice measures is best, to get prices right by itself is at least a step in the right direction. This is, however, not so. I have shown elsewhere that the right prices by themselves, without the complementary public sector action, can be ineffective or counterproductive (Streeten 1987). In Bangladesh, raising the price of rice without a land reform meant that some deficit farmers, who had pledged their tiny plots of land against loans to buy the higher priced food, lost their plots. Since output per acre is less on large than on small holdings, total output declined, and social justice suffered as well.

Japan and the Republic of Korea are often cited as examples of successful private-public sector cooperation. It is sometimes said that the relation is supportive, not antagonistic. But looking more deeply in the nature of successful state interventions, we note that the state in Japan and the Republic of Korea, as Bhagwati (1988) put it, issues prescriptions rather than proscriptions. The success of the East Asian governments rests on their ability to resist self-interested, destructive private pressure groups and to bear the national interest in mind. They intervene by encouraging and promoting selected activities, not by prohibiting and restricting. Of course, to be able to get credit for only one type of investment implies being prevented from doing another. Or to be prohibited from importing a good encourages domestic production. The distinction is not as clear-cut as it may seem.[8] The skill of these policies does not lie so much in the disputed art of "picking winners" as in creating winners. Korean shipbuilding was created without the existence of the requisite skills or raw materials, and today competes successfully with the previously pre-eminent Swedish industry. The highly successful Korean steel industry was created without indigenous iron or coal. Modern comparative advantage can be created by good government policies.

Japan uses government intervention to promote industrial productivity through export incentives, barriers to protect the domestic market, low-cost credit to selected investments, and policies that favor business and education. In addition, there are numerous more covert policies to favor companies that move into government-approved types of production, such as commercial intelligence services, nationalistic patent policies, etc. The government practices an art despised and condemned by most United States economists, who are minimalists: industrial policy.

The public-sector Pohang Iron and Steel Company (Posco) is one of the most efficient enterprises in the world (in spite of the complete absence of iron ore and coal in the Republic of Korea), while the Steel Authority of India is a testimony to bureaucratic inefficiency. The Korean firm has financial autonomy, seeks to make profits, has clear objectives, has operating independence, and is open to potential competition from domestic rivals and imports. It is not burdened with multiple social objectives and the incentive structure encourages it to export. The Indian Authority accepts losses, has confusing and multiple objectives, its finances overlap with the budget, it is subject to close political scrutiny and interference, its prices are politicized, and it is protected from competition through tariffs, import licensing, and legal restrictions on domestic entry.

The East Asian success stories, moreover, illustrate that the same types of intervention that in Latin America have impeded growth, such as subsidized interest rates, have been used by these governments to accelerate growth. The role of corruption and its control also contributes to explaining differential performance (see Myrdal 1968, Klitgaard 1988). It is now generally acknowledged that "getting prices right" has not been the principal, and certainly not a sufficient, recipe for the success of East Asian countries, although their government interventions have been "market-friendly", and the markets have been "people-friendly".

Differences in the institutional arrangements of the relations between managers of public enterprises and the public authority are also important. Managers are given sufficient autonomy to get on with their jobs, while remaining accountable to the public. With all the current talk about incorporating political variables in economic analysis, and endogenizing political change, there is remarkably little work done on how specific political and economic institutions function.

In Europe too, new forms of cooperation between local authorities, central government, and firms have been evolving. In the Third Italy and in Baden-Württenberg in Germany, methods of production, called by some as flexible specialization and by others as diversified quality production, have combined markets, firms, local government, and central government regulation successfully.

With the end of the Cold War, the differences between different types of capitalism have become more prominent. One type, the Jápanese and German, is characterized by close coordination between different firms, between firms and banks, between government and business, and between employers and workers; the other exhibits little coordination and conducts its relations at arm's length between firms, with no involvement of banks in the management of firms, and on the basis of hiring and firing within firms. One commits its resources to long-term goals, the other is more concerned with short-run financial flexibility. One emphasizes "flexible specialization" and product innovation, the other preset machinery whose performance does not depend on the skill of the workers, who are tightly controlled financially (see Albert 1993).

Economists are trained in the study of the operation of economic forces within political, social, and moral constraints.[9] This approach has to be supplemented (and in some cases replaced) by the study of the operation and manipulation of political, social, and psychological forces within economic limits. More fundamentally, the distinction between economic and noneconomic variables may not be tenable if the aim is to understand society.

Democracy, Capitalism, and Development

A common sense definition of democracy runs in terms of two institutions: regular, free elections, and a body of civil rights (as well as responsibilities). Both institutions limit the power of the state: the first by ensuring that the rascals can be thrown out of office, the second by making sure that the rascals cannot do certain things even while in office (see Berger 1992). Civil rights also protect minorities against the dictatorship of the majority.

Does democracy require a market economy, and does a market economy require democracy? The answer to the first question is yes, for there are no democracies that are not market economies, although the admixture of public ownership, management, and regulation varies widely; the answer to the second question is no, for there are many market economies that are not democracies.

What are the connections between democracy, human rights, and freedom on the one hand and development or economic growth on the other? There is a large literature on the links between freedom and economic growth. Ruttan (1991) draws on the political science literature (especially Huntington and Dominguez) and concludes that at early stages they are incompatible. The view is widespread that the tough measures necessary for successful development call for discipline and resistance to the pressures of special interest groups that can be provided only by authoritarian governments. *The Human Development Report 1991* (UNDP 1991) rejects this and shows that freedom, though not a necessary condition, is entirely consistent with growth and development, even at low levels. It compares the Human Freedom Index with the economic indicators. It is true that Japan's success and the East Asian "miracles" were not built by democratic governments. From this some have argued that democracy and human rights are a luxury that countries embarking on development cannot afford. This is what the killings of Tiananmen Square wanted to impress on 1.2 billion Chinese. But these experiences do not prove that authoritarian government was a necessary condition for the success of these countries. Their success depended on land reforms, mass education, and the timely switch to labor–intensive exports. Also, their experience was limited to a few countries and a relatively short period. Kohli (1986) has also shown that the growth rates of democracies have not been lower than those of undemocratic regimes. The United States in the nineteenth century, and more recently Botswana, Costa Rica, Israel, Malaysia, Mauritius, and Venezuela, have done well economically while remaining democracies. Przeworski and Limongi's careful review of the theoretical and statistical arguments of 18 studies of the links between political regimes and growth is inconclusive: "We do not know whether democracy fosters or hinders economic growth" (Przeworski 1992, Przeworski and Limongi 1993).

A recent study edited by Williamson (1994) looked at 13 cases of radical reform in rich and poor countries (trade liberalization, drastic changes in taxes, and public spending) and found that six of the successfully reforming governments were "unambiguously democratic": (Australia in 1983, Colombia in 1989, New Zealand in 1984, Poland in 1990, Portugal in 1985, and Spain in 1982). Bhalla, in an unpublished paper, subjects 90 countries to an econometric analysis for the relation between various kinds of freedom. He finds that civil and political freedoms promote economic growth. He ranks countries in a seven-mark scale, and concludes that, other things being equal, an improvement by one mark in civil and political freedom raises annual growth per head by roughly a full percentage point. It is often said that property rights, a necessary condition for economic growth, are securer in democracies and that these are less grasping than autocracies (Olson 1993)[10]. But how much private property, as opposed to public property, and how much state intervention are essential conditions for a democratic market economy to work is not known.

In an interesting unpublished paper, Campos (1994) reviews some of the empirical literature on the relation between democracy and development and concludes that there is a significant positive effect of democracy on development via education and, surprisingly, investment. Chatterji et al. (1993) find that politically free regimes in Asia have higher growth rates of real income per head than in other regions.

The connection between democracy and capitalism is, however, not that painted by ideologues of capitalism. When the invisible hand of the market causes suffering through excessive unemployment or exploitation or environmental degradation, democracy demands interventions with the free market. There is no evidence whatsoever that these interventions are bound to lead to slavery and despotism, as Friedrich von Hayek predicted. On the other hand, the owners and managers of private firms attempt to restrain democracy when it claims too many resources for mass consumption.

Economic growth is the product of the rate of investment and its productivity. Early writers emphasized the importance of stepping up the investment rate, and some dictatorships may have had an advantage there. The choice between what was thought to be freedom and economic growth used to be called "the cruel choice". Later, as the emphasis shifted

to its productivity, democracies could provide better incentives and institutions, and mobilize people's enterprise and initiative (Bhagwati 1992).
More recently, the interdependence between the investment rate and its
productivity has been explored.

What is, however, more important than attempts to show that freedom
and democracy are consistent with good development performance, is the
fact that human development (with improved health and education, as
well as higher incomes) and economic growth (with the creation of a middle
class) lead, sooner or later, to the irresistible call for freedom, as can be seen
historically in Europe and today in East Asia, Eastern Europe, South Africa,
and Latin America. Even an aberration such as Hitler lasted only 12 years.

I should like to give Albert Hirschman the last word for the present on
the complex relationship between democracy or political progress and development or economic progress. "What, then, is the point of my story? It
is to affirm once again that political and economic progress are not tied
together in any easy, straightforward, 'functional' way. There are the various on-and-off connections.... Then there are stories, intricate and often
nonrepeatable ... that look more like tricks history has up its sleeve than
like social-scientific regularities, not to speak of laws. To make an inven-
tory, to survey history's repertoire of such tricks, seems to me an appropriately modest way of trying to make progress with this difficult topic"
(Hirschman 1994, 347).

The Transition from Planned to Market Economies

Eastern Europe and the former Soviet Union have moved from the zoo
to the jungle. The people of Central and Eastern Europe and the former
Soviet Union are undergoing several interlinked dramatic and traumatic
transitions. Politically, they are moving from autocratic rule to greater
political freedom, participation, and democracy. Culturally, they are undergoing a transition from a restricted life to one of free movement and
travel across frontiers. Psychologically, they are experiencing a transition
from a life that relied on the state for many provisions to having to draw
on their private initiative and enterprise. And economically they are
transforming centrally planned economies, based on physical planning
and physical capital, into market-oriented ones, in which human, financial, and social capital also play important parts. But these desirable
moves are accompanied by upheavals, conflicts, pains, and a rapid
growth of crime and racketeering.

Human investment, resulting from free public services in education
and health, was always high in the ex-socialist countries. Life expectancy,
infant mortality, and literacy rates were those of much higher-income

countries.[11] But these achievements did not have an opportunity to manifest themselves in productive efforts. The rapid growth of small firms and of self-employment now, still largely confined to trade and services, is evidence of the existence of this human potential.

As many countries today wish to adopt democracy and markets, several questions arise: what is the right sequence of reforms, and what is their impact on employment and wages? Should political reform (*glasnost*) precede economic reform (*perestroika*) à la Gorbachev or should economic reform precede political reform à la Deng Xiaoping? Should economic reforms start with privatization, the capital market, the budget, reducing subsidies, freeing prices, or making the currency convertible? Which sequence minimizes unemployment and transitional poverty and hardships? Should the reforms be implemented gradually or all together in one "big bang" through "shock therapy" (or "cold turkey")? Is there anything the ex-socialist countries can teach the developing countries about the transition to democracy and markets, or learn from them?

The old socialist regimes were distinguished by the public ownership of all large firms, large subsidies to them, high levels of employment combined with low marginal labor productivity, restricted labor mobility between regions, administered and controlled prices, indexed wages, repressed inflation, and soft budget constraints for enterprises, as well as large levels of military expenditure. Plant and equipment were obsolete, labor and management poorly trained and motivated, labor efforts weak. Services, the knowledge industries, and the environment had been neglected. In the transition to a market economy, real wages have fallen drastically, unemployment has risen from nothing to as much as 10-15 percent and more (except in the Czech Republic which has succeeded in keeping it much lower), hours worked have been reduced, output has declined more sharply than employment, resulting in reduced labor productivity, investment has also declined, and bankruptcies have increased. All this has been accompanied by extremely high rates of inflation. Some groups are particularly hard hit, among them women, the young, the old, and some ethnic minorities, such as the Gypsies in Slovakia and the Turks in Bulgaria. In Russia, the choice is between even more inflation and even higher unemployment.

On the face of it, this looks paradoxical. For a previously inefficient system can be expected to offer scope for reallocating resources so that total output should rise and everyone should gain. But this is true only of the long run. In the short run, which can be quite long, the cessation of activities in inefficient enterprises is not accompanied by expansion in efficient ones. Workers lose their jobs, sometimes on a very large scale. If there are no alternative employment opportunities in other industrial firms or in agriculture, or if the skill requirements are quite different, or if finance is lacking, and if labor markets are competitive, real wages fall and unemployment rises.

The policies recommended for the transition involve fiscal and monetary restraint (the "hard budget constraint" for enterprises and a balanced budget; in the absence of financial instruments, the growing budget deficits have been almost entirely monetized, leading to repressed or open inflation), decontrol of prices and wages, an incomes policy, privatization of firms, the encouragement of competition, liberal trade, currency convertibility, and a social safety net to catch the victims of the transition. The present safety net is quite inadequate, both in terms of the amount of assistance given to the old and disabled, and of the groups of people left out, such as the "new poor" thrown out of employment. Large, long-term unemployment is both undesirable in itself and cannot fulfill the economic functions expected of unemployment, such as keeping wages down and helping restructuring in an expanding economy.

These reforms cause large dislocations, inflict hardships on many people, and are also opposed by special interest groups, who think that they will lose from market reforms, such as managers and workers in public enterprises, the military, the bureaucracy, and, in some cases (as in Russia), the legislature. Mass unemployment, often very long-lasting, and high inflation add to the troubles. Such dislocations may lead to a reversal and the call for a return to the old system or for a fascist dictatorship. Public works programs for the long-neglected physical infrastructure, housing, and environmental restoration can absorb some of the unemployed. Western financial and technical help and open markets can ease progress.

It is easy to show that some attempts at partial or gradual reform are bound to fail. "You do not cross a chasm in two leaps." There are three arguments for rapid and simultaneous reform. Firstly, it avoids internal contradictions. The story is told that, in the late 1980s, Poland had become an exporter of semitropical flowers. This was the result of the new freedom granted to managers in the economic reforms. But these exports were profitable only because the government's price for energy was a fraction of the world price. Greenhouses could be heated at practically no cost. What was profitable to the flower growers subtracted value from the point of view of the community: the cost of energy and materials was higher than the value of the flowers (*The Economist* 1992a). Similarly, free trade and currency convertibility without fiscal restraint and some consequential bankruptcies can lead only to spiralling inflation. Enterprises that can get any amount of subsidy from the state will bid any amount for the foreign currency to buy imports.

Secondly, there is the danger that a gradualist and piecemeal approach gives the opposition time to mobilize its pressures against the reforms, and gives time for vested interests to oppose progress that is in the interest of society as a whole.

Thirdly, after a "big bang", individuals and firms can react quickly and with confidence to the new economic incentives. Uncertainty is thereby reduced. All three arguments point to the conclusion that all reforms have to be carried out together—and within a short period, say two to three years. Its advocates argue that the large dislocations accompanying the reforms will be minimized if the reforms are rapid.

But there are great dangers in this shock therapy too. Weak economies and fledgling democracies may not be able to survive such shocks. They spell large dislocations: a large drop in output, an increase in unemployment, and accelerated inflation. The opponents of shock therapy point out that it took the United Kingdom 12 years to privatize a few enterprises, and the process is not yet complete. (Though the United Kingdom's privatized natural monopolies have to be replaced by regulation, which takes time, this is not true for many enterprises in the ex-socialist states.) Retraining people, reorienting trade, building up markets, and creating the climate for foreign investment are long-term processes. Specialized skills for heavy industry cannot be switched quickly to the demands of an amorphous market. Modern industries that can compete in world markets cannot be built overnight.

The critics say there are only small short-term gains from shock therapy, but the losses can be tremendous: there may be a complete breakdown of the economy, mass unemployment with political unrest, widespread economic distress, even hunger and famine. Though it is true that you cannot cross a chasm in two leaps, you can drop a bridge, and cross it gradually.

Operating on a wide front at the same time can be done in small steps, and is quite consistent with not doing everything in one fell swoop. The phasing or sequencing of reforms is one of the most difficult issues in the transition. There are sectors that even quite passionate free marketeers would exempt from complete liberalization. Wages are the most important of these. It is widely agreed that some form of incomes policy must be an element in the transitional policy package. Since the aim is to reduce the power of the bureaucrats, it could take the form of a tax-based incomes policy. Unwarranted price and wage increases would be taxed. The problem is to prevent inflationary wage increases, while getting wage differentials right, eliminating distortions, and improving incentives for the skilled and well-educated labor forces. Reallocating redundant workers to more efficient firms should be combined with increasing the efficiency of workers in all firms.

The economic reforms need to include five components: price reform, financial reform, privatization, trade reform, and institution-building. Prices serve as signals, incentives, and mobilizers. When scarce goods become more expensive, less will tend to be consumed, and more will tend to be produced, thereby reducing the scarcity. Financial reform applies to fiscal policy, monetary control, and banking regulation. Privatization has to be combined with encouraging competition. Trade reform combined with convertibility of the currency is one quick way of introducing competition, and at the same time of bringing domestic prices into line with world prices. Institutions that have to be created include laws regulating contracts, corporate ownership, bankruptcy regulations, a commercial and profitable banking and financial system, a fair tax system, accounting and bookkeeping conventions, etc.

It seems sensible to begin in economies where none of these items (or even the memory of them) exists, such as the former Soviet Union, with institutional reforms, followed by stabilization and the alignment of relative prices, and only finally to proceed to free markets.

The current slogans in the economic area are privatization, deregulation, liberalization, and decentralization.[12] Privatization and deregulation are intended to free people from the strangulating (or at best heavy) hand of the state, liberalization is intended to subject trade to foreign competition and world prices, and decentralization is intended to make administration cheaper, more transparent, more participatory, and more responsive to people's needs.

Privatization takes two different forms, (1) transferring previously state-owned enterprises into private ownership, control, and management; and (2) encouraging the growth of new, normally initially small, private enterprises. The reason for privatization is the inefficiency of many (though by no means all) public enterprises, and the heavy drain on public revenue that their subsidies constitute. An additional benefit can be the absorption of the liquidity overhang in many ex-socialist countries, if shares in the enterprise are sold and the receipts are not spent. In this way, inflationary pressures can be reduced. But the aim should not be to maximize receipts from the sale of assets, but rather to encourage competition.

Certain conditions have to be met to make privatization a success. In addition to the need for a capital market (which did not exist in the ex-socialist countries), there must be a competitive environment, so that public inefficiency is not just replaced by private inefficiency or by exploitation; or, if a monopoly is inevitable, it should be regulated. The premature freeing of prices in Russia led to vast price increases, which did not lead to more production because protection rackets kept out new entrants and skimmed off large profits.

Competitive firms in the United Kingdom, such as Jaguar, Rolls Royce, British Petroleum, Trustees Savings Bank, and British Airways, have faced fewer problems being privatized than "natural monopolies" such as British Telecommunication, British Gas, and the regional water companies. Corporate control created problems in the ex-socialist countries which privatization in the West did not face. The managers of enterprises, freed from the control of ministries, sought the perquisites of control rather than the rewards of ownership and enterprise. There was neither the Anglo-Saxon control of management by capital markets (and take-over bids), nor the German-Japanese control by the dominant shareholding of banks and other financial institutions. Such controls are absent in Russia, where shareholders are weak and dispersed. Without functioning capital and credit markets and without a soft budget constraint, efficient firms may be forced out of business for want of finance.

For successful privatization there must also be training facilities for the new entrepreneurs and the workers; there must be a legal framework for property rights; political consensus on privatization is desirable, which, in turn, presupposes transparency of proceedings and credibility of policies; and there should be provision for the workers dismissed from over-manned public enterprises.

Deregulation can be excessive and of the wrong kind. In the United States deregulation led to the savings and loan crisis. The greed of the managers and owners, released from controls, harmed the depositors and taxpayers, who had to bail them out. Similarly, in the case of the airlines, with their heavy investment in fixed assets, deregulation led to cut-throat competition, bankruptcies, monopolistic practices, and again bailouts and higher fares. When privatization leads to private monopolies, regulation is essential.[13]

Too rapid trade liberalization and currency convertibility can also be harmful. Eastern Europe can learn from East Asia not only how to "pick winners", but also to create winners. We have seen that the Republic of Korea's shipbuilding and steel industries, models of efficiency, were built with selective government support, without indigenous resources and initial skills. Efficient protection of promising industries, which later became successful exporters, has been the approach of Japan and the Republic of Korea. Efficient import substitution under protection has normally preceded successful exports. Rapid trade liberalization captures only the existing comparative advantage, confined to raw materials and industries with low value added. In order to gain a comparative advantage in high value-added industries (often the result of import substitution of previously imported inputs for exports) and modern technologies, government support is essential. And success in exports is achieved not by relying only on the invisible hand (though international competition is a disciplining force), but by the strong supporting visible arm of government. Countries that are often cited as shining examples of free markets have powerfully and efficiently intervened in the allocation of investment (steering the private sector by differential interest rates, industrial policy, and other interventions), have used a battery of import controls and export incentives, and have had a large, efficient public sector.

Should economic reform (*perestroika*, restructuring for liberalization) precede political reform (*glasnost*, democratization) or the other way round? A priori, one might choose the latter, for political reform, involving granting negative freedoms, is easier to implement; further, the goodwill created might then be mobilized for the implementation of the more difficult economic reforms. But the limited evidence that is available suggests that the former is preferable. The People's Republic of China appears to have done better than Russia. Paradoxically, the transition from a centrally planned to a market economy requires strong state action in designing the market economy. Given the historical legacy of institutions and practices, natural evolution of the market, as occurred in Western Europe, cannot be relied upon. In a young democracy following autocratic rule, there are not yet enough powerful interests to push for the reforms. Only a strong, ruthless, and perhaps undemocratic rule may be capable of resisting the privileged interests of the old order, who wish to undermine the efforts for change.

Many questions in this section had to be left unanswered. Neither economic theory nor experience has much to contribute to the problems of the transition. But the uncertainty, risks, and adjustment pains that these countries have to go through constitute a powerful argument for generous foreign financial and technical assistance and for keeping Western frontiers open to cultural and economic exchange, above all to the import of agricultural products. As one official at a conference on the problems posed by capitalism's victory over communism remarked, the choice boils down to Marshall Plan or martial law (cited in Keegan 1992).

I conclude that correctly phased gradual reforms on wide fronts are to be preferred in many situations to shock therapy in spite of its risks; that economic liberalization should precede political liberalization; that institutional reform should precede stabilization, and stabilization precede the freeing of markets, including foreign trade liberalization. Wages should be freed last unless firm agreement on an incomes policy has been reached.

There are lessons to be learned from the ex-socialist countries in transition for the developing countries. Both have tended to be over-regulated, and have suffered from ham-handed government interventions and an excessively large public sector producing things. Many developing countries have also suffered from a neglect of public action in basic social services. But simply introducing free markets may replace a government monopoly by a private one, often owned and run by foreigners. Institutional reform, including legal reform, again should lay the foundations for a working competitive market. Where monopolies are inevitable or to be preferred, they should be made accountable and consumers' voices should be made articulate. Educational reform, especially public action for girls and women, should have a high priority. For Asia, where much human capital has already been created, stepping up savings and investment and making the investment more productive, are among the main prerequisites of success. The activities of the state should be changed to produce an enabling environment for the private sector, to provide the physical, human, and social infrastructure and the institutions. Foreign assistance and foreign investment can help to make the transition less painful and accelerate economic growth.

The absence of civic traditions in post-Communist societies and developing countries alike may produce weak governments and economic stagnation. It is therefore important to build a civil society, a network of groups and voluntary grassroots organizations, clubs, guilds, cooperatives, and other associations, that provide the soil for initiative, enterprise and economic prosperity.

Decentralization

Decentralization and devolution have become popular in Europe, against the principles of Napoleon and Stalin, Europe's two great centralizers. France was the most centralized state, with 22 regional governments with directly elected representatives set up by the socialist government in 1986. Spain devolved power to 17 "autonomous communities" and Portugal did similarly. The regions spend 5.6 percent of GNP, 90 percent of it directly passed on from central government taxes. In Italy, new regional governments were created in 1970, and local authorities are now acquiring the power to raise property, income, and road taxes. Germany's constitution grants a lot of power to the *Länder*. They have veto power on central legislation through their seats in the Bundesrat, the upper house of Parliament. Eastern Europe now looks at Germany as its model. Norway, Sweden, Denmark, and Finland, with a longer history of decentralization, are experimenting. Local authorities can ask the central government to relax any control that they regard as inhibiting. It has become fashionable to talk in the European Community of a *Europe des régions,* with direct contact between Brussels and regional governments *(The Economist* 1992b)[14].

Decentralized government can be more responsive to citizens' needs, can mobilize resources more readily, for some purposes can be more effective in achieving its objectives, and can reduce costs and increase participation. But it also tends to aggravate regional inequalities, because the richer regions can raise more tax revenue and provide better services. And its advantages depend on a power structure in which access to power is widely distributed. Otherwise it can simply reinforce the grip of local power elites. It must also be confined to the appropriate areas of activity, and has to be supported by central action in others, e.g., monetary authority, human rights legislation, and judiciary action. Those concerned with the fate of the blacks in Mississippi would not wish to decentralize power to that state. Strong central government legislation backed by the Supreme Court, combined with empowering the minority blacks in the state, is a better way to achieving their civil rights. The Communist state in West Bengal also illustrates the success of strong (state) government action combined with participatory local organizations.

The Civil Society

States and markets do not exhaust the players in the game. Frequently, although they need each other, they also weaken and undermine each other. States damage markets by over-regulation, licensing, and bureaucratic red tape. Markets tend to corrupt governments through bribery, lobbying, and log-rolling. Therefore there is a need for the civil society. It can contribute to more constructive relationships between the two.

Private voluntary organizations have come to play an increasing role, next to governments and profit-seeking companies. They comprise the most diverse organizations: religious, political, professional, educational, recreational, and cooperative organizations, associations, clubs; pressure groups and interest groups; and institutions that are project-oriented, give technical assistance, provide disaster relief, or are concerned with disaster prevention, etc. Although they often claim to work without or even against governments, their contributions can sometimes best be mobilized by working jointly with governments.

The most successful NGOs in the Third World, such as the Self-Employed Women's Organisation based in Ahmedabad, India, or the Grameen Bank or BRAC of Bangladesh, depend for their continuing and expanding (though not for their initial) operations on access to, and support and replication by, governments. Of course, in some situations their function is to criticize and exhort governments, or fill gaps in government activities, or to do things at lower costs, with better results, and with more popular participation than governments. In other situations, when they promote their selfish interests against the wider interests of the community, or when they reflect the dominant power of particular groups, government may be justified in trimming their influence.

The relationship between NGOs and governments can be understood as one of cooperative conflict (or creative tensions), in which the challenge of the voluntary agencies and their innovative activities can improve both government services and the working of markets, and help to resolve tensions between them.

In some situations, the state plays a passive role, only responding to the pressures of interest groups. The outcomes will then be determined by the power of these groups, which in turn depends on their size, age, motivation, and enforcement mechanisms. In other cases, the state is more active, imposing regulations and restrictions that can give rise to competitive rent-seeking by private-interest groups. In yet other situations, both the private groups and the state work together for common objectives.

Functions are divided between the state and civil society. The institutions of civil society—churches, trade unions, interest groups, action groups, the media, and many others—are often quite undemocratic, in spite of their rhetoric. There is then a need for the empowerment of weak and neglected groups within them: women, the unemployed, ethnic minorities. There can be an undesirable concentration not only of economic and political, but also of social power.[15]

Though there is a need to strengthen both states and markets in the early stages of development, in fact, they often tend to weaken and undermine each other. It is the institutions of the civil society that can intervene and inhibit such weakening and undermining (Lipton 1991). Interactions between the state, markets, and civil society are complex. Some authors maintain that civil society is the reason why capitalism is necessary for democracy. But some autocracies, such as Bangladesh, had flourishing civil societies, while the democratic Prime Minister Margaret Thatcher proclaimed that there was no such thing as society, wishing to destroy the civil society. Both too weak and too strong a state can discourage the growth of civil society. And too strong private political and ethnic organizations can undermine the power of the state, as in Lebanon, Somalia, the former Soviet Union, Sri Lanka or Yugoslavia, and can lead to the dissolution of society.

The Politics of Aid

Aid policies, just like domestic policies, are motivated by a mixture of political and commercial pressures, national interests, idealism, and human solidarity. Military security, altruistic and Machiavellian motives, and profit-seeking export interests inspire foreign assistance policies. To technical, economic, and environmental conditionality has been added political conditionality about "good governance". It would be one-sided to criticize national policies for being subjected to political constraints without looking at international efforts in the same light. And it would be remiss in making recommendations about the redirection of aid, not to say anything about how political constraints can be overcome. Business interests are behind the provision of inappropriate, capital-intensive technologies (tractors and combine harvesters to countries with large rural surplus populations), and the interests of consultancy and training firms behind the provision of inappropriate technical assistance. Denmark and Sweden have bought off the business lobby by earmarking a fixed percentage of the aid program for programs of interest to businesses and the donor country (Mosley 1990). The answer to the pressures from consultancy firms and training institutions lies in decentralizing technical assistance programs to the donor offices in the developing countries. The local representatives who are in continual touch with the needs and people of the recipient countries are more likely to choose the right local people.

The interests of banks that have lent to developing countries and are eager to have their debts serviced are clearly partly behind the switch in donor policies from project aid to program lending. The policy conditionality that accompanies such lending is often based on the premature crystallization of flawed orthodoxies. Unfortunately or fortunately, depending on whose point of view one takes, policies, like projects, can be substituted for one another, and it is sometimes not difficult to evade the conditions imposed in program loans.

It is often said that aid is inevitably given in the national self-interest of the donor country; it is just a branch of foreign policy. A lot depends, of course, on how narrowly or broadly national self-interest is interpreted. It is, however, noteworthy that countries like Holland, Sweden, and Norway, whose aid programs are inspired by moral concerns of human solidarity, have given more aid, and of a better quality, than countries like the United States and the United Kingdom, which have defended aid in terms of national self-interest. Australia conducted a public opinion survey which showed that people regard development aid as an expression of human solidarity.

Frequently NGOs and action groups agitate for more and better quality aid. Expanding the role of NGOs would help in reducing the bias in favor of large projects that create few jobs, and might raise aid effectiveness. To some extent this has occurred. The success of the World Development Movement in England in suing the British Government and the Foreign Secretary Douglas Hurd over the misuse of aid funds for the Pergau dam in Malaysia, which was linked to a large arms contract, is a good example. But NGOs might object to becoming too dependent on government funds and government objectives. This objection might be met by expanding government contributions to NGOs more slowly, so that they can keep in step with nongovernmental contributions, and by permitting the NGOs to preserve their autonomy.

Frequently the obstacles to restructuring aid policies to the priority sectors do not lie with outside pressure groups but have to be sought within aid ministries. Reducing conditionality would reduce the amount of work to be done by the donor, but would also reduce leverage. It could be replaced by actually giving aid only to those who have shown a commitment to human development policies, or who are intent on doing so in the future. Quiet signalling can be more effective than ham-fisted conditionality imposed on unwilling recipients.

An objection to supporting human development programs consisting of basic education, primary health care, and family planning that has sometimes been raised by aid ministries, is that they involve supporting recurrent expenditure, with the complaint that they present a bottomless pit, indefinite donor commitment. The answer should lie in designing strategies with gradually growing recipient contributions, or with self-liquidating cost-recovery over a specified period. This may be accompanied by jointly working out new sources of tax revenue to finance the human development and antipoverty projects (e.g., water, nutrition, basic education, preventive health services, family planning) for which cost recovery and user charges would be wrong.

The Political Economy of International Support

International and bilateral agencies can be mobilized both as pressure groups and as sources of finance for human development, including the respect for human rights, an important aspect of governance. Feeding and educating deprived children has a powerful appeal to people everywhere. A well-designed human development program that benefits the poor in a poor country can count on support by citizens from all countries. Eliminating hunger and starvation in the world can be regarded as a public good. My satisfaction of being successful in this endeavor does not detract from yours. And providing each human being born into this world with the potential for the full development of his or her capacities is part of the enlightened self-interest of humankind.

The United Nations Children's Fund (UNICEF) has been a highly successful pressure group for protecting the poor, and particularly children and pregnant women, in the adjustment processes that began in the 1980s. Since 1985, UNICEF has propagated the use of growth charts and growth monitoring, oral rehydration, breastfeeding, and inoculation as cheap and effective methods of dramatically reducing child mortality and improving children's health. Through its book *Adjustment with a Human Face* (UNICEF 1987) and through its dialogues with the International Monetary Fund and the World Bank, its propoor advocacy influenced the policies on conditionality of these two institutions and other donors so that they moved away from a merely technical, economic approach for stabilization and balance of payments corrections, toward a more humane, compassionate approach, concerned with the human and social dimensions of stabilization and adjustment. It also drew attention to the need and the political advantages of protecting the poor (by a form of compensation) from the burdens of adjustment. There were, of course, groups inside these institutions and in some developing countries that had been responsive to propoor policies earlier, and that had been continuing the traditions of the basic needs strategy of the 1970s.

The success of UNICEF in getting governments to restructure their expenditure has been due to not only (1) the general appeal of improving children's health, but also (2) the low costs at which substantial improvements can be achieved, (3) external financial support for these measures, and (4) the fact that they included many children in the middle-income groups.

On the other hand, the political benefits to governments of the special campaigns that accompanied these drives may not be applicable to other areas with less public appeal, that are more narrowly aimed at the poor, that have fewer resources contributed by other sectors such as the military, and less external finance.

Donors have funded programs that compensate the poor during adjustment periods. The best known are the Bolivian Emergency Social Fund (ESF), started in 1986, and the Ghanaian Program of Action to Mitigate the Social Costs of Adjustment (PAMSCAD), which started in 1988. These are programs of employment creation through local public works, credit creation, and social services. They are mainly intended to be temporary and for workers dismissed from the tin mines in Bolivia and from the over-staffed public sector in Ghana. Local communities and NGOs played an important part in proposing and designing these programs. Bolivia's ESF in particular involved minimum government involvement and full delegation to local communities and private contractors. Another similar scheme is the Economic Management and Social Action Program in Madagascar. It includes measures to provide drugs and support family planning. The projects are broadly targeted so as to gain wide political support. The World Bank is planning similar programs for many other countries.

The Bolivian and Ghanaian programs have been criticized because the foreign funds were not additional to other aid, and in any case quite small compared with Bolivia's debt service and the drop in the world price of Ghana's principal export, cocoa. A second ground for criticism is that the poorest among the dislocated did not benefit. However, in countries like Bolivia and Ghana, with so many poor people, it is hard not to benefit some poor people with almost any scheme. A deeper criticism is that both projects are remedial to adjustment measures, whereas the desirable policy would incorporate human concerns right from the beginning in the very structure of the adjustment process.

If a country that has, in the past, neglected egalitarian human development now intends to adopt reforms that promote it, it runs into short-term problems. These may take the form of heavy burdens on the budget and on administration, or of political discontent and riots by those who are likely to lose from the reforms. If there is redistribution of income to the poor, there is likely to be an additional impetus to inflation arising from the sectors producing goods (especially food) on which the poor spend their money, because their supply is inelastic in the short run. This may be accompanied by unemployment in the trades that had previously catered for the rich, because it takes time to shift resources. There may be a reduction in productive investment and balance of payments problems caused by additional food imports and capital flight, as the rich try to get their money out of the country. If the reform-minded government has replaced a dictatorship, previously oppressed groups will assert their claims for higher incomes, with additional inflationary results. If some groups become disaffected, they may organize strikes, sabotage, or even *coups d' etat.* All these are familiar troubles for reform-minded governments that wish to change the course of policy in favor of the poor. They account for the regular disillusion after a honeymoon period.

In such critical situations, international aid agencies can help to make the transition less painful and disruptive, and more likely to succeed. They can help to overcome an important obstacle to reform—the fear that the cost of the transition to more appropriate policies is too high. They can add flexibility and adaptability to otherwise inert policies set on a damaging course. Structural adjustment loans have come to be accepted in other contexts, such as the transition to a more liberal international trade regime and more market-oriented domestic policies. By an extension of the same principle, adjustment loans should be given to the transition to a regime oriented more toward human development. They can take the form of financial or technical assistance for land reform or tax reform, well-designed food aid or international food stamps, or support of a national nutrition program. An international economic order built on international support of domestic efforts for human development, including good governance and poverty eradication, is more sensible and more likely to succeed than one built on the hope of trickle-down effects and intergovernmental transfers.

Combining development aid with conditions for policy reform, environmental protection, poverty reduction, social objectives, political freedom, human rights, and good governance has become popular among bilateral and multilateral donors. The concessionary component in the assistance buys, as it were, the policies that a purely commercial lender cannot insist on. In Zambia, for example, a housing subsidy was given to high-level bureaucrats who often did not pay even the small, subsidized rents they owed. The World Bank exercised pressure to raise the rents and use the revenue for sites and services schemes for the poor.[16]

It is controversial how desirable and feasible such conditionality is. Some observers have said that conditions can be successfully imposed only if the recipient government is committed to the policies anyway. Complaints have been voiced that conditionality imposed by foreigners is intrusive, incompatible with national sovereignty, and can be counterproductive if it discredits domestic groups aligned with such reforms. It can also be evaded by substituting other undesirable policies for the ones eliminated by conditionality. The same objectives can be achieved by adopting a quieter style than by imposing performance criteria, by supporting regimes determined to promote human development, withdrawing aid from those that do not, and thereby signalling unobtrusively to all recipients the conditions for receiving aid. Alternatively, institutional innovations might be considered that put a mutually trusted intermediary between donors and recipients, who would insist on the condition of poverty reduction, briefly discussed in the next section.

It is important for conditionality on governance and human rights to distinguish between three types of human rights. First, human rights in the narrow sense: not to be tortured, imprisoned without trial, etc. Second, civil rights, such as access to an independent judiciary, i.e., the rule of law. In Tudor, England there was no democracy, but these rights were respected. Third, political rights, multiparty system, free elections, etc. The status of these three kinds is quite different. In the third, there is a danger that only a parliamentary or presidential democracy is accepted, which may be inappropriate for some cultures. But human rights in the narrow sense are universally acknowledged, and I for one know with greater certainty that it is wrong to torture people than that an exchange is overvalued. Another question is whether the conditionality referring to governance and human rights is additional in two senses: (1) Are the conditions added to other conditions? (2) Are additional funds available if the conditions are met? Robert McNamara's Redistribution with Growth and Basic Needs approaches in the 1970s were accompanied by additional money.

Buffers between Donors and Recipients

The question of monitoring aid, though it may appear to be a purely recording effort, does, however, raise policy issues. On the one hand, monitoring of poverty reduction and income distribution by donors is regarded by recipient countries as intrusive and perhaps even violating national sovereignty. On the other hand, donors believe that their responsibility to the taxpayer is to account for the use of aid funds and to ensure that poverty reduction is achieved, if this is the purpose of the aid. Donor institutions are distrusted by recipients, because they fear that extraneous criteria may enter into the process; recipients' institutions are distrusted by donors, because they may wish to conceal unsuccessful performance. To resolve this conflict it is necessary to design institutions that are trusted by both sides, and to monitor reliably and objectively.

In addition to having to gain the trust of both sides and be responsive to their needs and demands, these institutions would have to fulfill the function of buffers between donors and recipients, be sensitive to social and political conditions, and have the expertise to judge the impact of programs on poverty reduction. They should also be helpful in building up the indigenous capacity of poverty monitoring in developing countries.

One possible solution would be to adopt the method that the Organization of European Economic Cooperation (the forerunner of the OECD) practised under Marshall Aid. The US generously withdrew from the monitoring process and encouraged European governments to monitor each other's performance. Analogously, groups of developing countries, such as those of East Africa or of Central America, would get together, and one, say Uganda, would monitor the performance of another, say Kenya or Tanzania, and vice versa. Technical assistance would initially be needed to acquire or strengthen the professional capacity to do this.

Another solution would be to appoint a mutually agreed council of wise men and women, with a component secretariat, who would perform the monitoring, possibly again combined with technical assistance for the strengthening of indigenous capacity. A third solution would be to aim at the creation of a genuine global secretariat, with loyalties to the world community, that is socially sensitive and technically competent. The secretariats of existing international organizations such as the World Bank have not quite reached that point, and are not perceived by recipients as being truly global. Reforms in recruitment, training, and promotion would be needed, and perhaps in the governance and location of these institutions. Decentralization with strong regional offices in daily contact with the local population and policymakers would be necessary.

Whatever institutional solution might be adopted, there is virtue in introducing a degree of competition into the monitoring process, so that a variety of methods may be tested against each other. At the moment, it is feared that the large international financial institutions exercise a monopoly of power and wisdom, and propagate at times prematurely crystallized orthodoxies. The proposed buffer procedures or buffer institutions should contribute to the building and strengthening of indigenous research and monitoring capacities of the recipient developing countries. For research on poverty and action against poverty tend to go together, as the investigations of Charles Booth and Seebohm Rowntree at the beginning of the century, and of Sidney and Beatrice Webb, of the World Bank, of the regional development banks, and of the specialized UN Development Agencies, have shown.

Theories of the State

We now have a menu of theories of the state to choose from. According to the one I was taught when an undergraduate, an idealistic, competent and well-informed government, like Platonic guardians, or perhaps more like Fabian bureaucrats, reigns above the interest conflicts and promotes the common good. It is implicit in the writings of Pigou, Lerner, Tinbergen, and Meade. According to this old romantic theory, the government can do no wrong.

The opposite theory, represented by the new classical Chicago economists, neoclassical political economists, and the public choice school (better named the self-interest school), holds that the government can do no right. Citizens, politicians, bureaucrats, and states use the authority of government to distort economic transactions for their benefit. Citizens use political influence and pressures to get access to benefits allocated by government; politicians use government resources to increase their hold on power; public officials trade access to government benefits for personal reward; and states use their power to get access to the property of citizens (Grindle and Thomas 1991). The result is an inefficient and inequitable allocation of resources, general impoverishment, and reduced freedom.

A narrow interpretation of the selfish political man (and to a lesser extent woman), pursuing ruthlessly his or her interests, can lead to mutual impoverishment. According to one version, the predatory officials and bureaucrats or politicians promote actively their selfish quest for money or power; according to another, they respond passively to powerful pressure groups so as to stay in power. "The model of government motivations" has been simplified "into a single-track form, supplying the public sector with a brain transplant straight out of the marketplace" (Lewis 1990).[17] Any intervention by this "predatory state" with the "magic of the market place" is bound to make matters worse. Government action is not the solution (as it is in the first theory), it is the problem—"invisible feet stomping on invisible hands" (Colander 1984). As has been said above, while according to the Platonic theory the government intervenes in order to correct "distortions", according to the public choice theory all distortions are due to government interventions. But according to both these apparently opposite views, the state is an optimizing agency. According to the Platonic view it optimizes the welfare of the people as a whole; according to the public choice view only that of special interest groups or those on whose support the politicians rely, such as bureaucrats, the army, or the politicians themselves. The Platonic view is normative (or naive); the public choice view crudely cynical.[18]

Even if it were true that politicians, bureaucrats, and interest groups pursue always only their self-interest, this is open to different interpretations; some of these may be in conflict with one another and with the interests of others, others may be in harmony. There may, for instance, be a conflict between smaller present and larger future gains; between "hot" impulsive, and "cool" deliberated interests; between concentrated smaller and more widely dispersed larger gains; between certain smaller and uncertain larger gains; or, perhaps as important as interest conflicts between groups, the conflict between perceived smaller and actual but non-perceived larger gains.

Amartya Sen (1995) pointed out in his Presidential address to the American Economic Association, that one does not have to subscribe to either the "high-minded sentimentalism" that public servants constantly try to promote some selfless "social good", or to the "low-minded sentimentalism" that everyone is constantly motivated entirely by personal self-interest, to assume that public servants have their own objective functions. To point to the need to fill in this gap in the theory of resource allocation does not imply assuming either Platonic guardians or *homo economicus*.

A third theory, propounded by Downs (1957) and applicable only to democracies, holds that politicians maximize their own welfare by selling policies for votes. Since not many (though a growing number of) developing countries are democracies, this theory would not have wide application among them.

Then there are social contract theorists, from Hobbes, Locke, and Rousseau to Rawls and Olson. They say that citizens surrender some of their rights or liberties in return for protection against aggression, provision of collective goods, benefits from externalities, and other services from the state.[19] A limited sacrifice of individual autonomy—by increasing the prospects of avoiding related traps such as prisoners' dilemmas, the isolation paradox, the free rider (and, worse, the sucker) outcome, and the tragedy of the commons—gives each citizen greater freedom and more benefits. The undersupply of public goods and the oversupply of public bads can be avoided by some enforced action by the central government.

Marxist theory says that the government is the executive committee of the ruling class and always serves the economic interest of that class. But this is open to different interpretations. Some Marxists regard the state as acting in the interest of international, metropolitan capital, extracting surpluses from the periphery for the benefit of the centre. This is the view of neo-Marxist dependency theorists and was Marx's view of the relation of Ireland to England. Others regard the state as acting in the interest of an indigenous capitalist class, sometimes against the interest of the capitalists at the centre. According to both these views, the state acts in the interest of a ruling class. A more sophisticated version of this theory holds that it is the function of the state to reconcile differences of interest within the ruling class, so as to maintain its power and the capitalist mode of production. According to this version, it is possible for the government to impose measures in the interest of the exploited workers and small peasants, in spite of the loss of profit that this involves, if these measures save the system from revolt or revolution. It can also be that higher wages or a land redistribution, while reducing the profits of particular groups, raise total savings and/or lower capital/output ratios so as to increase the volume of the total surplus, though not the ratio of surplus to GNP. Others again regard the state as the agent of a "state class" or a bureaucracy.

Palaeo-Marxists like Warren (1979, 144-168)[20] hold that peripheral capitalism is a progressive, revolutionary force, making for productivity growth and economic progress. They make Seers' remark about the convergence of "Marxism and other neoclassical doctrines" comprehensible (see Seers 1979). And it is ironical that both neoclassical political economy and Marxism, two largely hostile and noncommunicating groups, conclude that thinking and research about government policy for poverty reduction or income redistribution are futile. According to both, the predatory state inevitably acts in its own interest and that of powerful pressure groups; there is no place for disinterested, benign, altruistic government policies; only the forces of the free market are capable of advancing the good of society.

It is worth remembering, in the debate over market versus state, that real states fall under neither extreme. Dogmatism here leads to error even more than usual. A more commonsensical view, borne out by overwhelming evidence, holds that many governments are neither monolithic nor impervious to pressures for rational and altruistic policies. Moreover, if there is scope for a positive-sum game (as there is bound to be in the reversal of rent-seeking movements away from the Pareto frontier), and if the government can hold on long enough to tax this sum, the possibility of rational policies is opened up, even on the narrow assumption about predatoriness of the public choice school.

The structure of government decision making consists of many departments, ministries, and agencies, and many layers from central government via provinces (or states in a federation) to village or town councils (see Lipton 1989). Power in some countries is divided between the legislature, the judiciary, and the executive. Each of these pulls in a different direction. The obstacle to "correct" policymaking is neither solely stupidity nor solely cupidity, neither just ignorance nor simply political constraints or monolithic selfishness. On occasion, governments, like charitable foundations, universities or voluntary associations, do act disinterestedly and in the public interest, particularly, but not only, if there are pressure groups behind them. It is the existence of these pressure groups with some power or influence that constitutes the "trustees for the poor" (Meier 1986), and the "guardians of rationality" (Arrow 1974)[21]. Count Oxenstierna may not have had the whole explanation, but knavery has no monopoly either.[22]

At the same time, there are areas in which a better analysis and a clearer sense of direction would help, just as there are areas where it is fairly clear what should be done, but vested interests, whether those of the policy makers or of pressure groups on whose support they depend, prevent it from happening. Governments sometimes create rents and encourage rent-seeking; at other times they destroy rents and reduce wasteful competition in their pursuit. The private sector also creates and seeks rents. Some government officials act sometimes in their selfish interest; at other times the same ones and others are, or want to be seen as, moral agents, acting in the common interest. Some pressure groups, individual or collective, domestic or foreign, are motivated by reason, solidarity, and morality.

According to this commonsense theory, for which there is overwhelming evidence, the state does not optimize anything, neither public welfare nor self-interest. It compromises, attempts to resolve conflicts, manages bargaining between groups, and occasionally leads. Myrdal's (1968) notion of the South Asian "soft state", in which declared policies are not implemented or not enforced, fits into this picture. But so does that of the East Asian hard state, which, having set its face against the pressures of particular interests, pursues successfully both growth and equity.

Some Policy Conclusions for Good Governance

For Governments

- Educate, train and instill the right attitudes for a competent civil service, willing and able to resist self-interested pressure groups and dedicated to serve the public.
- Build the right checks and balances for government, private sector, civil society, and family, so that governments do not overregulate firms, private firms do not corrupt government, and civil society does not destroy society, but makes government accountable.
- Provide opportunities for popular participation in decisions that affect the life and work of the people, access to power and accountability of those in power.
- Keep the macro economy stable, avoiding inflation, large-scale unemployment, and imbalances in the balance of payments.
- Enforce property rights and contracts.
- Encourage government interventions in order to (1) make free markets work efficiently, correcting for market failure, and (2) provide opportunities for the poor so that they can become self-reliant, correcting for market success. This means giving the poor access to resources and power: land, food, health services, education, training, public employment, credit, and a social safety net.
- Give higher priority in welfare policies to women and children over men, to rural over urban residents, to the poor over the better-off, and to neglected minorities discriminated against over the established majority.
- Always treat people as ends, never as mere production fodder.

For Donor Agencies

- Practice humility, adopt a quiet style in giving, avoid laying down ham-fisted conditionality.

- Remember that economics is not a science, that different circumstances call for different responses, and listen.

- Devote a high proportion (say 20 percent) of aid to social priority sectors such as nutrition, primary and secondary education, preventive rural health services, water and sanitation, and family planning.

- Use development aid not to fill resource or foreign exchange gaps, but to add flexibility to policy making and reforms.

Notes

1. Some of the material of this paper are an expansion of Streeten (1993). The revision of the paper has benefited from comments by Cayetano Paderanga, Rahul Khullar, and R. Swaminathan, to whom I am grateful.

2. The terms are due to Michael Lipton.

3. The widely used notion of price "distortions" is not as clear as it may seem. Distortion is the deviation of the actual from some natural, proper, legitimate, norm. But there is no reason to believe that prices determined in free markets under laissez-faire reflect such a norm. Any one of an infinite number of income distributions would produce a different set of relative prices. Free market prices also reflect monopoly power, and do not reflect externalities in consumption (such as my wearing a tie only because you wear one) or in production (such as pollution). In conditions of widespread unemployment and underemployment, wage rates do not reflect the opportunity cost of labor. In an economy already "distorted", an additional distortion may move it toward an improvement. For reasons such as these, the notion that government interventions "distort" an otherwise correct set of signals and incentives is highly misleading. In the presence of such "private distortions," the addition of "public distortions" can be a beneficial corrective.

The flawed agenda of the governments in many developing countries is well summed up in the 1662 Prayer Book: "We have left undone those things which we ought to have done; And we have done those things which we ought not to have done. And there is no health in us."

4. There are clearly exceptions to this. Albert Hirschman (1967) has pointed out that an alternative to exit is voice. Competition with public sector enterprises is not always efficient. He writes:

"The presence of a ready alternative to rail transport makes it less, rather than more, likely that the weaknesses of the railways will be fought rather than indulged. With truck and bus transportation available, a deterioration in rail services is not nearly so serious a matter as if the railways held a monopoly for long-distance transport—it can be lived with for a long time without arousing strong public pressures for the basic and politically difficult or even explosive reforms in administration and management that would be required. This may be the reason public enterprise, not just in Nigeria but in many other countries, has strangely been at its weakest in sectors such as transportation and education where it is subjected to competition: instead of stimulating improved or top performance, the presence of a ready and satisfactory substitute for the services public enterprise offers merely deprives it of a precious feedback mechanism that operates at its best when the customers are securely locked in. For the management of public enterprise, always fairly confident that it will not be let down by national treasury, may be less sensitive to the loss of revenue due to the switch of customers to a competing mode than to the protests of an aroused public that has a vital stake in the service, has no alternative, and will therefore "raise hell".

5. Lance Taylor (in an oral presentation) distinguished between the four possible combinations of weak/strong states and competitive/cartellized or rigged markets. The weak state combined with competitive markets is Buchanan's heaven. The strong state combined with atomistic markets is Lal's heaven. The weak state combined with monopolistic markets is Olson's hell. And the strong state combined with monopolistic markets is North's hell.

6. Contrasted with Taylor's heaven and hells, this might be considered earth, or the real world.

7. There are some exceptions, such as Lal quoted above and Olson. Another asymmetry has been identified by Shapiro and Taylor. While it is pointed out that bureaucrats have no special talent for running an economy, they are called upon to do so in the authoritarian state that dismantles the controls.

8. Myrdal anticipated the emphasis on encouragement or what he called "positive controls". The term is unfortunate, for controls suggest prevention.

9. A recent book, whose contributors are mainly political scientists and historians, is entitled *The Economic Limits to Modern Politics* (Dunn 1990). But this is not quite the needed companion volume to the political limits to modern economics.

10. In the nineteenth century it was widely thought that democracy would destroy private property, for the majority of the poor would vote to expropriate the rich. Other explanations of the link between the market economy and democracy include the provision of: "the social space" for a civil society (Berger 1992) and the possibility of political dissent (Bhagwati 1992).

11. The fact that many socialist and ex-socialist countries are "outliers" if one traces income per head against human indicators such as life expectancy is open to two interpretations: they may have done especially well on the human performance, or especially badly on the economic performance.

12. The comprehensive package of measures recommended to Eastern Europe is known as a program of stabilization, liberalization, and privatization. Stabilization refers to a stable macroeconomic environment.

13. Albert (1993) writes: "In the US (and, to some extent in the UK), it is increasingly obvious that the major `winners' in the drive to deregulate the economy have been the lawyers, for whom chaos in the airlines industry and bankruptcy among the savings and loan associations have been an unqualified boon...The US now has more lawyers than farmers." (p. 10)

14. An interesting plea for decentralization to the states in the USA is made by Alice M. Rivlin (1994) appointed Deputy Director of the Office of Management and Budget by President Clinton.

15. Usually participation and democratization are discussed only in the political domain. But the other three sectors, the private sector, the civil society, and the familial society also need democratization.

16. It should be noted that attempts at cost recovery in squatter-upgrading projects showed that default rose with income.

17. It should be noted that even in the market place individuals do not always behave selfishly.

18. In advocating maximum delegation to markets as morally neutral systems of coordination, the self-interest school also ignores the fact, pointed out by many authors, that markets presuppose generalized moral norms, and particularly trust. See, for example, Arrow (1971, 1973) and Platteau (1991). See also MacPherson (1984) and Hausman and MacPherson (1993).

19. Some countries, like Italy, give the impression that their citizens have entered with their governments into an *anti*-social contract: we shall not pay taxes, and in return we do not expect any public services.

20. Marx himself, of course, originated this view in his writings on India.

21. Without these two groups there is no Archimedean point from which any political economy that endogenizes politicians can lift itself out of full determinism and make room for the possibility of reform. If we accept determinism, we have no choice.

22. Thomas Balogh dedicated his book *The Dollar Crisis* to Lord Lindsay of Birker, the Master of Balliol College, Oxford, "who never quite could convince me that Oxenstierna had the whole explanation..." Count Oxenstierna had written to his son in 1648 "An nescis, mi fili, quantilla prudentia regitur orbis?" ("Dost thou not know, my son, with how little wisdom the world is governed?") Balogh, disagreeing with Lindsay, believed that it was knavery more than foolishness that was responsible for the world's troubles.

References

Albert, M., 1993. *Capitalism against Capitalism*. London: Whurr Publishers.

Arrow, K., 1971. "Political and Economic Evaluation of Social Effects and Externalities." In M. Intriligator, ed., *Frontiers of Quantitative Economics*. Amsterdam: North-Holland.

———, 1973. *Information and Economic Behavior*. Stockholm: Federation of Swedish Industries.

———, 1974. *The Limits of Organization*.

Barro, R., 1989. "A Cross-country Study of Growth, Saving and Government." NBER Working Paper No. 2885. National Bureau of Economic Research, Cambridge, Massachusetts.

Berger, P. 1992. "The Uncertain Triumph of Democratic Capitalism." *Journal of Democracy* 3(3):10-12.

Bhagwati, J., 1988. *Protectionism*. Cambridge: M.I.T. Press.

———, 1992. "Democracy and Development." *Journal of Democracy* 3(3):37-44.

Bhalla, S., undated. "Free Societies, Free Markets and Social Welfare." Unpublished.

Blejer, M., and M. Khan, 1984. "Government Policy and Private Investment in Developing Countries." *IMF Staff Papers* 31:379–403.

Campos, N., 1994. "Why Does Democracy Foster Economic Development? An Assessment of the Empirical Literature." Department of Economics, University of Southern California Los Angeles, October. Unpublished.

Chakravarti, S., 1987. *Development Planning: The Indian Experience.* Oxford: Clarendon Press.

Chatterji, M., B. Gilmore, K. Strunk, and J. Vanasin, 1993. "Political Economy, Growth and Convergence in Less-Developed Countries." *World Development* 21(12):2029–38.

Colander, D., ed., 1984. *Neoclassical Political Economy.* Cambridge: Ballinger.

Commission on Global Governance, 1994. *Update.* September.

———, 1995. *Our Global Neighbourhood.* Oxford: Oxford University Press.

Downs, A., 1957. *An Economic Theory of Democracy.* New York: Harper and Row.

Dunn, J., ed., 1990. *The Economic Limits to Modern Politics.* Cambridge: Cambridge University Press.

The Economist, 1992a. February 8th, p. 49.

———, 1992b. August 8th, p. 51.

Grindle, M. S., and J. W. Thomas, 1991. *Public Choices and Policy Change: The Political Economy of Reform in Developing Countries.* Baltimore: Johns Hopkins University Press.

Haussman, D., and M. S. MacPherson, 1993. "Taking Ethics Seriously: Economics and Contemporary Moral Philosophy." *Journal of Economic Literature* 21(2):671-731.

Hirschman, A. O., 1967. *Development Projects Observed.* Washington: Brookings Institution. Cited in *Exit, Voice and Loyalty,* 1970. Cambridge: Harvard University Press.

———, 1994. "The On-and-Off Connection Between Political and Economic Progress." *American Economic Review, Papers and Proceedings* 84(2):343-48.

International Monetary Fund, 1994. *IMF Survey.* Washington, D.C.

Klitgaard, R., 1988. *Controlling Corruption.* Berkeley and London: University of California Press.

Keegan, W., 1992. *The Spectre of Capitalism; The Future of the World Economy after the Fall of Communism.* London: Radius.

Kohli, A., 1986. "Democracy and Development." In J. P. Lewis and V. Kallab, eds., *Development Strategies Reconsidered.* Washington: Overseas Development Council.

Krueger, A. O., 1974. "The Political Economy of the Rent-Seeking Society." *American Economic Review* 64:291–303.

Lal, D., 1983. *The Poverty of Development Economics.* Cambridge: Harvard University Press.

Landel-Mills, P., and I. Serageldin, 1992. "Governance and the External Factor." Proceedings of the World Bank Annual Conference on Development Economics 1991, Supplement to the World Bank Economic Review and the World Bank Research Observer. World Bank, Washington, D.C.

Lateef, K. S., 1992. "Comment on 'Governance and Development' by Boeninger." Proceedings of the World Bank Annual Conference on Development Economics 1991, Supplement to the World Bank Economic Review and Research Observer, World Bank, Washington, D.C.

Lewis, J. P. 1990. "Government and National Economic Development." In F. X. Sutton ed., *A World to Make: Development in Perspective.* New Brunswick and London: Transaction Publishers.

Lipton, M., 1989. "Agriculture, Rural People, the State and the Surplus in Some Asian Countries: Thoughts on Some Implications of Three Recent Approaches in Social Science." *World Development* 17:1553–71.

———, 1991. "The State-Market Dilemma, Civil Society and Structural Adjustment." *The Round Table* 317:21–31.

MacPherson, M. S., 1984. "Limits on Self-Seeking: the Role of Morality in Economic Life." In D. Colander, ed., *Neoclassical Political Economy: The Analysis of Rent-Seeking and DUP Activities.* Cambridge: Ballinger.

Meier, G. M., 1984. *Emerging from Poverty, The Economics that Really Matters.* Oxford: Oxford University Press.

Mosley, P., 1990. "Increased Aid Flows and Human Resource Development in Africa." Innocenti Occasional Papers Number 5. UNICEF International Child Development Centre.

Myrdal, G., 1968. *Asian Drama.* Harmondsworth: Penguin.

Nelson, J., 1992. "Comment on 'Governance and Development' by Boeninger". Proceedings of the World Bank Annual Conference on Development Economics 1991, Supplement to the World Bank Economic Review and the World Bank Research Observer. Washington, D.C., World Bank.

Ohlin, G., 1994. "A Plea for Realism in Discussing International Cooperation." Participant Paper 52 for the Roundtable on Global Change. Saltsjobaden, UNDP, 22–24 July 1994.

Olson, M., 1993. "Dictatorship, Democracy and Development." *American Political Science Review* 87(3):567-76.

Ortiz, G., and C. Noriega, 1988. "Investment and Growth in Latin America." Washington: International Monetary Fund.

Platteau, J-P., 1991. "The Free Market is not Readily Transferable: Reflections on the Links between Market, Social Relations, and Moral Norms." Paper prepared for the 25th Jubilee of the Institute of Development Studies, Sussex, Cahiers de la faculté des sciences économiques et sociales, facultés universitaires Notre-Dame de la Paix, Namur, Belgium, November 1991.

Przeworski, A. 1992. "The Neoliberal Fallacy." *Journal of Democracy* (July):58–9.

Przeworski, A., and F. Limongi, 1993. "Political Regimes and Economic Growth." *The Journal of Economic Perspectives* Summer:51–69.

Putnam, R., with R. Leonardi and R. Y. Nanetti, 1993. *Making Democracy Work.* Princeton: Princeton University Press.

Rivlin, A., 1994. *Reviving the American Dream: The Economy, the States and the Federal Government.* Washington: The Brookings Institution.

Ruttan, V., 1991. "What Happened to Political Development?" *Economic Development and Cultural Change* 39(2):265-92.

Seers, D., 1979. "Introduction: The Congruence of Marxism and Other Neoclassical Doctrines." In *Toward a New Strategy of Development*, A Rothko Chapel Colloquium. New York and Oxford: Pergamon Press.

Sen, A., 1995. "Rationality and Social Choice." *American Economic Review* 85(1):1-24.

Shapiro, H., and L. Taylor, 1990. "The State and Industrial Strategy." *World Development* 18(6):861-78.

Streeck, W., 1989. "The Social Dimensions of the European Community." Paper prepared for the 1989 meeting of the Andrew Shonfield Association, Florence, September 14–15.

Streeten, P., 1987. *What Price Food?* Basingstoke: Macmillan, and Ithaca: Cornell University Press.

———, 1993. "Markets and States: Against Minimalism." *World Development* 21(8):1281–98.

UNDP, 1991. *Human Development Report 1991.* Published for the United Nations Development Program. New York and Oxford: Oxford University Press.

UNICEF, 1987. *Adjustment with a Human Face, Vol. 1: Protecting the Vulnerable and Promoting Growth.* Oxford: Oxford University Press.

Wade, R., 1990. *Governing the Market.* Princeton: Princeton University Press.

Warren, B., 1979. "The Postwar Economic Experience of the Third World." In *Toward a New Strategy for Development*, A Rothko Chapel Colloquium. New York and Oxford: Pergamon Press.

Williamson, J., ed., 1994. *The Political Economy of Policy Reform.* Washington: Institute for International Economics.

World Bank, 1989. *Sub-Saharan Africa: From Crisis to Sustainable Growth. A Long-Term Perspective Study.* Washington, D.C.

———, 1991. *World Development Report 1991: The Challenge of Development.* Oxford University Press.

Chapter 3

Democracy: A Recipe for Growth?

Robert J. Barro

E conomic freedoms, in the form of free markets and small governments that focus on the maintenance of property rights, are often thought to encourage economic growth. This view receives support from the present study, which uses data since 1960 from many countries. The results confirm the importance of economic freedom and provide some quantification of the linkages among growth rates, market distortions, rule of law, and other variables.

The connection between political and economic freedom is more controversial, as stressed in the theoretical parts of the recent surveys by Sirowy and Inkeles (1990) and Przeworski and Limongi (1993). Some observers, such as Friedman (1962), believe that the two freedoms are mutually reinforcing. In this view, an expansion of political rights—more "democracy" — fosters economic rights and tends thereby to stimulate growth. But the growth-retarding features of democracy have also been stressed. These features involve the tendency to enact rich-to-poor redistributions of income (including land reforms) in systems of majority voting and the enhanced role of interest groups in systems with representative legislatures.

Authoritarian regimes may partially avoid these drawbacks of democracy. Moreover, nothing in principle prevents nondemocratic governments from maintaining economic freedoms and private property. A dictator does not have to engage in central planning. Examples of autocracies that have expanded economic freedoms include the Pinochet government in Chile, the Fujimori administration in Peru, and several previous and current regimes in East Asia. Furthermore, as stressed by Schwarz (1992), most Organisation for Economic Co-operation and Development (OECD) countries began their modern economic development in systems with limited political rights and became full-fledged representative democracies only much later.

The effects of autocracy on growth are adverse, however, if a dictator uses his power to steal the nation's wealth and to carry out nonproductive investments. Many governments in Africa, some in Latin America, some in the formerly planned economies of eastern Europe, and the Marcos administration in the Philippines seem to fit this pattern. Thus, history suggests that dictators come in two types, those whose personal objectives often conflict with growth promotion, and those whose interests dictate a preoccupation with economic development. This perspective accords with Sah's (1991, 70-71) view that dictatorship is a form of risky investment. In any event, the theory that determines which kind of dictatorship will prevail is presently missing.

Democratic institutions provide a check on governmental power and thereby limit the potential of public officials to amass personal wealth and to carry out unpopular policies. Since at least some policies that stimulate growth will also be politically popular, more political rights tend to be growth-enhancing on this count. Thus, the net effect of democracy on growth is theoretically inconclusive.

Another question concerns the impact of economic development on a country's propensity to experience democracy. A common view since Lipset's (1959) research is that prosperity tends to inspire democracy; this idea is often described as the Lipset hypothesis.[1] Theoretical models of the processes that underlie the positive effect of economic development on democracy are not so well developed.[2] But, in any event, the cross-country evidence in the present study strongly supports the Lipset hypothesis: increases in various measures of the standard of living tend to generate a gradual rise in democracy. In contrast, democracies that arise without prior economic development—sometimes because they are imposed from outside—tend not to last.

Framework of the Empirical Analysis

The framework for the growth analysis is an extension of the neoclassical growth model to include governmental functions and other elements.[3] The long-run or steady state level of per capita output in this model depends on an array of choice and environmental variables.[4] The private sector's choices include fertility and saving rates, each of which depends on preferences and costs. The government's choices involve spending in various categories, tax rates, extent of distortions of markets and business decisions, maintenance of the rule of law and property rights, and degree of political freedom. Also relevant are the terms of trade, typically given to an individual country by international conditions.

For a given initial level of per capita output, an increase in the steady state level of per capita output raises the per capita growth rate over a transition interval. For example, if the government improves the climate for business activity—say by reducing the burdens from regulation, corruption, and taxation, or by enhancing property rights—the growth rate increases for a while. Similar effects arise if people decide to have fewer children or (in a closed economy) to save a larger fraction of their incomes. In all of these cases, an increase in the long-run level of per capita output translates into a transitional increase in the economy's growth rate. Moreover, because the transitions tend to be lengthy, the growth effects persist for a long time.

For given values of the choice and environmental variables, a higher starting value of per capita output leads to a lower per capita growth rate. This relation reflects primarily the presence of diminishing returns to capital in the neoclassical model. As an economy prospers, the return on investment declines, and the growth rate tends accordingly to decrease. This effect may be modified by endogenous responses of the saving rate, fertility, work effort, and migration. However, if diminishing returns apply, then the force toward lower growth rates tends eventually to dominate.

The inverse relation between the growth rate and level of per capita output leads to a well-known convergence property: poor economies tend to grow faster per capita than rich ones and tend thereby to catch up to the rich ones. The discussion already implies that this convergence force applies in the neoclassical model only in a conditional sense. For given values of the choice and environmental variables, a lower starting value of per capita output tends to generate a higher growth rate. But a poor country that has a low steady state level of per capita output—because, for example, it has political institutions that are inhospitable to investment—need not grow faster than a rich country. Since countries are likely to be poor or rich precisely because the underlying determinants of their steady states are unfavorable or favorable, the model does not predict any clear pattern of simple correlation between growth rates and starting positions.

The diffusion of technology provides another force toward convergence. Since imitation is usually cheaper than innovation, follower countries have an advantage here. However, as the stock of adaptable but uncopied ideas decreases, this advantage declines. The growth rates of follower economies accordingly tend to decrease with the level of per capita output, much as in the neoclassical growth model with diminishing returns to investment. The convergence predicted by technological diffusion is also conditional on government policies and other elements that influence the returns from introducing modern techniques to a follower economy. For example, a backward country that does not respect property rights and has few infrastructure services will not import much modern technology and will not grow rapidly.

The capital stock accumulated in the neoclassical model can be broadened to include human capital (in the forms of education, experience, and health), as well as physical capital and natural resources (see Lucas 1988, Rebelo 1991, Caballe and Santos 1993, Barro and Sala-i-Martin 1995). The economy tends toward target ratios for the various kinds of capital, but these ratios may depart from their target values in an initial state. The extent of these departures generally affects the rate at which initial per capita output approaches its steady state value. For example, a country that starts with a high ratio of human to physical capital (perhaps because of a war that destroyed mainly physical capital) tends to grow rapidly, because physical capital is more amenable than human capital to rapid expansion. A supporting force is that the adaptation of foreign technologies is facilitated by a large endowment of human capital (see Nelson and Phelps 1966, Benhabib and Spiegel 1993). This element implies an interaction effect whereby a country's growth rate is more sensitive (inversely) to its starting level of per capita output the greater its initial stock of human capital.

Empirical Findings on Growth across Countries

Table 3.1 shows the results from regressions that use the framework of the previous section. See the Appendix Table for means and standard deviations of the variables that appear in the analysis. The regressions apply to a panel of roughly 100 countries observed from 1960 to 1990. The dependent variables are the growth rates of real per capita gross domestic product (GDP) over three periods: 1965-1975, 1975-1985, and 1985-1990.[5] (The first period begins in 1965, rather than 1960, so that the 1960 value of the level of real per capita GDP can be used as an instrument; see below.) Henceforth, the term GDP will be used as a shorthand to refer to real per capita GDP.

The estimation uses an instrumental-variable technique, where some of the instruments are earlier values of the regressors.[6] This approach may be satisfactory because the residuals from the growth-rate equations for the various periods exhibit little correlation. In any event, the regressions describe the relation between growth rates and prior values of the explanatory variables.

Table 3.1: **Regressions for Per Capita Growth Rate**

Variable	(1)	(2)	(3)	(4)	(5)
log(GDP)	-.0290	-.0266	-.0264	-.0247	-.0247
	(.0029)	(.0031)	(.0029)	(.0029)	(.0029)
male schooling	.0149	.0096	.0168	.0141	.0164
	(.0038)	(.0040)	(.0037)	(.0037)	(.0036)
female schooling	-.0139	-.0080	-.0142	-.0122	-.0134
	(.0052)	(.0041)	(.0052)	(.0050)	(.0049)
log(life expectancy)	.0419	.0413	.0443	.0432	.0442
	(.0120)	(.0131)	(.0120)	(.0126)	(.0128)
log(GDP)*human capital	-.65	-.75	-.53	-.45	-.38
	(.22)	(.29)	(.17)	(.19)	(.17)
log(fertility rate)	-.0149	-.0123	-.0126	-.0163	-.0138
	(.0054)	(.0057)	(.0054)	(.0056)	(.0054)
government consumption	-.127	-.111	-.111	-.104	-.107
ratio	(.028)	(.028)	(.027)	(.027)	(.026)
public educational	.178	.140	.150	.200	.206
spending ratio	(.089)	(.090)	(.088)	(.089)	(.092)
black market premium	-.0221	-.0216	-.0231	-.0208	-.0210
	(.0056)	(.0051)	(.0054)	(.0053)	(.0052)
rule-of-law index	.00432	.00403	.00403	.00360	.00423
	(.00096)	(.00097)	(.00094)	(.00092)	(.00092)

table continued next page.

Notes: The system has three equations, where the dependent variables are the growth rate of real per capita GDP for 1965-1975, 1975-1985, and 1985-1990. The variables GDP (real per capita gross domestic product), schooling (years of attainment at the secondary and higher levels), and life expectancy at birth are observed at the beginning of each of the periods. The rule-of-law index applies to the early 1980s (one observation for each country). The terms-of-trade variable is the growth rate over each period of the ratio of export to import prices. The variable log(GDP)*human capital is the product of log(GDP) (expressed as a deviation from the sample mean) and the estimated effect of the schooling and life-expectancy variables (also expressed as deviations from samples means). The other variables are measured as averages over each period. These variables are the log of the total fertility rate, ratio of government consumption (exclusive of defense and education) to GDP, ratio of public educational spending to GDP, black market premium on foreign exchange, ratio of gross investment (private plus public) to GDP, and democracy index. The first dummy variable for democracy takes on the value 1 if the average of the democracy index is between 0 and 0.33 and 0 otherwise. The second one takes on the value 1 if the average of the democracy index is between 0.33 and 0.67 and 0 otherwise. The variables sub-Saharan Africa, Latin America, and East Asia are dummies, which take on the value 1 for countries in the respective area and 0 otherwise.

notes continued next page.

Table 3.1. continued.

Variable	(1)	(2)	(3)	(4)	(5)
terms-of-trade change	.117	.098	.127	.130	.138
	(.028)	(.029)	(.028)	(.028)	(.029)
investment ratio	.031	.022	.035	.023	.024
	(.023)	(.023)	(.021)	(.021)	(.022)
democracy index	--	--	-.0074	--	.053
			(.0060)		(.027)
democracy index squared	--	--	--	--	-.056
					(.024)
democracy index dummy for (0, 0.33)	--	--	--	.0046	--
				(.0044)	
democracy index dummy for (0.33, 0.67)	--	--	--	.0155	--
				(.0044)	
Sub-Saharan Africa	--	-.0049	--	--	--
		(.0044)			
Latin America	--	-.0090	--	--	--
		(.0035)			
East Asia	--	.0035	--	--	--
		(.0041)			
R^2	.65, .61, .24	.64, .63, .32	.66, .62, .24	.69, .55, .30	.66, .59, .29
number of observations	82, 89, 84	82, 89, 84	78, 89, 84	78, 89, 84	78, 89, 84

Individual constants (not shown) are estimated for each period. Estimation is by instrumental variables. The instruments are the five-year earlier value of log(GDP) (for example, for 1960 in the 1965-1975 equation); the actual values of the schooling, life-expectancy, rule-of-law, and terms-of-trade variables; and earlier values of the other variables. For example, the 1965-1975 equation uses as instruments the averages of the black market premium and government spending and investment ratios for 1960-1964. The estimation allows for different error variances in each period and for correlation across these errors. The estimated correlation of the errors for column (1) is -0.03 between the 1965-1975 and 1975-1985 equations, 0.06 between the 1965-1975 and 1985-1990 equations, and 0.25 between the 1975-1985 and 1985-1990 equations. The pattern is similar for the other columns. The estimates are virtually the same if the errors are assumed to be independent over the time periods. Standard errors of the coefficient estimates are shown in parentheses. The R^2 values and numbers of observations apply to each period individually.

The regression shown in column (1) includes explanatory variables that can be interpreted as initial values of state variables or as choice and environmental variables. The state variables include measures of human capital in the form of schooling and health, and the initial level of GDP. This GDP level reflects the endowments of physical capital and natural resources (and also depends on effort and the unobserved level of technology). The choice and environmental variables are the fertility rate, government spending for consumption and education,[7] the black-market premium on foreign exchange, an index of the maintenance of the rule of law, the ratio of gross investment to GDP, and the change in the terms of trade. A later analysis adds an index of democracy.

Initial Level of GDP

For given values of the other explanatory variables, the neoclassical model predicts a negative coefficient on initial GDP, which enters in the regression in logarithmic form.[8] The coefficient on the log of initial GDP has the interpretation of a conditional rate of convergence. If the other explanatory variables are held constant, then the economy tends to approach its long-run position at the rate indicated by the magnitude of the coefficient. The estimated coefficient of -0.0290 (s.e.= 0.0029) is highly significant. This estimate implies a conditional rate of convergence of 2.9 percent per year.[9]

Initial Level of Human Capital

Initial human capital appears in four variables in the regressions: male and female average years of attainment in secondary and higher schools for the adult population at the start of each period, the log of life expectancy at birth at the start of each period, and an interaction between the log of initial GDP and an overall human-capital variable. Overall human capital is the sum of the levels of male and female school attainment and the log of life expectancy, where each variable is multiplied by its coefficient in the regression.[10]

The column (1) regression indicates a significantly positive effect on growth from initial human capital in the form of health; the coefficient on the log of life expectancy is 0.042 (0.012). The results on education show the puzzling pattern described in Barro and Lee (1994) in which the estimated coefficient on male attainment is significantly positive, 0.015 (0.004), whereas that on female attainment is significantly negative, -.014 (0.005). If life expectancy is included in the regressions, as in Table 3.1, then it seems to proxy for the level of human capital; the level of educational attainment then has no additional explanatory power for growth. An additional positive effect on growth emerges, however, when male attainment is high relative to female attainment. A possible interpretation is that the gap between male and female schooling is an indicator of an economy's backwardness, and that greater backwardness induces a higher growth rate through the familiar convergence mechanism.

The interaction term between initial GDP and human capital is significantly negative, -0.65 (0.22), in column (1) of the table. The result indicates that a country with more overall human capital tends to converge faster toward its long-run position. The estimated coefficient on the interaction variable turns out, however, to be dominated by a small number of outlying observations and is accordingly sensitive to minor changes in specification. Therefore, the estimated effect may not be reliable.

Educational Spending

A likely difficulty with the educational variables is that they measure years of attainment but do not adjust for school quality. The construction of a broad data set on measures of quality—including school days per year, estimated salaries of teachers in relation to country wage rates, teacher/pupil ratios, and the frequency of school dropouts and repeaters—is ongoing. The ratio of public educational spending to GDP, included in the regressions in Table 3.1, is intended as an imperfect proxy for school quality. The estimated coefficient of this variable, 0.18 (0.09), is positive and marginally significant.

Fertility Rate

If the population is growing, then a portion of the economy's investment is used to provide capital for new workers, rather than to raise capital per worker. For this reason, a higher rate of population growth has a negative effect on the steady state level of output per effective worker in the neoclassical growth model. Another reinforcing effect is that a higher fertility rate means that increased resources are devoted to child rearing, rather than to production of goods (see Becker and Barro 1988). The regression in column (1) shows a significantly negative coefficient, -0.015 (0.005), on the log of the total fertility rate.

Fertility decisions are surely endogenous; previous research has shown that fertility typically declines with measures of prosperity, especially female education (see Schultz 1989, Behrman 1990, Barro and Lee 1994). The estimated coefficient of the fertility rate in the regression of column (1) can be interpreted as the response of growth to higher fertility, for given schooling, life expectancy, GDP, and so on. Since the average of the fertility rate over the preceding five years is used an instrument, the coefficient likely reflects the impact of fertility on growth, rather than vice versa. (In any event, the reverse effect would involve the level of GDP, rather than its growth rate.) Thus, although population growth cannot be described as the most important element in economic progress, the results do suggest that an exogenous drop in birth rates would raise the growth rate of per capita output.

Government Consumption

The regression in column (1) also shows a significantly negative effect on growth from the ratio of government consumption (measured exclusive of spending on education and defense) to GDP. The estimated coefficient is -0.13 (0.03). (The period-average of the ratio enters into the regression, and the average of the ratio over the previous five years is used as an instrument.) The particular measure of government spending is intended to approximate the outlays that do not enhance productivity. Hence, the conclusion is that a greater volume of nonproductive government spending —and the associated taxation—reduces the growth rate for a given starting value of GDP. In this sense, big government is bad for growth.

Measures of Market Distortions: The Black Market Premium and the Rule-of-Law Index

The black market premium on foreign exchange is a widely available and apparently accurate measure of a particular price distortion (the gap between the official exchange rate and the rate available to nonfavored market participants). The premium likely serves as a proxy for governmental distortions of markets more generally. One difficulty with the variable is the likelihood of reverse causation; economic difficulties may pressure governments into exchange controls and other policies that lead to high black market premiums. This problem is mitigated by the use of an average of the premium over the previous five years as an instrument. (The period-average of the premium appears in the regressions). The estimated coefficient, -0.022 (0.006), is significantly negative, thereby suggesting that distortions of markets are adverse for economic growth.

Knack and Keefer (1994) discuss a variety of subjective country indexes prepared for fee-paying international investors by International Country Risk Guide. The measures gauge the maintenance of the rule of law, political corruption, risk of repudiation of contracts, and so on. The rule-of-law index (measured on a 0 to 6 scale, with 6 the most favorable) appeared, a priori, to be the most relevant of these indicators for gauging the attractiveness of a country's investment climate. Thus, the rule-of-law variable is entered into the column (1) regression and has a significantly positive coefficient, 0.0043 (0.0010). (The other measures of investment risk are insignificant in the growth regression if the rule-of-law index is also included.) The desired interpretation is that greater maintenance of the rule of law is favorable to growth.

A major problem is that figures on the rule of law and the other subjective indicators are available from International Country Risk Guide starting only in the early 1980s.[11] The results shown in Table 3.1 use a single observation—that for the earliest year available in the 1980s—for each country. The equations for growth in 1965-1975 and 1975-1985 therefore use as an explanatory variable a later or contemporaneous value of the rule-of-law index. The justification for this procedure is that a country's institutional structure that governs the enforcement of laws and contracts tends to persist over long periods. Therefore, the value for the early 1980s is typically a good proxy for the values that prevailed earlier and later. The possibility of reverse causation—low growth stimulating the deterioration of law enforcement (or influencing the perceptions of International Country Risk Guide)—is, however, especially serious for the 1965-1975 regression.

Knack and Keefer (1994) provide information from another consulting service for the early 1970s on the quality of the bureaucracy, the degree of contract enforcement, and some other variables. The figures apply, however, to a much smaller number of countries. These data can be used as instruments for the rule-of-law index for the 1975-1985 equation. The system then loses the 82 observations for 1965-1975, has 44 observations (instead of 89) for 1975-1985, and retains 84 observations for 1985-1990 (for which the rule-of-law variable enters as an instrument). In this case, the estimated coefficient on the rule-of-law variable is 0.0031 (0.0019), now only marginally significant, but not significantly different from the value shown in column (1) of Table 3.1. Since the point estimate changes little when these instruments are used, it is plausible that the estimated coefficient in column (1) reflects mainly the effect of the rule of law on growth, rather than vice versa.

Another issue is the use of the rule-of-law index as a cardinal variable. As already mentioned, the index takes on the 7 possible integers from 0 to 6. Although the values may be meaningful on an ordinal scale—that is, a higher number signifies more respect for the rule of law—there is no guarantee that the variable has a cardinal meaning. Thus, even if the relation between the growth rate and some cardinal measure of the rule of law were linear, the relation with the ordinal index need not be linear.

Linearity can be checked by using dummy variables: specifically, one dummy variable is defined to equal 1 for places in rule-of-law categories 0, 1, and 2 and to equal 0 otherwise; another dummy equals 1 for places in categories 3 and 4 and equals 0 otherwise. Places with values of 5 and 6 have both dummies set to 0. The mean value of the rule-of-law index over the relevant sample of countries is 1.2 for the first group (only Guyana and Haiti have index values of 0), 3.5 for the second group, and 5.8 for the third group.

The system from column (1) of Table 3.1 was reestimated with the two dummy variables replacing the rule-of-law index. The estimated coefficient on the first dummy is -0.021 (0.004) and that on the second is -0.016 (0.004). (The other results are similar to those shown in column [1].) Thus, the countries in the lowest groups for the rule-of-law variable had the worst growth performance, those ranked in the middle came second, and those ranked highest did the best. If the relation were linear, then the coefficient on the first dummy would be roughly twice that on the second dummy (based on the means of the rule-of-law index within each group). A test of this restriction has a p-value of 0.05. Thus, although strict linearity would be barely rejected at the 5 percent level, the hypothesis is not greatly at odds with the data. The remainder of the analysis therefore retains the form in which the rule-of-law index enters directly as a regressor.

Investment Ratio

In the neoclassical growth model for a closed economy, the saving rate is exogenous and equal to the ratio of investment to output. A higher saving rate raises the steady state level of output per effective worker and thereby raises the growth rate for a given starting value of GDP. Some empirical studies of cross-country growth have also reported an important positive role for the investment ratio; see, for example, DeLong and Summers (1991) and Mankiw, Romer, and Weil (1992).

Reverse causation is, however, likely to be important here. A positive coefficient on the contemporaneous investment ratio in a growth regression may reflect the positive relation between growth opportunities and investment, rather than the positive effect of an exogenously higher investment ratio on the growth rate. This reverse effect is especially likely to apply for open economies. Even if cross-country differences in saving ratios are exogenous with respect to growth, the decision to invest domestically, rather than abroad, would reflect the domestic prospects for returns on investment, which would relate to the domestic opportunities for growth.

The regression in column (1) of Table 3.1 contains the period/average investment ratio as an explanatory variable but uses the average of the investment ratio over the preceding five years as an instrument. The estimated coefficient, 0.031 (0.023), is positive, but not statistically significant. In contrast, the estimated coefficient is more than twice as high and statistically significant if the period/average investment ratio is included as an instrument. These findings suggest that much of the positive estimated effect of the investment ratio on growth in typical cross-country regressions reflects the reverse relation between growth prospects and investment. The direct effect of exogenously higher investment on growth—which is perhaps shown by the estimated coefficient in column (1)—is much smaller than usually thought. (Blömstrom, Lipsey, and Zejan 1993 reach similar conclusions in their study of investment and growth.)

Terms of Trade

Changes in the terms of trade have often been discussed as an important influence on developing countries, which typically specialize their exports in a few primary products. The effect of a change in the terms of trade—measured as the ratio of export to import prices—on GDP is, however, not mechanical. If the physical quantities of goods produced domestically do not change, then an improvement in the terms of trade raises real domestic income and probably consumption, but does not affect real GDP. Movements in real GDP result only if the shift in the terms of trade stimulates a change in domestic employment and output. For example, an oil-importing country might react to an increase in the relative price of oil by cutting back on its employment and production.

The result in column (1) of Table 3.1 shows a significantly positive coefficient on the growth rate of the terms of trade: 0.12 (0.03). (The change in the terms of trade is regarded as exogenous to an individual country's growth rate and is therefore included as an instrument.) Thus, an improvement in the terms of trade apparently does stimulate an expansion of domestic output.[12]

Dummies for Africa, Latin America, and East Asia

Previous research, such as Barro (1991), indicates that countries in sub-Saharan Africa and Latin America grow at significantly lower rates even after holding fixed a set of explanatory variables in a regression. This kind of analysis suffers from a selection bias in that the choice of which dummy variables to consider for geographical areas is dictated by the prior observation that some places have especially low or high growth rates. Nevertheless, the confidence in the growth-rate specification would be enhanced if the regressors included already explained why the typical country in sub-Saharan Africa and Latin America grew at below-average rates.

The regression in column (2) of Table 3.1 adds dummy variables for sub-Saharan Africa, Latin America, and East Asia (a high-growth area). The result is that only the estimated coefficient for Latin America, -0.009 (0.004), is individually statistically significant at usual critical levels. The coefficient for sub-Saharan Africa is negative, -0.005 (0.004), but insignificant, whereas that for East Asia is positive, 0.004 (0.004), but also insignificant. A joint test that the coefficients of all three dummy variables are zero has a p-value of 0.031. Thus, although there is still an indication of an omitted adverse effect on growth in Latin America, the present specification accounts well for the high average growth in East Asia and is much better than previous specifications in explaining the low average growth in sub-Saharan Africa.

Democracy

The measure of democracy is the indicator of political rights compiled by Gastil and his followers (1982-1983 and subsequent issues) from 1972 to 1993. A related variable from Bollen (1990) is used for 1960 and 1965.[13] The Gastil concept of political rights is indicated by his basic definition: "Political rights are rights to participate meaningfully in the political process. In a democracy this means the right of all adults to vote and compete for public office, and for elected representatives to have a decisive vote on public policies" (Gastil, 1986-1987 edition, 7). In addition to the basic definition, the classification scheme counts as less democratic countries that have dominant political parties in which minority groups have little influence on policy.

Operationally, the concept of political rights is applied on a subjective basis to classify countries annually on a scale from 1 to 7, where 1 is the highest level of political rights. The classification is made by Gastil and his associates based on an array of published and unpublished information about each country. Unlike the rule-of-law index discussed before, the subjective ranking is not made directly by local observers.

The ranking from 1 to 7 has been converted here to a scale from 0 to 1, where 0 corresponds to the fewest political rights (Gastil's rank 7) and 1 to the most political rights (Gastil's rank 1). The scale from 0 to 1 corresponds to the system used by Bollen.

Figure 3.1 shows the time path of the unweighted average of the democracy index for 1960, 1965, and 1972-1993. The number of countries covered rises from 98 in 1960, to 109 in 1965, and 134 from 1972 to 1993. The figure shows that the mean of the democracy index peaked at 0.66 in 1960, fell to a low point of 0.44 in 1975, and rose subsequently to 0.57 in 1992-1993.

Figure 3.1
Democracy in the World, 1960-1993
(values plotted for 1960, 1965, and 1972-1993)

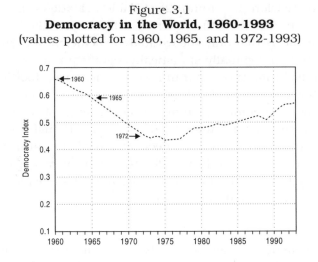

Figures 3.2 and 3.3 demonstrate that the main source of the decline in democracy after 1960 was the experience in sub-Saharan Africa. Figure 3.2 indicates that many of the African countries began with democratic institutions when they became independent in the early 1960s, but most had evolved into nondemocratic states by the early 1970s (see Bollen 1990 for further discussion). For countries outside sub-Saharan Africa, Figure 3.3 shows that the average of the democracy index fell from 0.69 in 1960 (72 countries) to 0.54 in 1975 (91 countries) and then returned to 0.68 in 1990-1992 (but fell to 0.67 in 1993).

Figure 3.2
Democracy in Sub-Saharan Africa, 1960-1993
(values plotted for 1960, 1965, and 1972-1993)

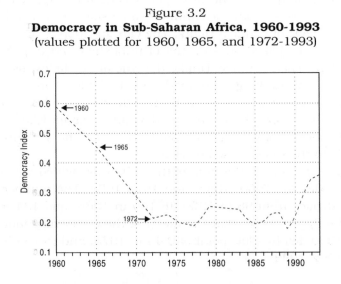

Figure 3.3
Democracy Outside of Sub-Saharan Africa, 1960-1993
(values plotted for 1960, 1965, and 1972-1993)

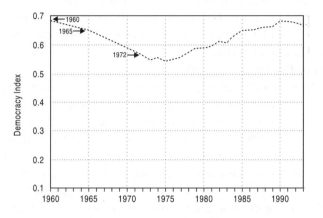

The discussion in the introduction indicated that the net effect of more political freedom on growth is theoretically ambiguous. Column (3) of Table 3.1 shows the regression results when the democracy index is included as an explanatory variable in the growth equations. The estimated coefficient, -0.0074 (0.0060), is negative, but not statistically different from 0 at conventional critical levels. The point estimate implies that a one standard deviation increase in democracy (by 0.3 in the indicator, see Appendix Table) reduces the growth rate by 0.002 per year. Thus, the results are consistent with a moderate adverse influence of democracy on growth.

Some previous studies, such as Kormendi and Meguire (1985) and Scully (1988), report favorable effects of political freedom on growth.[14] It is possible to replicate these kinds of results within the present framework by eliminating some of the other independent variables from the regressions. For example, if the variables for the rule of law, schooling, life expectancy, and fertility are omitted, then the estimated coefficient of democracy becomes significantly positive, 0.0141 (0.0067). A reasonable interpretation is that democracy looks favorable for growth in this specification only because democracy is positively correlated with some omitted country characteristics that are themselves growth-enhancing. Once these other variables are held constant, the marginal contribution of democracy to growth becomes moderately negative.[15]

Democracy may also indirectly influence growth by affecting some of the explanatory variables that are held constant in the regressions. For example, more political rights might stimulate female education (by promoting equality among the sexes), which in turn reduces fertility and thereby promotes growth. However, if fertility and female schooling are omitted from the growth equations (but male schooling, life expectancy, and the rule-of-law index are retained), then the estimated coefficient on the democracy variable is still negative, -0.009 (0.006). Hence, the channel through female schooling and fertility is not sufficient for democracy to show up as a positive influence on growth.

Another possibility is that democracy encourages maintenance of the rule of law. Tests of this hypothesis are hampered by the limited availability of time-series information on the rule-of-law concept. For a sample of 47 countries, it is possible to consider the dynamic relation between the rule-of-law index, which applies to the early 1980s, and the previously discussed measures of bureaucratic delay and contract enforcement, which apply to the early 1970s. A regression for the rule-of-law variable that includes these two measures, along with log(GDP) for 1975, log(life expectancy) for 1970-1974, and democracy for 1975 has a coefficient of -0.61 (0.71) on democracy. Thus, this limited evidence suggests that democracy does not promote the maintenance of the rule of law.

The analysis thus far has considered only linear relations between growth and democracy. The relation may be nonlinear because the democracy index—based on Gastil's (1982-1983) seven subjective categories—has only an ordinal meaning and also because the true relation between growth and democracy could be nonlinear. For example, in the worst dictatorships, an increase in political rights might be growth-enhancing because of the benefit from limitations on governmental power. But in places that have already achieved a moderate amount of democracy, a further increase in political rights might impair growth because of the intensified concern with income redistribution.

Column (4) of Table 3.1 shows the results when the democracy index is replaced by two dummy variables. The first dummy equals 1 if the democracy index is between 0 and 0.33 and equals 0 otherwise, and the second dummy equals 1 if the index is between 0.33 and 0.67 and equals 0 otherwise. The estimated coefficients are 0.005 (0.004) for the first dummy and 0.016 (0.004) for the second. The p-value for the joint significance of the two dummy variables is 0.001. (The hypothesis of linearity—requiring that the coefficient of the first dummy be roughly double that of the first—is strongly rejected.)

The results indicate that the middle level of democracy is most favorable to growth, the lowest level comes second, and the highest level comes third. The strongest part of this finding is the superiority of the middle level over the other two; the lowest and highest groups do not have significantly different growth rates (given the values of the other independent variables).

Similar conclusions emerge if the democracy index is entered directly in a quadratic form. Column (5) of Table 3.1 shows that the estimated coefficient on the linear term is positive, 0.053 (0.027), whereas that on the squared term is negative, -0.056 (0.024). The p-value for joint significance of the two terms is 0.02. In this form, the results suggest that, at low levels of democracy, more political freedom enhances growth. The growth rate reaches a peak at a middle level of democracy—the point estimate is 0.47—and then diminishes if democracy continues to rise.

Figure 3.4 shows the nature of the partial relation between the growth rate and the level of democracy. The vertical axis plots the part of the growth rate that is unexplained by the independent variables other than the democracy index and its square (from the regression in column [5] of Table 3.1).[16] The scatter diagram shows how this "partial residual" relates to the democracy index. An inverse u-shape can be discerned in the plot, with many of the low and high democracy places exhibiting negative residuals. Only a few of the countries with middle levels of democracy (e.g., Argentina and Peru) have negative residuals. However, the overall relation is far from perfect; for example, a number of countries with little democracy have large positive residuals. Also, the places with middle levels of democracy seem to avoid low growth rates but do not have especially high growth rates. Thus, at this point, there is only the suggestion of a nonlinear relation in which more democracy raises growth when political freedoms are weak but depresses growth when a moderate amount of freedom is already established.

Figure 3.4
Partial Relation between Growth and Democracy

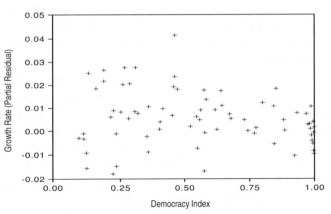

Sources of Growth

Table 3.2 uses groups of slow and fast-growing countries to illustrate how the fitted growth rates break down into contributions from the individual explanatory variables. The countries considered fall into the lowest or highest quintiles of growth rates from 1965 to 1990. Group I in the table has 15 slow-growing sub-Saharan African countries, group II has 6 slow-growing Latin American countries, group III has 9 fast-growing East Asian countries, and group IV has 6 fast-growing European countries. The table can be used to see how the model "explains" or fails to explain the sharp differences in growth performance among the four groups of countries.

The fitted growth rates in Table 3.2 come from a regression that excludes the democracy variable; that is, the one shown in column (1) of Table 3.1. These fitted values are expressed relative to the sample mean in each period (see Appendix Table). For a typical poor country, the contribution to fitted growth from log (GDP) is positive, but this effect is offset by negative contributions from human capital and fertility (because GDP is strongly positively correlated with human capital and strongly negatively correlated with fertility). For this reason, it is helpful to think of a net convergence effect, which combines the contributions from log (GDP) with those from human capital and fertility. The contribution to fitted growth from this net convergence effect is shown along with the individual elements in Table 3.2.

The table shows that the net convergence effects for the African and European countries are each close to zero in the 1965-1975 period. For Africa, the positive effect from low GDP is offset by low values of human capital and high values of fertility, whereas in Europe, the negative effect from high GDP is offset by high values of human capital and low values of fertility. In contrast to these experiences, the East Asian countries have a substantial positive contribution from net convergence, 0.019, because human capital (especially male schooling) starts out high relative to GDP.

For the Latin American countries, a noteworthy result is the adverse contribution from high market distortions, especially toward the end of the sample. For 1985-1990, the contributions to growth are -0.013 from the black market premium and -0.008 from the rule-of-law index (which does not vary over time). The African countries also suffer from large distortions, whereas the East Asian and European countries benefit from small distortions. High government consumption is another negative contributor for Africa. The terms-of-trade change, although often mentioned as a key element in Africa, is not a major element for any of the groups.

Table 3.3 uses the same approach to illustrate sources of growth by time period for 35 individual countries. In this case, the breakdown by components is less detailed, consisting of the net convergence effect, the

Table 3.2
Sources of Growth for Slow and Fast Growers

	1965-1975	1975-1985	1985-1990
I. Fifteen slow-growing sub-Saharan African countries			
Per capita GDP growth rate	.000 (15)	-.022 (15)	-.010 (15)
Growth relative to sample mean	-.030 (15)	-.034 (15)	-.021 (15)
Fitted growth, relative to mean	-.020 (6)	-.031 (7)	-.025 (7)
Contributions to fitted growth:			
Net convergence effect	.000 (10)	.004 (10)	.009 (10)
of which:			
initial GDP	.024 (15)	.032 (15)	.042 (15)
male schooling	-.010 (10)	-.014 (10)	-.018 (10)
female schooling	.007 (10)	.011 (10)	.015 (10)
life expectancy	-.014 (15)	-.012 (15)	-.011 (15)
initial GDP*human capital	-.003 (10)	-.005 (10)	-.008 (10)
fertility rate	-.005 (15)	-.007 (15)	-.009 (14)
Government consumption	-.012 (13)	-.010 (13)	-.009 (11)
Educational spending	-.001 (11)	-.001 (11)	-.002 (11)
Rule of law	-.003 (10)	-.003 (10)	-.003 (10)
Black market premium	-.002 (12)	-.010 (13)	-.005 (14)
Investment ratio	-.004 (15)	-.004 (15)	-.003 (15)
Terms of trade	-.001 (14)	.000 (14)	-.002 (14)

continued.

Table 3.2. continued.

	1965-1975	1975-1985	1985-1990
II. Six slow-growing Latin American countries			
Per capita GDP growth rate	.014 (6)	-.023 (6)	-.027 (6)
Growth relative to sample mean	-.016 (6)	-.035 (6)	-.038 (6)
Fitted growth, relative to mean	-.016 (5)	-.016 (6)	-.015 (6)
Net convergence effect	-.008 (6)	-.001 (6)	.008 (6)
of which:			
initial GDP	-.006 (6)	-.002 (6)	.008 (6)
male schooling	-.005 (6)	-.005 (6)	-.006 (6)
female schooling	.002 (6)	.003 (6)	.002 (6)
life expectancy	.000 (6)	.001 (6)	.001 (6)
initial GDP*human capital	.003 (6)	.004 (6)	.004 (6)
fertility rate	-.002 (6)	-.002 (6)	-.001 (6)
Government consumption	.000 (6)	.000 (6)	.001 (6)
Educational spending	-.001 (6)	-.001 (6)	-.001 (6)
Rule of law	-.008 (6)	-.008 (6)	-.008 (6)
Black market premium	.000 (5)	-.003 (6)	-.013 (6)
Investment ratio	-.001 (6)	-.001 (6)	-.001 (6)
Terms of trade	.002 (6)	-.002 (6)	.000 (6)

continued.

Table 3.2. continued.

	1965-1975	1975-1985	1985-1990
III. Nine fast-growing East Asian countries			
Per capita GDP growth rate	.059 (9)	.052 (9)	.058 (9)
Growth relative to sample mean	.028 (9)	.040 (9)	.047 (9)
Fitted growth, relative to mean	.031 (8)	.031 (8)	.022 (8)
Net convergence effect	.019 (8)	.012 (8)	.001 (8)
of which:			
initial GDP	.004 (8)	-.002 (9)	-.013 (9)
male schooling	.008 (8)	.007 (8)	.012 (8)
female schooling	.000 (8)	.000 (8)	-.005 (8)
life expectancy	.002 (9)	.004 (9)	.004 (9)
initial GDP*human capital	.003 (8)	.001 (8)	-.001 (8)
fertility rate	.001 (9)	.005 (9)	.007 (9)
Government consumption	.004 (8)	.006 (8)	.007 (8)
Educational spending	-.001 (8)	-.001 (8)	-.001 (8)
Rule of law	.005 (8)	.005 (8)	.005 (8)
Black market premium	.002 (8)	.004 (8)	.005 (8)
Investment ratio	.001 (9)	.003 (9)	.003 (9)
Terms of trade	.001 (9)	.000 (9)	.001 (9)
IV. Six fast-growing European countries			
Per capita GDP growth rate	.050 (6)	.026 (6)	.038 (6)
Growth relative to sample mean	.020 (6)	.014 (6)	.027 (6)
Fitted growth, relative to mean	.019 (6)	.013 (6)	.013 (6)
Net convergence effect	.004 (6)	-.004 (6)	-.007 (6)
of which:			
initial GDP	-.017 (6)	-.023 (6)	-.028 (6)
male schooling	.002 (6)	.002 (6)	.007 (6)

continued.

Table 3.2. continued.

	1965-1975	1975-1985	1985-1990
female schooling	-.002 (6)	-.002 (6)	-.005 (6)
life expectancy	.010 (6)	.009 (6)	.008 (6)
initial GDP*human capital	.002 (6)	.001 (6)	.001 (6)
fertility rate	.009 (6)	.009 (6)	.011 (6)
Government consumption	.004 (6)	.004 (6)	.003 (6)
Educational spending	.000 (6)	.000 (6)	-.001 (6)
Rule of law	.006 (6)	.006 (6)	.006 (6)
Black market premium	.003 (6)	.004 (6)	.006 (8)
Investment ratio	.004 (6)	.003 (6)	.002 (6)
Terms of trade	-.001 (6)	.000 (6)	.004 (6)

Notes: The groups of countries are selected from those in the lowest or highest quintile of growth rates of real per capita GDP from 1965 to 1990. The 15 slow-growing sub-Saharan African countries are (in increasing order of growth rates) Chad, Mozambique, Madagascar, Zambia, Uganda, Zaire, Somalia, Benin, Niger, Mauritania, Comoros, Central African Republic, Sierra Leone, Ghana, and Sudan. The six slow-growing Latin American countries are Nicaragua, Guyana, Venezuela, Peru, Haiti, and Argentina. The nine fast-growing East Asian countries (in decreasing order of growth rates) are the Republic of Korea; Singapore; Taipei,China; Hong Kong; People's Republic of China; Indonesia; Japan; Thailand; and Malaysia. The six fast-growing European countries are Malta (included with Europe), Portugal, Ireland, Italy, Greece, and Finland.

Fitted values are from the growth-rate regression shown in column (1) of Table 3.1. The figure in parentheses is the number of observations over which the value is averaged (reflecting the availability of data). The fitted values (expressed as deviations from sample means) are broken down into components, which correspond to the explanatory variables in the regression. See the text and the notes to Table 3.1 for definitions of variables.

The net convergence term encompasses the effects from initial real per capita GDP, male and female secondary and higher school attainment, life expectancy, the interaction between initial real per capita GDP and human capital (schooling and life expectancy), and the fertility rate. Since the rule-of-law index has only one observation per country, the estimated contribution from this variable does not vary over time.

total influence of government consumption and public education (a government spending effect), the combined impact from the rule-of-law index and the black market premium (an overall distortions effect), the influence of the investment ratio, and the effect of the change in the terms of trade.

Effects of Economic Development on Democracy

Inspection of the cross-country data suggests that countries at low levels of economic development typically do not sustain democracy. For example, the political freedoms installed in most of the newly-independent African states in the early 1960s did not tend to last. Conversely, nondemocratic places that experience substantial economic development have a tendency to become more democratic. Examples include Chile; the Republic of Korea; Portugal; Spain; and Taipei,China.

Table 3.4 contains regressions that test the idea that prosperity stimulates the development of democratic institutions; that is, the hypothesis associated with Lipset (1959). The dependent variables are the averages of the democracy indexes over three periods of roughly a decade, 1965-1974 (based on data for 1965 and 1972-1974), 1975-1984, and 1985-1993. The explanatory variables are indicators of the level of the standard of living, GDP, life expectancy at birth, and educational attainment. The schooling figures that turn out to be important here are the years of attainment at the primary level for males and females.

The framework amounts to an error-correction model: the long-run target for democracy depends on the standard of living, and democracy tends to rise or fall depending on whether the target is above or below the current level of democracy. Thus, column (1) of Table 3.4 includes as a regressor the lagged value of democracy; 1960 in the 1965-1974 equation, 1972 (1970 is unavailable) in the 1975-1984 equation, and 1980 in the 1985-1993 equation. The measures of standard of living refer, respectively, to 1965, 1975, and 1985.

The significantly positive coefficients on log (GDP) and log (life expectancy) indicate that the target level of democracy is increasing in these indicators of the standard of living.[17] Female school attainment is also significantly positive, whereas male attainment is significantly negative. This finding is reminiscent of the results in the growth regressions, where a larger gap between male and female attainment was viewed as a signal of greater backwardness. In Table 3.4, a smaller excess of male over female attainment signals less backwardness—that is, a more advanced society—and thereby raises the target level of democracy.

In column (1) of Table 3.4, the estimated coefficient on the lag of democracy, 0.46 (0.04), is significantly positive, but also significantly less than one. This result indicates that a country's level of democracy tends to move roughly half the way toward the value associated with its standard of living in a decade.

In column (2), the process of adjustment is related to two lags of democracy. (Because of lack of data before 1960, this system includes only two equations.) The estimated coefficients on the lagged democracy variables, 0.36 (0.05) and 0.13 (0.05), are each significantly positive. Thus, this pattern of adjustment depends not only on the most recent value of democracy but also on the longer-term history. The pattern still implies that democracy adjusts gradually toward the values implied by the indicators of the standard of living. The estimated coefficients on these indicator variables in column (2) are similar to those in column (1).

The results from Table 3.4 can be used to forecast changes in the level of democracy from the last value observed, 1993, into the future. These forecasts are based on 1990 values of GDP and life expectancy, and on 1985 values of educational attainment (the latest figures available). The projections can be viewed as applying roughly to the year 2000.

Table 3.5 displays the results for cases in which the forecasted change in democracy has a magnitude of at least 0.14, which corresponds to a shift by one category in the Gastil ranking. For the equation from column (2) of Table 3.4, 20 of 101 countries with all of the necessary data are projected to increase democracy by at least 0.14, whereas 15 are projected to decrease by at least 0.14.

The group with large projected increases in democracy, on the left side of Table 3.5, includes some countries that have virtually no political freedom in 1993. Some of these are among the world's poorest countries, such as Sudan and Haiti, for which the projected level of democracy in 2000 is also not high. Sudan is forecasted to raise its democracy from 0 in 1993 to 0.24 in 2000, and Haiti is also expected to rise (perhaps with the assistance of the United States) from 0 to 0.24. Some other countries that have essentially no political freedom in 1993 are more well-off economically and are therefore forecasted to have greater increases in democracy; for example, the projected value in 2000 is 0.43 for Indonesia, 0.33 for Algeria, and 0.32 for Syria.

Expectations for large increases in democracy also apply to some reasonably prosperous places in which the measured level of political freedoms lags behind the standard of living. Singapore is projected to increase its democracy index from 0.33 in 1993 to 0.61 in 2000; Mexico is expected to go from 0.50 to 0.72 (a change that has probably already occurred with the 1994 elections); Fiji is anticipated to advance from 0.50 to 0.68; and Taipei,China is forecasted to rise from 0.50 to 0.64. Japan, which fell from 1.00 in 1992 to 0.83 in 1993 because of the political cor-

Table 3.3
Sources of Growth for Selected Countries

Country	Per Capita Growth Rate	Growth Relative to Sample Mean	Fitted Value	Net Convergence	Government Spending	Distortions	Investment Ratio	Terms of Trade
I. 1965-1975								
Botswana	.085	.055	.024	.016	.002	.009	.002	-.006
Ghana	.001	-.029	.000	.015	.003	-.017	-.004	.003
Kenya	.031	.001	-.001	.012	-.004	-.007	.000	-.002
South Africa	.032	.002	-.008	-.011	-.001	.005	.001	-.002
Zaire	.015	-.015	-.024	.012	-.011	-.018	-.005	-.002
Canada	.035	.004	.004	-.029	.013	.016	.002	.002
Haiti	-.005	-.035	-.022	.007	-.010	-.010	-.005	-.003
Mexico	.034	.003	-.003	-.013	.004	.007	-.001	.000
United States	.015	-.015	-.010	-.039	.014	.016	.002	-.002
Argentina	.019	-.011	-.011	-.004	.002	-.006	-.002	-.001
Brazil	.064	.034	.011	.005	.002	.005	.001	-.002
Chile	-.012	-.042	-.029	-.008	-.004	-.012	-.004	-.001
Peru	.021	-.009	-.012	-.008	.004	-.008	.000	.000
Venezuela	.000	-.030	-.013	-.036	.008	.003	-.001	.013
Hong Kong	.047	.017	.030	.007	.005	.015	.000	.002
India	.010	-.020	.003	.014	-.002	-.006	-.001	-.002
Indonesia	.046	.016	.013	.015	.003	-.011	-.003	.009
Iran	.054	.024	-.002	-.018	.009	-.007	-.001	.016
Japan	.064	.034	.025	-.001	.006	.016	.006	-.002
Rep. of Korea	.081	.051	.050	.045	.005	.000	.001	-.001
Malaysia	.047	.017	.022	.013	.004	.007	.000	-.003
Philippines	.028	-.002	-.004	.013	-.004	-.008	-.002	-.003

continued.

Table 3.3. continued.

Country	Per Capita Growth Rate	Growth Relative to Sample Mean	Fitted Value	Net Convergence	Government Spending	Distortions	Investment Ratio	Terms of Trade
Singapore	.097	.067	.056	.025	.009	.015	.004	.002
Taipei,China	.061	.031	.036	.031	-.008	.014	.001	-.002
Thailand	.040	.010	.019	.017	.001	.003	.000	-.001
Finland	.039	.009	.015	-.017	.009	.016	.006	.000
France	.033	.003	.001	-.025	.006	.016	.004	.000
West Germany	.023	-.007	.000	-.024	.004	.016	.004	.000
Ireland	.040	.010	.009	-.010	.004	.011	.003	.000
Italy	.037	.007	.004	-.014	.005	.011	.004	-.003
Portugal	.059	.029	.030	.011	.002	.015	.003	-.001
Spain	.046	.016	.004	-.009	.002	.011	.004	-.003
Sweden	.024	-.006	-.003	-.029	.008	.016	.003	.000
United Kingdom	.020	-.010	-.005	-.024	.004	.016	.001	-.002
Australia	.026	-.004	-.005	-.032	.009	.016	.004	-.002
II. 1975-1985								
Botswana	.051	.040	.003	.002	-.003	.007	.003	-.005
Ghana	-.015	-.026	-.037	.031	-.010	-.051	-.004	-.002
Kenya	-.006	-.017	.005	.010	-.003	-.003	-.001	.002
South Africa	-.004	-.016	-.019	-.012	-.001	.005	.001	-.003
Zaire	-.035	-.047	-.019	.014	-.005	-.025	-.004	.001

continued.

Table 3.3. continued.

Country	Per Capita Growth Rate	Growth Relative to Sample Mean	Fitted Value	Net Convergence	Government Spending	Distortions	Investment Ratio	Terms of Trade
Canada	.024	.012	.005	-.029	.014	.017	.002	.000
Haiti	.007	-.004	-.003	.016	-.009	-.008	-.003	.002
Mexico	.013	.002	.006	-.010	.005	.006	.000	.004
United States	.021	.009	.005	-.029	.015	.017	.001	.001
Argentina	-.014	-.026	-.013	-.007	.006	-.007	-.001	-.005
Brazil	.013	.002	-.001	-.005	.003	.003	.001	-.004
Chile	.011	.000	.005	.004	-.003	.010	-.002	-.004
Peru	-.018	-.029	-.006	-.002	.001	-.003	.001	-.004
Venezuela	-.019	-.031	-.008	-.025	.008	.000	.001	.008
Hong Kong	.065	.053	.026	.002	.006	.017	.001	-.001
India	.023	.011	.028	.032	-.002	.001	.000	-.003
Indonesia	.055	.044	.019	.019	-.001	-.005	.001	.005
Iran	-.023	-.034	-.020	-.019	.010	-.022	.002	.008
Japan	.034	.022	.017	-.015	.010	.017	.005	-.001
Rep. of Korea	.061	.049	.050	.035	.009	.003	.003	-.001
Malaysia	.044	.033	.039	.013	.010	.009	.003	.003
Philippines	-.006	-.018	-.004	.014	-.007	-.006	.000	-.006
Singapore	.049	.037	.040	.004	.010	.017	.006	.002
Taipei,China	.057	.046	.034	.020	-.003	.017	.003	-.002
Thailand	.037	.026	.020	.017	.001	.004	.000	-.003
Finland	.021	.010	.009	-.021	.007	.017	.005	.000
France	.015	.004	.005	-.024	.008	.017	.003	.001
West Germany	.021	.010	.006	-.018	.005	.017	.003	.000
Ireland	.023	.011	.013	-.012	.008	.013	.003	.001
Italy	.027	.015	.006	-.014	.004	.013	.002	.001

continued.

Table 3.3. continued.

Country	Per Capita Growth Rate	Growth Relative to Sample Mean	Fitted Value	Net Convergence	Government Spending	Distortions	Investment Ratio	Terms of Trade
Portugal	.014	.003	.019	.003	.001	.015	.002	-.001
Spain	.002	-.010	.006	-.013	.004	.013	.002	.000
Sweden	.012	.000	-.001	-.027	.007	.017	.001	.000
United Kingdom	.021	.010	.008	-.018	.006	.017	.000	.003
Australia	.016	.005	.001	-.028	.011	.017	.003	-.002
III. 1985-1990								
Botswana	.055	.045	--	-.004	-.006	.009	.000	--
Ghana	.013	.002	-.002	.034	-.016	-.009	-.004	-.008
Kenya	.033	.022	.013	.019	-.002	.000	-.001	-.001
South Africa	-.010	-.020	-.003	-.007	-.002	.008	.000	-.002
Zaire	-.025	-.036	.024	.027	-.005	-.005	-.003	.010
Canada	.021	.010	.003	-.034	.014	.019	.004	.001
Haiti	-.029	-.040	-.018	.016	-.011	-.022	-.003	.001
Mexico	.003	-.007	-.002	-.008	.004	.007	-.001	-.003
United States	.021	.010	.002	-.037	.017	.019	.002	.001
Argentina	-.021	-.031	-.003	-.002	.007	-.007	-.003	.001
Brazil	-.002	-.013	.006	-.006	.004	.000	.000	.008
Chile	.042	.031	.027	.006	.004	.011	-.001	.007
Peru	-.039	-.050	.008	.011	.003	.001	.000	-.007
Venezuela	-.009	-.020	-.023	-.016	.009	-.014	.000	.000
Hong Kong	.060	.050	.010	-.018	.006	.019	.001	.002

continued.

Table 3.3. continued.

Country	Per Capita Growth Rate	Growth Relative to Sample Mean	Fitted Value	Net Convergence	Government Spending	Distortions	Investment Ratio	Terms of Trade
India	.034	.024	.042	.040	-.003	.004	.000	.001
Indonesia	.035	.025	.007	.014	-.003	-.005	.004	-.003
Iran	-.052	-.062	-.052	-.007	.007	-.056	.002	.003
Japan	.042	.032	.019	-.023	.010	.019	.006	.007
Rep. of Korea	.087	.076	.044	.020	.012	.005	.005	.002
Malaysia	.037	.026	.025	.004	.012	.010	.003	-.004
Philippines	.028	.017	.008	.017	-.006	-.004	-.001	.001
Singapore	.059	.048	.025	-.012	.011	.019	.006	.001
Taipei,China	.077	.067	.025	.008	-.002	.018	.003	-.001
Thailand	.075	.064	.025	.014	.001	.006	.001	.003
Finland	.032	.021	.010	-.025	.006	.019	.005	.004
France	.027	.016	.009	-.026	.009	.019	.003	.003
West Germany	.029	.018	.010	-.023	.005	.019	.003	.005
Ireland	.046	.035	.012	-.014	.008	.015	.002	.001
Italy	.028	.018	.007	-.017	.002	.015	.003	.005
Portugal	.052	.041	.030	.006	-.001	.017	.001	.006
Spain	.049	.039	.022	-.005	.004	.015	.003	.004
Sweden	.017	.006	.000	-.030	.006	.019	.002	.003
United Kingdom	.032	.021	.004	-.023	.005	.019	.001	.002
Australia	.009	-.001	.005	-.030	.010	.019	.004	.002

Notes: See the notes to Tables 3.1 and 3.2. The growth rate is for per capita real GDP. The net convergence term is the combination of the effects from initial real per capita GDP, male and female school attainment at the secondary and higher levels, life expectancy at birth, and fertility. The government spending term combines the effects of government consumption (exclusive of defense and education) and public educational spending. The distortions term includes the rule-of-law index and the black market premium on foreign exchange.

Table 3.4
Regressions for Democracy Index

Variable	(1)	(2)
constant	-1.56	-1.66
	(.37)	(.50)
democ$_{t-1}$	.457	.365
	(.037)	(.050)
democ$_{t-2}$	--	.129
		(.046)
log(GDP)	.054	.048
	(.024)	(.031)
male primary schooling	-.077	-.086
	(.022)	(.027)
female primary schooling	.081	.085
	(.021)	(.026)
log(life expectancy)	.37	.40
	(.12)	(.16)
R^2	.76, .70, .75	.72, .76
number of observations	72, 95, 102	87, 102

Notes: System (1) has three equations, where the dependent variables are the average value of the democracy index for 1965-1974 (estimated from the observed values in 1965 and 1972-1974), 1975-1984, and 1985-1993. System (2) contains only the two equations for 1975-1984 and 1985-1993. The variable democ$_{t-1}$ is for 1960 in the 1965-1974 equation, 1972 in the 1975-1984 equation, and 1980 in the 1985-1993 equation. System (2) includes also democ$_{t-2}$, the value for 1960 in the 1975-1984 equation and 1972 in the 1985-1993 equation. The variables log(GDP), male and female primary schooling (years of attainment at the primary level), and life expectancy at birth apply to 1960 in the 1965-1974 equation, 1970 in the 1975-1984 equation, and 1980 in the 1985-1993 equation. Each system contains only one constant, as shown. Estimation is by the seemingly unrelated technique. The estimated correlation of the errors is 0.00 between the 1965-1975 and 1975-1984 equations, 0.22 between the 1965-1974 and 1985-1993 equations, and 0.12 between the 1975-1984 and 1985-1993 equations. The estimates are virtually the same if the error terms are assumed to be independent over the time periods. Standard errors of the estimated coefficients are shown in parentheses. The R^2 values apply to each period individually.

Table 3.5
Countries Forecasted to Experience Major Changes in Democracy

Projected to Be More Democratic			Projected to Be Less Democratic		
Country	Democracy 1993	Democracy 2000	Country	Democracy 1993	Democracy 2000
Indonesia	.00	.43	Mali	.83	.44
Bahrain	.17	.52	Benin	.83	.50
Hong Kong	.33	.67	Zambia	.67	.35
Algeria	.00	.33	Central African Rep.	.67	.36
Syria	.00	.32	Niger	.67	.37
Singapore	.33	.61	Gambia	.83	.54
Iran	.17	.41	Bangladesh	.83	.56
Yugoslavia	.17	.41	Bolivia	.83	.58
Sudan	.00	.24	Congo	.67	.42
Haiti	.00	.24	Nepal	.83	.60
Mexico	.50	.72	Hungary	1.00	.81
Tunisia	.17	.38	Pakistan	.67	.48
Iraq	.00	.21	Mauritius	1.00	.81
Swaziland	.17	.35	Papua New Guinea	.83	.65
Fiji	.50	.68	Botswana	.83	.66
Sri Lanka	.50	.67			
Peru	.33	.51			
South Africa	.33	.47			
Japan	.83	.97			
Taipei,China	.50	.64			

Notes: Democracy 1993 is based on the 1993 value of the Gastil concept of political rights, as described in the text. The measure runs from 0 to 1, with 0 representing the fewest rights. Democracy 2000 is the projected value for roughly the year 2000, based on the regression from column (2) of Table 3.4. The countries listed on the left side of the table are the 20 out of 101 places included that show projected increases of at least 0.14 in the democracy indicator. Those on the right side are the 15 with projected decreases of at least 0.14.

ruption scandals, is projected to return to 0.97 by 2000. For Peru, where the democracy index declined from 0.83 in 1989 to 0.33 in 1993 (and in which economic freedoms were strengthened), the model projects an increase to 0.51 in 2000.

South Africa is also included on the left side of the table, with a projected rise in the democracy index from 0.33 in 1993 to 0.47 in 2000. However, the political changes in South Africa in 1994 have probably overshot the mark, and the model would likely forecast a substantial decline of political freedom in this country after 1994.

The examples of large expected decreases in democracy, shown on the right side of Table 3.5, consist mainly of relatively poor countries with surprisingly high levels of political freedom in 1993. Many of these cases are African countries in which the political institutions recently became more democratic: Benin, Central African Republic, Congo, Mali, Niger, and Zambia. The regression predicts that, as with the African experience of the 1960s, democracy that gets well ahead of economic development will not last. Three other African countries, Botswana, the Gambia, and Mauritius, have maintained democratic institutions for some time, but the regression still predicts that political freedoms will eventually diminish in these places. (A military coup in July 1994 has already reduced Gambia's level of political freedom.)

For poor, but relatively democratic countries outside Africa, the forecast for large decreases in democracy applies to Bangladesh, Bolivia, Nepal, Pakistan, and Papua New Guinea. Hungary, which has a higher standard of living, is projected to decline from its fully democratic condition of 1.00 in 1993 to 0.81 in 2000.

The interplay between democracy and economic development involves the effect of political freedom on growth and the influence of the standard of living on the extent of democracy. With respect to the determination of growth, the cross-country analysis brings out favorable effects from maintenance of the rule of law, free markets, small government consumption, and high human capital. Once these kinds of variables and the initial level of GDP are held constant, the overall effect of democracy on growth is weakly negative. There is some indication of a nonlinear relation in which more democracy enhances growth at low levels of political freedom but depresses growth when a moderate level of political freedom has already been attained.

With respect to the effects of economic development on democracy, the analysis shows that improvements in the standard of living—measured by a country's real per capita GDP, life expectancy, and education—substantially raise the probability that political institutions will become more democratic over time. Hence, political freedom emerges as a sort of luxury good. Rich places consume more democracy because this good is desirable for its own sake, even though increased political freedom may have a small adverse effect on growth. Basically, rich countries can afford the reduced rate of economic progress.

The analysis has implications for the desirability of exporting democratic institutions from the advanced Western countries to developing nations. The first lesson is that more democracy is not the key to economic growth, although it may have a weak positive effect for countries that start with few political rights. The second message is that political freedoms tend to erode over time if they are out of line with a country's standard of living.

The more general conclusion is that the advanced Western countries would contribute more to the welfare of poor nations by exporting their economic systems, notably property rights and free markets, rather than their political systems, which typically developed after reasonable standards of living had been attained. If economic freedom can be established in a poor country, then growth would be encouraged and the country would tend eventually to become more democratic on its own. Thus, in the long run, the propagation of Western-style economic systems would also be the effective way to expand democracy in the world.

Acknowledgment
    The author is grateful to Jong-Wha Lee and Jordan Rappaport for help with the underlying data. This research has been supported in part by the National Science Foundation and the Bradley Foundation.

Appendix Table
Means and Standard Deviations of Variables

	Mean	Standard Deviation
I. 1965-1975 period, 87 observations or as indicated		
Growth rate of GDP, 1965-75	.030	.023
log(GDP), 1965	7.56	.94
GDP, 1965	2943	2838
Male primary school, 1965[a]	3.17	1.84
Female primary school, 1965[a]	2.53	2.04
Male secondary school, 1965	.74	.68
Female secondary school, 1965	.52	.64
Male higher school, 1965	.113	.125
Female higher school, 1965	.053	.091
log(life exp. at birth, 1960-64)	4.00	.21
log(fertility rate), 1965-74	1.53	.45
Government consumption ratio, 1965-74	.092	.065
Public educational spending ratio, 1965-74	.038	.015
Black market premium, 1965-74	.147	.200
Rule-of-law index[b]	3.2	2.0
Terms-of-trade change, 1965-75	.000	.036
Investment ratio, 1965-74	.199	.099
Democracy index, 1965-74[c]	.56	.30
II. 1975-1985 period, 97 observations or as indicated		
Growth rate of GDP, 1975-85	.011	.026
log(GDP), 1975	7.83	.96
GDP, 1975	3873	3556
Male primary school, 1975[d]	3.26	1.84
Female primary school, 1975[d]	2.64	2.05
Male secondary school, 1975	1.05	.94
Female secondary school, 1975	.78	.91

continued.

Appendix Table. continued.

	Mean	Standard Deviation
Male higher school, 1975	.176	.197
Female higher school, 1975	.089	.133
log(life exp. at birth, 1970-74)	4.05	.20
log(fertility rate), 1975-84	1.37	.53
Government consumption ratio, 1975-84	.101	.072
Public educational spending ratio, 1975-84	.045	.017
Black market premium, 1975-84	.224	.357
Rule-of-law index[e]	3.1	2.0
Terms-of-trade change, 1975-85	-.013	.035
Investment ratio, 1975-84	.193	.085
Democracy index, 1975-84	.53	.34

III. 1985-1995 period, 97 observations or as indicated

	Mean	Standard Deviation
Growth rate of GDP, 1985-90[f]	.011	.033
log(GDP), 1985	7.95	1.04
GDP, 1985	4597	4404
log(GDP), 1990[f]	8.02	1.10
GDP, 1990[f]	5193	5091
Male primary school, 1985[d]	3.79	1.68
Female primary school, 1985[d]	3.10	1.96
Male secondary school, 1985[d]	1.42	1.08
Female secondary school, 1985[d]	1.10	1.04
Male higher school, 1985[d]	.268	.246
Female higher school, 1985[d]	.159	.193
log(life exp. at birth, 1980-84)	4.12	.18
log(life exp. at birth, 1985-89)	4.15	.17
log(fertility rate), 1985-89	1.26	.55
log(fertility rate), 1990	1.23	.54
Government consumption ratio, 1980-84	.101	.074
Public educational spending ratio, 1980-84	.046	.018
Black market premium, 1985-89	.301	.514
Terms-of-trade change, 1985-90	-.009	.046
Investment ratio, 1985-89	.171	.086
Democracy index, 1985-93	.61	.33
Projected democracy index, 2000	.65	.28

Notes: The data and detailed definitions of the variables are contained in the Barro-Lee data set available from Ingrid Sayied, Economics Department, Harvard University, Cambridge MA 02138.

[a] 81 observations.

[b] 82 observations for figures from early 1980s.

[c] 83 observations, based on data for 1965, 1972-1974.

[d] 96 observations.

[e] 89 observations for figures from early 1980s.

[f] 95 observations. Some of the data for GDP in 1990 came from the World Bank rather than Summers and Heston.

Notes

1. Lipset (1959, 75) apparently prefers to view it as the Aristotle hypothesis: "From Aristotle down to the present, men have argued that only in a wealthy society in which relatively few citizens lived in real poverty could a situation exist in which the mass of the population could intelligently participate in politics and could develop the self-restraint necessary to avoid succumbing to the appeals of irresponsible demagogues."

2. Lipset (1959, 83-84) stresses increased education and an enlarged middle class as elements that expand "receptivity to democratic political tolerance norms" (a phrase that I do not understand). He also stresses the role of private organizations and institutions as crucial checks on dictatorship. The importance of private organizations has been emphasized on different grounds by Putnam (1993), who finds that the propensity for civic activity is the key underpinning of good government in the regions of Italy. Unfortunately, however, the empirical work defines good government mostly as activist government (including as positives the standard array of social programs associated in the United States with the New Deal and the Great Society). For Huber, Rueschemeyer, and Stephens (1993), the crucial theoretical idea is that capitalist development lowers the power of the landlord class and raises the power and ability to organize of the working and middle classes. It is however, hard to tell from their case-study approach whether the data support their hypothesis.

3. The theory comes from Ramsey (1928), Solow (1956), Swan (1956), Cass (1965), and Koopmans (1965). For an exposition, see Barro and Sala-i-Martin (1995, Chs. 1 and 2). Previous empirical applications of the model include Barro (1991); Mankiw, Romer, and Weil (1992); and Barro and Sala-i-Martin (1995, Ch. 12).

4. With exogenous, labor-augmenting technological progress, the level of output per worker grows in the long run, but the level of output per *effective* worker approaches a constant.

5. Most of the GDP figures are from version 5.5 of the Summers-Heston data set (see Summers and Heston 1991, 1993 for general descriptions). These values adjust for estimated differences in purchasing power across countries. World Bank figures on real GDP growth rates (based on domestic accounts only) are used for 1985-1990 when the Summers-Heston figures are unavailable.

6. Countries are equally weighted in the regressions, but the estimation allows for different error variances for each period and for correlation of the errors across the periods. The results are virtually identical, however, if the error terms from the different periods are treated as independent. See notes to Table 3.1 for additional information.

7. Data problems prevent consideration of marginal tax rates and some other components of government spending, such as transfers and infrastructure services. See Easterly and Rebelo (1993) for a discussion of these data. The ratio of defense spending to GDP turned out to be insignificant in the growth regressions.

8. The variable log (GDP) in Table 3.1 refers to 1965 in the first period, 1975 in the second period, and 1985 in the third period. Five-year earlier values of log (GDP) are used as instruments. The use of these instruments lessens the estimation problems associated with temporary measurement error in GDP.

9. This result is only approximate because the growth rate is observed as an average over ten or five years, rather than at a point in time. The implied instantaneous rate of convergence is slightly higher than the value indicated by the coefficient. See Barro and Sala-i-Martin (1992) for a discussion.

10. The interaction term measures log(GDP) and human capital as deviations from sample means. The procedure makes it easier to interpret the regression coefficients on log(GDP), male and female schooling, and log of life expectancy.

11. The information appeared contemporaneously starting in the 1980s and could not therefore be influenced by a country's subsequent experience, including its rate of economic growth.

12. Barro and Sala–i–Martin (1995, Ch. 12) consider some other regressors. One variable included in that framework and in Alesina and Perotti (1993) is political instability, measured by the frequencies of revolutions and other disruptions. The political instability variables are, however, not significantly related to growth when the rule–of–law index is also included in the regressions. King and Levine (1993) explore the effects of financial development, and Cukierman (1992) assesses the influences from inflation and central bank independence.

13. See Gastil (1991) for a discussion of the methods that underlie his data series. Inkeles (1991) provides an overview of measurement issues on democracy. He finds (p. x) a "...high degree of agreement produced by the classification of nations as democratic or not, even when democracy is measured in somewhat different ways by different analysts." Bollen (1990) suggests that his measures are reasonably comparable to Gastil's. It is difficult to check comparability directly because the two series do not overlap in time. Moreover, many countries—especially those in Africa—clearly experienced major declines in the extent of democracy from the 1960s to the 1970s. Thus, no direct inference about comparability can be made from the higher average of Bollen's figures for the 1960s than for Gastil's numbers for the 1970s.

14. Sirowy and Inkeles (1990) and Przeworski and Limongi (1993) contain broad surveys of the empirical evidence.

15. A possible argument is that the index of political freedom has so much measurement error that true democracy is more correlated with some of the other variables than with the democracy variable. It is unclear, however, that the subjective measure of political rights is less accurate than some of the other variables, especially for the poorer countries.

16. The estimated coefficients come from the regressions that include all of the variables. But the contributions from the democracy variables are omitted in the calculations of the residuals shown on the vertical axis of Figure 3.4.

17. Helliwell (1994, Table 3.1) finds that the Gastil measures of political rights and civil liberties are positively related to levels of GDP and secondary school enrollment ratios.

References

Alesina, A., and R. Perotti, 1993. "Income Distribution, Political Instability, and Investment." Working Paper No. 4486. National Bureau of Economic Research, Cambridge, Massachusetts.

Barro, R. J., 1991. "Economic Growth in a Cross Section of Countries." *Quarterly Journal of Economics* 102(2):407-33.

Barro, R. J., and J-W Lee, 1994. "Sources of Economic Growth." Carnegie-Rochester Conference Series on Public Policy.

Barro, R. J., and X. Sala-i-Martin, 1992. "Convergence." *Journal of Political Economy* 100(2):233-51.

_____, 1995. *Economic Growth.* New York: McGraw Hill.

Becker, G. S., and R. J. Barro, 1988. "A Reformulation of the Economic Theory of Fertility." *Quarterly Journal of Economics* 103(1):1-25.

Behrman, J. R., 1990. "Women's Schooling and Nonmarket Productivity: A Survey and a Reappraisal." University of Pennsylvania. Unpublished.

Benhabib, J., and M. M. Spiegel, 1993. "The Role of Human Capital and Political Instability in Economic Development." New York University. Unpublished.

Blömstrom, M., R. E. Lipsey, and M. Zejan, 1993. "Is Fixed Investment the Key to Economic Growth?" Working Paper No. 4436. National Bureau of Economic Research, Cambridge, Massachusetts.

Bollen, K. A., 1990. "Political Democracy: Conceptual and Measurement Traps." *Studies in Comparative International Development* (Spring):7-24.

Caballe, J., and M. S. Santos, 1993. "On Endogenous Growth with Physical and Human Capital." *Journal of Political Economy* 101(6):1042-67.

Cass, D., 1965. "Optimum Growth in an Aggregate Model of Capital Accumulation." *Review of Economic Studies* 32(July):233-40.

Cukierman, A., 1992. *Central Bank Strategy, Credibility, and Independence.* Cambridge: MIT Press.

De Long, J. B., and L. H. Summers, 1991. "Equipment Investment and Economic Growth." *Quarterly Journal of Economics* 106(2):445-502.

Easterly, W., and S. Rebelo, 1993. "Fiscal Policy and Economic Growth: An Empirical Investigation." *Journal of Monetary Economics* 32 (December):417-58.

Friedman, M., 1962. *Capitalism and Freedom.* Chicago: University of Chicago Press.

Gastil, R. D., and followers, 1982-83 and other years. *Freedom in the World.* Westport: Greenwood Press.

Gastil, R. D., 1991. "The Comparative Survey of Freedom: Experiences and Suggestions." In A. Inkeles, ed., *On Measuring Democracy.* New Brunswick: Transaction Publishers.

Helliwell, J. F., 1994. "Empirical Linkages Between Democracy and Economic Growth." *British Journal of Political Science* 24:225-48.

Huber, E., D. Rueschemeyer, and J.D. Stephens, 1993. "The Impact of Economic Development on Democracy." *Journal of Economic Perspectives* 7(Summer):71-85.

Inkeles, A., 1991. *On Measuring Democracy.* New Brunswick: Transaction Publishers.

King, R. G., and R. Levine, 1993. "Finance, Entrepreneurship, and Growth: Theory and Evidence." *Journal of Monetary Economics* 32 (December):513-42.

Knack, S., and P. Keefer, 1994. "Institutions and Economic Performance: Cross-Country Tests Using Alternative Institutional Measures." American University. Unpublished.

Koopmans, T. C., 1965. "On the Concept of Optimal Economic Growth." *The Econometric Approach to Development Planning.* Amsterdam: North-Holland.

Kormendi, R. C., and P. G. Meguire, 1985. "Macroeconomic Determinants of Growth." *Journal of Monetary Economics* 16:141-63.

Lipset, S. M., 1959. "Some Social Requisites of Democracy: Economic Development and Political Legitimacy." *American Political Science Review* 53:69-105.

Lucas, R. E., Jr., 1988. "On the Mechanics of Development Planning." *Journal of Monetary Economics* 22(1):3-42.

Mankiw, N. G., D. Romer, and D. N. Weil, 1992. "A Contribution to the Empirics of Economic Growth." *Quarterly Journal of Economics* 107(2): 407-37.

Nelson, R. R., and E. S. Phelps, 1966. "Investment in Humans, Technological Diffusion, and Economic Growth." *American Economic Review* 56(2):69-75.

Przeworski, A., and F. Limongi, 1993. "Political Regimes and Economic Growth." *Journal of Economic Perspectives* 7(Summer):51-69.

Putnam, R. D., with R. Leonardi and R. Y. Nanetti, 1993. *Making Democracy Work, Civic Traditions in Modern Italy.* Princeton: Princeton University Press.

Ramsey, F., 1928. "A Mathematical Theory of Saving." *Economic Journal* 38(December):543-59.

Rebelo, S., 1991. "Long-Run Policy Analysis and Long-Run Growth." *Journal of Political Economy* 99(3):500-21.

Sah, R. K., 1991. "Fallibility in Human Organizations and Political Systems." *Journal of Economic Perspectives* 5(Spring):67-88.

Schultz, T. P., 1989. "Returns to Women's Education." PHRWD Background Paper 89/001. Population, Health, and Nutrition Department, The World Bank, Washington, D.C.

Schwarz, G., 1992. "Democracy and Market-Oriented Reform—A Love-Hate Relationship?" *Economic Education Bulletin* 32(5).

Scully, G. W., 1988. "The Institutional Framework and Economic Development." *Journal of Political Economy* 96(3):652-62.

Sirowy, L., and A. Inkeles, 1990. "The Effects of Democracy on Economic Growth and Inequality: A Review." *Studies in Comparative International Development* 25(Spring):126-57.

Solow, R. M., 1956. "A Contribution to the Theory of Economic Growth." *Quarterly Journal of Economics* 70(1):65-94.

Summers, R., and A. Heston, 1991. "The Penn World Table (Mark 5): An Expanded Set of International Comparisons, 1950-1988." *Quarterly Journal of Economics* 106(2):327-68.

_____, 1993. "Penn World Tables, Version 5.5." Available on diskette from the National Bureau of Economic Research, Cambridge, Massachusetts.

Swan, T. W., 1956. "Economic Growth and Capital Accumulation." *Economic Record* 32(November):334-61.

Chapter 4

Can Anything Be Done About Corruption?

Abhijit Banerjee

The economic consequences of corruption, while (inevitably) poorly measured, seem unambiguous. The one relatively rigorous empirical study of the relation between growth and corruption in a cross-section of countries finds a positive and significant correlation (see Mauro 1993). Hines (1995), using the same data set, finds that United States companies invest significantly less in more corrupt countries.

There are a number of channels through which corruption might affect economic performance and growth. One effect which is clearly of the first order is the loss of government revenue. Lost revenues include tax revenues lost when tax inspectors are bribed to overlook unreported income, output, or imports. They also include wasted subsidies allocated to undeserving claimants (what in the United States is called "pork") and what amounts to the same thing, giving away resources controlled by the government to private parties at a fraction of their market price.

The magnitude of this loss can be substantial. To get a sense of the size of just the losses inside the tax collection system, consider the report by Acharya et al. (1986) that in India approximately 50 percent of legally reportable income goes untaxed (cited in Chander and Wilde 1992). Chu (1990) cites a survey by the city government of Taipei where 94 percent of all taxpayers claimed to have paid a bribe. Goswami et al. (1990) cite a study by The Policy Group which reported that three quarters of all Indian tax auditors accept bribes, and 68 percent of those who file their taxes through Certified Public Accountants admit to having paid bribes.[1]

A consequence of the loss of revenue is a cutback in government expenditure or a switch to inflation and other less desirable forms of taxation. It is well known, for example, that the fraction of government revenue in India that comes from direct taxes has declined very sharply over the last 40 years. Cutbacks in government expenditure may also turn out to be regressive since it is expenditure for the poor that is often easiest to cut. The cutbacks may also have direct undesirable growth effects since infrastructural investment is another area where, in the short run, it is easy to cut government expenditure. Barro (1991) finds that government investment has desirable growth effects.

To the various sources of loss of revenue on the collection side must be added the losses from direct stealing by those who are supposed to spend the money.[2] In some of the kleptocracies of present day Africa, in Trujillo's Dominican Republic, or in Somoza's Nicaragua, the loss from this kind of stealing may be of a magnitude comparable to the amount of the public debt.

Corruption has a different but potentially equally costly effect when the person being corrupted has a punitive role—say a policeman, a judge, or a pollution inspector. In each case, the goal of corruption is to exchange the more costly punishment that has been earned for a smaller cash payment to the agent who is supposed to do the punishing. The net result is to reduce the effective punishment for violating the law. The extreme version of this phenomenon is what apparently has happened in parts of both India and Pakistan: the law has broken down to the point where, for a price (paid to the police) one can buy the right to murder another human being.

The human costs of such a breakdown of the legal system are almost too frightening to contemplate. In terms of something more concrete, Wade (1984, 34) reports that corruption in the soil conservation bureaucracy in India is allowing top soil to wash away even though "top soil is India's most precious resource; each inch of top soil takes roughly 1000 years to form".

A related problem arises when corruption affects the allocation of a publicly provided private good like education or health care. These are goods that the market is unlikely to supply effectively, both because there are expenditures and because those buying them tend to be credit-constrained. To the extent that corruption reintroduces market forces into the allocation of these goods, it brings back precisely the distortions the original intervention was intended to avoid. To take an example, say that government was supplying education at a below-market price because it wanted the poor to avail of it. With corrupt bureaucrats, the price will go back to the market price and the poor will be priced out of the market. Corruption frustrates any attempt to do something to help the poor.

There are also the costs of the apparatus that is set up to try to detect corruption. The most obvious cost comes from all the rules that government bureaucrats have to follow and all the records they have to keep (the so-called "paper trail").

A more subtle cost comes from the structure of the law against corruption. As argued elsewhere (Banerjee 1995), these laws tend to be relatively insensitive to the scale of the corruption—once someone is caught it matters relatively little whether he has been dishonest only occasionally or all the time. As a result, the bureaucrat has a fairly drastic choice between breaking the law and staying within it, and consequently there will be those who will remain uncorrupted and those who embrace corruption wholeheartedly. From the point of view of someone who has to deal with a bureaucrat, this heterogeneity in bureaucratic behavior constitutes additional uncertainty. This uncertainty is compounded by the fact that the bribe is rarely a posted price—it is something that is usually set through haggling, and haggling is usually an uncertain process. In addition, it is typically illegal to pay a bribe and the briber suffers utility losses when he has to bribe someone. These utility losses may be particularly large for foreign firms, since such firms are likely to be the object of investigation when there is an anticorruption drive. It is therefore no surprise that Hines (1995) finds a significant negative effect of a country index of corruption on United States investment in that country.

Can anything be done about corruption? This chapter tries to identify some possible directions for reform aimed at combating corruption. The next two sections look at the possibilities of reform purely from a mechanism designer's point of view, i.e., assuming that if corruption reform is in the social interest it will not lack political support. The concluding section considers possible political constraints on corruption reform and discusses how these reforms should be implemented.

Reforming the Current System

This section and the next confront the problem of corruption from the point of view of a mechanism designer. In other words, we will presume that if there is a change in the set of rules for bureaucrats that will clearly enhance social welfare, then it will be implemented. To go along with this, we will adopt the fiction that there is something called "the government" which decides on these rules and that the government's decisions are based on a desire to promote social welfare. This is, of course, at best a very partial view of what governments do and desire, but it is a convenient abstraction that allows us to postpone political economy issues till the last section.

This section focuses on interventions aimed at improving the existing system of incentives for bureaucrats. While countries differ substantially with respect to the scope of what governments do, there seems to be a relatively uniform system of incentives for bureaucrats within the governmental sector. One distinguishing feature of this system is the very stringent restrictions on private transactions between the bureaucrats and their clients. Another distinguishing feature is the virtual absence of high-powered financial incentives for bureaucrats—bureaucrats are rarely allowed to retain any more than a small fraction of any moneys they collect on behalf of the government.

The rest of this section considers reforms that retain these basic features of the system. The next section will then consider reforms that alter the system in more drastic ways—specifically emphasizing the option of legalizing profit-making by government bureaucrats. This section will be built around a case study of tax farming with some remarks on legalization in other settings.

There is now a substantial literature on how to reduce corruption while working within the current system. Klitgaard (1988) and Mookherjee (1994a, 1994b) in particular provide very useful discussions of actual efforts to reduce corruption, and attempt to identify the key ingredients of successful anticorruption programs. Their key recommendations (which are largely quite standard in this literature) are summarized below, with some of the limitations of this route to corruption reform.

Adequate Rewards for Bureaucrats

One common recommendation is that bureaucrats need to be paid enough, and that there should be some rewards for good performance. At some theoretical level this would seem obvious, even uninteresting. After all, if bureaucrats are paid a high enough wage, even a small chance of losing their jobs would discourage them from being corrupt. The reason why corruption is such an issue is that governments are unwilling to pay these salaries to get rid of corruption.[3] Yet, if obvious, the message that low salaries promote corruption seems to have been overlooked all too often. Klitgaard (1991) reports that in Equatorial Guinea, if the average government monthly real salary was spent entirely on food, it still would not buy enough food to feed four people for a month. In Jamaica, the real salary of a top bureaucrat dropped to at most one sixth of its initial level between 1972 and 1982. In Ghana, the real salary of a top bureaucrat in 1982 was a sixth of what it was in 1975. In Uganda, the real salary of a secretary in the government in 1988 was 3 percent of what it was in 1975. Faced with a drop in real salary of this magnitude, even the most rigidly honest bureaucrats will be tempted to go beyond the law to preserve their standard of living.

While this tells us about what kinds of salaries are clearly not going to work, it does not tell us much about the level at which the salary should be set if our goal is to make the average bureaucrat hesitate before he takes a bribe (rather than to eliminate all corruption). It would be interesting to know whether the answer to this question comes to an amount that a government might consider worth paying.[4]

Better Record Keeping

A second recommendation of those who seek to improve the current system is an improvement in the technology of record keeping. Mookherjee (1994a), in particular, argues that an efficient system of record keeping makes it easy for a supervisor to detect misrepresentation and argues that this has reduced corruption significantly where it has been used.

While this is quite plausible, it leaves open two problems: (a) it only helps in a situation such as tax collection, where multiple independent sources of information on the same transaction of the same person may be automatically available—it is much less likely to help when the corruption is in pollution inspection, unless a system for gathering multiple independent pieces of information is set up; and (b) it works only if the supervisor is honest, which in itself may be quite hard to achieve.

Selecting the Right Bureaucrats

The literature emphasizes that it is important to invest a lot in the selection of bureaucrats and, in particular, to build up a core of incorruptible agents. The hope is that these people will put pressure on the rest of the bureaucracy both by setting an example and by reporting on them. Klitgaard (1988) argues that this was an important step in the clean-up of the Philippine tax administration by Justice Plana.

One problem with this scheme is that someone needs to do the screening—and dishonest people cannot be relied on to select honest people. In fact, as Wade (1982) has described with great effectiveness, a big part of the problem of corruption in the irrigation bureaucracy in South India is that the officials in charge of allocating jobs are corrupt. They know exactly which jobs afford maximum scope for corruption and reserve those jobs for those who will pay them a price. This, of course, guarantees that only the corrupt get these jobs.

Another related problem is that once the bureaucracy gets a reputation for being corrupt, it will typically have a hard time attracting honest people, since the honest people expect to be sidelined and allocated to the least influential jobs.

Reducing Discretion

Reduced discretion for bureaucrats certainly reduces the scope for corruption. With less discretion, the things a bureaucrat can and cannot do are relatively well defined and therefore, it is easy to detect deviations.

However, there are a number of problems with reducing discretion. Discretion exists because it serves a social function; it allows the rules to be more responsive to individual circumstances. For example, a flat tax would almost certainly eliminate a lot of tax evasion, but it may not be a choice we are willing to make. Clearly, we need to trade off the unfairness caused by inflexible rules with the unfairness caused by un-implemented rules, and there is no reason to believe the existing systems are in any way optimal. Nevertheless the scope for change may be quite limited.

Another problem with reduced discretion is that it makes the job uninteresting, and this may further discourage principled, ambitious people from joining the bureaucracy.

To conclude this section, it should be emphasized that we are *not* saying that reforms of the current system cannot have a significant impact. We are merely suggesting that there are limits to how much is possible.

Reducing Corruption by Changing the System

Corruption arises under the current system because of the combination of restrictions on voluntary transactions and the absence of any direct rewards for bureaucrats. One obvious response to corruption is therefore to remove all restrictions on private transactions between government bureaucrats and their clients and to allow the bureaucrats to retain any money that they collect on behalf of the government. This would, almost by definition, eliminate corruption since there would be no laws to violate, and will be referred to as "legalization". Of course, legalization might have other effects that may need to be weighed against the obvious benefit that it gets rid of corruption. The effects of legalization in the context of tax collection and the implications for dealing with corruption in other contexts are discussed below.

Tax Farming: A Case Study of Legalization

Legalization is an old idea, at least in the context of tax collection. In many countries of the premodern world, tax collection was carried out by private agents who bought the right to collect taxes. The government would set the tax rates for various categories of taxpayers and then sell the right to collect taxes for a fixed sum of money. The tax collectors would then be responsible for determining the liabilities of individual taxpayers as well as collecting the money from them.

A Simple Model of Tax Farming

To understand the consequences of legalization better, it is useful to set up a simple and extremely stylized model of this process. Assume that there is a population of taxpayers who would each like to pay as little in taxes as possible. Some of these taxpayers are richer than others; specifically let there be two classes of taxpayers. Let us denote these two classes by H and L and adopt the convention that H are those who have an income of y_H and L are those who have an income of y_L (where y_L is smaller than y_H).

The sequence of actions is as follows. At first the government sets the tax liabilities, t_H and t_L, for the two categories of taxpayers. Then it sells the right to collect these taxes to a tax farmer. The tax farmer now has to assign the various taxpayers whose taxes he has bought to different categories.

If the taxpayers were totally honest this would of course be trivial—but it seems more reasonable to assume that if all taxpayers were asked to report their incomes personally and there was no way to check on their reports, they would all claim that they belonged to category L (making the reasonable assumption that $t_H > t_L$). As a result, the tax collector needs to have access to a mechanism which, in principle, can sort between the two types. We model it as a test, assuming that if a type H who claims to be a type L has been tested for a length of time T, the probability that he has been exposed is $\Psi(T)$, where Ψ increases with T. It is also assumed that the cost of being tested is the same for both types, and the cost per unit of time of being tested is denoted by δ. Let the cost of testing be v per unit of time independent of the type of the taxpayer (this is borne by those who actually do the testing, i.e., the tax collectors).

If the government had honest tax collectors, it would set taxes and the level of testing for the two types in order to maximize social welfare (say, a utilitarian social welfare function) subject to the constraint that it raises at least an amount R in revenue. This maximization will generate a certain level of utility for the two types. We will refer to these as the social welfare-maximizing levels.

Under the current system, the problem is usually that the tax collectors are not honest. If the government simply assigns them to collect taxes on its behalf, the tax collectors will want to cheat the government and try to maximize their private revenue.

Tax farmers, on the other hand, have no incentive to cheat the government. Rather, all the problems with tax farming arise from the possibility of extortion of taxpayers by the tax collector. To see why this may be a serious problem, consider what happens if the tax collector demands that a taxpayer pay him more than the taxpayer is legally obliged to pay. The taxpayer could, of course, refuse to pay, but then the tax collector could report him for nonpayment of taxes.

What should happen in the event of such a disagreement between the tax collector and the taxpayer? If the taxpayer is allowed to get away with it, no one would have the incentive to pay any taxes. As a result, the government would not want to give such blanket protection to the taxpayers. Let us therefore focus on cases where there is some compulsion for the taxpayer to pay.

Alternate Sets of Rules for Tax Collectors
Case 1: Unlimited Tax Collector Power

If the tax collector always has his way in the event of a dispute, he will try to squeeze as much out of the taxpayer as he possibly can. For the type *L* taxpayer, this would mean being pushed to the point where he is prepared to refuse payment and face the consequences. It may not, however, be possible to push the type *H* taxpayer to this point. The reason is that a type *H* can always claim to be a type *L* and, if he is not discovered, he can pay taxes as type *L*. Now the probability that a type *H* who claims to be a type *L* will be discovered depends on the amount of testing of those who claim to be *L* types. Raising the amount of testing encourages *H* types to tell the truth, but it also reduces the utility of the *L* types and thereby reduces the amount that the *L* types are willing to pay the tax collector. As a result, it may not be in the tax collector's interest to try to squeeze the maximum out of the type *H* taxpayer.

This is, of course, just an example of the general fact that those who can benefit from lying about their type are often able to keep some rents in screening-type models. In this context, the only reason to remark on it is that it makes the richer people relatively more able to resist extortion by the tax collector. This reinforces all the political advantages the rich already have—such as friends in the right places who might be able to make the tax collector desist.

Case 2: Tax Collector Power Limited by a Right of Review

Consider now what would happen if taxpayers were given the right of review in the event of a dispute about a tax claim. Specifically, let there be a tax court where the taxpayer can take his case and complain about the tax collector's demands. The court now has to adjudicate between the two.

Let us assume that the court has access to the same tests as the tax collector, which it can use to distinguish between different categories of taxpayers. However, let us also assume that the court is less efficient than the tax collector as a tester in the sense that the unit cost of being tested by the court, δ', is larger than the unit cost of being tested by the tax collector, δ.[5]

Let us also assume that the courts are all honest. (Nothing important changes if instead we assume that some fraction of the courts are dishonest.) Also assume that when the court decides that a particular taxpayer is of a specific type, the taxpayer gets to pay exactly the amount he really owes.

Now note that the court has no reason to test a self-declared type H. Therefore any type H can guarantee that he pays no more than t_H at no additional cost to himself. A self-declared type L, by contrast, must be tested by the court. Since testing by the court is less efficient than testing by the tax collector, the taxpayer would be better off paying the tax collector somewhat more than t_L to avoid having to go to court.

Thus, while the H type pays no more than what he owes under this system, the L type pays strictly more.[6] Once again, there is over-collection relative to the official tax rates and once again, but for a different reason now, the rich seem to have an advantage in dealing with tax farming.

Case 3: Tax Collector Power Limited by a Right to Review
and Compensation

The conclusion above was that the L-type pays more than what he legally owes. This result is, however, only partial, since it takes the legal tax rates as given when they are in fact chosen by the government. An obvious question to ask is therefore whether the legal tax rates can be chosen in such a way that the L-type taxpayer ends up paying no more than what he would have paid if the tax collector had been the social planner. This question may be rephrased in the following way: Is it possible to set official tax rates so that a type L taxpayer who goes to court is guaranteed a utility level equal to what he would get in the social welfare-maximizing outcome? If this is possible, the tax collector will be forced to offer the L-type at least that level of utility.

What limits the court's ability to offer a L-type a high level of utility is its inability to distinguish costlessly between the types. The key question is whether a combination of testing and official tax rates for L types can be set in such a way that the L-types get the desired level of utility but those who are type H do not want to claim to be type L.

It has been argued elsewhere (see Banerjee 1995) that the answer to this question is yes and, in fact, there always exists an official tax rate that delivers any particular desired level of utility for the L-type. Intuitively, it is always possible to choose a very high level of testing for all L-types and then set the official tax rate at an extremely low level so that the L type's utility is set at the required level. But once the level of testing is set at a sufficiently high level, no H-types would want to claim to be type L since they will almost always get caught.

Note that this argument relies on the possibility that the official tax rate may be negative. It is therefore perhaps better thought of as part compensation for L-types who are forced to go to court.

This argument extends directly to the case where a (possibly large) fraction of the courts are corrupt and act exactly like private tax collectors, as well as the case where there is a fixed cost of going to court. In each case, all that happens is that the compensation part of the L-type's official tax rate has to be made larger to accommodate the fact that only some of the courts will pay the compensation (the rest will ask for bribes).

We thus have the result that, in a range of environments, the court system can be set up in such a way that the tax collectors are forced to offer the L-types the socially desired level of utility. The corresponding result for H-types holds automatically by virtue of the fact that a type H will never pay more than the official tax rate for type H.

How much revenue would the tax collector collect? Recall that the social welfare-maximizing utility levels were obtained by maximizing the sum of taxpayer utilities subject to the constraint that at least R amount of revenue is raised. In this case, by contrast, the tax farmers are maximizing revenue subject to the constraint that each taxpayer gets at the least the utility that he got in the social welfare-maximizing outcome. Therefore, the tax farmers must be able to collect at least R in revenue—

simply by choosing the tax rates and the amount of testing that the social welfare-maximizing government would have chosen. (Actually the tax farmers will end up collecting exactly R in revenue.)

What price would the government get by auctioning the right to collect taxes? In general, the answer to this question will depend on the supply of tax collectors but, if there are enough risk-neutral potential tax collectors who are not credit-constrained, the price for the right to collect taxes should be equal to the revenue the tax collectors expect to collect, less the cost of the tax collector's time and effort. In other words, the government will get as much revenue as it would have got if it had honest tax collectors and the taxpayers will be exactly as well off as they would be in the social welfare-maximizing outcome.

While this is clearly an extreme case, it suggests that a system of legalized private tax collection backed up by a court system that protects and compensates the taxpayers may actually work rather well. It is true that it only works if a fraction of tax courts are honest, but this fraction can be quite small (if one takes the model strictly, the fraction can be anything as long as it is not exactly zero). What is more, the total number of courts necessary for the system to function can be quite small. Even if there were only a few courts, according to the logic of the proposition, there is no reason to expect that these courts would be swamped with work since, in equilibrium, no one goes to tax court—it is simply an option that sustains the equilibrium.

The Historical Record of Tax Farming

Rather in contrast with the conclusion of the previous section, in the popular mind tax farming has a rather negative image—it is viewed as something that served rapacious governments well but not the people. The Ferme Generale in France and the system of tax farming in the 17th and early 18th-century Dutch Republic, for example, have reputations for being so inequitable and inefficient that they drove people to revolt (Higgs 1928, on France; de Vries 1976, on the Dutch Republic).

There is no reason to doubt that this reputation was largely well-earned.[7] As argued above, how well tax farming works is very much a function of how well the rights of the taxpayers are protected by the courts. In a country such as pre-revolutionary France, it is not clear that there was any authority that really wanted to protect the taxpayers. Collins (1988) notes that, in 16th-century France, anybody paying taxes of less than five louis (which was roughly two thirds of the population) could only complain about their tax assessment to the *élus,* who were precisely the people who did the assessment.

In the absence of a system for protecting the taxpayers, it is not implausible that tax farming would work less well than a system of tax collection by a public bureaucracy that is not allowed to profit from the taxes it collects. In particular, we have already established that if the government sets tax rates at their social welfare-maximizing levels but either offers no right of review to the taxpayer (Case 1) or provides a right of review but no compensation (Case 2), there will be over-zealous tax collection. What is more, it is plausible that it is the poor who will end up paying more than they are legally obliged to. This inequality of treatment is only going to be exacerbated if, as in 16th-century France, the right of review is reserved for the rich.

The view that tax farming leads to over-zealous collection and that it is the poor who resent tax farming most is consistent with the record of decentralized tax collection[8] in pre-modern France (Collins 1988, chapter 4) and England (see Cam 1930). It is from England that we have the following rather vivid lament about the ways of the tax collectors:

> Even as the children of the night—the owl, the nighthawk and the vulture—love darkness rather than light, so from King's Court are sent sheriffs, undersheriffs and beadles ... men who at the outset of their office swear before the highest judge to serve honestly and faithfully God and their master, but being perverted by bribes, tear the fleeces from the lambs and leave the wolves unharmed (Walter Map, about 1181, quoted in Cam 1930).

Some Practical Limitations of the Legalization Approach

While the relevance of the historical experience of tax farming is discounted for the evaluation of a properly designed scheme for private tax collection, we are not arguing that the proposed version of legalization (Case 3) is unproblematic. There are a number of concerns with this kind of scheme that deserve to be taken seriously.

- *Endogenous levels of honesty in the tax courts.* The assumption that the fraction of honest tax courts is exogenous is clearly rather dubious. It is more realistic to assume that while many bureaucrats put some weight on social welfare, they will deviate from that ideal if the temptation is strong enough. It seems more reasonable to assume that the fraction of tax courts which are oriented toward making money is some increasing function of the amount a taxpayer gains by ending up at an honest court. Now as the fraction of honest courts falls, the amount that an honest court has to award the taxpayer as compensation increases. This, by our assumption above, causes the fraction of honest courts to fall even further. It is not clear that this process converges. If it fails to converge, then it will not be possible to ensure that the *L*-type taxpayer gets paid an adequate compensation.

While this is indeed a serious constraint, it must be remembered that the government is able to influence the level of honesty in the judiciary. In particular, since the government could be rid of the burden of trying to get honest behavior out of a large bureaucracy by using our scheme, it may find it relatively easy to improve the level of honesty within the judiciary.

- *Trying to influence the choice of judges.* Here we have assumed that taxpayers are assigned judges randomly. In fact, they have every incentive to attempt to find out the identities of good judges and try to take their cases to them. If this happens, the whole approach falls apart since the good judges would be swamped. While this could be forbidden by law, one could imagine people trying to bribe some intermediary to ensure that they get a good judge. A policy that would make this harder is one where judging is anonymous, since then it is less likely that people would know the identities of the good judges and it would be harder for an intermediary to make a credible commitment to assign the case to a good judge. However, anonymity is not costless—which is why we do not have anonymous judging in our courts.
- *Miscalculations by the tax collector.* The model set up above rules out any miscalculation by the tax collector about how much the taxpayer would pay before he goes to court. If there are many such miscalculations, the load on the tax courts could increase dramatically. However, such miscalculations could be reduced significantly by fining the tax collector every time there is a complaint against him or her; the tax collector would then be wary of pushing the taxpayer too hard.
- *Coordination losses in the tax collection process.*[9] There is a significant need for coordination among tax collectors. This stems from the fact that an easy way to detect false claims by taxpayers is by cross-checking these against claims made by other taxpayers relating to the same transaction. Therefore each tax collector needs to have access to the tax returns of those who are not his own clients. Under the present system, this sharing of information is not a problem since all tax collectors belong to the same organization. Under the proposed system, this would no longer be true. However, there seems no obvious reason why one tax collector would

not make the information available to another tax collector on a quid pro quo basis: while they are competitors they only compete ex ante, ex post they all have the same interest.

• *The supply of tax collectors.* Another potential problem with private tax collection is the potential lack of competition in the market for the right to collect taxes. What conditions must be satisfied if the market for the right to collect taxes is to work well? The first thing to note is that tax collection requires training; a tax collector has to be able to read tax forms and interpret tax laws. As a result, tax farming is likely to be a full-time or semi-full-time occupation rather than something someone does on the side. But to make full use of each tax collector would require that each collector collects a relatively large amount of money. Efficient tax farming requires that the collector should be able to pay a price up to the full value of taxes he will collect before he becomes the tax collector. In other words, each tax collector will either have to be very rich or have good access to credit. Further, in order to avoid collusion in the market for tax farming, there must be a large number of such potential tax collectors.

Is this a serious constraint? In countries where the class of wealthy people is very small, it may very well be (note that this does not necessarily have much to do with inequality as measured by say the Lorenz ratio since the poor are typically tax exempt— what matters is rather the relative sizes of the middle class and the upper class in the population). On the other hand, it seems unlikely to be a significant constraint in a number of the larger third world countries such as Brazil, India, Indonesia, and Mexico. Indeed, for the case of India we have Wade's (1982) claim that on the deltas in South India, an executive engineer in charge of irrigation may pay (as bribe) up to 14 times his annual salary in order to obtain a two-year tenure at a particular location. The fact that such high prices are paid suggests that these government engineers are in a position to raise very large amounts of money in order to buy into specific jobs; there seems no reason why this would not be equally true of tax collectors.

Even in countries where we cannot rely on the existence of a large wealthy class, legalization could be made to work by making the amount of money collected by each collector relatively small. This can be achieved in part by making the period for which the rights are sold shorter, and in part by allowing part-time tax collection. Making the period shorter should not create large inefficiencies for taxes that are paid round the year—such as customs and sales taxes.[10] It may be harder to shorten the period in the case of income taxes and agricultural taxes because of their natural periodicity. One can attempt to get around this by staggering the dates at which different people pay taxes. Unfortunately this runs into a number of other problems. First, staggering the collection dates would create problems in how to treat husbands and wives who want to file jointly if they have different filing dates. One could of course get around this by having the same filing dates for those who file jointly. But if they have different employers, this would essentially imply that all employers have to be prepared to issue W2 forms (or their equivalents) on demand.

This would certainly imply some extra costs for the employers, but it is hard to imagine that they would be very significant. In any case, there is relatively little tax evasion among employees whose taxes are deducted at source—it is the self-employed and those who have asset income who are the focus of our proposal.

A more important problem with staggering the dates has to do with the fact, discussed above, that tax collectors need to cross-check the returns from different people. This would be significantly harder if all tax returns were not filed at the same time.

The alternative to staggering is part-time tax collection. This would certainly lead to a loss of some scale economies, but it may be possible to make these losses small by making the tax code relatively simple, since the fixed cost comes mainly from the costs of mastering the tax code.

- *Enforcement of tax payments.* Under the current system, tax payment is enforced by the law; those who do not pay go to jail. The same kind of enforcement power has to be accessible to private tax collectors. It is unclear that the government would be as willing to enforce tax payments when what is at stake are no longer payments to the government.

A related issue is what happens if the government is perceived by private tax collectors to be an inefficient enforcer and they turn to private enforcement. One could easily imagine this leading to serious violations of people's civil rights. The reported penetration of the mafia into the Italian tax collection process suggests that this may be a serious issue. On the other hand, private agents do seem to use the court system to resolve disputes at least for the most part; therefore a move toward private enforcement does not seem inevitable.

- *The commitment to compensate.* One thing that makes our scheme work is the payment of large amounts in compensation. Ex post, the government may want to renege on paying this compensation, which could destroy the whole scheme. Note however that this is essentially like an increase in the population of corruptible judges and therefore does not go beyond the discussion under the first point above.

Taking Stock: Can Legalization Really Work?

The discussion essentially makes four points about legalization of tax collection: (i) for legalization to work well, it must be combined with a system of tax courts that will protect and compensate taxpayers in the event of a dispute with the tax collector; (ii) with an appropriately designed system of tax courts and compensations for wronged taxpayers, under some additional conditions, tax farming may work very well indeed—it can be designed to yield the outcome that maximizes social welfare; (iii) some of the key conditions for tax farming to work well, such as the presence of some irrevocably honest tax courts and a supply of rich potential tax farmers, may be relatively easy to satisfy in some of the bigger less developed countries, and governments can choose policies to ensure that these conditions are met; (iv) there is a set of other potentially serious problems with our scheme for tax farming which need to be assessed empirically and compared with the costs of the current system before we make up our mind.

We are not, therefore, at the stage where we are prepared to suggest tax farming as the way to reform tax collection. We are, however, prepared to suggest that it should enter the discourse on tax reform as an option worth taking seriously. In the next subsection, we ask whether the same kinds of ideas have any relevance for dealing with other kinds of corruption.

Combating Corruption in Other Sectors of the Government

The one other kind of corruption which has a structure very similar to the tax collection case is corruption in the enforcement of penalties for pollution and other crimes for which the entire punishment consists of a fine. In these situations, those who have really committed the crime can be thought of as type H and those who have not as type L. The mechanism for detecting pollution corresponds to our testing mechanism. The same results therefore hold—the social welfare-maximizing outcome can be obtained if the review and compensation mechanism is set up in the appropriate way.

Legalization probably will not work where the penalty is partly or entirely noneconomic. Particularly in the case of noneconomic crimes, there are good reasons why the punishment needs to be noneconomic as well—think of a psychopathic murderer who might do it again and therefore needs to be kept off the streets.[11] Corruption arises in such cases because the criminal may have the incentive to bribe the police or the judge to let him not suffer the noneconomic penalties; in other words, he may substitute an economic penalty for a noneconomic one in a situation where, from society's point of view, these are not substitutes. Legalization clearly does not solve this problem.

Another situation which has more or less the same structure as our tax collection example, is where there is corruption in the provision of a publicly provided private good such as education, health care, irrigation water, and various government permits. Some of these goods have limited externalities and are demanded mainly by those who are not credit-constrained. In such situations, allocating the goods through an open auction makes a lot of sense and as long as the government can commit to an open auction, there should not be much corruption.[12]

The less transparent case is one in which there are either externalities or credit constraints so that it is not optimal to sell all the goods to the highest bidders. If, however, the government tries to implement some rule which does not involve selling to the highest bidder, there is at least the possibility of corruption.

Legalization will, of course, eliminate corruption, but in this context it is not necessarily going to deliver the social welfare-maximizing outcome. The problem arises from the fact that the social welfare-maximizing outcome may well be one in which people of the same type end up with differing levels of utility (particularly if the good is indivisible). But the scheme we propose above gives each L-type person the same guaranteed minimum utility. Therefore this particular scheme will not necessarily sustain the efficient outcome.

Legalization clearly will not solve the problem of pure theft. If a bureaucrat is diverting money from the construction of a bridge to the construction of his mansion, legalization can at best legitimize his malfeasance.

Legalization is therefore no panacea—it works, if at all, in specific circumstances to solve specific problems. Of course, even if it works there is no guarantee that it would be adopted by the powers that be.

The Political Economy of Corruption

Any reform of the current system that reduces the extent of corruption is likely to be resisted by the beneficiaries of corruption. These are potentially both influential and numerous. They include not only the bureaucrats but also politicians, companies which avoid taxes and fines, taxpayers who save on taxes, public sector workers who get paid more than they would otherwise, investors who get a permit they do not deserve. In many countries it also includes the head of state. In other words, the Olson model (1965) would predict that the supporters of corruption should be expected to wield a great deal of power (they have a lot to lose and they are numerous but not so numerous that organization costs are impossibly large).

The power of this group is, of course, limited by the extent of popular power. But it is becoming clear from recent theoretical work on voting that, even with one man/one vote, there are limits to the power of the people to elect an anticorruption politician. A simple example might make this clear. Assume that the ethnic groups H and T together have an overwhelming majority in a particular country. Now both Hs and Ts dislike corruption, but what they dislike even more is being ruled by a corrupt person from the other ethnic group, since it is known that such persons divest all resources in favor of their own ethnic group. More specifically, say that there are three candidates, A, B, and C. A is from ethnic group H and is known to be corrupt. B is from ethnic group T and is also known to be corrupt. C is an honest person who is known not to favor anyone on the basis of ethnicity. The preferences of both ethnic groups are as follows: They both prefer C to the other candidates, but if C is not going to win they prefer to vote along ethnic lines.

In this situation there can be an equilibrium where all the Hs vote for A and all the Ts vote for B. Given that the Hs are voting for A, the Ts feel that the risk of victory by A is substantial enough that a vote for B is the optimal strategy.[13]

Balancing these rather depressing theoretical conclusions (and the depressing empirical picture from most of the world) is the fact that Plana's much publicized clean-up of the Bureau of Internal Revenue in the Philippines was, after all, initiated by Ferdinand Marcos, the notoriously corrupt president. Klitgaard (1988) lists other instances of corruption elimination programs initiated by corrupt governments. This should not be surprising; even a corrupt government cares about how much money it can make over the duration of its rule; therefore it might care about policies that promote growth (which means its take in the future)[14] or increase its popularity (which increases its expected duration) (see

Clague 1994). Now, of course, these corrupt power blocks within the country will not support full elimination of corruption. But they may very well agree to limit its scope and to remove some of the more egregious inefficiencies associated with it.

To take an example, consider the possibility of implementing the efficient tax farming scheme described in the previous section. Fully implemented, this scheme leaves the existing tax bureaucracies with nothing and therefore is likely to meet with much resistance. However, the scheme may be easily modified to give preferences to the existing tax collectors at the auction stage. In other words, the existing tax collectors may be given the first option on the tax farm, and the price for the tax farm may be set below its market clearing level. In fact, even if the price is set so low that the tax collectors are left with the same net income as they had under the previous system, the economy may benefit from this reform: first, because the various distortions created by the existing system (discussed in the first section) will be removed and second, because the existence of corruption typically means that the taxpayers pay less than they owe, the elimination of corruption should raise the total amount of revenue collected.

The general point goes back to Coase (1960). If a change in some rule is likely to increase general welfare but hurts some section of society, there should be the possibility of compensating that group for their losses. It is important, however, to stress what we are not saying here—we are *not* saying that if compensations are possible all corruption can be eliminated. This is because, as we have seen, there is not always a feasible change in rules which, once put in place, eliminates all corruption.

It is also important to emphasize that these compensations are not always easy to arrange. In a series of recent papers, Shleifer and Vishny (1993, 1994) have argued that a large part of the costs of corruption come precisely from the limitations on the ability to pay compensations. In their 1993 paper, they stress the consequences of lack of coordination between different groups within a corrupt bureaucracy. The idea is quite easily explained by using the following metaphor: imagine that there is a bridge with two toll booths on it instead of one. If the toll is not set by the two groups of bureaucrats in the two toll booths acting in cooperation, one toll booth will be shut down and the other will set the toll at the monopoly level. However, if neither group of bureaucrats can commit not to put up a toll booth, they will end up competing to set the tolls; each group will choose their toll, taking the other's toll as given, and society will end up with a higher aggregate toll than even the monopoly level. Thus, while both social welfare and the bureaucrats' private welfare is enhanced if one of the two groups can be bought off, in equilibrium it does not happen.

The paper does not develop a theory of this lack of coordination. It does, however, make the useful point that this problem is likely to be most serious when the government is weak. This is best seen by considering the extreme case where the government cannot prevent new toll booths from being set up. In this situation, every time the existing toll collectors manage to coordinate and set the tools at the monopoly level, some new toll collector will come in and put up a new toll booth.

While the basic point of this example, that intersecting bureaucratic jurisdictions can lead to a multiplication of regulations, seems plausible enough, I am not convinced that the source of the problem is a purely physical inability to collude on the part of the bureaucrats. After all, new regulations are publicly observable and the relation between the bureaucrats is long-term.

The preferred hypothesis therefore is that the inability to collude derives from an inability to make the relevant transfers. This connection is made explicit in the later paper by Shleifer and Vishny (1994). The paper develops a simple model of a public sector firm in which corruption only has efficiency effects if there are limitations on the extent of transfers. While the reason for the restriction on transfers is not explicitly modeled, the paper suggests that certain transfers may not be possible because of a "decency" constraint on the government. Specifically, they distinguish between direct, nondistorting gifts from the government to their model firm and indirect, distorting gifts in the form of wage subsidies, and argue that the former may be less politically acceptable than the latter.

Why should the political system discriminate against the most efficient way to make transfers? There are three possible explanations. First, it may not always be clear that the transfer is being made to the right party. In the context of the Shleifer-Vishny model, wage subsidies have the advantage of making sure that at least the money does not go to enrich the management. Within the context of our more general inquiry, the issue is whether the government can convincingly establish that the transfer was all going to buy off corrupt bureaucrats who would not otherwise agree to an efficiency-enhancing change in the rules. If the government allocates a certain amount of money in its budget for this purpose, the people may be justly suspicious of whether this is really how the money will be used (especially since the public does not usually know who all the corrupt bureaucrats are).

A second reason why efficient transfers are not always possible has to do with the reluctance of governments to admit to the existence of corruption. This reluctance would certainly be rational if the people at large were broadly unaware of the extent of corruption.[15] However, in many cases this seems like a relatively small risk since most people in these countries are already very cynical about the government. There is, however, a related problem which may persist even where the populations have no illusions about the government. Most people in most countries want governments to be honest. When they encounter corruption they are inclined to view it as a failure of the specific government rather than as an endemic problem of all governments. As a result, they may be unwilling to give up on the hope of an honest government by establishing new rules that do not even encourage people to be honest. Consequently, they may be hostile to governments that ask them to make deals with corrupt people.

A third limitation on efficient transfers derives from an institutional constraint. Even if the existence of corruption is publicly known and broadly acknowledged, corrupt bureaucrats cannot simply start open negotiations with the representatives of the public. There is no forum or institution under whose aegis such a negotiation could be carried out. Without such an institution, it is easy to see why the bureaucrats may be afraid to start negotiations. For example, they may legitimately fear that once they acknowledge their complicity, the public might want to lynch them out of sheer vengefulness. It is therefore essential that there is some institutionalized mechanism for guaranteeing that bureaucrats do get paid what they were promised.

The existence of these restrictions on transfers has important implications for the design of a corruption reform project:

- Reforms which are rapid and hard to reverse also have the advantage that they only require cutting a deal with the current group of bureaucrats. This will typically reduce the cost of buying off the bureaucrats very substantially since the current bureaucrats will not internalize the costs (in terms of best opportunities to make money) that the reform inflicts on future generations of bureaucrats.
- Sweeping reforms which involve shutting down a complete section of the bureaucracy and replacing it with a newly-created section with an entirely new staff have the advantage that the change and the transfers that go with it (the golden parachutes for bureaucrats on their way out) are easily observed by the public.
- Another advantage of retiring current bureaucrats as a part of the reform proposal package is that it focuses the negotiation on the size of the severance payment, which is obviously something that can be openly negotiated and even enforced by courts.
- Reforms that have a built-in mechanism for rewarding the current bureaucracy may be easier to implement, at least initially. In this

vein, Basu and Li (1994) have argued that the Chinese economic reforms of the late 1970s and 1980s succeeded because at first they freed up profit-making opportunities without substantially reducing the ability of the bureaucracy to extract rents. As a result, the growth in profits actually benefited the current bureaucracy who, therefore, largely supported the reforms.

A problem with this kind of argument for a certain gradualism is that it creates an incentive within the bureaucracy for initially supporting reforms and then, once their goals have been achieved, to start resisting further change. Basu and Li actually address this problem and therefore it is worth spelling out their basic idea. The first step of the reforms in their model is to deprive the bureaucrats of direct control rights over a class of firms. However, the initial reforms do not do away with all regulations: in particular, enough regulations are retained so that it becomes useful to hire a consultant to deal with these regulations. And the existing generation of bureaucrats, having been central to the aid system, are ideally placed to be the consultants. The next generation of bureaucrats, however, never having enjoyed much power within the system, are not going to be nearly as useful as consultants and therefore will not have the incentive to resist the second stage of the reform when the remaining rules are removed.

While this is quite ingenious, it is not clear if this mechanism has wide applicability (nor is it clear why the current generation of bureaucrats could not have been simply pensioned off). The general point, however, is important. It may be possible to design mechanisms that take advantage of the conflict of interest between various segments of the bureaucracy and thereby minimize the cost of the transition (see Dewatripont and Roland 1992). More generally, practical recommendations for bureaucratic reform need to be based on a more secure understanding of the process of negotiation between the reformers and the bureaucrats and the rest of the population. In the real world, the real constraint on corruption reform may not be the economist's ability to come up with a better mechanism, but rather the political economist's ability to design a process that would allow this mechanism to be put in place.

Acknowledgment

The author thanks the discussants at the Asian Development Bank Third Conference on Development Economics, Elisabetta Marmolo, Dilip Mookherjee (in particular for the Walter Map quote and a host of other useful comments), and M. G. Quibria for their comments. The author alone is responsible for the views expressed here as well as any remaining errors.

Notes

1. The numbers for revenue loss in the allocation of governmental license under the current regime seem comparable: the Santhanam Committee appointed to investigate bureaucratic corruption in India reported that "it is common knowledge that each (import) license fetches between one hundred percent to five hundred percent of its face value" (on the illegal market). Legalization could transfer a large part of this lost revenue to the government.

2. This is not necessarily distinct from the previous point since some of the stealing takes the form of gifts to oneself or to one's brother.

3. This point was first made by Becker and Stigler (1988) and developed by Besley and McLaren (1993).

4. This is no empty question: India is currently going through a debate on whether it may be optimal to raise the salaries of top bureaucrats by five times.

5. Once one goes to court one needs a lawyer and there are various legal procedures to go through.

6. This proposition can be extended to the case where there are more than two types. It is easy to see that poorer people will need to be tested more in any incentive-compatible mechanism. Therefore poorer people have more to lose by going to court and are more vulnerable to extortion by the tax collector.

7. Stella (1990) echoes this view of tax farming.

8. Actually since historically the principal direct tax was a land tax, the corruption entered at the point of assessment rather than at the point of collection—an important difference in practice, but from the point of our abstract model, essentially a relabelling.

9. I am grateful to Peter Diamond for emphasizing this point.

10. Azabou and Nugent (1988) in their very interesting piece on tax farming in Tunisia suggest that this is exactly the reason why the right to collect taxes at various market places is sold for periods as short as a month.

11. There are other less utilitarian reasons as well.

12. The recent F.C.C. auctions in the United States suggest that governments may now be more willing to move in this direction.

13. Myerson (1993) makes a related point.

14. Of course there are others like, say, Mobutu, who know that their reputations are sufficiently bad that they might as well maximize their short-run take.

15. Coate and Morris (1993) formally model this idea.

References

Azabou, M., and J. Nugent, 1988. "Contractual Choice in Tax Collection Activities: Some Implications of the Experience with Tax Farming." *Journal of Institutional and Theoretical Economics* 144 (4):684-705.

Banerjee, A.V., 1994. "A Theory of Misgovernance." Mimeo.

———, 1995. "Eliminating Corruption." Mimeo.

Barro, R., 1991. "Economic Growth in a Cross-section of Countries." *Quarterly Journal of Economics* 106(2):407-43.

Basu, S., and D. Li, 1994. "Corruption and Reforms." University of Michigan. Mimeo.

Besley, T., and J. Mclaren, 1993. "Taxes and Bribery." *Economic Journal* 103(416):119-41.

Becker, G., and G. Stigler, 1988. "Law Enforcement, Malfeasance and Compensation of Enforcers." In *Chicago Studies in Political Economy*. Chicago and London: University of Chicago Press.

Cam, H., 1930. *The Hundred and the Hundred Rolls: An Outline of Local Government in Medieval England.*

Chander, P., and L. Wilde, 1992. "Corruption in Tax Administration." *Journal of Public Economics* 49(3):333-49.

Chu, C. Y. C., 1990. "Income Tax Evasion with Venal Tax Officials—The Case of Taiwan." *Public Finance* 45(3):392-408.

Clague, C., 1994. "Bureaucracy and Economic Development." *Structural Change and Economic Dynamics* 5(2):273-91.

Coase, R., 1960. "The Problem of Social Cost." *Journal of Law and Economics* 3:1-44.

Coate, S., and S. Morris, 1993. "On the Form of Transfers to Special Interests." Mimeo.

Collins, J.B., 1988. *Fiscal Limits of Absolutism*. Berkeley and London: University of California Press.

de Vries, J., 1976. "The Economy of Europe in an Age of Crisis, 1600-1750." Cambridge: Cambridge University Press.

Dewatripont, M., and G. Roland, 1992. "Economic Reform and Dynamic Political Constraints." *Review of Economic Studies* 59:703-30.

Goswami, O., A. Sanyal, and I. Gang, 1990. "Corrupt Auditors: How They Affect Tax Collection." Indian Statistical Institute. Mimeo.

Higgs, H., 1928. "The French Revolution." In *The Cambridge Modern History*, Vol. 8. New York: Macmillan.

Hines, J., 1995. "Forbidden Payment: Foreign Bribery and American Business after 1977." Mimeo.

Klitgaard, R., 1988. *Controlling Corruption*. Berkeley: University of California Press.

———, 1991. *Adjusting to Reality*. International Center for Economic Growth.

Mauro, P., 1993. *"Essays on Country Risk, Asset Markets, and Growth."* Ph.D. dissertation. Harvard University.

Mookherjee, D., 1994a. "Recent Trends in Tax Administration in CIAT Countries." Mimeo.

———, 1994b. "Reforms in Income Tax Enforcement in Mexico." Mimeo.

Myerson, R., 1993. "Effectiveness of Electoral Systems for Reducing Governmental corruption: A Game Theoretic Analysis." *Games and Economic Behavior* 5(1):118-32.

Olson, M., 1965. *The Logic of Collective Action*. Harvard University Press.

Shleifer, A., and R. Vishny, 1993. "Corruption." *Quarterly Journal of Economics* 108(3):599-618.

———, 1994. "Politicians and Firms." *Quarterly Journal of Economics* 109(4):995-1025.

Stella, P., 1993. "Tax Farming: A Radical Solution to Developing Country Problems?" *IMF Staff Papers* 40(1):217-25.

Wade, R., 1982. "The System of Administrative and Political Corruption: Canal Irrigation in South India." *Journal of Development Studies* 18(3):287-328.

———, 1984. "The Market for Public Office: Why the Indian State is not Better at Development." Discussion Paper DP 194. Institute of Development Studies, Sussex, England.

Chapter 5

Ethics, Values, and Economic Development

Basant K. Kapur

hile economic thinkers in previous centuries, such as Adam Smith and Alfred Marshall, devoted a fair amount of attention to issues of values, the subject tended to recede from the concerns of mainstream economists of the 20th century. Over the past two decades or so, however, there has been a gradual resurgence of interest in the subject (e.g., Hausman and McPherson 1993, Rabin 1993, Sen 1988), and indeed one may safely claim that it now constitutes a branch of economics in its own right—and one that may come increasingly to influence other areas of the discipline in the future.

Space and relevance considerations do not permit a survey here of the evolution of this field over the past 20 years (Hausman and McPherson 1993, Cheng 1994). Instead, in the next section we discuss, in an admittedly selective manner, what appear to be some of the central themes in the emerging literature—themes which, moreover, stand in a consistent, "holistic" relationship with each other. The following section goes on to explore the relevance and applicability of these themes to issues in economic development, and proposes a preliminary agenda for further work in this area.

Ethics and Values in Economics—A Discussion[1]

The Problem Posed

The fundamental behavioral postulates on which mainstream, or "neoclassical", economics rests have been succinctly stated by Hirshleifer (1985): "Economic man is characterized by *self-interested goals* and *rational choice of means*" (p. 54; emphases in original).

Now, there are certainly many areas of economics that can usefully be explained through the application of models based on these two postulates. Consumer demand analysis, based on the result that utility-maximizing individuals will equate marginal rates of substitution to commodity price ratios, is one example.[2] However, difficulties begin to arise as economic theorizing seeks to progressively widen its domain of applicability (Hirshleifer 1985), while retaining the above basic postulates. Even many economists, not to mention laymen, are, for example, likely to view with raised eyebrows the following assertion by a well-known Chicago economist: "A person is reliable if and only if it is more advantageous to him than being unreliable ... someone is honest only if honesty, or the appearance of honesty, pays more than dishonesty" (Telser 1980 as quoted by Frank 1988, 75).[3]

Extraordinary as Telser's statement may appear, it is by no means a "fringe" view among economists. Indeed, it underlies the principal-agent framework, which has become the dominant paradigm for the examination of an extremely wide range of economic issues. In this framework, agent deceptiveness is taken for granted: "The agent could commit himself morally to pursue an action that is determined jointly with the principal. Then it is the principal's doubt concerning the morality of the agent that creates the problem" (Laffont 1989, 180). As Laffont thereafter specifies, the "principal's doubt" is well founded.

An important reason for such totally amoral conceptions is that the utility functions of economic actors are typically conceived very narrowly. Not only are economic actors viewed as entirely self-interested, but self-interest is specified in highly materialistic terms. For example, in modern labor economics, the utility function of the worker almost invariably contains only two arguments, real income and work effort (viewed as a source of disutility) (for example, Gibbons 1987, Aron 1986). The same applies in respect of the utility functions of managers (vis-à-vis their dealings with owners) while in modeling the behavior of investors, it is quite common to view them as concerned only with their consumption streams over time.[4] Economic actors are thus specified as being entirely indifferent—or perhaps more appropriately, oblivious—to the purely ethical dimensions of their conduct, involving issues such as honesty, trustworthiness, or reliability, except insofar as these are modeled as impinging upon their material prospects over time. Such modeling is itself comparatively rare.[5]

There are three questions which can, perhaps, be raised in regard to such a circumscribed view of human motivation in the economic sphere. First, although such a question may not find favor with a confirmed Friedmanite, is it descriptively accurate? Do social and ethical considerations play no intrinsic roles in workers' dealings with firms and with each other, or managers' dealings with shareholders? Is it possible that such considerations do play a role, which varies from one society to another or within the same society over time? To stimulate the reader into perhaps devoting some thought to these issues, one may refer to the renowned economist Edward Denison (1979, 73), who cites "the apparent decline in the ability to rely on the honesty of other people (including employees)" as a factor in reduced United States productivity growth in the 1970s (see also Dickens et al. 1989).

Second, is it predictively accurate, in the sense that models based on it are capable of generating predictions that are not empirically refuted? Here, too, doubts are increasingly being expressed. Stiglitz (1991, 21-22) points out that "many predictions of the incentives paradigm do not seem to be borne out", and gives a number of examples from observed compensation schemes. Frank (1991, 278) asserts even more categorically that "the self-interest model, which assumes that everyone behaves opportunistically, is destined to make important errors in predicting actual behavior". Among the reasons that Frank gives in support of this assertion is that, "without taking into account concerns about fairness, we cannot hope to predict what prices stores will charge, what wages workers will demand, how long business executives will resist a strike, what taxes government will levy, how fast military budgets will grow, or whether a union leader will be re-elected" (p. 277).

Third, is it prescriptively fruitful? This question itself raises two sets of issues. The first relates to individual attitudes and behavior. So pervasive has economic logic and modes of thinking become that "twentieth-century man is led to believe he is obligated to act in his own self-interest, in the interests of efficiency, and in aid of the invisible hand" (Maital 1982, 279).[6] Economists are of course aware of the numerous qualifications to the invisible hand theorem, but this awareness does not appear to have filtered down to the lay public at large—hence the above observation.

Not only is self-interested behavior thus not always optimal in the economic sphere, but the issue can also be raised as to whether individuals who always behave self-interestedly in the economic sphere are capable of behaving non-self-interestedly in other spheres—as friends, relatives, community leaders, and the like. This is obviously a very profound issue, which we cannot explore within the confines of this paper. By way of provoking thought on it, however, consider the following observation on a great 20th-century Japanese entrepreneur: "Matsushita foresaw that a lifetime's organizational experience shapes one's character indelibly. It was unthinkable, in his view, that work, which occupies at least half of our waking hours, should be denied its powerful role. The firm, therefore, had an inescapable responsibility to help the employees' inner selves" (Pascale and Athos 1981, 50).[7]

The second set of issues has to do with policy recommendations. If people are taken to be immutably self-interested, then only measures that appeal to their self-interest can be contemplated when seeking to influence their behavior in directions that are regarded as desirable from a policy standpoint. Hence the economist's standard reliance on a variety of taxes, subsidies, and regulatory and other pecuniary-oriented measures—even when dealing with quasi-social issues such as procreation, marriage, care of the aged, public service, and the like. The government's role in moral suasion, and in seeking to influence or mould the ethical climate of the society generally, invariably fails to enter into the economist's frame of reference when thinking about policy issues.

Some Philosophical Perspectives

Having posed the problem, it is necessary next to begin thinking about approaches toward a resolution of it. Some "depth" may be added to the discussion if we begin with some philosophical perspectives, before proceeding in the next subsection to the more specifically economic analyses.

The first, and rather fundamental, point that needs to be made in this connection is that virtually all the great religious and cultural traditions of the world are unanimous in enjoining non-purely-self-interested behavior—and surely, when there is unanimity on such a grand scale, it deserves to be given very serious consideration. Beginning from the West, and working our way progressively Eastwards, we may adduce some very revealing quotations on this issue:

> "You shall love your neighbour as yourself.[8]
>
> "The structural edifice of social life (in Islam) is pervaded by very deep and sincere feelings of love, goodness, and brotherhood. The whole social life is a true picture of co-operation and mutual help ... The Holy Prophet said ... "None of you is a true believer in Islam until and unless he loves for his fellow men what he loves for himself" (Rahman 1980, 381-380).
>
> "Love ... is identifying yourself with all beings in the world. When we accept that all the world is the One Supreme Self, we must love all beings literally as ourselves" (Parthasarathy 1988, 14).
>
> "To study Buddhism is to study oneself. To study oneself is to forget oneself. To forget oneself is to realize oneself as

all things [in the world]" (Dogen, *Shobogenzo*, as quoted in Yoshifumi 1967, 170).

"Heaven loves all. A *jen* man also loves all. To love all is to be a *jen* man, and to be a *jen* man is to follow man's way, which is also Heaven's way" (Chang 1980, 319).

Consider also the view of another leading Confucian scholar: "The cultivation of the self ... requires an unceasing struggle to eliminate selfish and egoistic desires" (Tu 1985, 137). This quotation from Tu carries two further implications. First, unselfish behavior and attitudes are not something that one can simply choose to adopt "overnight": an "unceasing struggle" is required "to eliminate selfish and egoistic desires", because, presumably, such desires exist not only on the conscious plane for each individual, but also at the subconscious, "instinctual" level. Second, this unceasing struggle is a requirement for the "cultivation of the self"—or what is termed progressive "self-realization" by other writers. To quote, for example, an eminent Christian philosopher, "'He that findeth his life shall lose it: and he that loseth his life for my sake, shall find it.' This paradox ... calls attention to the fact that egoism is self-defeating, while self-sacrifice actually leads to a higher form of self-realization. Thus self-love is never justified, but self-realization is the unintended but inevitable consequence of unselfish action" (Niebuhr 1948, 63-4).

There is a further aspect to this unfolding process of self-realization that is worthy of note. As a person becomes progressively less selfish, his concerns become wider: his "consciousness" expands in the sense of his becoming able to empathize with increasingly larger groups of others. To quote again from Tu (1985, 134): "The enlargement of the self, with its eventual union with Heaven as the most generalized universality, travels the concrete path of forming communions with a series of expanded social groups".

There is a profound similarity between this insight and the views of the great Greek philosopher Aristotle. Space does not permit a detailed discussion of the latter, which may, however, be found in Kapur (1995b). Aristotle also viewed "social engagement" as a virtually indispensable means for self-realization: although his discussion focused mainly on political involvement and concern with the affairs of the State, he was well aware that the State is an "association embracing other associations, like the family" (Barker 1959, 228), and that the individual should be constructively engaged with these other associations as well. Engagement with the State and other associations *in a spirit of "justice and friendship"* (p. 235) would serve to progressively neutralize the individual's instinctual selfish tendencies (or what Barker [p. 243] terms "elements of appetite and passion") and make him a better person: "Progress in political science ('in its widest sense') is not so much to know more as to be better—not an increase of knowledge, but of goodness through knowledge. It means self-knowledge, *and with that self-control*" (Barker 1959, 242).[9]

In summary, we wish to draw three lessons from the foregoing philosophical discussion, which are—as we argue further in the subsequent discussion—of relevance to economic analysis. First, there is a strong normative prescription of non-purely-self-interested behavior in the great religious and cultural heritages of the world. Second, endeavors toward such behavior serve to gradually widen and deepen the individual's social concerns—which means that his utility function may change in a fairly systematic way over time. Third, such a progressive process serves to—also progressively—neutralize the "elements of appetite and passion" in the individual, and thereby increase his "self-control"—or, as economists would say, his ability to make consistent, rational choices. These three considerations are all integral aspects of the pursuit of self-realization on the part of individuals.

Rather striking empirical support for the third proposition above has been provided by the sociologist Rushton (1980), one of the world's leading investigators into altruistic behavior (Frank 1988). Rushton's investigations led him to the findings (p. 84) that "the consistently altruistic person is likely to have an integrated personality", and that such persons "behave consistently more honestly, persistently, and with greater self-control than do nonaltruists". All in all, it is hoped that we now have a fairly fertile basis for the more specifically economic discussions in the next subsection.

Some Economic Perspectives

In this subsection, we discuss some economic analyses and findings in which issues of ethics and values play significant roles, and attempt to relate them to the discussion in the preceding subsection. We begin with the important work of Frank (1988). Frank argues that emotions play an important role in economics, and gives two central reasons for this. The first is that people are often not capable of making consistent intertemporal choices. The primary reason for this is the tendency, on which experimental psychology furnishes ample evidence, for current rewards or penalties to appear much more "vivid" in people's imaginations than future ones. People (and animals) have a "psychological reward mechanism" that assigns "disproportionate weight to near-term rewards", thus creating a "self-control" or "impulse-control" problem (Frank 1988, 82-3).[10] It would appear that one of Aristotle's "elements of appetite and passion" has, in modern analysis, become this psychological reward mechanism.

Frank then goes on to argue that "a person who cares only about material rewards" (p. 82) is likely to succumb to this self-control problem, and make ill-advised short-term choices—for example, by cheating "even when it is not prudent to do so" (ibid.). It is here that emotions have a role to play. A person with a conscience—in other words, an ingrained aversion to cheating simply because it is cheating—will be better able to solve the self-control problem, and to make the prudent decision not to cheat even though it may appear attractive to do so.

Frank goes on to provide other illustrations of situations in which emotions can help people to make consistent intertemporal choices.[11] However, the general point is clear, and indeed, raises a profound issue— namely, that the two fundamental postulates that have been advanced by Hirshleifer (1985) as characterizing Economic Man—the pursuit of self-interest, and rational behavior—may in many situations be incompatible with each other, on account of the self-control problem. The implications of this are far-reaching, and will be explored further as we proceed.

The second is that emotions help to solve what he terms the "commitment problem". In Prisoner-Dilemma-type situations, self-interested persons will inevitably choose the noncooperative strategy, and, knowing this of each other, are unlikely to voluntarily enter into such arrangements. However, if two individuals have emotional predis-positions toward cooperative, "honest" behavior for its own sake, and if such predispositions can be at least partially identified by the other party, then they are likely to enter into such arrangements, and to adopt the cooperative strategy within them, to the benefit of both.

A difficulty with Frank's argument here, which he recognizes, is that in the case of repeated games, adoption of the well-known "tit-for-tat" strategy by both parties is often sufficient to ensure cooperative behavior on the part even of self-interested individuals. Emotions are therefore not necessary for this purpose. Frank's response is that we often observe cooperative behavior even in "one-shot" situations. This may well be the case, but, if repeated game situations represent the most common and economically important ones, then the application of the principle of Occam's Razor might well dictate retention of the self-interest paradigm in explaining the prevalence of cooperation in such settings.

There is, however, an alternative approach to strengthening Frank's argument. This is to adopt the framework, not of repeated prisoner's dilemma games, but of repeated principal-agent games, in which there is an additional source of uncertainty that affects outcomes beyond simply that regarding the other player's actions.[12] In such a setting, an important paper by Radner (1981) has shown that almost fully efficient outcomes can be achieved provided both parties know that the game will be played sufficient times, and provided that the principal and the agent attach a zero (or, more informally, a very low) discount rate to future utilities. Here, however, is the rub. If, as argued above, self-interested persons tend to attach a "disproportionate weight to near-term rewards",[13] then this latter condition will not be satisfied, and efficient outcomes will not result.[14]

As Frank himself appears to recognize (pp. 88-9), therefore, the commitment model itself rests fundamentally on the self-control problem that is argued to characterize purely self-interested persons.[15] The two models are, however, applicable in somewhat different contexts, the self-control model applying to choices made by the individual "in isolation", and the commitment model to choices made in settings involving interpersonal interactions. We discuss important economic issues in these two contexts below.

Let us turn next to the important area of savings behavior. One of the salient features of the postwar United States, according to the historian Lasch (1978), has been the progressive development of "a culture of competitive individualism" (p. xv), and the associated gradual decline of what, in economic terms, may be termed the degree of intergenerational altruism. "To live for the moment is the prevailing passion—to live for yourself, not for your predecessors or posterity. We are fast losing the sense of historical continuity, the sense of belonging to a succession of generations originating in the past and stretching into the future. It is the waning of the sense of historical time—in particular, the erosion of any strong concern for posterity—that distinguishes the spiritual crisis of the 1970s from earlier outbreaks of millenarian religion, to which it bears a superficial resemblance" (Lasch 1978, 5).

Now, it would appear that the progressive and sustained decline in the US savings rate in the postwar period can indeed be attributed to a significant degree to this decline in intergenerational altruism. To quote Kotlikoff (1986, as reprinted 1989, 299), "it appears clear that the country is experiencing a long-term decline in saving which may well be the result of the unreported but enormous economic deficits associated with Social Security and other unfunded federal government retirement programs in the last three decades". The postwar period witnessed significant increases in the coverage and value of Social Security benefits paid to retirees (Aharoni 1981, 78-85), which were substantially financed, not by their own prior contributions, but by levies on younger, working individuals. The fact that intergenerational transfers on a scale so large as to seriously affect the nation's long-run savings rate were mandated appears only to be explicable by the "waning of the sense of historical time" and the "erosion of any strong concern for posterity" that Lasch identifies.[16]

In preceding parts of this paper, the proposition was also advanced that self-interested individuals would be less capable of making consistent intertemporal choices. Space does not permit a detailed discussion of the evidence here, but some pieces are suggestive:

- The first is a recent study of the US credit card market by Ausubel (1991), who shows that the US credit card market exhibits significantly noncompetitive outcomes despite the presence of a large number of credit-card issuers, and his explanation "crucially relies on the assumption that there are consumers who do not intend to borrow but continuously do so" (p. 71). There appears to be "a substantial breakdown in optimizing behavior among credit card holders" (p. 72), and Ausubel further suggests—very revealingly, from our standpoint—that these consumers "face a commitment problem: consumers cannot commit their future selves not to borrow" (p. 70).

- Consider, next, the following observation in respect of the US by Hatsopoulos et al. (1989, 9): "sophisticated managers have a tendency to ratchet up their consumption in response to a high bonus during a year of record earnings, although they are fully aware of the temporary nature of such a payment. Because of this, many large corporations accrue bonuses and pay them over a number of years". By contrast, in Japan—arguably a significantly more "communitarian" society than the US over the postwar period —the bonus system is viewed as leading to an increased, or at the least an unchanged, savings rate, but not as inducing a ratcheting-up of consumption.

- Another "puzzle" was uncovered in a recent survey-based study by Shapiro and Slemrod (1993). "In 1992, the income tax withholding tables were adjusted so that less would be taken out of workers' pay and, as a result, year-end tax refunds would be smaller" (p. 4). Economic analysis predicts that this would not affect consumers' spending, "since only the timing of income would change, not the total amount". Very surprisingly, however, Shapiro and Slemrod found that 43 percent of the persons they surveyed "said they would spend the extra cash that resulted from a change in the timing of tax payments". Moreover, Shapiro and Slemrod found "no link to liquidity in the spending promises of the survey respondents"—and they were thus left with no plausible explanation, based on conventional theory, for their finding.

•   Consider, lastly, another important recent study by Viard (1993). As with Kotlikoff (1986), Viard focuses on the decline in the US savings rate, but restricts himself to the 1973-1990 productivity slowdown period. He points out (p. 549) that the permanent income hypothesis "generally predicts that a productivity slowdown, by lowering future expected income, will stimulate saving .... However, the US national saving rate instead fell to a postwar low after the productivity slowdown". He also argues that "other economic events during this period cannot explain this discrepancy", that "the savings shortfall ... constitutes a large deviation from the permanent income hypothesis", and that (p. 562) "the highest research priority in this field should be the development of models that can explain these events."

Our next area has to do with interpersonal interactions in the economic sphere, and, to make the discussion more "concrete", we place particular emphasis on interactions within the firm. Before doing so, however, let us review some philosophical perspectives. Consider again the previously-quoted insight of Tu, "The enlargement of the self, with its eventual union with Heaven as the most generalized universality, travels the concrete path of forming communions with a series of expanded social groups."

In another study, Tu (1989, 113) has conceptualized the above series of expanded social groups as a "series of concentric circles". In pre-modern times, this series could well consist of the family (with the individual at the center), the town or village, the district, the province, the nation, and so on. However, in modern times, the firm might well be regarded as constituting one of these communities. Some suggestions to this effect may be found in the following observations, one from the West and the other from the East: "many of the best companies (in the US) really do view themselves as an extended family" (Peters and Waterman 1982, 261);[17] "(with) the change-over to an industrial economy in the 1880s and 1890s (in Japan)...company affiliation automatically replaced the clan, and to some extent the family as well, in the social fabric of the country" (De Mente 1981, 132).

A subsequent observation by De Mente (1981, 133) is also of interest: "It must be recognized that the relationship between the larger Japanese employer and his employees is not strictly an economic one. The average employer gets from his workers a degree of loyalty, cooperation and effort that is seldom surpassed anywhere. In turn, the employer feels responsible not only for the economic welfare of his employees, but also takes an interest in their social and spiritual well-being."[18]

Similar views have been expressed by others: sociologist Dore (1987), for example, goes so far as to elaborate what he terms the "community model" of the Japanese firm. The analysis here fits in very neatly with the theory advanced by Frank (1988): regarding their firms as communities which they identify with (and which in turn identify with them) provides Japanese workers and managers with a strong emotional propensity to engage in cooperative acts and behavior over a sustained period of time.[19]

The question that one may then wish to ask is whether purely self-interested behavior, under an appropriately designed system of incentives, is capable of generating the same cooperative outcomes. In order to answer this question, we have first to consider briefly the changing competitive environment we live in. The progressive globalization of markets that has occurred over the past quarter-century or so has, as described by Aoki (1988), been accompanied by two basic developments: the "increasing diversity of consumers' preferences" (p. 20), and "rapidly changing market and technological environments" (p. 18). As both Aoki and Dertouzos et al. (1989) have argued, therefore, the traditional mass-production system is, in many industries, ill-equipped to cope with current challenges, which require production of a wide range of varieties in fairly small batches, continual flexible adaptations of the product mix in response to changing market conditions, and continual technological upgrading.

In turn, quick-changing and unpredictable marketing and technological situations necessarily place a premium on technical competence, versatility, and "retrainability" on the part of workers. Moreover, the fact that all possible contingencies cannot be foreseen in advance implies that initiative, flexibility, and a team-oriented approach to problem-solving are likely to be very advantageous attributes. Workers have to undergo job rotations and continual retraining, and Aoki further points out (p. 50) that "job demarcation is ... fluid and ambiguous ... in the J(Japanese-type)-firm".

The question therefore arises whether purely self-interested behavior—with individuals' utilities depending solely on their expected incomes and leisure—can sustain "optimal", cooperative outcomes in such settings. There are at least three reasons why this is highly unlikely to be the case:

- The first is contained in the following observation by Aoki (p. 76): "applicants hoping to enter the ranking hierarchy of the J-firm characterized by the relatively low initial pay and the relatively higher intrafirm upward mobility reveal themselves to be of the type who are willing to endure the long training needed to accumulate contextual skills and willing to wait for the financial returns, which are realizable only after long periods".[20] It is very unlikely, however, that self-interested persons, subject to Frank's self-control problem, are prepared to wait for "long periods" for their financial returns. Moreover, such persons may not exercise the degree of initiative that the "fluid and ambiguous" nature of job assignment demands (since to them work is a source of disutility), and—being individualistic—are likely to find the emphasis on teamwork irksome. On balance, therefore, the short-term costs are likely to weigh much more heavily in the calculation of self-interested persons than the long-term benefits, precluding them from displaying the same degree of cooperativeness as more "communitarian-minded" individuals would.

- It should be noted that the changing competitive environment we have described above pertains primarily to the fast-changing and technologically dynamic sectors of the economy—what are generally referred to as "high-tech" industries. It may appear, therefore, that self-interested persons may be induced to work in these sectors by paying them a sufficiently large premium over the wage earned in the other, less dynamic, sectors of the economy, as well as by instituting more elaborate systems of monitoring their performance. The problem, however, is that higher wages and monitoring expenses add to the costs of the firms concerned, and in the highly integrated world economy of today, weaken their international competitiveness. One might indeed hypothesize that, owing to these costs, a highly individualistic society is likely to experience serious difficulty in maintaining a comparative advantage in industries for which the J-firm is the most suitable organizational form, over more communitarian-oriented societies.[21] Some examples from Dertouzos et al. (1989) are consistent with this hypothesis: (a) "Among the industries studied, consumer electronics provides the clearest illustration of an innovative, high-growth industry that has been virtually eliminated in the United States by overseas competition" (p. 217). Among the reasons cited by Dertouzos et al. for this are the facts that in Asia "such professionals as engineers and managers...worked longer hours at lower salaries" (p. 218), and that "the Japanese emphasis on teamwork and quality gave them advantages over American firms" (p. 219). (b)

"In semiconductors the effect of the competition has been ruinous .... By 1987 the American share of the world market had shrunk to 40 percent .... The big winners were the Japanese, whose global market share almost doubled in 10 years from 28 percent to 50 percent ... American companies ... subcontract manufacturing to Japanese companies to reduce costs" (pp. 248-9).

These examples are sobering indeed. One would expect a highly developed, presumably human-capital-rich, country such as the United States to have a comparative advantage in high-technology production—the higher salaries paid to workers engaged in such production should be more than offset by their higher skills and productivity. Instead we appear to have been observing the converse. There has of course in very recent years been a partial revival of US competitiveness in high-tech industry, but, while the causes of this have not been fully studied, one prominent cause appears to be the substantial decline in the US dollar[2]—and, associatedly, a decline in the US terms of trade, and hence in US living standards, which does not appear to be a preferred means, in general, of stimulating competitiveness.

- Another important feature of high-tech industry is its very significant reliance on research and development (R&D). This is an area in which self-interested behavior can create another, very significant problem—which appears to have manifested itself empirically. Consider an employee (or a group of employees) assigned by a firm to work on an R&D project. This is a situation of asymmetric information par excellence; such an employee is likely to acquire much more information about the project than the firm's management. After working on the project for a number of periods—at the firm's expense, and while on its payroll—the individual may realize that he is fairly close to a breakthrough. It might then very plausibly be to his interest to quit the firm, set up his own firm, complete the remainder of the project, and garner the resulting profits all for himself, instead of having to share much of it with the original firm. Moreover, it would be very difficult for the latter to take legal action against him, since it is likely to have much less information regarding the status of the project at the time the individual left the firm.[23]

The foregoing scenario has apparently been played out quite a few times in the US semiconductor industry: "The larger, more mature firms (including Motorola, Fairchild, Intel, and AT&T) suffered major disruptions as entire advanced-development groups broke away to form new companies (a practice that gave rise to the term "vulture capitalism"). The new firms were often quite innovative at first, sometimes pioneering whole new sectors of the business. Then after two or three rounds of venture-capital financing, they would sell stock to the public, which made the founders overnight multimillionaires. Later the companies frequently languished and fell behind the fast-moving technology" (Dertouzos et al. 1989, 255).[24]

Japan, however, presents a rather different picture: "Independent venture formation and mass defections are almost nonexistent in the Japanese semiconductor industry. Personnel raiding is rare and considered unethical. Salaries are controlled, and when companies invest in research and development and training, they are confident of receiving the benefit" (Dertouzos et al. 1989, 260).

The consequence has been that large Japanese companies have been considerably more successful in conducting R&D on a sustained, long-term basis, as well as in exploiting "synergies" between R&D and "product optimization, design for manufacturability, fabrication methods, and quality" (p. 251). Not only have they taken the lead in semiconductor manufacture, but they have also overtaken American industry in one of the most "high-tech" areas of all: applied research and development: "Relative performance in research and development ... has also changed dramatically. The United States is still leading in many areas of theoretical research but trailing in applied research and development.... A 1987 study by a Defense Science Board Task Force concluded that the United States continues to lead in only three of more than a dozen critical semiconductor technologies surveyed" (p. 249).

Lastly, while the discussion in this part has dealt with cooperation within the firm, similar analyses are applicable in respect of cooperation in other economic contexts, which is what we would expect given Tu's "concentric circles" vision (Kapur 1995a, see chapter 5). Indeed, in their far-reaching diagnosis of US economic problems, Dertouzos et al. devote an entire chapter to "Failures of Cooperation" and observe (p. 94), "Our studies have shown a lack of cooperation at several levels. The relationships affected include those between individuals and groups within firms, between firms and their suppliers or their customers, among firms in the same industry segment, and between firms and government" (as well as, we may add, between firms and their sources of finance).

The conclusion that emerges from the entire discussion in this part, then, is that untrammeled self-interest is a very poor substitute for an altruistic orientation, or Sen's "other-regarding concerns" (1988), on the part of workers and managers as far as the attainment of organizational efficiency is concerned. It is very ironic that an extreme focus on material gain can result in an economy becoming less competitive, materially, than another economy with a different focus. Given that economists, no matter how strongly they are committed to the self-interest axiom, are also committed to strengthening economic competitiveness and achieving continuing, reasonably fast growth in living standards, it becomes all the more imperative for them to consider whether there are any internal inconsistencies in their view of the world.

There is of course a variety of other economic issues in which considerations of values play important roles. Space constraints preclude a comprehensive enumeration and discussion of them, however, a brief mention of some of them would appear to be warranted.

The first has to do with the growing literature on "fairness" concerns. A valuable reference is Kahneman, Knetsch, and Thaler (1986), who also demonstrate the predictive usefulness of their approach; also noteworthy is Fehr et al. (1993).

The second—which embraces sociological as well as economic concerns—has to do with the very important role played by the family. Under the onslaught of the "me-first" mentality (and other influences), the family as an institution has weakened very considerably in the United States. When we juxtapose this with the findings of the Coleman Report—whose "basic conclusion was that the quality of the family that a child was reared in proved to be a major determinant of educational success .... Other researchers later came to similar conclusions" (Donohue 1990, 168)—we have here a basic reason for the decline in American educational performance, and hence also in American productivity performance (Bishop 1989). Of importance in this context are also the observations by Dertouzos et al. that "the problems of public education in this country go well beyond the classroom to basic social and economic conditions" (p. 152), that "the task of upgrading the primary and secondary schools is probably the single most important challenge facing the country" (p. 152), and that "unless the nation begins to remedy these inadequacies (in basic education and technical literacy) it can make no real progress on all the rest" (p. 142).

Our final issue is put forward more in the nature of a conjecture than anything else. So far, we have placed considerable emphasis on the self-control problem as a basic reason why self-interested behavior fails to result in optimal, cooperative outcomes. A further reason, however, may be that of "bounded rationality" (Simon 1957). In the highly complex, interdependent society of today, any action taken by an individual may have manifold consequences, direct as well as indirect, immediate as well as delayed. It is virtually impossible for any individual—self-interested or otherwise—to be precisely aware in advance of all these possible consequences. If, however, it is true that in essence "the whole social life is a true picture of cooperation and mutual help" (Rahman 1980), then in most of these situations, individuals, and society generally, would be better off if they had, at the outset, chosen the cooperative mode of behavior, even though they were not aware of all the possible consequences. Altruistic persons are, of course, likely to do so, on account of their very nature, but self-interested persons might well fail to make the correct choice in many such situations.[25]

Ethics and Values in Economic Development

There does not appear to have been much systematic work on ethical issues in modern development economics, with the exception of concerns relating to the provision of basic needs, discussed further below. However, some fundamental lessons may be learned from the discussion in the preceding section, and some extensions thereof. We discuss these in sequence here, beginning at the most aggregative level, and proceeding on to more disaggregated levels and more specific issues.

The Societywide Level

One of the most basic lessons of the preceding section is that the ethical codes of a society, as embodied in its prevailing culture, do matter, as far as its economic performance (short-run and long-run) is concerned. Most if not all developing societies can be said to have notable communitarian elements in their respective cultures, and it should be recognized that these elements constitute an economically valuable resource, in as far as they emotively predispose, to varying degrees, participants in these cultures toward cooperative modes of behavior.

By way of illustration, consider the following observation in respect of Japan (in past as well as present eras): "The *Shinto* concept that is most explicit in Japan's management philosophy is belief in *musubi* (moo-sue-bee), or 'the undifferentiated coexistence of men, nature and the gods' .... The Way of the Gods *(Shinto)* teaches that every man is his brother's keeper, and that to achieve and practice *amae* (indulgent love) all men must be selfless ... in the main, *Shintoism* resulted in the majority of the Japanese, until modern times, being strongly influenced by the concept of 'instinctive unselfishness' and harmonious behavior" (De Mente 1981, 40).

At the same time, we should be careful not to overstate our argument. Not all elements of traditional cultures are favorable to economic development: superstition, conservatism for its own sake, feudal modes of social and economic organization, and the like are all to be abjured. A Japanese executive has spoken of "the balancing of the rationalism of the West with the spiritualism of the East" (Pascale and Athos 1981, 52), and this captures well the flavor of what we have in mind. In heterogeneous societies, moreover, very careful attention should be paid to emphasizing the common ethical elements across the various constituent cultures of such societies, as we have, for example, endeavored to do above.

From the foregoing, we wish to draw three lessons, the first of which relates to the discussion in the preceding section, and the other two specifically to developmental issues. The first is that there is a compelling need for a much more interdisciplinary approach to the study of many economic issues. Issues of values, cooperation, and the like can only be satisfactorily explicated if the insights and approaches of a variety of disciplines—philosophy, psychology, sociology, history, political science, and of course economics—are systematically utilized, and progressively integrated. This increasingly appears to be the view of leading members of our profession,[26] and implies a very substantial agenda for future work.

The second lesson, following from the first, is that it is very important that interdisciplinary approaches be adopted in the study of particular societies, even in respect of what might appear to be narrowly "economic" issues. If indeed cultural factors do influence—and are influenced by—economic variables,[27] then it is essential that these linkages be systematically studied. Working together, social scientists studying particular societies may hopefully be able to learn how the "balancing of rationalism with spiritualism" may best be achieved within each society.

The third lesson has to do with the role of the government. It should be recognized that, in the realm of culture and values, there is an important advocacy role that governments should play. They should not uncritically accept that "Westernization"—in all its aspects—is either an inevitable or a desirable concomitant of the process of economic development in their societies. Basing, hopefully, on the work of the social scientists mentioned above, they should endeavor to sensitize their populations to those elements of their heritages that are worth preserving, and those that should be discarded. A continual process of education and "moral suasion" is called for. Some examples along these lines are Indonesia with its Pancasila philosophy, Singapore with its fairly recently proposed core values (one of which is "society before self"), and, as cited above, Japan.[28] As Keynes observed, ideas play a much more powerful role than is commonly appreciated.

The Political System

At the outset, it may be useful to distinguish between two very different conceptions of the political system. The first is typified by the political economy approach (see, for example, Magee et al. 1989; Olson 1982; Tirole 1994): it views actors in the political system as being basically self-interested. Thus, interest groups lobby for their own advantage, and political parties, including the ruling one, respond to lobbying pressures in such a manner as to maximize their chances of election or reelection. In some extensions, bureaucratic officials are viewed as prone to "capture" by special-interest groups (see, for example, Laffont and Tirole 1991). "Rent-seeking" is viewed as a pervasive phenomenon within the political system.

An extremely interesting alternative view is presented by the Japanese political scientist Okimoto (1988, 1989)[29] (see also Mansbridge ed., 1990). Okimoto begins by arguing (1988, 211) that in Japan "the state is not, as in some Western countries, simply an administrative appendage, superimposed on society with the responsibility of allocating resources, laying down equitable rules and norms, and adjudicating conflict through the operation of the legal apparatus". Instead, "state and society form mutually reinforcing parts of a whole". Japan can, he argues (p. 214), "be characterized as a 'network', a 'relational' or 'societal' state in the sense that government power is intertwined with that of the private sector. It hinges on its capacity to work in concert with the private sector, with each side making an effort to take into account the needs and objectives of the other".

State-society interactions are, in fact, "embedded" in a matrix of deeply held communitarian values: indeed, in the absence of such an encompassing framework, it would be virtually impossible for these interactions to produce the beneficent outcomes that they have over sustained periods of time. Okimoto (1989, 237) includes in these communitarian or "relational" values "the emphasis on the group over the individual; the stress on harmony; cooperation and competition; achievement and ascription; hierarchy and equity; obligation; long-term, "no-exit" commitments; reciprocity; the sharing of risks, costs and benefits; and mutual trust".

Given this setting, it is not surprising that the "state's central role is to function as guardian of the public welfare ... its responsibility is to serve the public" (Okimoto 1988, 211). As indicated earlier, in order to do so effectively, it has (for informational and other reasons) to work in close concert with the private sector, and is facilitated in doing so by the similarly communitarian orientation of the latter. Okimoto (1989, 155) points out that "policy networks ... include informal relationships between government officials and industry leaders ... If its officials did not devote so much time and energy to cultivating personal relationships with key leaders in the private sector, MITI (the Ministry of International Trade and Industry) would not be nearly as effective as it is. Indeed, early consultation, on-going negotiation, conflict resolution, and consensus formation—the sine qua non of effective industrial policy and close government-business relations—hinge, to a large extent, on the existence and utilization of informal networks".

It might appear that such close public-private relationships create the possibility of severe conflicts of interest, divided loyalties, and resultant (witting or unwitting) abuse of authority by public officials. Okimoto argues (1989, 156-7) that a check on this is, for example, the organization of MITI along both "horizontal" and "vertical" lines: the vertical bureaus liaise closely with the various industries "assigned" to them, but their advocacy of industry interests is monitored and modulated by the horizontal, coordinating bureaus. While this is certainly an important consideration, it is hard to believe that it is the sole, or even the most important, safeguard: the underlying communitarian ethos of the society, which has been discussed earlier, and which substantially influences the outlook and behavior of both public and private sector participants, almost certainly plays an indispensable role in neutralizing the acerbity of sectional demands and discouraging opportunistic or devious behavior, such as the exploitation of confidential information for personal or private gain.[30]

How, then, do we relate the discussion so far in this subsection to the situation of the developing countries? In the first flush of independence from colonial rule, many of these countries were imbued with a sense of national pride, and there appeared to have been a genuine commitment on the part of both the political leadership and the society at large to the task of nation building.[31] As years have gone by, however, the dream has turned sour for many countries. While there are various reasons for this, one of the most basic ones, in my view, has been the adoption of poorly designed, inward-looking economic policies, which have resulted in the proliferation of bureaucratic controls, distortion of market forces, sluggish economic growth, and the diversion of huge amounts of talent and energy into lobbying and rent-seeking activities

(Krueger 1993, 61), which have sapped both the economic and the moral vitality of these societies.

However, the situation is not irreversible. There is now a wide-spread consensus that outward-looking policies and a strategy of economic liberalization must, either quickly or gradually, be adopted, and over time the scope for rent-seeking behavior, relative to productive activities, should be reduced.[32] In such an environment, people's historical memories of the early post-independence years of nation-building can perhaps be fruitfully—and, again, gradually—revived (although it should be emphasized to them that in our highly interde-pendent world nation building must go hand-in-hand with a spirit of international cooperation). If the loyalties of actors in the political system and of the society at large can be constructively channeled to the nation as a whole, as in the case of postwar Japan, then the political system of these societies may gradually evolve from the "rent-seeking" to the "relational" kind, with considerable benefits to the countries concerned.[33] Again, the responsibilities in terms of moral exhortation and example-setting of the political leadership of these countries are crucial.

The Issue of Basic Needs

Any ethics-based approach to economic development must pay careful attention to the issue of basic needs. As Moon (1991) eloquently puts it, "the normative case for concern with the poor is unassailable, universal, and compelling. There is virtually no major strand of religious, or, indeed, secular humanist philosophy which does not recognize the virtue, if not the moral imperative, of charity in the face of need. The challenge that "the measure of a society is the way it treats its poor" strikes a resonant chord.... Anyone who has seen the blank stare of a hungry child need look no further for an incentive to cope better with the problem of abject poverty" (p. 7).

There is by now an extensive literature on basic needs; however, Moon's recent work (1991) appears to encapsulate much of the "state of the art" in this area. As he points out, basic needs concerns address themselves to fundamental aspects of the well-being of the "mass citizenry" (p. 3) in many less developed countries. He also defines "basic needs" pragmatically: "The needs considered basic are those minimally required to sustain life at a decent material level. Conventionally, these are defined in terms of adequate food, water, health care, shelter, and minimum education. Adequacy is defined in a minimum way and measured in terms of observable outcomes rather than in relation to income or consumption of such basic "goods". Thus, the most common indicators of national achievement of basic needs are life expectancy, infant mortality, and literacy" (p. 5).

Moon also observes, sensibly, that in his study "basic needs attainment is accepted as a development goal, but commitment to the meeting of basic needs does not entail commitment to any particular strategy for bringing it about" (p. 6).[34] He then embarks on a detailed study of the "broad-scale social, political, and economic processes that yield basic needs outcomes" (p. 9). It is not possible to present all his findings here. However, there is one finding that deserves some comment. "Though Buddhism is dominant in relatively few nations, the particular nations involved have such a distinctive basic needs record that a causal connection has to be entertained. On the basis of the model [of Table 93], for example, the nation with the largest positive deviation from expected PQLI level is Thailand. A second Buddhist society, Sri Lanka, is perhaps the best-known example of a society whose basic needs performance exceeds expectations based on GNP ... and its PQLI exhibits the fourth greatest positive deviation ... it appears that the fine basic needs performance ascribed to Asian countries in general is actually found in only the nine countries coded as Buddhist" (pp. 250, 252).

The point of the above finding is not, of course, to suggest that we should all become Buddhists. Rather, it is adduced as an indication of the fact that cultural variables—and the values embodied in them—can and do play an important "autonomous" role additional to that of economic and political variables, in helping to determine significant economic outcomes. If this is recognized, then there may be a greater acceptance of the potential usefulness of—as suggested in earlier subsections—a more systematic, comprehensive, and on-going endeavor to infuse the "body politic", as well as the "body economic" and the "body social", with the appropriate values.

A related issue is that of inequality of income and wealth. Most economists would agree that, other things being equal, less inequality is preferable to more. The catch, of course, lies in the phrase "other things being equal". However, it is noteworthy that, in a very recent study, Persson and Tabellini (1994) have found that, empirically, among democratic societies, including the less developed ones, those with more equal income distributions tend to have a stronger growth performance. The authors are careful to point out that this empirical finding does not imply that any measure to promote greater equality will be as effective as any other in terms of achieving more rapid growth. Nonetheless, their finding does raise the distinct possibility that, rather than being inherently conflicting, ethical desiderata and faster economic growth could well be mutually consistent in more situations than are generally appreciated.

Other Issues

If indeed ethical considerations are as important and pervasive as we have argued them to be, then they should have a bearing on a great many economic, as well as noneconomic, issues. To mention just a few in addition to those discussed earlier: the issue of material versus nonmaterial incentives in economic life; the issue of the appropriate degree of inequality; the issue of democracy versus authoritarianism, and so on.

Each of the abovementioned issues is highly complex, and examining them would require separate analyses in their own right. Nor is it claimed that resort to ethical considerations alone can serve to fully resolve them. What I do wish to claim, however, is that a careful consideration of the ethical dimension would constitute an integral part of such resolutions, and that in the absence of such an incorporation any proposed resolution would remain incomplete and unsatisfactory. Moreover, it is also hoped that the discussion in this paper provides a framework for thinking about ethical issues that is both useful and valuable for such further investigations.

An important part of our ethical framework is that it emphasizes the responsibilities of the individual, and not solely his rights. The individual has responsibilities to the society, as well as to his own self-realization, and indeed his discharge of the former contributes integrally to the latter. To quote from Barker's (1959) rendering of some of Aristotle's views, "the true end of the State must be not to make its members one, but to raise them to the fullness of their being, by encouraging the highest activities of a good life" (p. 405). Ironically enough, man moves closest to "a perfect freedom" when (referring back to our discussion above) "reason, the highest element of the soul and the peculiar differentia of man, has become conscious of itself and has learned to use its powers" (p. 427).[35]

Finally, our emphasis on self-realization as an ongoing process implies that it is likely to be preferable to adopt a "relativistic" approach to various important policy concerns, such as the appropriate degree of inequality, or the appropriate mix between democracy and authoritarianism. Tu's observation forms a fitting end to this paper:

> ontologically we are infinitely better and therefore more worthy than we actually are. In the ultimate sense we, as persons, form a trinity with Heaven and Earth. From this transcending perspective, it is not at all inconceivable that every particular pattern of social relations is only instrumentally important and is therefore deprived of ultimacy (Tu 1985, 137).[36]

Acknowledgment

The author would like to thank M. G. Quibria, as well as the discussants, Jeffrey Liang, Salim Rashid, and Byung-Nak Song, for their most valuable comments. This paper was partly written while the author was visiting the Department of Economics of the University of Melbourne, whose hospitality, as well as comments of Jurgen Eichberger and Peter Stemp, are gratefully acknowledged. Comments by Michael McAleer are also deeply appreciated. The usual disclaimer applies.

Notes

1. Many of the issues in this section are examined in significantly greater detail in Kapur (1995a).

2. Even here, however, there may be exceptions. For example, consumers may well refrain from consuming a particular species of fish—even though it is both sumptuous and affordable—if they believe that continuing consumption is likely to lead to its extinction. 'Ethical' considerations may well be germane to more areas of economic choice than is generally appreciated.

3. Note that Telser's statement in effect denies that people behave in accordance with the golden rule of ethics: "do unto others as you would have others do unto you".

4. As both Quibria and Liang point out, there is nothing inherent in neoclassical economics which prevents it from incorporating altruistic or other-regarding concerns in the utility functions of economic agents. There is a fairly extensive economic literature on altruism, associated with the names of Gary Becker, Oded Stark, B. Douglas Bernheim, and others. However, in practice, in large areas of economics this literature is ignored. A great deal of recent analytical work on managerial and worker behavior in organizations, for example, adopts the narrow specifications of utility functions described in the text. On a related point, as some writers have, in my view, correctly argued, to describe an altruistic person as self-interested because he still seeks to maximize his utility function (which includes the utilities of others) is to reduce the notion of self-interest to a tautology. If Hirshleifer's statement, quoted above, is to have significant substantive content then the notion of self-interest has in general to be conceived rather narrowly.

5. Perhaps the most important examples of such models are those dealing with reputational considerations. However, it is not uncommon for reputational models to have multiple equilibria: depending on the structure of payoffs, which in turn may depend upon the beliefs of economic actors, it is just as possible to have a low-reputation equilibrium as a high-reputation one. Examples of such multiple equilibria possibilities are Allen (1984) and Guttman (1992).

6. Maital is approvingly describing here the argument of Hirsch (1976).

7. Stiglitz (1993) also recognizes this possibility: "How work is organized may not only affect the productivity of workers, but how they view themselves and their world, and how they behave outside the work place" (p. 112). In his

written comment on this paper, Rashid argues that, fundamentally, "ethics and values are prior to the market": referring to the enforcement of property rights, for example, he points out that "before capitalism, a system of greedy individuals pursuing their self-interest, is to function we need a set of judges who are individuals not motivated by greed". Rashid further argues that historically, the requisite value system, as part of what we might term the institutional framework of capitalism, was provided by Christianity. The issue that one might wish to raise here is whether an institutional framework that "looks beyond self-interest" (Rashid), and capitalist economic behavior, based essentially on self-interest, can coexist indefinitely. This is a profound issue that we cannot explore here, but the interested reader may find it worthwhile to read the works of such writers as Bell, Lasch, and Bellah (all three authors are cited and briefly discussed by Donohue [1990, 17-19], although his criticisms of their views is, in my opinion, misplaced).

8. From the Bible, as quoted by Stark (1989, 86). Continuing, Stark observes, "This rule for regulating relations between pairs of individuals has two elements : first, it mandates altruism. Second, it prescribes a specific dosage of it. The rule instructs individuals to care not only about their own component of the social state, and to attach a weight to the well-being of another individual that is exactly equal to the weight they attach to their own well-being". As a practical matter, Stark further argues that in various situations assigning a weight of less than half to the other person's welfare— but *not* an arbitrarily small weight—would suffice to generate efficient outcomes.

9. There is thus a two-way process at work: a certain initial degree of unselfishness serves to incline the individual toward constructive social engagement, and the experience of social involvement in turn leads to greater self-awareness and further deepening of the individual's unselfish tendencies.

10. In support of this, Frank (pp. 76-7) adduces the results of the following experiment. When subjects were asked to choose on a given day between $100 to be received 28 days later and $120 to be received 31 days later, they made, correctly, the latter choice. However, when they were then asked to choose between "$100 today" and "$120 three days from now", they chose the former—a clear case of choice inconsistency. "The behavioral psychologist's explanation for the inconsistency goes roughly as follows: With respect to the first pair of alternatives the psychological reward mechanism regards each payoff as temporally remote. Something 28 days away seems virtually as far off as something 31 days away. One can't get immediate gratification anyway, so why not settle for the more valuable reward? In the second pair of alternatives, however, the immediacy of the first reward is, for many subjects, just too vivid to ignore. It floods their consciousness and overwhelms their judgment" (Frank 1988, 78).

11. A difficulty with Frank's analysis is that, in the wide-ranging examples that he provides (pp. 82-3), an equally wide-ranging set of emotions— ranging from having a conscience to being "predisposed to feel anger when wronged" or to feel "envious and resentful" upon getting less than one's fair share—is adduced by him as being helpful in solving impulse-control problems. One can well imagine that anger, for example, while it may help in

solving some kinds of self-control problem, is itself likely to create other kinds of self-control problem for the individual (especially as emotions, by their very nature, cannot be precisely modulated so as to be aroused only in some situations and not in others—a predisposition "to feel anger when wronged" may quite readily develop into a tendency to be bad-tempered in general). Not all classes of emotions are therefore conducive to self-control across a wide variety of situations.

12. Frank alludes to this in one of his examples ("The non-cheater's low return is not a reliable sign of having been cheated, since there are many benign explanations why a business might do poorly" [p. 47]), but in his formal discussions makes use only of the prisoner's dilemma framework.

13. This may be due to the self-control problem, or, Frank points out (p. 82, footnote), to such persons employing "excessively high exponential rates of discounting".

14. The magnitude of the resulting efficiency loss is, of course, an empirical matter, and could well vary from one principal-agent setting to another: however, the discussion later suggests that it could well be substantial.

15. I am indebted to Professor Kenneth Chan of McMaster University for first suggesting this to me.

16. A recent paper by Lord and Rangazas (1993) provides further support for this basic argument. It might appear that the growth of social security was a response to various socioeconomic challenges, such as the desire to protect the basic living standards of a generation whose earning opportunities had been adversely affected by the Great Depression and World War II. While such considerations may have played a part, they appear unable to account for the magnitude of the transfers that have been mandated over time. To quote Thurow (1985, 249), "the average elderly family now enjoys a standard of living higher than that of the non-elderly. Much of this progress can be traced to social security". Aharoni (1981, 83) points out that 'A worker who entered the system in 1937 and paid the maximum tax for thirty years before retirement would have paid a very small fraction of the benefits received. Today, high-income workers may pay far more than they will receive in benefits.' In their empirical study, Altonji et al. (1992) find little evidence of intergenerational altruism in US data.

17. Interestingly, Peters and Waterman also quote the Chairman of 3M, Lew Lehr, as pointing out that companies with such an orientation have "filled the void" resulting from the breakdown of institutions such as communities, schools, and churches as social centers.

18. De Mente was of course writing in 1981, before the very recent, ongoing social, economic, and political changes in Japan. These changes merit a separate analysis in their own right, but all the same De Mente's observations may be viewed as applicable in respect of a considerable part of 20th century Japanese experience.

19. Consider also the following (noncountry-specific) observation by Stiglitz (1993, 111-2): "Simon (1991) has provided a convincing case that agency problems are often overcome best by attempting to change the preferences of workers, making them "identify" with the firm with which they work, and that successful firms manage to do this." Sen (1994) also mentions

the Japanese company ethic as an example of "other-regarding concerns" (p. 389).

20. Aoki has earlier (pp. 50-1) described contextual skill ("which is developed over a relatively long period of time") as "a relatively wide range of skills (integrative skills) that have been developed and are useful in the context of the nonhierarchical information structure (of the J-firm)".

21. Copeland (1989) arrives interestingly at a similar conclusion in his efficiency-wage model: "given two otherwise identical economies, the country with the lower disutility of effort will have a comparative advantage in the good which is relatively intensive in jobs which are costly to monitor" (p. 234).

23. Presumably, it would be "rational" for him to misrepresent this status to the firm at the time of, as well as before, his departure from it.

24. See also Megna and Klock (1993), whose finding (for the US) that "rivals' stocks of R&D expenditures have a positive effect on (Tobin's) q ... is consistent with the conventional wisdom that knowledge from R&D in the semiconductor industry is frequently transferred by defecting employees" (p. 269).

25. It might appear that, once this is realized, self-interested persons could decide to behave cooperatively out of pure self-interest. Consider, however, the following observation of the great philosopher, Immanuel Kant (quoted in Collard 1981, 176): "Commencing good from obligation through habit we can end by doing it from inclination, and to this extent love can be commanded."

26. See, for example, the 1991 Centenary Issue of the *Economic Journal*. As a small sample of some of the views expressed therein: "if, as I expect, economists become less wedded to a narrow interpretation of self-interested behavior, then they will draw increasingly on ideas and perspectives from other social sciences" (Pencavel, p. 85); "instead of theorems we shall need simulations, instead of simple transparent axioms there looms the likelihood of psychological, sociological and historical postulates ... There will be a change of personnel, and economics will become a 'softer' subject than it now is" (Hahn, p. 47).

27. One good example is the study of group-based rural credit programs, exemplified by the well-known case of the Grameen Bank in Bangladesh. See Riedinger (1994) and Banerjee et al. (1994), and the references cited therein. On the causation in the reverse direction—from economic variables to cultural factors, including values—it is certainly true, as Quibria suggests, that such a relationship exists. Donohue (1990, 17), for example, points out that in advanced countries "social and geographic mobility, coupled with increasing economic independence, has diminished the central role that community relations once played". However, this is not to imply that we subscribe to a rigid determinism relating culture to economics. While economic trends do influence cultural factors, there is, in my view, considerable scope for selective adaptation and adjustment of the latter to the former, and for further refinement of a society's values in accordance with its own evolving ethical consensus, and it is in these areas that research, discussion, and policy have important roles to play.

28. Consider also Tu's (1988, 41) observation on certain aspects of the role of the state in East Asian countries, quoted by Byung-Nak Song in his written comments on the present paper: "comprehensive leadership is obligated, in a classical Confucian sense, 'to provide, to enrich, and to educate' the people. Bureaucrats are not merely government functionaries but leaders, intellectuals and teachers." Emphasis is placed, inter alia, on "the primacy of education as character building", and on "the importance of exemplary leadership in politics" (Tu 1988, 35).

29. Okimoto indicates in the former that his paper is an extract from the latter, but some differences in the degree of amplification of certain points remain between the two versions. An insightful discussion of the two different conceptions of the political system may also be found in the chapter by Paul Streeten in this volume.

30. Again, we remind the reader that we are considering the postwar period in Japan generally, rather than the events of the recent past, which merit a separate analysis.

31. "A strong case be made that in many countries immediately after independence the leaders had the well-being of their people at heart and wanted to be benevolent social guardians. This certainly appears to have been the case with Jawaharlal Nehru in India and Kemal Ataturk in Turkey" (Krueger 1993, 61).

32. Valuable discussions of the economic and political issues that have to be attended to in order to achieve successful liberalization may be found in Krueger (1992, 1993), Johnson (1994), and Sturzenegger and Tommasi (1994).

33. In this connection, the unpublished paper by Lal (1992) (see also Lal and Myint 1990) should also be noted. As summarized by Sturzenegger and Tommasi (1994, 245-6), Lal distinguishes between 'platonic' ("in which the government coincides with a social planner"), 'predatory', and 'factional' developing states, and shows that platonic states (which in his study comprised Hong Kong, Singapore, Malta, Turkey, and Malawi) have in general had the most favorable growth performance over the 1960-1985 period.

34. Squire (1993), whose recent review of poverty reduction efforts in developing countries "suggests three broad conclusions. First, economic growth that fosters the productive use of labor, the main asset owned by the poor, can generate rapid reductions in poverty. Second, public spending has been an important factor driving improvements in the health status and educational attainment of the poor, but judging from rate-of-return estimates it still has a long way to go in most countries before it would generate trade-offs with economic growth. Third, of the total transfer to the poor, basic social services, rather than cash, have been the preferred delivery mechanism possibly for political reasons, but also because they achieve their intended objective of increasing the consumption of health and education services" (p. 381).

35. Our emphasis on the individual's responsibilities contrasts with current trends in thinking among economists, and perhaps in contemporary Western society in general. By way of illustration, the May 1994 *Papers and Proceedings* of the American Economic Association contains papers devoted to issues such as poverty and welfare, the situation of the working poor, and the

economic support of child raising. The fact that all of these issues have strong normative (as well as more "technocratic") dimensions is hardly noticed in these papers. A good example of the "flavor" of these analyses is the following: "Rhetorical appeals for a return to "family values" are unlikely to make headway against the problem of child poverty.... A more efficacious and humane approach to the cure of child poverty would be to take the weakening of marriage as a given and to look for politically acceptable ways of capturing more economic resources for children in single-mother families. Such policies may further weaken the incentives to marriage, but that may be unavoidable" (Bergmann 1994, 76). Child poverty certainly represents a tragic phenomenon, and Bergman may well be right that what she refers to as "rhetorical appeals" are not likely to work in the short run: however, what is disturbing is the absence of any reference to the moral responsibilities involved in marriage and parenthood, even as an issue that could be effectively raised over a longer time horizon. Consider also an observation by Folbre (1994): "as children become increasingly public goods, parenting becomes an increasingly public service" (p. 86).

36. "Neo-Confucian Religiosity..." (Tu 1985, 137). Niebuhr (1948, 68, 71) takes a similar position.

References

Aharoni, Y., 1981. *The No-Risk Society*. New Jersey: Chatham House Publishers Inc.

Allen, F., 1984. "Reputation and Product Quality." *Rand Journal of Economics* 15(3):311-27.

Altonji, J. G., F. Hayashi, and L. J. Kotlikoff, 1992. "Is the Extended Family Altruistically Linked? Direct Tests using Micro Data." *American Economic Review* 82(5):1177-98.

Aoki, M., 1988. *Information, Incentives, and Bargaining in the Japanese Economy*. Cambridge: Cambridge University Press.

Aron, D. J., 1987. "Worker Reputation and Productivity Incentives." *Journal of Labor Economics* 5(4/2):S87-106.

Ausubel, L. M., 1991. "The Failure of Competition in the Credit Card Market." *American Economic Review* 81(1):50-81.

Banerjee, A. V., T. Besley, and T. W. Guinnane, 1994. "Thy Neighbor's Keeper: The Design of a Credit Co-operative with Theory and a Test." *Quarterly Journal of Economics* 109(2):491-515.

Barker, E., 1959. *The Political Thought of Plato and Aristotle*. New York: Dover.

Bergman, B. R., 1994. "Curing Child Poverty in the United States." *American Economic Review* 84(2):76-80.

Bishop, J. H., 1989. "Is the Test Score Decline Responsible for the Productivity Growth Decline?" *American Economic Review* 79(1):178-97.

Chang, C. Y., 1980. *Confucianism: A Modern Interpretation*. Taipei,China: China Academy.

Cheng, A. K., 1994. "Economist's Perceptions of the Role of Altruism in Economic Life." Unpublished Honor's Thesis. Department of Economics and Statistics, National University of Singapore.

Collard, D., 1978. *Altruism and Economy: A Study in Non-Selfish Economics.* Oxford: Martin Robertson.

Copeland, B. R., 1989. "Efficiency Wages in a Ricardian Model of International Trade." *Journal of International Economics* 27:221-44.

De Mente, B., 1981. *The Japanese Way of Doing Business.* Englewood Cliffs: Prentice-Hall. (Reissued as *Japanese Etiquette and Ethics in Business.* Illinois: NTC Business Books, 1994).

Denison, E., 1979. *Accounting for Slower Economic Growth.* Washington, D.C.: The Brookings Institution.

Dertouzos, M. L., R. K. Lester, R. M. Solow, and The MIT Commission on Industrial Productivity, 1989. *Made in America: Regaining the Productive Edge.* Cambridge: The MIT Press.

Dickens, W., L. Katz, K. Lang, and L. H. Summers, 1989. "Employee Crime and the Monitoring Puzzle." *Journal of Labor Economics* 7(3):331-47.

Donohue, W. A., 1990. *The New Freedom: Individualism and Collectivism in the Social Lives of Americans.* New Brunswick: Transaction Publishers.

Dore, R., 1987. *Taking Japan Seriously: A Confucian Perspective on Leading Economic Issues.* London: The Athlone Press.

Economic Journal, 1991. Centenary Issue. 101(404):47-50; 81-87.

Fehr, E., G. Kirchsteiger, and A. Riedl, 1993. "Does Fairness Prevent Market Clearing? An Experimental Investigation." *Quarterly Journal of Economics* CVIII(2):437-59.

Folbre, N., 1994. "Children as Public Goods." *American Economic Review* 84(2):86-90.

Frank, R. H., 1988. *Passions Within Reason: The Strategic Role of the Emotions.* New York: W.W. Norton and Co.

———, 1991. *Microeconomics and Behavior.* New York: McGraw-Hill.

Gibbons, R., 1987. "Piece-Rate Incentive Schemes." *Journal of Labor Economics* 5(4/Part 1):413-29.

Guttman, J., 1992. "The Credibility Game: Reputation and Rational Cooperation in a Changing Population." *Journal of Comparative Economics* 16(4):619-32.

Hatsopoulos, G. N., P. R. Krugman, and J. M. Poterba, 1989. *Overconsumption: The Challenge to U.S. Economic Policy.* Washington, D.C.: American Business Conference.

Hausman, D. M., and M. S. McPherson, 1993. "Taking Ethics Seriously: Economics and Contemporary Moral Philosophy." *Journal of Economic Literature* 31(2):671-731.

Hirsch, F., 1976. *Social Limits to Growth.* Cambridge: Harvard University Press.

Hirschleifer, J., 1985. "The Expanding Domain of Economics." *American Economic Review* 75(6):53-68.

Johnson, O. E. G., 1994. "Managing Adjustment Costs, Political Authority, and the Implementation of Adjustment Programs, with Special Reference to African Countries." *World Development* 22(3):399-411.

Kahneman, D., J. L. Knetsch, and R. Thaler, 1986. "Fairness as a Constraint on Profit Seeking: Entitlements in the Market." *American Economic Review* 76(4):728-41.

Kapur, B. K., 1995a. *Communitarian Ethics and Economics.* Aldershot: Avebury.

———, 1995b. "A Communitarian Utility Function." Mimeo.

Kotlikoff, L. J., 1986. "Deficit Delusion." *Public Interest.* Reprinted in L. J. Kotlikoff, 1989. *What Determines Savings?* Cambridge: The MIT Press.

Krueger, A. O., 1992. *Economic Policy Reform in Developing Countries.* Oxford: Basil Blackwell.

———, 1993. *Political Economy of Policy Reform in Developing Countries.* Cambridge: The MIT Press.

Laffont, J. J., 1989. *The Economics of Uncertainty and Information.* Cambridge: The MIT Press.

Laffont, J. J., and J. Tirole, 1991. "The Politics of Government Decision-Making: A Theory of Regulatory Capture." *Quarterly Journal of Economics* LVI(4):1089-127.

Lal, D., 1992. "Why Growth Rates Differ: The Political Economy of Social Capability in 21 Developing Countries." UCLA Working Paper No. 642. Los Angeles, California.

Lal, D., and H. Myint, 1990. *Poverty, Equity and Economic Growth.* World Bank Comparative Study. Mimeo.

Lasch, C., 1978. *The Culture of Narcissism.* New York: Norton.

Lord, W., and P. Rangazas, 1993. "Altruism, Deficit Policies, and the Wealth of Future Generations." *Economic Inquiry* 31(October):609-30.

Magee, S. P., W. A. Brock, and L. Young, 1989. *Black Hole Tariffs and Endogenous Policy Theory.* Cambridge: Cambridge University Press.

Maital, S., 1982. *Minds, Markets, and Money: Psychological Foundations of Economic Behavior.* New York: Basic Books.

Mansbridge, J. J., ed., 1990. *Beyond Self-Interest.* Chicago: University of Chicago Press.

Megna, P., and M. Klock, 1993. "The Impact of Intangible Capital on Tobin's q in the Semiconductor Industry." *American Economic Review* 83(2): 265-9.

Moon, B. E., 1991. *The Political Economy of Basic Human Needs.* Ithaca: Cornell University Press.

Niebuhr, R., 1948. *An Interpretation of Christian Ethics.* 4th ed. London: SCM Press Ltd.

Okimoto, D. I., 1988. "Japan, the Societal State." In D. I. Okimoto and T. P. Rohlen, eds., *Inside the Japanese System: Readings on Contemporary Society and Political Economy.* Stanford: Stanford University Press.

———, 1989. *Between MITI and the Market: Japanese Industrial Policy for High Technology.* Stanford: Stanford University Press.

Olson, M., 1982. *The Rise and Decline of Nations*. New Haven and London: Yale University Press.

Parthasarathy, S., 1988. "Commentary on *Kaivalyopanishad*." In K. Brown, ed., *The Essential Teachings of Hinduism*. London: Rider.

Pascale, R. T., and A. G. Athos, 1981. *The Art of Japanese Management: Applications for American Executives*. New York: Simon and Schuster.

Persson, T., and G. Tabellini, 1994. Is Inequality Harmful for Growth?" *American Economic Review* 84(3):600-21.

Peters, T. J., and R. H. Waterman, Jr., 1982. *In Search of Excellence: Lessons from America's Best-Run Companies*. New York: Warner Books.

Rabin, M., 1993. "Incorporating Fairness into Game Theory and Economics." *American Economic Review* 83(5):1281-1302.

Radner, R., 1981. "Monitoring Cooperative Agreements in a Repeated Principal-Agent Relationship." *Econometrica* 49(5):1127-48.

Rahman, A., 1980. *Islam: Ideology and the Way of Life*. Singapore: Pustaka Nasional Pte. Ltd.

Riedinger, J. M., 1994. "Innovation in Rural Finance: Indonesia's Badan Kredit Kecamatan Program." *World Development* 22(3):301-13.

Rushton, J. P., *Altruism, Socialization and Society*. New Jersey: Prentice-Hall, Inc.

Sen, A. K., 1988. *On Ethics and Economics*. Oxford: Basil Blackwell.

———, 1994. "The Formulation of Rational Choice." *American Economic Review* 84(2):385-90.

Shapiro, M., and J. Slemrod, 1993. *Consumer Response to the Timing of Income: Evidence from a Change in Tax Withholding*. NBER Working Paper No. 4344. National Bureau of Economic Research, Cambridge, Massachusetts.

Simon, H., 1957. *Models of Man*. New York: Wiley and Sons.

Squire, L., 1993. "Fighting Poverty." *American Economic Review* 83(2):377-82.

Stark, O., 1989. "Altruism and the Quality of Life." *American Economic Review*. 79(2):86-90.

Stiglitz, J. E., 1991. "Symposium on Organizations and Economics." *Journal of Economic Perspectives* 5(2):15-24.

———, 1991. "Post Walrasian and Post Marxian Economics." *Journal of Economic Perspectives* 7(1):109-14.

Sturzenegger, F., and M. Tommasi, 1994. "The Distribution of Political Power, the Costs of Rent-Seeking, and Economic Growth." *Economic Inquiry* 32(2):236-48.

Telser, L. G., 1980. "A Theory of Self-Enforcing Agreements." *Journal of Business* 53(1):27-44.

Thurow, L. C., 1985. *The Zero-Sum Society*. New York: Simon and Schuster.

Tirole, J., 1994. "The Internal Organization of Government." *Oxford Economic Papers* 46(1):1-29.

Tu, W. M., 1985. "Neo-Confucian Religiosity and Human-Relatedness." In W. M. Tu, *Confucian Thought: Selfhood as Creative Transformation*. Albany: State University of New York Press.

————, 1988. "A Confucian Perspective on the Rise of Industrial East Asia." *The American Academy of Arts and Sciences Bulletin* 52 (1).

————, 1985. *Centrality and Commonality: An Essay on Confucian Religiousness.* Albany: State University of New York Press.

Viard, A. D., 1993. "The Productivity Slowdown and the Savings Shortfall: A Challenge to the Permanent Income Hypothesis." *Economic Inquiry* XXXI(4):549-63.

Yoshifumi, U., 1967. "The Status of the Individual in Mahayana Buddhist Philosophy." In C. A. Moore, ed., *The Japanese Mind: Essentials of Japanese Philosophy and Culture.* Honolulu: East-West Center Press.

Chapter 6

Regulation, Privatization, and Incentives in Developing Countries

Jean-Jacques Laffont

Regulation and privatization are two possible instruments for promoting development. They may appear at first sight contradictory, since privatization is designed to a large extent to keep the government's hands off enterprises, and regulation means government control. Actually they are not since, even in a world where all firms are privatized, we still have to worry about monopolistic behavior and competitive policy is required. The extreme form of this required public intervention concerns natural monopolies, which fall in the domain of regulation. We will restrict our analysis to this case of natural monopolies because we are more interested here in defining what is the proper role of an economic state in developing countries than in the study of the process by which a planned economy can be transformed into a market economy. The fact that some form of public intervention is needed in the case of natural monopolies is undisputed. The debate centers around the type of intervention and the real domain of natural monopolies. Also it is well recognized today that the inadequacy of physical infrastructures such as telecommunications, transport, and energy, the privileged domains of natural monopolies,[1] is a major handicap for development (as in the People's Republic of China for example), and this topic requires more attention than it has received so far in development economics.[2]

We are not going to specifically discuss areas that have been shown or at least argued to be highly important for development, such as technological innovation, human capital, learning by doing, or infrastructures. A specific study of these issues from the point of view of incentives would be welcome and we hope to carry it out in the future. In this paper, we want to pursue the more modest task of reviewing the arguments that have been put forward to defend certain types of regulation (such as the promotion of price cap regulation in the last decade) and the wide-spread privatization programs for developing countries.

Much has been written recently about the privatization issue, in particular for Eastern European Countries (e.g., on the theoretical side Tirole 1991, Dewatripont and Roland 1992, Bolton and Roland 1992, Maskin 1991, Aghion and Burgess 1992), but not with particular reference to natural monopolies. We will not survey this literature, but rather attempt to draw from the recent advances of economic theory, a general view on the role of incentives in regulation and privatization for natural monopolies given the specificities of developing countries. Hopefully, it will be useful to provide an intellectual framework and to appraise some difficulties in the much needed reforms of state enterprises in developing countries such as the People's Republic of China.

The next section lists the specificities we will be taking into account. The third section examines the question of regulation of natural monopolies both from the point of view of cost reimbursement rules and pricing methods, and the following section discusses privatization. Conclusions are drawn at the end of each section. A general conclusion ends the paper.

Specificities of Developing Countries

An essential concept in the theories of regulation and privatization is the notion of marginal price of public funds, that is to say the social price of raising one unit of money. This price includes a dead-weight loss (that we will refer to as the cost of public funds) because government revenue is raised with distortive taxes.[3]

Of course, the dead-weight losses of taxes depend on the type of tax used since the tax systems are not generally optimized, but a common estimate of this cost for developed countries is around 0.3.

In developing countries this cost is considered to be much higher. Several studies by the World Bank (see Jones, Tandon and Vogelsang 1990 for a synthesis). situate this number well beyond 1, for example, Malaysia 1.20, Philippines 2.48, and Thailand somewhere between 1.19 and 1.54.

The first specific feature of developing countries that we will take into account is therefore the high cost of public funds[4] even though precise figures cannot be selected as they depend in particular on the stage of development.

Auditing of costs is also an essential part of the ability of a regulatory agency to control that will be crucial in choosing between alternative modes of regulation or privatization. Developing countries often lack elaborate accounting systems and proper auditing staffs and administrations. The poor functioning of audits is due to at least three phenomena:

first, the political and social difficulty of paying incentive salaries to auditors that induce effort and discourage corruption (Gould and Amaro-Reyes 1983); second, the poor technology of auditing itself which makes it harder to discover cost padding, and third, the inability (due to stronger limited liability constraints of many economic agents) to impose high penalties when wrongdoing is documented.

The inefficiency of auditing clearly makes corruption more wide-spread, but our concern here will be more with the effect of this ineffi-ciency on the choice of regulatory institutions and privatization proce-dures than with the analysis of corruption itself.

Related to auditing is the concept of internal cost of side transfers. When two parties, such as a firm and an auditor, or a bidder and the or-ganizer of a privatization auction, design side transfers to arrange a pri-vate deal, they must take into account the costs of being identified and the necessity of using indirect compensations (for example the revolving door phenomenon) that are less efficient than money. The cost of these internal transfers is expected to be smaller than in developed countries, because side transfers are more difficult to identify and because social norms may value positively some types of side transfers (for example when they take place within families, villages, or ethnic groups).

Two features (even if they are quite imperfect) characterize devel-oped countries and are often missing in developing countries: a constitu-tional control of the government and some ability to commit and write long-term contracts.

The lack of the checks and balances provided by well-functioning democracies, Supreme Courts, government auditing bodies (Cour des Comptes, General Accounting Office) and other counter powers makes the government more easily captured by interest groups and more able to fa-vor excessively the voters supporting it. We will be consequently led to emphasize the political economy aspects of regulation and privatization in our analysis.

Also, the lack of political democracy and well-functioning political institutions increases the uncertainty of future regulations and makes it difficult for the government and regulatory institutions to make credible commitments to long-run policies.[5] Consequently, the economic policies of developing countries are even more sensitive to ratchet effects and rene-gotiation constraints.

Finally, we will take into account the well-documented feature of poorly developed capital markets as well as the sheer lack of wealth which make limited liability constraints more binding.[6]

Regulation and Development

A Recap of the New Economics of Regulation

Following the pioneering application of incentive theory to regulation by Loeb and Magat (1979), and Baron and Myerson (1982), the 1980s have witnessed the emergence of a new theory of regulation which emphasizes the asymmetries of information between government, regulatory commissions, firms, and various interest groups (see Laffont 1994a for a survey of this literature). The insights of these new theories have not been examined in the light of the specificities of developing countries.

Let us recap intuitively some of the lessons we have learned from these theories. Consider the regulation of a natural monopoly which has private information both on its technological characteristics (adverse selection parameter) and on an effort variable (moral hazard) which decreases costs but creates a nonmonetary disutility to the firm's management.

Cost is ex post observable by the regulator who can determine the pricing rule and the cost reimbursement rule.[7] However, when high costs are observed, the regulator does not know if it is because the firm is technically inefficient or because of low effort levels. This asymmetric information about the firm's costs implies that an informational rent must be given up to the firm when it is efficient, since it can always mimic the inefficient firm and realize the same cost with a lower effort level.

Assuming a utilitarian regulator, social welfare equals the sum of the net surplus of consumers and the firm utility level minus the social cost of the net transfer from the regulator to the firm. Because of the need to use distortive taxation to finance this transfer, we use the social cost of funds to evaluate it. This social cost of funds implies that it is socially costly to give up a rent to the firm, since any dollar that can be captured from the firm enables the government to decrease by one dollar the distortive taxes, which cost more than one dollar to society. The regulator will want to decrease this costly rent and will be led to distorting the allocation of resources for this purpose, i.e., to accept inefficiencies.

Optimizing expected social welfare under incentive and individual rationality constraints of the firm, the regulator determines the optimal trade off between efficiency and rent extraction, and optimal pricing.

The trade off between efficiency and rent extraction is determined by the cost reimbursement rule. Full reimbursement of cost enables the regulator to perfectly control the rent given up to the firm, but induces large inefficiencies because there is no incentive for cost minimization. At the other extreme, payments independent of cost induce proper behavior of cost minimization, but in general leave large rents to the firm.

The optimal cost reimbursement rule is equivalent to a menu of linear sharing rules of overruns. Firms can choose from a menu that may include either a fixed payment and no reimbursement of cost (a fixed-price mechanism) or a smaller payment and full reimbursement of cost (cost-plus mechanism) as well as intermediary mechanisms which specify partial reimbursement of costs. Firms self-select from this menu. In particular, the most efficient firm chooses a fixed-price mechanism (which induces a high level of effort since the firm is then a residual claimant of its cost savings) and less-efficient firms choose cost-sharing mechanisms that induce less effort. So the innate efficiency differentials are enlarged by the firm's response to the optimal menu of cost-reimbursement rules.[8]

The second part of optimal regulation is the pricing rules, which reduce here to the Ramsey pricing rules. More specifically, relative deviations of prices from the marginal costs evaluated for the effort level induced by the cost-reimbursement rule are inversely proportional to the superelasticities of the commodities considered.[9] The coefficient of proportionality is increasing in the cost of public funds. If this cost is zero, we have marginal cost-pricing. If it becomes very large, we have monopoly pricing.

High Cost of Public Funds

As we have stressed above, a major characteristic of developing countries is the high cost of public funds. It is easy to see that this high cost calls for higher prices of the commodities produced by the natural monopoly and for lower-powered incentive schemes (high shares of cost reimbursement). Before giving the intuitive reasoning for these results, let us emphasize the assumptions we are making of perfect observability of cost and full commitment of the regulator.

The intuitions are as follows. A higher cost of public funds means a higher cost of giving up rents and also a higher cost of inefficiencies, but relatively the cost of rents increases faster. This is because when an additional rent is given up to a type of firm to support an improvement of efficiency by this firm, by incentive compatibility it must also be given up to all firms more efficient than this one. The optimal regulation sacrifices some efficiency to decrease those rents. It is therefore an argument favoring cost-plus schemes vis-à-vis fixed-price schemes, or rate of return regulation versus price-cap in the language of regulation theory.

A higher cost of funds also means that it is more valuable to price above marginal cost, i.e., to use prices of public utilities to finance the fixed costs and the government's budget. In particular, it is a mistake to advocate marginal cost pricing for public utilities in developing countries.

The implied difference in pricing between developed and developing countries can be substantial, since a move from a cost of funds of 0.3 to 1 translates into a relative deviation from marginal cost which is double in the second case. Since effort levels also decrease as cost reimbursement rules are tilted toward cost-plus schemes, marginal costs are higher and therefore prices should be even higher in developing countries.

For example, as a concrete application, for defining access pricing rules to networks in developing countries one should incorporate deviations from marginal costs to finance the fixed cost of the network even more than in developed countries (see Laffont and Tirole 1994 for an extensive study of access pricing rules). Similarly, if asymmetric information concerns the level of quality, a higher value of the cost of funds calls for lower quality. More generally, such a high cost means a higher relative cost of rents and an arbitrage toward less efficiency. Here again the relative inefficiency of the tax system calls for a higher deviation from first-best efficiency.

We have assumed so far that transfers between the regulator and the firm are feasible. As shown in Laffont and Martimort (1994), it may be interesting to regulate with multiple regulators to decrease the costs of capture. An application of this result could be that the regulator controls costs and chooses prices but does not make any transfer to the firm, which must apply for funds on the credit markets. The higher cost of funds militates for this type of structural separation even more in developing countries, because the gains derived from weaker collusion proof constraints are higher.[10] Structural separation provides an alternative way to fight corruption than paying supervisors.

Note finally that with budget-balanced regulation, the social cost of funds does not play any direct role in the determination of optimal regulation (Laffont and Tirole 1993). However, the strength of the budget balance constraint affects regulation in the same way as the social cost of public funds, and is itself affected by the taxes and subsidies incurred by the firm.

Monitoring

Monitoring of effort generally enables the regulator to reduce the informational rents and calls for higher-powered incentive schemes. A less-efficient monitoring technology will call for relatively less-powerful incentive schemes. Indeed, low incentives and monitoring are substitute instruments to extract the firm's rent. A decrease of the use of one instrument makes the other instrument more attractive. An increase in the cost of public funds induces low incentives both directly and indirectly through a decrease of the more costly monitoring.

We have emphasized so far the strong assumption of perfect observability of costs. In practice, costs are imperfectly observable. Noisy cost observation in itself is not a problem as long as risk neutrality can be maintained, but one must also take into account the possibility of cost padding, i.e. the many ways in which a firm can divert money. Cost can now be increased by undue charges which benefit the management and the workers. Note that the existence of cost padding is itself the result of the regulator's desire to extract the firm's rent. Cost padding would never arise if the regulator offered a fixed price contract, since it would pay the entirety of each unit of money diverted.

The analysis (Laffont and Tirole 1992) shows that the imperfect auditing of cost padding calls for a shift toward higher-power incentive schemes. In the extreme, if auditing did not exist, only fixed-price contracts would be possible. Indeed they would be the only ones preventing unlimited cost padding by making firms residual claimants of their costs. It is therefore very intuitive that a deterioration of the auditing technology, as can be expected in developing countries, will induce an even higher desire to shift toward fixed-price mechanisms. This effect is reinforced by the savings of auditing costs allowed by fixed-price mechanisms in countries with high cost of public funds. This conflicts with the findings of the previous section and we will return to it.

Hierarchical Regulation

The next consideration we want to integrate is the necessary decentralization of regulation to regulatory agencies or ministries. A main role of these institutions is to bridge partially the informational gap between the public decision maker and the regulated firm. But then a new issue appears, the possible capture of the regulatory agency by the firm.

Such a collusion will occur with greater probability if the stakes of collusion are high, if the cost of side transfers between the firm and the regulator are low, and if no incentive mechanism is in place for the regulators.

The stake of collusion amounts to the informational rent that an efficient firm obtains when the regulator hides the fact that it is efficient. From our previous analysis, it is increasing with the level of effort chosen by the less-efficient firm (since it is equivalent to the gain obtained by an efficient firm when it mimics an inefficient one).

The maximum bribe that a firm will be willing to offer to the agency is this stake. However, it should be discounted by the price of internal transfers, which includes the costs of being discovered as well as the need to use often indirect transfers that are less efficient than monetary transfers.

Capture is avoided if the agency is paid an amount larger than the discounted value of the stake of collusion when it reveals the firm is efficient (we will call this constraint the collusion-proof constraint).

In the simplest cases, the regulatory response to the fear of capture is to satisfy the collusion-proof constraint at the lowest possible cost. This includes shifting optimal regulation toward cost-plus to decrease the stake of collusion, and improving monitoring to increase the cost of side transfers.

Three features of developing countries call for even higher shifts toward cost-plus mechanisms. First, we can expect a lower cost of internal transfers because of less monitoring of illegal activities. Second, incentive payments to the agency are more costly because of the higher cost of public funds. Third, it may be politically more difficult to create such strong incentive payments.

So far we have dealt with a case where the optimal regulatory response entails no corruption. If we extend the framework to a case where, for example, regulators are more or less susceptible to being corrupted (some requiring low bribes, others requiring higher bribes), it may be optimal to let some corruption occur if the proportion of regulators requiring low bribes is small enough. Creating incentive payments which suppress the corruption of this type of regulators would be too costly, because the high payments required to fight corruption would have to be incurred even for the other type of regulators, for which they are not necessary. Then, the same features of developing countries which militate in favor of low-powered incentive schemes (high cost of public funds, poor auditing technologies) suggest that it is optimal to let more corruption happen at the equilibrium.

We argued above that bad auditing technologies of costs favor fixed-price mechanisms. Furthermore, auditing mechanisms are also sensitive to corruption.[11] However, the consequences of easier collusion possibilities on optimal regulation when auditing of cost padding can be corrupted are somewhat involved. This is because now an efficient firm has two ways to mimic an inefficient firm, either by under-effort of cost minimization or by cost padding. The effects on the power of incentives depend finely on the values of the parameters, because they depend on which incentive constraint is binding. On the one hand collusion impairs audits, which raises the desirability of high-powered schemes. On the other hand, high-powered schemes induce more cost-reducing effort, which must be compensated by high transfers to the firm. These high transfers raise the stakes of collusion because the firm loses more when the auditor reveals cost padding. Thus, the threat of collusion calls for low-powered schemes to reduce the stakes. Either of these two effects may dominate. So more corruption of auditing has ambiguous effects on optimal regulation. Another interesting result also emerges: the maximal penalty result of auditing theory does not necessarily hold because high penalties increase the stakes of collusion in auditing (see Laffont and Tirole 1992 for a more detailed analysis). This alleviates somewhat the constraints coming from limited liability constraints.

Political Constraints

Let us now examine the implications of the existence of less control by constitutional rules of the government in developing countries. We will interpret this feature as the fact that the majority holding power can pursue its own objectives more easily than in more developed countries, where the various counter powers force the government to take a better account of social welfare (see Laffont 1995).

Suppose for simplicity that we have two groups of consumers and that one group (type 1) owns the regulated private firm (we will study the privatization issue in the next section). Consider first the same regulatory environment as above. Maximization of social welfare leads to an incentive scheme that arbitrates between inefficiencies and rent extraction.

Now suppose that the political majority is in the hands of type 1 consumers. Then type 1 consumers take into account the rent of the firm in their objective function (since they appropriate it), and their preferred regulation favors rents more than optimally because they share the rents between themselves and not with the whole population, as when social welfare is maximized (at least if pricing cannot be discriminatory of the first degree).

However, if the political majority belongs to type 2 consumers, since the majority does not appropriate the firm's rent it arbitrates more favorably toward a decrease of the rent, i.e., a less powerful incentive scheme. A change of government (from left to right, if we assume that the right owns the monopoly) is likely to strengthen incentives, more specifically might trigger a change from cost-plus regulation toward fixed-price (or price-cap) regulation. This is consistent (because fixed-price regulation is a commitment to let the firm enjoy the benefits of its investments) with Levy and Spiller's observations (1993, 237) that, in the Philippines, "a repeated pattern appears of substantial private investment in telecommunications immediately after a government comes to power that is aligned with the group controlling the telecommunications utility" or that in Chile after 1930, "Within twenty years social forces had arisen that were hostile to profitable participation in utilities. Consequently, by the late 1940s private investment began to lag" (Levy and Spiller 1993, 237).[12]

Suppose now that an independent agency monitors the firm. If type 2 has the majority, the firm will want to protect its rent, which is not valued by the government, and will have incentives to bribe the agency. On the other hand, if type 1 has the majority, one may argue that the firm then has no incentive to such bribes.

Then we can ask the question of whether or not to set up incentive payments for the agency constitutionally. If no such incentives are created, corruption will happen with majority 2 resulting in social losses. However, creating a costly incentive system for the agency is useless with majority 1.

Forbidding incentive payments constitutionally is better when the cost of public funds is high and the cost of internal transfers low, two features of developing countries. As it is more costly to fight political interference, it may be optimal to let it happen, here in the form of a less powerful administration.

These political economy considerations run partially against our previous conclusions. A powerful administration and efficient auditing regulatory institutions are a good thing with decision makers who maximize social welfare. It is less clear when they have private agendas.

Again under the assumption of good auditing of cost, these considerations favor cost-plus mechanisms since they destroy political competition for appropriating the rents of regulated monopolies.

What about pricing of regulated monopolies? Suppose type 1 consumers like the commodity produced more than type 2, and let us start from the optimal second-degree price discrimination rules. Price discrimination will be smaller (greater) than optimal if type 1 (type 2) has the majority. The intuition runs as follows. Price discrimination trades off distortions in consumption patterns with informational rents given up to the consumers who like the commodity more. If type 1 has the majority, it will value the informational rents more and consequently create less distortions of consumption, i.e., less price discrimination. These distortions of pricing will be greater in developing countries from our assumption of less control by government.

This may have a bearing on issues such as the regulation of bypass activities. Suppose that there exists a possibility for type 1 consumers to bypass the monopoly, but that the bypass activity would be socially wasteful (for example, excessive development of self-generation of electricity). It would be optimal for a benevolent social maximizer to forbid bypass rather than distort the price system to keep type 1 consumers with the monopoly. However, in a political economy setting like here, allowing bypass activities constitutionally may be a good policy because it prevents the type 2 majority from designing excessively discriminating policies.

In a developing country, it may even be more advisable to prevent price-discriminating policies and to limit the power of regulatory authorities than in more developed countries. Of course, the approach above is quite naive or at least optimistic. It presumes the existence of a benevolent constitutional stage. In practice, political alternation is often missing and the analysis of this section then simply shows how industrial policy can be used in favor of ruling groups.

Commitment

Let us consider now the important issue of commitment, more specifically the fact that governments in developing countries have even less credibility to commit to long-run regulatory rules than those in developed countries.

A lack of commitment puts the ratchet effect into motion. Faced with incentives in the first periods, firms fear that taking advantage today of these incentives (efficient firms make more money by having low costs) will lead to more demanding incentive schemes in the future. The way to commit credibly to not expropriate rents in the future is to learn nothing today about the firms' efficiency. Instead of offering, as in the static case, a menu of contracts with variable sharing of overruns which induces self-selection, the extreme attitude is to offer a single contract which induces under-effort of the good types and higher than first-best effort of the bad types. The inefficiency created by the lack of commitment is an inappropriate provision of effort levels over the various periods, which has no simple interpretation in terms of the power of incentive schemes. In the case of linear schemes it can be shown (Freixas et al. 1985) that the ratchet effect pushes toward high-powered schemes which create higher rents in the first period to induce the revelation of types. More generally, the less commitment ability there is, the less the regulator should try to separate types and the more so if the cost of public funds is high.

The lack of ability of regulators to commit can be mitigated by the repetition of their relationship with the firms and the building of the regulators' reputation of not expropriating the rents derived from improvement of efficiency in the future (see Croker and Reynolds 1989; Gilbert and Newbery 1988; and Salant and Woroch 1988 for models of infinitely repeated contracting in which some collusive equilibria do not exhibit the trading inefficiencies associated with shorter horizons). It can be expected that this substitute to commitment of institutions will be less easy to achieve in developing countries.

No general analysis exists of how easy commitment is depending on the type of regulatory regime. Regulatory institutions must be particularly scrutinized in developing countries for their ability to provide long-run incentives through their power of commitment. For example, price-capping has been pushed in the Western world as a way to provide high-powered incentives. However, price caps can be easily renegotiated while a commitment to a fair rate of return might be less prone to costly renegotiations (Greenwald 1984).

Financial Constraints

Financial constraints compound the difficulties of asymmetric information for regulation in many circumstances. The basic intuition can be stated in simple moral hazard control problems with risk neutrality. Moral hazard in a delegated activity can be controlled without giving up a rent to the agent if penalties are possible even when the observation of the performance is noisy. However, if such penalties are not possible because of limited liability constraints, only rewards for good performance can induce appropriate effort levels, i.e., informational rents must be given up.

The greater the financial constraints the greater those rents. Both the strength of financial constraints and the high cost of public funds favor a shift toward less powerful incentive schemes in developing countries. The irony of the situation is that, even though these countries should make more effort to emerge from underdevelopment, inducing effort is much more difficult in developing countries.[13] This line of reasoning can be extended even further. Suppose that these various effort levels we have been talking about also affect learning abilities in a learning-by-doing framework. All the arguments we have given to explain the rationally lower optimal effort levels in developing countries will explain a growing disparity of efficiencies between developed and some developing countries.

Promotion of Competition

We have restricted the analysis of this paper to natural monopolies to concentrate on the difficult case where a simple appeal to full-blown competition cannot be invoked. However, we cannot avoid a discussion of competition for a number of reasons. First, because of the informational rents it may be optimal to duplicate fixed costs and induce a duopoly structure, in view of the informational gains derived from the yardstick competition then made possible (Auriol and Laffont 1993). Second, the scope and nature of regulation may be more or less pro-competitive, for example the type of access-pricing rules, the constraint put on the monopoly in markets where it faces some competition, the constraints on bypass activities of the monopoly's network. Third, ex ante competition can be created by auctioning the right to be a regulated monopoly. Note here the word regulated. In the design of the auction appropriate regulation must be committed to in order to avoid the distortions of monopolistic behavior. Auctions may be nevertheless quite useful to decrease the informational rents (Laffont and Tirole 1993).

However, results are rather ambiguous.[14] Yardstick competition requires the duplication of fixed costs to decrease the rents of asymmetric information. A higher cost of public funds affects both the gains from and the benefits of yardstick competition. As we saw all through this section, regulation is less efficient in developing countries. Limiting regulation to core activities of natural monopolies to provide counter powers to discretionary political and bureaucratic behaviors seems particularly welcome in developing countries. Nevertheless, it should be remembered that it also makes the multiplication of costly rents possible in countries where competition is often insufficient. Finally, let us recall the lack of proper administration, the lack of credibility, and the risks of favoritism that make the organization of successful auctions in developing countries difficult.

Conclusions about Regulation

This section has shown that very many arguments favor a move toward less-powerful incentive schemes (and therefore a move toward less efficiency) in developing countries. However, the use of performance evaluation to improve the fundamental trade off between efficiency and rent extraction presumes a perfect or at least unbiased auditing of those performances. The main argument against such advice is the cost padding effect and the corruption of the audit of costs which, on the contrary, militate in favor of fixed-price mechanisms which, in addition, save all the auditing costs.

Maybe we can then distinguish three stages of development concerning regulation. In stage one of development, which might be the current situation in the People's Republic of China, the auditing mechanisms are so bad that powerful incentive schemes should be advocated. They promote short-run efficiency in activities that are immune to ratchet effects, but they strongly favor ex post inequality[15] (since the efficient types make more money than the inefficient ones), they encourage some types of corruption of regulatory and political institutions, and they are costly for the rest of the economy because of the money drain toward the regulated monopolies they create.

This stage one should be used to develop a good auditing system. For example, it seems to be a national priority in the People's Republic of China to improve the accounting system and to create a national body of reliable and efficient accountants. Once this auditing system is in place, one can move rather discontinuously to stage two of development by moving toward less powerful incentive schemes for the reasons explained above. Then, as development continues, it will be optimal to slowly move toward more powerful incentive schemes in stage three. The quality of regulation in each of these stages depends critically on the ability of the governments to commit credibly to the implementation of the schemes.

Privatization

Conventional Arguments
We will be concerned here only with the privatization of natural monopolies, i.e., of firms which, once privatized, will still have to be regulated. We review the conventional wisdom about the pros and cons of privatization[16] and then explain why the arguments put forward seem so undecisive in the framework of complete contracting theory. First, we discuss the costs of public ownership:

Absence of Capital Market Monitoring
The argument here is that the managers of a public enterprise may mismanage its assets because they do not have appropriate incentives. They invest too little because they are not given the stocks and stock options that would encourage them to take a long-term perspective. Stock market prices contain information about the firm's future prospects and thus about the managers' long-term decisions. In addition, a public enterprise is not subject to takeovers, and its managers are therefore less concerned about losing their jobs.

First, the government may, and sometimes does, retire only a fraction of the firm's stocks when nationalizing. Further arguments, for example the low volume of trade in the stock market or regulatory and political uncertainties, are needed to explain why the stock price in a mixed firm would be less informative about managerial performance than that of the same private firm (Holmstrom and Tirole 1993). Second, economists have never demonstrated that the stock market is the only instrument, or even the most efficient instrument, to obtain outside information about a firm's health. Why can't the government mimic the stock market's incentives? The absence of financial takeovers argument is clearer but not conclusive either. Managers of public enterprises are fired and political takeovers occur.

Soft Budget Constraint

A public enterprise is not subject to the discipline of the bankruptcy process because the government always bails it out in case of difficulties. This reduces managerial incentives.

Public enterprises can be shut down. One expects this would occur less frequently than if the firm were private, but one needs an explanation of this phenomenon. Why can't the government mimic the market? Furthermore regulators (and governments) do bail out private regulated firms in difficulty, by raising allowed prices or even by direct subsidies.

Expropriation of Investments

Managers of public enterprises refrain from investing because, once investments are sunk, the government may use these investments for purposes they were not intended to serve. Hence managerial investments may be expropriated.

One has to explain why appropriate contracts to protect those investments cannot be written and why the shareholders of a private firm would not expropriate managerial investments in a similar situation?

Lack of Precise Objectives

The multiplicity, fuzziness, and changing character of government's objectives exacerbate the problem of managerial control in public enterprises.

This argument also fails to distinguish between ownership structures, since government's goals will also affect the behavior of private regulated firms.

Lobbying — Government Interference

Governments are subject to the pressure of interest groups to direct the behavior of public enterprises and enhance the welfare of these groups (Shleifer and Vishny 1994). Again, this argument works against private regulated firms as well and one has to explain why the constitutional rules allow this type of interferences.

On the positive side of public ownership we can list:

Social Objectives

In economies with many market inefficiencies (environmental problems, public goods, incomplete markets), public ownership is an additional instrument to achieve social goals that include, but are not confined to, profit maximization.

This argument is persuasive if governments want to maximize social welfare, but it does not explain why the government cannot achieve the same goals in a regulatory framework.

Centralized Control

By letting the government be responsible for both internal and external control, nationalization prevents conflicts of objectives between the firm's regulators and owners.

This argument suggests a potential inefficiency associated with the multimasters feature of private regulated firms, but remains vague about the nature of the inefficiency, given that centralized control has its own costs.

Incomplete Contracting: A Needed Framework

The difficulty of the discussion is actually quite complex from a theoretical point of view. In a world of complete contracting with a benevolent constitution, ownership does not matter (Williamson 1985; Grossman and Hart 1986; Sappington and Stiglitz 1987). Anything privatization achieves can be mimicked by an appropriate contract.[17]

In the following discussion we will maintain the assumption that, when the constitution is drawn, maximization of social welfare is the objective.

The analysis can then proceed from the point of view of incomplete contracting. The main consequence of this incompleteness is that the private objectives of decision makers will affect the outcomes, because they cannot be perfectly controlled by appropriate contracts and depend on the nature of existing institutions.

Contracts require a benevolent judicial system, which may not be available. Contracts can be incomplete in many dimensions and many states of nature are not even forecastable at reasonable cost. Flexibility requires leaving some discretion in decision making. Big mistakes can be punished ex post, but many other decisions will remain discretionary at no cost.

This phenomenon explains why a constitution cannot perfectly control politicians and why the issues of politicians' private agendas and of the qualities of the democratic process are so essential for our analysis. This lack of controllability itself induces further contractual limitations, such as the limits put on decision makers to commit for the future. If we could control politicians we could let them commit for the future. Without such control, it may be better (to avoid great mistakes) to limit their power in the short run as well as the long run.

These contractual difficulties spur another round of problems in organizations since they affect coalitional behavior. The ability to capture, to form successful coalitions, is itself affected by internal contractual limitations (lack of a benevolent third party to arbitrate conflicts and costs of contracting), but is also affected by the way incomplete contractness is dealt with at higher levels. For example, coalitional behavior is affected by the structure of the organization (see Laffont and Martimort 1994).

The eventual lack of a benevolent third party to enforce contracts (which is related to the problems of incentives of the judicial system) and the complexity of the possible futures, can explain other forms of contractual incompleteness, such as: limits in ability to commit credibly to the future through the need for flexibility and for correcting past mistakes, limits associated with the nonverifiability paradigm that many authors transform into noncontractability (fundamentally due to the two above phenomena), limits in ability to prevent profitable renegotiation, and limits in the coalitional opportunities within the organization.

Our inability, for now and for a long time to come, to model how human beings deal with the complexity of the future will make any incomplete contracting modeling somewhat ad hoc. On the other hand, only such an approach can shed some light on the privatization issue.

The theoretical literature has proceeded by combining various contractual limitations and studying their impact on privatization. We will review here these arguments from the point of view of developing countries. An interesting research program would be to try to understand how the specificities of developing countries that we considered above are related to these fundamental contractual difficulties. In the next section we will continue to take the specificities as given.

Some Tradeoffs

The Shapiro-Willig Model

Two contractual hypotheses underlie the Shapiro and Willig (1990) argument. First, it is assumed that governments have noncontrollable private agendas. This can be traced to the simplicity of the constitutional-judicial rules which make this control quite imperfect. The political evolution of countries tends to improve this control over time as more complex institutions are set up and citizens become more informed. Therefore, we can expect that politicians will have a greater ability to pursue their private agendas in developing countries.

The second building block is that privatization is a commitment not to learn all the private information of the firm. This argument is far from being clear if we restrict our analysis to natural monopolies. Why would a regulatory agency of a private monopoly have less information than the ministry controlling a public firm?

The question can be rephrased as, Does ownership provide information which cannot be obtained from outside? Due to the complexity of information it is likely that ownership and management create an informational advantage (Riordan 1987, 1990; Sappington 1986).[18] But such an informational advantage will also appear for the manager of the public firm. Why then is the incentive problem between the government and the public firm's manager different from the incentive problem between the regulatory agency and the private firm's managers and owners? The manager of the private firm is selected by the owners, whose interest is to hide information. The manager of the public firm is hired by the government who wants the information. So the argument seems to hold unless the managers of the public firms have enough power to resist political pressures and, for example, collude with the workers to protect the firm's informational rent.

Clearly this argument is quite sensitive to the quality and horizon of the bureaucracy in charge of public firms. A good bureaucracy may be more informed than a regulatory agency, but it will develop its own agenda, which may be closer or further away from the social objectives than the politicians' own agenda.

What matters here is the ability of the institutions to commit to have less control over the private firm than over the public firm. If we accept that public firms are more controllable, then an argument in favor of privatization may appear. Less control means some inefficiencies and in particular higher informational rents for the firm, but it also limits the ability of the government to pursue its private agenda. Privatization is a costly instrument for preventing political interference.

Clearly, in a developing country, the cost is higher but the gain may be higher also. The answer depends crucially on the quality of the democratic institutions. The worse they are the higher the gains from privatization will be from this particular point of view.

The Schmidt Model

Schmidt (1990) also takes as given the fact that privatization is a commitment not to learn some information about the firm and therefore it is a credible commitment to give an informational rent to the firm. The other building block is that managers can realize or not noncontractable investments in the firm, which increase the efficiency and the potential rent of asymmetric information. Under public ownership, the government is informed and expropriates the rent. Therefore managers have no incentive to realize those noncontractable investments.

For a small cost of public funds, the argument in favor of privatization here is strong, but it decreases as this cost increases since appropriate incentives for those noncontractable investments are bought at the price of a costly, inefficient regulation including costly rents. On the other hand, as we saw above, managers of public firms in a developing country may be able to capture a rent (due to an inefficient public auditing system) as well and be provided with better incentives for investment this way.

If under privatization the manager of the firm does not hold the shares, the previous reasoning breaks down. The manager is expropriated by the private owners under privatization as he is under nationalization. Schmidt then introduces a more subtle argument with a nonappropriable private benefit for the manager that increases with the level of output. Then, public ownership eliminates the ex post output distortion due to asymmetric information (since the government is fully informed), but it reduces the sensitivity of output to the efficiency parameter and, through the private benefit, reduces the manager's incentive to invest. Nationalization reduces allocative inefficiency but decreases managerial investment.

Summing up, the costs of privatization seem higher in developing countries for two main reasons, a high level of cost of public funds and therefore a high cost of foregone rents because less information means higher rents, and a bad auditing system, which favors high rents. On the other hand, the imperfections of public management confer some of the same features as private firms on nationalized firms (the government remains uninformed and rents are captured by employees, bureaucrats, etc.).

The Laffont-Tirole Model

The cost of privatization here (Laffont and Tirole 1991b) is due to the multiprincipal structure obtained, since both the regulator of this private monopoly and the owners of the firm attempt to control the managers who have private information about the firm's efficiency. The result of this dual control is that each principal fails to internalize the effects of contracting on the other principal and provides socially too few incentives for the firm's insiders.[19]

The impact of these lower incentives on the efficiency of the regulated private firm will be lower in developing countries in stage 1 of the previous section (due to bad auditing) and higher in stage 2 (due to a high social cost of funds).

Here also managers can realize noncontractable investments which yield noncontractable private benefits. The government cannot commit not to expropriate managers' investments in order to maximize ex post public use of investment. Government often has ex post incentives to reallocate the benefits of the investments to other parties (if the firm has become more efficient, it can force the firm to keep more employees than needed). Given the greater congruence of objectives between managers and stockholders, this reallocation of benefits to outsiders seems less likely in a privatized firm, at least if privatization has a strong content of noninterference in the internal management of the firm.

Here, the argument against privatization is less strong than in the Schmidt model because the inefficiency generated is not accompanied by higher rents. On the other hand, it is certainly less robust to political economy considerations. We know that to decrease the cost of capture, governments will often be structured with several regulators of the same firm (the Ministry of the Industry and the Ministry of Finance). So the multiprincipal feature is also present in the public ownership case, reducing the cost of privatization of this model.

The basic question turns around the ability of the government to commit to leave some of the gains of their investments to managers. If the government has the ability to commit not to learn information about the firm (as in the Schmidt and Shapiro-Willig models), this provides an incentive for those investments but at a high cost in terms of foregone rents and inefficient regulation, particularly so in a developing country.

But then one can then ask the following question: If the government has the ability to commit not to learn information, why does it have the ability to sign contracts with the managers of the public firms which leave them the rents needed for investment without the associated inefficiencies (as the French "Contrats de Plan" try to do)?

The reason must be looked for in the ratchet phenomenon or in the "whipping the fast cows" phenomenon, as the Chinese put it. Unless extremely powerful contractual institutions can be set up, it is clear that the only way for a principal to commit not to expropriate the regulated agents from their efficiency gains is not to learn anything about their efficiency.

We cannot expect those institutions to exist in developing countries. We come then to the conclusion that privatization would be the only way available to induce incentives for these types of investments, with the further condition that renationalization should not be feared by the economic agents. However, it should be remembered that it is a particularly highly costly way to achieve this goal in developing countries because of the high cost of rents, and that the alleged fact that privatization is a credible way to commit not to learn information is controversial.

Political Economy Issues

Let us now return to political economy issues already present in the Shapiro-Willig model. Let us assume that, through voting, politicians represent majorities which have particular interests. For example, and somewhat caricaturally, if we have a rightist majority which owns the stocks of the regulated firms, we can expect the government to internalize the rents captured by these firms in its objectives. On the other hand, if it is a leftist majority, which has no stake in the rents of the regulated firms, it will settle for a different trade off between efficiency and rents in the regulation of these firms, actually for less rents and less efficiency.

In the case of public firms, we can argue that by definition they belong to the majority in power and that regulation will be the same whatever the majority, since the firm's rent will always be taken into account (in this case excessively).[20] Therefore, changes of majorities will affect the incentives of regulated firms.

If we take now an ex ante maximin point of view, public ownership has the advantage of enabling the "poor" when it has the majority to capture the rent of the public firm. On the other hand, when it is the minority, it can expect the majority to set up high-powered incentive schemes which lead to high rents and the poor may have to participate in funding these rents through the general budget. The constitutional choice of privatization or nationalization is then centered around these two effects.[21] A high cost of public funds favors privatization. Clearly, to make further progress a deeper political science analysis is needed here.

Financial Constraints

Finally, the absence of good financial markets in developing countries also has an enormous impact on what can be expected from privatization.

First, since we are concerned with private regulated monopolies, it is clear that the information derived from the valuation of stocks will depend more on the expectations about regulation than on the quality of management. It will therefore provide little help to structure the control of the managers, whose incentives to affect regulation will be much higher than the incentives to run their firms efficiently. Furthermore, the quality of the stock market valuations to monitor the management will be poor because of the lack of competitiveness of this market.

Second, privatization will be more difficult since the individuals and groups with the best management abilities may not be able to participate easily in the privatization process because of their budget constraints. One way to alleviate those difficulties is to structure the bidding process in a way which enables bidders to pay in the future. However, such mechanisms may be difficult to implement because limited liability limits ex post the possible penalties which would induce proper behavior (Bolton and Roland 1992; Aghion and Burgess 1992; Maskin 1992). The ex post moral hazard problems created by these mechanisms of deferred payments associated with first-price or second-price auctions have been noted in the literature,[22] but the attraction of all-pay auctions to mitigate this problem has not been studied.

To open the privatization process to foreign firms, which have both the financial capabilities and the information needed to provide good management, is tempting. However, given the fact that these firms will remain regulated, the ability of the government to commit to a stable regulatory framework will again be crucial for a successful privatization program. Also one has to worry about the problem of favoritism in the organization of these auctions. Clearly, for such complex auctions one would ideally like to use any additional available information about the bidders to choose the winner and not only the sizes of the bids. However, this opens the possibility of favoritism by the organizer of the auction (see Laffont and Tirole 1991a for an analysis of favoritism in auctions). This problem can be expected to be even more serious in developing countries, and decreases the benefits of the privatization program.

Privatization and Governments' Budget Constraints

Governments' budget problems are often given as a motivation for privatization. This would suggest a strong case for privatization in developing countries, but it would be misleading. Indeed, if the government could commit to high-powered incentive schemes ensuring efficiency and then auction the firm in competitive bidding, the government could raise a lot of money while at the same time obtaining efficient production of the monopoly (Demsetz 1968). Many reasons militate against a smooth functioning of this scheme. Financial constraints of potential bidders, lack of competition, but more importantly political and economic uncertainties and the likely inability to commit not to change the regulation ex post, will make privatization a very ineffective tool for raising public funds in developing countries. From the pure point of view of raising funds, it seems fairly clear that privatization of natural monopolies should be delayed until a credible regulatory environment is built. This point is reinforced by the fact that public firms in developing countries are often the most efficient tools for raising tax revenues. Too hasty a privatization will produce little revenue and quickly precipitate a sharp increase in the government deficit.[23]

Conclusions about Privatization

For a number of reasons discussed in this section, the success of the privatization of natural monopolies in developing countries seems to rest crucially on the ability to establish a credible and stable set of regulatory rules which avoid future political interference (and interference by other interest groups) and therefore provide new incentive structures. Privatization alone is clearly not enough to achieve this goal.[24]

On the other hand, we saw above that it is desirable to alter the regulatory rules as the setting up of a good auditing system proceeds. It is therefore very important to be able to commit to a well-defined timing of regulatory reforms. The following scheme could then be suggested:

In the beginning, a commitment to a price-cap type of regulation for four to six years is made, with the collaboration of international institutions to resist the capture problems which exist in the definition of these price caps.[25] At the same time, and hopefully helped by the funding of these international institutions, a large program for building a good accounting system and a reliable set of public accountants is set up which will take over the regulation of these firms in four to six years. Meanwhile, restructuring measures concerning incentives within the firm, vertical disintegration, managerial and technological transfers, and infrastructures should be implemented to bring the public firms close to profit maximizing behavior.

Once these commitments have been made credible, and only then, the question of privatization should be addressed.[26] The major consideration to be taken into account in privatization decisions is the quality of the political and bureaucratic institutions. Public management may still be preferred in a country with bad financial institutions and good political institutions.

We have attempted to see what recent economic theory suggests for the design of regulatory rules and privatization programs for national monopolies in developing countries. The discussion of privatization programs for natural monopolies cannot be disconnected from the discussion of their current and future regulation. Successful privatization of these industries seems much harder than the privatization of competitive industries. Efforts should be devoted first to the setting up of good regulatory institutions, before envisioning privatization.

A very obvious conclusion is that it is unfortunately going to be more costly and less efficient to carry out these programs in developing countries. We have suggested that the help of international institutions should be particularly fruitful at this stage of development. However, only if these institutions develop a nonpolitical and specific vision of what programs would best fit developing countries will the required acceptance by those countries of what could look as interference in internal affairs be obtained.

Acknowledgment

The author is grateful to Philippe Aghion, Beatriz Armendariz, Fan Gang, T. Hoschka, Morimitsu Inaba, Jean Tirole, and the participants to the Third ADB Conference on Development Economics for their comments.

Notes

1. Of course what is a natural monopoly is an empirical question and may vary over time. This is particularly true in telecommunications.

2. See however the 1994 World Bank Development report.

3. See Browning 1976, 1987; Rosen 1978; Ballard, Shoven and Whalley 1975, for various approaches to estimate the cost of public funds generated by distortive taxes.

4. Another reason for this high cost is the lack of access to national and international borrowing due itself to the lack of credibility of the institutions in developing countries and to their wealth constraints.

5. This point is debatable. Some nondemocratic governments have sometimes been able to develop a reputation for stability and commitment, at least for the medium run if not for the very long run. See Barro (1994).

6. See Stiglitz (1993) for a discussion of market failures in financial markets.

7. Therefore we assume that monetary transfers are possible between the regulator and the firm. This is by no means essential but it enables us to separate more clearly the incentive issues and the pricing issues. We will come back to this assumption in the next section.

8. The analysis is presented here with risk neutrality. Risk aversion calls also for less powerful incentive schemes (Laffont and Rochet 1994).

9. Actually, in the most general theory, distortions of pricing from Ramsey pricing occur also in an attempt to decrease the informational rent of the firm. Appropriate separability assumptions of the cost function eliminate this distortion. The principles stated in the text constitute a useful benchmark (see Laffont andTirole 1993).

10. See corollary 1 in Laffont and Martimort (1994).

11. See Laffont (1994b) for an analysis of the implications of corruption in tax auditing for the decentralized tax system of the People's Republic of China.

12. Since high powered incentives favor investments which decrease costs.

13. This neglects income effects which might run in the opposite direction.

14. This is not denying the fact that, if potentially competitive segments can be isolated in the natural monopoly's activity, they should be open to competition.

15. However, for an ex ante maximin criterion they are good because they maximize welfare in the bad state.

16. We are only marginaly involved in the analysis of the process of privatization itself. In particular attention should be devoted to the incentives of the stakeholders in the public firm to participate in the privatization process. See Vickers and Yarrow (1988), Aghion and Burgess (1992).

17. Note that the argument is valid even for economies where information is decentralized and moral hazard, adverse selection, and nonverifiability issues plague the economy. Sometimes the optimal contract can be implemented by a well-chosen attribution of property rights (see Tirole 1994).

18. See also Aghion and Tirole (1994), who show that in an incomplete contracting framework ownership is associated with discretion in decision making. Consequently, as ownership will eliminate the need for bargaining, it will create more incentives to acquire information (which is more valuable).

19. The model here can be viewed as a particular case of the multiprincipal framework (Martimort 1991; Stole 1990) where the activities of the agent for the principals are either substitutes or complements. Here there are strict complements. Then, when a principal decreases the incentives for his own activity, he achieves that by decreasing the level of the activity. It is then in the interest of the other principal to decrease his own activity (by complementarity). Therefore the first principal does not internalize the decreasing incentive effect that will be implemented by the other principal. As a consequence, too little incentives are provided at the Nash equilibrium of the contractual offers by the two principals.

20. Actually the way it is taken into account depends on the size of majorities.

21. We have considered here the simplistic case where majorities can appropriate the monetary rents of public firms. Constitutional controls often force the majorities to give away rents in the form of underefforts.

22. It is often presented as the equivalent problem of overleveraged firms in the post-privatization period.

23. The eventual reduction of slack due to privatization will also produce layoffs and welfare expenses (see Aghion and Blanchard 1994).

24. For example, privatization as a credible commitment to enforce bankruptcy laws and hard-budget constraints will not work until the political and social costs associated with liquidation have been reduced, and more so with essential natural monopolies.

25. If corruption of the government is hopeless, immediate privatization may be advocated but it is then doubtful that it will be successful or even implemented.

26. The case for this timing is even greater when the state sector is very large (as in the People's Republic of China today), and privatization of the competitive sectors should take place first.

References

Aghion. P., and O. Blanchard, 1994. "On the Speed of Transition in Central Europe." Nuffield. Mimeo.

Aghion, P., and R. Burgess, 1992. "Financing and Development in Eastern Europe and the Former Soviet Union." Oxford. Mimeo.

Aghion, P., and J.Tirole, 1994. "Formal and Real Authority in Organizations." Institut d'Economie Industrielle. Mimeo.

Auriol, E., and J.J. Laffont, 1993. "Regulation by Duopoly." *Journal of Economics and Management Strategy* 2:507-33.

Ballard, C., J. Shoven, and J. Whalley, 1975. "General Equilibrium Computations of the Marginal Costs of Taxes in the U.S." *American Economic Review* 195:128-38.

Baron, D., and R. Myerson, 1982. "Regulating a Monopolist with Unknown Costs." *Econometrica* 50: 911-30.

Barro, R. J., 1994. "Democracy: A Recipe for Growth?" Paper presented at the Third ADB Conference on Development Economics, 24-27 November 1994, Manila, Philippines. Mimeo.

Bolton, P., and G. Roland, 1992. "The Economics of Mass Privatization." Ecole Polytechnique No. 375. Paris.

Browning, E., 1976. "The Marginal Cost of Public Funds." *Journal of Political Economy* 84: 283-98.

———, 1987. "On the Marginal Welfare Cost of Taxation." *American Economic Review* 77: 11-23.

Croker, K., and K. Reynolds, 1989. "Efficient Contract Design in Long Term Relationships: The Case of Air Force Engine Procurement." WP 10-89-1. Pennsylvania State University.

Demsetz, H., 1968. "Why Regulate Utilities." *Journal of Law and Economics* 11: 55-65.

Dewatripont, M., and G. Roland, 1992. "Economic Reform and Dynamic Political Constraints." *Review of Economic Studies* 59: 703-30.

Freixas, X., R. Guesnerie, and J.Tirole, 1985. "Planning under Incomplete Information and the Ratchet Effect." *Review of Economic Studies* 52: 173-92.

Gilbert, R., and D. Newbery, 1988. "Regulation Games." WP 8879. University of California.

Gould, D., and J. Amaro-Reyes, 1983. "The Effects of Corruption on Administrative Performance." World Bank Staff Working Paper No. 580. Washington, D.C.

Greenwald, B., 1984. "Rate Base Selection and the Structure of Regulation." *Rand Journal of Regulation* 15:85-95.

Grossman, S., and O. Hart, 1986. "The Costs and Benefits of Ownership: a Theory of Lateral and Vertical Integration." *Journal of Political Economy* 94: 691-719.

Holmström, B., and J. Tirole, 1993. "Market Liquidity and Performance Monitoring." *Journal of Political Economy* 101:678-709.

Jones, L., P. Tandon, and I. Vogelsang, 1990. *Selling Public Enterprises : A Cost Benefit Methodology.* Cambridge: MIT Press.

Laffont, J. J., 1994a. "The New Economics of Regulation Ten Years After." *Econometrica* 62: 507-37.

———, 1994b. "Incentives in China's Decentralized Tax System." Mimeo.

———, 1995. "Industrial Policy and Politics." *International Journal of Industrial Organization.* Forthcoming.

Laffont, J. J., and D. Martimort, 1994. "Separation of Regulators against Collusive Behavior." Institut d'Economie Industrielle. Mimeo.

Laffont, J. J., and J.C. Rochet, 1994. "Regulation of a Risk Averse Firm." Institut d'Economie Industrielle. Mimeo.

Laffont, J.J., and J. Tirole, 1991a. "Auction Design and Favoritism." *International Journal of Industrial Organization* 9:9-42.

———, 1991b. "Privatization and Incentives." *Journal of Law, Economics and Organization* 7: 84-105.

———, 1992. "Cost Padding, Auditing and Collusion." *Annales d'Economie et Statistique* 25-26:205-226.

———, 1993. *A Theory of Incentives in Regulation and Procurement.* Cambridge: MIT Press.

———, 1994. "Access Pricing and Competition." *European Economic Review.* Forthcoming.

Levy, B., and P. Spiller, 1993, "Regulation, Institutions, and Commitment in Telecommunications: A Comparative Analysis of Five Country Studies." Proceedings of the World Bank Annual Conference of Development Economics, Supplement to the World Bank Economic Review and the World Bank Research Observer, 215-252.

Loeb, M., and W. Magat, 1979. "A Decentralized Method of Utility Regulation." *Journal of Law and Economics* 22:399-404.

Martimort, D., 1991. "Multi-principaux avec sélection adverse." IDEI. Mimeo.

Maskin, E., 1992. "Auctions and Privatization." Harvard University. Mimeo.

Riordan, M., 1987. "Hierarchical Control and Investment Incentives in Procurement." WP E-87-44. Hoover Institution, Stanford University.

———, 1990. "What is Vertical Integration ?" In M. Aoki et al., eds., *The Firm as a Nexus of Treaties.* London: Sage Publications.

Rosen, H., 1978. "The Measurement of Excess Burden with Explicit Utility Functions." *Journal of Political Economy* 86:121-35.

Salant, D., and G. Woroch, 1988. "Trigger Price Regulation." GTE Laboratories, Waltham. Mimeo.

Sappington, D., 1986. "Commitment to Regulatory Bureaucracy." *Information, Economics and Policy* 2:243-58.

Sappington, D., and J. Stiglitz, 1987. "Privatization, Information and Incentives." *Journal of Policy Analysis and Management* 6: 567-82.

Schmidt, K., 1990. "The Costs and Benefits of Privatization." DP A-330. University of Bonn.

Shapiro, C., and R. Willig , 1990. "Economic Rationales for the Scope of Privatization." DP 41. Princeton University.

Shleifer, A., and R. Vishny, 1994. "Politicians and Firms." Mimeo.

Stiglitz, J., 1993. "The Role of the State in Financial Markets." Proceedings of the World Bank Annual Conference on Development Economics, World Bank.

Stole, L., 1990. "Mechanism Design under Common Agency." Massachusetts Institute of Technology. Mimeo.

Tirole, J., 1991. "Privatization in Eastern Europe: Incentives and the Economics of Transition." National Bureau of Economic Research, Cambridge, Massachusetts.

————, 1994. "Incomplete Contracts: Where Do We Stand?" Institut d'Economie Industrielle. Mimeo.

Vickers, J., and G.Yarrow, 1988. "Economic Perspectives on Privatization." Oxford University. Mimeo.

Williamson, O., 1985. *The Economic Institutions of Capitalism.* New York: The Free Press.

Chapter 7

Trade Liberalization
and Economic Development

Rodney E. Falvey

The last two decades have seen a major shift in emphasis for the trade policies of many developing countries, away from the inward-oriented, import-substitution (IS) policies that most had pursued since independence, toward more outward-oriented policies, often referred to as "export-promotion" (EP) policies, aimed at improving growth performance, raising export earnings, and improving the efficiency of domestic industries by increasing their exposure to international competition. A considerable theoretical and empirical literature now exists comparing the relative merits of IS and EP as growth strategies and explaining why this shift in emphasis has occurred.

The adoption of IS strategies by the newly independent developing countries in the 1950s and 1960s broadly reflected the conventional wisdom in development economics at the time. Development (in the sense of sustained increases in real per capita income) required industrialization—a shift of resources out of low productivity agriculture into higher productivity manufacturing. This had been the pattern of changes in the shares of various activities in gross domestic product (GDP) in the developed economies as their real income per capita increased in the past. The policy question was how best to promote this structural transformation in the then primarily agricultural and raw material-producing and exporting developing world. New industries were required, but these industries could be primarily targeted at domestic or at international markets. Since imports of manufactures were evidence of domestic demand, IS policies could simply replace these imports with domestic output, reducing developing countries' reliance on primary exports (whose prices were both variable and believed to be in long-term decline relative to manufactures) and achieving industrialization in the process. This approach was also consistent with the prevailing "structuralist" view that developing economies lacked flexibility, being inhibited by obstacles, bottlenecks, and constraints (Little 1982).

The limitations of a growth strategy based on industrial expansion aimed at domestic markets became obvious in the 1960s and 1970s. After some initial success, those countries that followed the IS approach grew more slowly than those with a more outward orientation. Rather than reducing the economy's dependence on trade, the anti-export bias of IS policy reduced the growth rate of exports. Further, the substitution of domestic production for marginal imports left the economy vulnerable to trade fluctuations for essential imports. Highly protected, uncompetitive IS industries could not reorient into producing exports. It was also recognized that the developing countries were not as constrained by structural rigidities as had been supposed. The IS trade strategy is now largely viewed as a failure. These observations, combined with the sustained growth performance of the East Asian newly industrializing economies (NIEs), has seen the adoption of EP as the preferred trade strategy for development. It is recognized that, as practiced, the EP strategy really assists both import-competing and exporting industries, in that it provides equal incentives to value added in all manufacturing industries, whether output is sold in domestic or foreign markets. The East Asian NIEs rely on international markets and have relatively few distortions, but the philosophies and policies of most governments are far from noninterventionist.

This experience has generated a substantial theoretical and empirical literature that investigates the links between trade policy, or "openness", and "growth". The primary focus of trade theory in investigating the "gains from trade" has been on the *level* of income rather than its *growth*. This is largely because, until recently, economic theory had relatively little to say about any links between trade policy and growth (in contrast to the extensive literature on the effects of growth on trade). While it is useful in theory to draw a distinction between the effects of trade policy on income through the improved allocation of existing resources (the "reallocation" effect) and its effects on the long-term rate of growth of income through changes in resource accumulation and technical progress (the "growth" effect), it is very difficult to separate these two effects in the data. Both effects take time, overlap, and can be confounded with the effects of other shocks. Because of this, and the problem of data availability, the empirical literature on openness and growth typically considers five to 10-year averages of annual growth rates, hoping thereby to exclude cyclical components. It is recognized, however, that some cyclical components may remain, and that these averages are not the steady state growth paths that the theory is based on.

The existence of beneficial resource allocation effects from general trade liberalization is widely accepted, and most of the liberalization debate has concentrated on exceptions. This despite the fact that, under the standard assumptions (constant returns to scale in production and perfect competition in all markets in particular), the estimated benefits to be obtained through trade liberalization were very, one might even say implausibly, small. In the past this has left proponents of trade liberalization falling back on unspecified "dynamic gains". Recent developments in theory have expanded the range of potential resource reallocation gains from trade liberalization and offered the prospect of investigating the dynamic implications of trade reform.

The trade policy implications of recent research on endogenous growth theory are potentially of major importance. Though still in its formative stages, this work has already generated a number of interesting explanations of the growth process. The prevalence of externalities in these explanations signals an important role for policy (even if it is just "staying out of the way"). A country's international links determine the extent to which it participates in the international transfer of technology, and knowledge more generally, which is recognized as an essential ingredient in the growth process. Even if policy changes can only generate small changes in the growth rate, these small differences can have a significant impact on living standards in the long run.

Two further points should be noted before we proceed. First, there is no space here for an extended discussion of what is meant by "economic development" and how it should be measured. This chapter concentrates on changes in real income per capita as a measure of the effects of trade liberalization on development, recognizing that this captures only an essential component and is not a comprehensive measure. The effects of trade liberalization on domestic income distribution, for example, will also be relevant. Second, most countries face the issue of trade reform at some point in their development. For a variety of reasons, governments in poor countries are relatively dependent on trade taxes as a revenue source (Burgess and Stern 1993). The causes of this dependence tend to diminish as development proceeds and alternative, broaderbased taxes become more attractive. There is also an unresolved debate in the literature over whether passage through some period of IS is a necessary prerequisite to the implementation of a successful EP strategy (although IS is never a viable strategy for very small economies). Thus questions of when and how to liberalize, and which trade measures, if any, should remain will emerge on each developing country's policy agenda at some point in time.

Empirical Evidence on Openness and Growth

The empirical literature on openness and growth has been quite comprehensively reviewed in a recent paper by Edwards (1993) (but see also Thomas et al. 1991, and Greenaway and Sapsford 1994). It remains to briefly examine some further evidence, and to summarize the important findings. The evidence for the relationship between openness and growth reported in Edwards comes from two sources: intensive multi-country studies and cross-section econometric studies. Two major collections of multicountry studies are available: the National Bureau of Economic Research (NBER) studies (of 10 countries) summarized in Bhagwati (1978) and Krueger (1978), and the World Bank study (of 19 countries) summarized in Michaely et al. (1991). Individual country studies have the advantage that country-specific factors can be held constant as an economy is tracked through a variety of different trade regimes. Inferences can then be drawn on the importance of trade regime for growth and other performance indicators for this country. Such studies are costly to undertake, however, and only a limited number are available. To draw general inferences, some method for comparing individual country experiences is needed, and this requires the construction of an index of a country's trade orientation.

Countries trade many goods and services and, in general, trade in some goods is restricted while trade in other goods may be encouraged. To characterize a country's trade regime then requires aggregating these trade interventions (or their outcomes) into some meaningful index of "trade orientation". No matter how this aggregation is done, it is likely that countries with quite different distributions and types of interventions will end up with the same index value. This aggregation is particularly difficult in developing countries because quantitative restrictions have traditionally constituted their most significant interventions (see Anderson and Neary 1994 for a measure designed to encompass all forms of restriction). The use of the terms "import substitution" and "export promotion" to contrast different strategies of openness is also unfortunate, given that both appear to involve movements away from free trade (albeit in different directions). One might define a "neutral" regime as one for which the incentives for IS and EP balance. A free trade regime then ensures neutrality by having no incentives in either direction. But there is a difference between eliminating an IS bias and neutralizing it with export incentives. In practice, it is a move toward (away from) a neutral position that is treated as the adoption of an EP (IS) strategy. Such an approach works because there are very few instances of policy regimes that have both high levels of protection for import-competing activities and large incentives for export promotion.

The NBER studies used the ratio of the effective exchange rate (EER) paid to importers to that paid to exporters, where the EER measure attempts to capture the price effects of all taxes, subsidies, and quantitative restrictions, as a general index of trade orientation. The NBER authors also allocated trade regimes into five categories—from most restrictive (category I) to fully liberalized (category V)—in an effort to ease comparability. In the World Bank study, each author was explicitly requested to construct an index of trade liberalization for their country, from most restrictive (1) to fully liberalized (20). Again this index defines trade liberalization as any change that moves the trade regime toward neutrality. The resulting indices are clearly subjective (with the consequent risk that they may simply reflect the ex post policy views of the authors) and, while useful for tracking intracountry changes in trade policy, are of limited value for making intercountry comparisons (Greenaway 1993).

Cross-section econometric studies are an attempt to draw inferences using standard aggregate data from larger samples of countries. Summarizing the results of this body of work is difficult, since different authors use different models, sets of explanatory variables, panels of countries, and data periods. There are also difficulties in interpreting the results, as noted below. Of all the hypotheses tested, those of most relevance here are whether the export sector generates a positive externality for production in the remainder of the economy, and, more generally, whether the data indicate that there is any relationship between a country's trade orientation and its rate of growth.

Feder (1982) used a simple two-sector model to simultaneously test two hypotheses: first, the export externality noted above, and, second, whether there is also evidence of a (uniform) productivity differential for all factors in favor of the export sector. Feder derived the resulting gross national product (GNP) growth equation and estimated it for a cross-section of countries, including investment, labor force growth, and export growth as explanatory variables. The evidence supported both hypotheses. A voluminous literature has since evolved, aimed at amplifying and clarifying these results (testing, for example, whether the relationship between exports and growth changed after the first oil shock). Clearly many issues need investigation. One would like to know the source of this externality, and whether it diminishes as exports grow or development proceeds. One is also concerned about causality, given that both exports and growth are endogenous.

The Two-Gap model, for example, suggests that the externality that exports may be generating is really associated with the relaxation of a binding foreign exchange constraint. Increased exports allow increased

imports of essential intermediate and capital goods, thereby relieving domestic production bottlenecks, and it is these imports that are generating
the apparent externality. As Esfahani (1991) observes, it may be important to distinguish this bottleneck-clearing externality from any other potential externalities associated with outward-oriented policies, because
while the latter may only be achieved through EP, the former can result
from foreign assistance or borrowing. If imports are rationed, it is appropriate to include an import shortage term in the Feder equation. Since
exports and imports are highly correlated, omitting this term may bias
upward the coefficient on export growth. Esfahani estimates an import
shortage index from the residuals of a regression of the import-to-GDP
ratio on log terms in GDP per capita, labor force, and land area. When
this import shortage term is added to the Feder regression, it has a positive coefficient, and the coefficient on export growth loses its statistical
significance. Esfahani concludes that once the import supply effect is
taken into account, no significant further externality effect remains. That
is, the externality generated by exports comes through their important
role in relieving import shortages. These results hold even when the si-
multaneity problem is dealt with by estimating a system of equations.

Once one starts considering the policy implications of any export
externality, one moves to the more general hypothesis noted above. Is
there a relationship between trade orientation and growth? The early
cross-section evidence (for example Balassa 1982) simply correlated export growth or the export share with output growth and found a positive
result. But to use this to draw conclusions concerning, say trade liberalization and growth, one must assume that liberalization leads to faster
growth in exports. The difficulty in using a characteristic such as an ex-
port-to-GDP ratio as a measure of a country's policy orientation, is that
such characteristics may differ across countries for reasons that are unrelated to any policy stance. One response to this difficulty has been to
measure openness using the deviations of the actual values of some
trade-related variable from the predicted values of this variable based on
a country's characteristics other than its (trade) policy stance. For example, Balassa (1985) constructs such an index using differences between
actual export volumes and those predicted by regressing exports on income per capita, population, and mineral resource availability. When GNP
growth is regressed on this index, it has a significant positive coefficient.
Recall that the same type of index for imports has been interpreted by
Esfahani as measuring any "import shortage". Both measures are related
to openness but have different interpretations.

Of course it would be desirable to test policy variables directly.
Attempting to do this returns us to the problem of constructing meaning-

ful policy indices. Several approaches have been tried, of which the NBER (EER and five categories) and World Bank (subjective index) indices were noted above. Krueger (1978) uses the NBER index and finds some evidence that more liberal trade regimes result in higher rates of growth of exports, and that higher exports (relative to the average over a period) have a positive effect on GNP growth. Heitger (1987) interprets a country's level (average effective rate of protection [ERP]) and structure (standard deviation of ERPs across commodities) of tariff protection as indicating its willingness to engage in international trade. When these variables are added to an extended Feder-type growth equation, they have negative, statistically significant coefficients. If instead the export share, adjusted for country size (by regressing log share on log GDP and taking the residuals), is included, it is not significant. But Heitger notes that this could be explained by the high correlation between the residual export share and capital accumulation.

While these results are interesting, the use of an index based on tariffs alone provides only a partial answer to our problem, since tariff policy is only a partial indicator of outward orientation, or openness. Indeed, one difficulty in assessing the specific impact of trade liberalization on growth is that successful trade reforms are usually accompanied by other policy reforms in both the micro and macro economies (including encouragement of foreign investment). Trade liberalizations in the absence of these complimentary reforms have a lower probability of success.

Other authors have attempted to construct more comprehensive measures of trade orientation. Dollar (1992) constructs an index from data on the real exchange rate (the relative price of traded goods in terms of nontraded goods). He argues that outward orientation is really a combination of two factors—a level of the real exchange rate that provides incentives to exporters, and policies that maintain stability in the real exchange rate so that incentives are consistent over time. He then uses ICP data on relative price levels (RPLs) to construct a cross-country index of the real exchange rate distortion. These RPLs differ across countries due to trade barriers and differences in the prices of nontraded goods. To correct for the latter, Dollar regresses the RPL on real per capita GDP and population density (plus interactive terms and some dummy variables), uses the estimated relationship to predict the RPL, and then takes the ratio of the actual RPL to the predicted RPL as index of distortion. The mean of this index is the level of distortion, the variation around this mean is the variability in the distortion. When per capita GDP growth is regressed on capital accumulation and these level and variability measures, growth is positively related to the former and negatively related to both of the latter.

Easterly (1993) uses the ICP data in a similar fashion, but at a more disaggregated level, to test the effects of price distortions on growth. In this case, an index of price distortions is constructed from the variance in the prices of individual commodities (relative to their price in the United States). Again the prices are first adjusted by regression on per capita income. Since Easterly's focus is on the effects of price distortions on growth through distortions in the composition of the aggregate capital stock, he computes separate indices for consumer goods and for intermediate and investment goods (where the latter includes human capital inputs such as health and education). In the estimated growth equation, the distortions in consumer goods prices are not significant, whereas the distortions in input prices are negative and significant. Lee (1993) also models and tests for the effects of trade interventions on growth through their impact on the use of foreign inputs in domestic production. The results indicate that trade interventions reduce both the growth rate and the investment rate. This evidence also appears to confirm the hypothesis that policies that affect the relative prices of inputs and investment goods can affect an economy's rate of growth, through reducing both the rate of capital accumulation and its efficiency. Alternatively, it might just indicate that otherwise growth-oriented economies tend not to distort these prices.

Dowrick (1994) investigates the hypothesis that openness stimulates growth. His measure of openness is trade intensity (exports plus imports divided by GDP) adjusted for country size (since small countries are "naturally" more open). This adjusted trade intensity is obtained from a double log regression of trade intensity on population (whose coefficient is significantly negative). The empirical results indicate that openness has a positive impact on growth, working partly through increasing investment rates, and that the coefficients on openness are the same when the sample is split into developed and developing countries. The strength of the correlation between openness and growth is dependent on the experience of the East Asian NIEs, however, for if they are excluded, openness has no statistically significant effect. There is a strong relationship between openness and investment for developing countries (and this is not dependent on the East Asian NIEs), but not for developed countries. Dowrick also finds that the growth of openness is strongly significant in explaining growth rates in developing countries, but is insignificant for developed countries.

A common finding in the literature is that any relationship between exports or openness and growth is likely to vary across countries depending, inter alia, on their levels of development. Many of the studies considered above exclude the sub-Saharan African countries (or "poor" countries more generally) and some of the oil exporters, because their growth patterns are typically very different and are extremely difficult to model (Dowrick 1994). Their data may also be relatively less reliable. In the context of the Feder equation, the hypothesis implied by excluding the poor countries is that a minimum level of development may be required before export growth generates any externality. Helleiner (1986) sets out to test this hypothesis. He also observes that policymakers in sub-Saharan Africa emphasize problems with export instability because of the bottleneck problems familiar from the Two-Gap model. To test this, an instability index is added to the Feder equation. The results show no significant link between export growth (here change in export share) and GDP growth for the poor countries. While the import instability index is statistically insignificant for the full sample of poor countries, it has a significantly negative effect for the sub-Saharan Africa subsample. Helleiner concludes that, for the sub-Saharan African countries, stabilizing the import volume is of greater concern than increasing the degree of outward orientation.

The considerable literature that now exists using cross-country regressions to search for empirical linkages between long-run average growth rates (and investment share of GDP) and other variables has recently been scrutinized by Levine and Renelt (1992). They note that typically only a small number of variables are included in any particular regression, but that over 50 variables have been found to be significantly correlated with growth in this way. Levine and Renelt seek to determine which results are robust enough to withstand slight alterations in the list of explanatory variables. They find that few are, in general, apart from a positive and robust correlation between average growth rates and the average share of investment in GDP. When investigating the relationship between growth and some of the openness measures discussed above (i.e., export, import, and total-trade indicators; more direct estimates of trade policy; and estimates of the distortion between domestic and international prices), three important results emerge. First, if imports or total trade are substituted for exports in cross-country growth or investment regressions, essentially the same coefficient estimates and standard errors are obtained. Because of the high correlation between imports and exports, it is unlikely that their effects in these equations can be separated. Second, the share of trade in GDP is robustly positively correlated with the share of investment in GDP. Open economies may grow faster through some link between trade and investment. This suggests that attitudes to foreign direct investment may be important. Finally, once the share of investment in GDP is controlled for, Levine and Renelt are unable to find a robust independent relationship between any trade or international price-distortion indicator and growth. They conclude that any relationship between trade and growth may be based on enhanced resource accumulation and not necessarily on the improved allocation of resources.

Since countries are composed of many productive sectors, growth rates depend on worldwide trends in the country's key sectors as well as country-specific factors that influence all sectors in the economy. Most theories of growth concentrate on steady state relationships, which imply that one is looking for long-run trends in the data, rather than cyclical variations or transitions, for empirical testing. One difficulty is that the five-year averages most researchers are constrained to rely on may contain cyclical components. If structural changes occur frequently, economies are always in transition. In fact, the data do not conform to steady state notions. Cross-period correlations of five-year growth rates yield weak, and in some cases negative, correlations. Easterly et al. (1993) emphasize the significance of this result. They note that much of the literature concentrates on country characteristics as the dominant determinants of growth. Yet country growth rates are highly unstable over time while country characteristics (including the wide range of variables considered by Barro 1991, plus other indices of policy and rates of factor accumulation) are highly persistent. Easterly et al. argue that shocks, particularly shocks to the terms of trade, are an important determinant of variations in growth rates, and that they help explain the low persistence. They also note that shocks affect policies. If shocks affecting relative prices are important, then they are unlikely to fall evenly across all sectors. This is confirmed by the low contemporaneous correlations of growth rates across sectors. But this low correlation could also reflect longer term sectoral shifts as a result of changing comparative advantage. The difficulty illustrated here is one of separating the long-term growth rate, which might be explained by the persistent factors, from short-term fluctuations in output that result from the shocks and policy reactions to them.

What should one conclude from this brief discussion of the empirical literature? The value of the information contained in individual country case studies is widely recognized. For example Levine and Renelt (1991, 24) observe that "a careful reading of these studies would make it very difficult for even a sceptical reader to conclude that trade liberalization does not hold favorable implications for growth." Edwards (1993) agrees that country studies have had important effects on policy discussions. But individual country studies also have their limitations. There are relatively few of them, and there is a natural tendency to concentrate on the more "interesting" cases. If developments in theory indicate that a new variable or relationship could be important in explaining growth, it will be difficult to test this using past studies unless they are remarkably comprehensive, and costly in terms of both time and resources to undertake a representative set of new studies.

This is where the cross-country regressions can play a useful role. Perhaps the results are sometimes "unconvincing" (Edwards 1993, 1389) or even "vacuous" (Bardhan 1995, 221), and the data may often be "very shaky" (Bardhan 1995, 221), but this data is easily available and tests based on it can perform a useful screening role. As we develop a better knowledge of the empirical relationships among variables, we get a sense of which hypotheses are likely to be important. One impediment to progressing in this direction is the ad hoc nature of many of these cross-country regressions. A variable of interest is simply added to the equation for example, or the trade volume is adjusted for country size effects in an ad hoc way. These equations only acquire economic content when we have a theoretical framework for understanding the relationships involved (Levine and Renelt 1991). Most do not represent behavioral relationships, and hence are best viewed as establishing patterns of correlations. The development of more tightly specified models will put more content into the regressions. "Models matter because they shape the point of view that we adopt, and our point of view directly influences how we process, interpret, store, and recall the large quantity of evidence that is available to us" (Romer 1994a, 36). At this stage one is inclined to agree with Levine and Renelt (1991, 28) who argue that "...we should not base our support or opposition to export promotion policies on existing cross-country growth regressions involving exports." But, conversely, is any hypothesis that has difficulty surviving a cross-country screening likely to appear a promising candidate for an expensive multicountry study?

Growth in per capita income can arise from two sources—factor accumulation and improvements in total factor productivity (TFP). Further evidence on the effects of trade policy on growth in per capita income can be obtained from studies of international differences in factor productivity. Nishimizu and Page (1991) investigate the relationship between an economy's market orientation and its growth in TFP. They emphasize that the choice of instrument of protection (tariffs versus quantitative restrictions, for example) can have an impact on the domestic industry's productivity performance. Quantitative restrictions have a tendency to insulate the domestic market by blocking the transmission of price signals which convey information on productivity changes in the rest of the world. Because they make the productivity performance of their foreign competitors less relevant to domestic firms, one should expect to see lower TFP growth in countries that rely heavily on quantitative restrictions. Similarly, market-oriented economies generally provide a more competitive environment and should therefore tend to have higher rates of TFP growth. Nishimizu and Page report evidence that export growth is positively correlated with TFP growth in the industrial sector, but only in economies that follow market-oriented policies, and, of these, only in those that do not make extensive use of quantitative restrictions. They also report a significant negative relationship between import penetration and TFP growth since 1973 for open market economies. This negative association is still present, but much weaker, for countries where industries are protected by quantitative restrictions. For non-market economies, there is no relationship. There appears to be no relationship between import penetration and TFP change before 1973. Nishimizu and Page do not investigate causality, however, so a conclusion that exports (imports) *cause* TFP growth (decline) is not warranted on this evidence.

Tybout (1992) surveys the evidence from previous international studies of TFP growth, and reports evidence from a recent World Bank research project. Using industry-specific TFP indices, this project finds that output expansion and TFP growth are positively related (Verdoorn's Law), and that it matters whether demand expands because of domestic market growth, export growth or import substitution, but that the pattern is country-specific and no general conclusions can be drawn. While earlier evidence is that larger plants are more likely to be exporters, the results of this study do not confirm the conjecture that opening an economy leads to efficiency gains through the exploitation of plant-level scale economies. If anything, it appears that increases in trade exposure tend to contract plants (in terms of employment). Other studies provide evidence of large intra-industry differences in TFP and relatively low average TFP in countries pursuing an IS strategy. But the evidence also indicates that trade liberalization gives a one-off improvement in TFP, rather than improvements in the long-run rate of growth of TFP.

Helliwell (1992) finds evidence that openness (as measured by trade intensity) has positive effects on both the level and the rate of growth of productivity in industrial countries. But recent work by Young (1993, 1994) suggests that rapid growth in per capita output in the East Asian NIEs has been due more to rapid factor accumulation than to TFP growth. Young (1993, 15) even concludes that it would be a mistake to view the East Asian NIEs as prime examples of the potential dynamic gains from outward-oriented policies. This is not to say that outward orientation is unimportant, but most of its beneficial effects are related to static gains from factor accumulation and the sectoral reallocation of resources.

Finally, note that this section has concentrated on the empirical literature dealing with openness (broadly interpreted) and growth. There is a much larger literature that investigates the general determinants of growth (see, for example, Barro 1991; Barro and Lee 1993). This literature is reviewed in Hammond and Rodriguez-Clare (1993) and in Pack (1994).

Trade Liberalization and the Level of Real Income Per Capita

The real income gains that result from the reallocation of existing resources along the lines of comparative advantage when trade is liberalized are well known. In view of this familiarity, we need only present a brief review of the issues here, concentrating on more recent developments. Under standard assumptions (constant returns to scale in production, no externalities, and perfect competition in all markets in particular), free trade is the optimal policy for a small country. Trade interventions distort domestic prices away from world prices (which represent opportunity costs for the small country), inducing domestic agents to take decisions that are private welfare-improving but social welfare-reducing. Even when these assumptions are relaxed, it is only where a country has monopoly power in international markets or there is some externality associated with trade per se, that the optimal (first-best) policies involve border interventions. Otherwise, trade interventions only appear as second-best policies, and most economists are reluctant to rely on second-best arguments to support policy initiatives when the outcome is as likely to be detrimental as beneficial.

One of the oldest and most widely-accepted arguments (at least in principle) for trade intervention is the optimum tariff argument. This argument is based on a country exploiting any ability it has to improve its terms of trade. A more recent debate over strategic trade policy has been built around arguments for strategic government intervention in oligopolistic markets. Circumstances can be specified where an appropriate intervention will induce responses in the behavior of the domestic and foreign market participants such that the profits of the domestic competitor increase by more than any costs of the intervention itself. Enthusiasm for this approach has waned considerably, however, as the severe informational requirements for successful intervention have become apparent. The present consensus is that small developing countries are likely to have very few opportunities for beneficial strategic interventions of this kind, and far too many opportunities to undertake interventions that are detrimental.

Alternative arguments for intervention could be based on the existence of externalities associated directly with trade in specific products. Such externalities might be confined within an export sector or activity. If such externalities exist, an "infant exporter" argument might be constructed, in analogy to the older "infant industry" case, and analyzed in the same way. The existence of such externalities for "new" exporters could rationalize the export subsidies offered by many developing and developed countries. Alternatively, these externalities could have the wider application proposed by Feder (1982), who argues that exporting activities provide incentives for adopting improved technologies and more efficient management techniques due to competitive pressures from abroad. The fairly inconclusive evidence on this was discussed in the preceding section. The debate concerning the use of an IS strategy purely as a prerequisite for subsequent EP, can also be phrased in these terms (Taylor 1991). But past experience with a too uncritical application of assistance to supposed "infant industries" (Bell et al. 1984) indicates considerable caution is advised before accepting these arguments.

Aside from these cases, domestic externalities call for domestic interventions, and the first-best forms of these are often production subsidies. The payment of subsidies does require a revenue source, however, and as has been noted above, developing countries are relatively dependent on trade taxes for revenue in general. This consideration leads Balassa (1982, 67) to advocate some use of tariffs as second-best interventions, arguing that "...the welfare loss caused by the distortions in consumption patterns associated with the tariff-induced changes in relative prices is difficult to gauge, and it is unlikely to outweigh budgetary considerations in most developing countries." If this second-best strategy is indeed followed by countries in the early stages of development, it will generate subsequent trade liberalizations as development proceeds and alternative, less distortionary tax bases become viable.

Taking these arguments into account, and considering the widespread use of trade restrictions in developing countries, the small magnitude of the estimated benefits from trade liberalization as calculated under the standard assumptions has been puzzling. While a permanent one percent increase in GDP is undoubtedly worth having, even its discounted value may not convince those who will bear the repercussions of the inevitable adjustment costs that trade liberalization is the policy to follow. But there is a widespread belief that these are underestimates of the true benefits available from trade liberalization, because important benefits have not been quantified.

Recent developments have extended the scope of calculations of the benefits from liberalization (or equivalently the "costs of protection") in a number of directions (see Feenstra 1992 for a discussion and estimates for the United States). First, relaxing the assumptions to allow increasing returns to scale and imperfect competition provides further dimensions in which trade reform can affect welfare. Liberalization can allow domestic consumers access to a wider range of products, and induce domestic producers to specialize in a narrower range of products thereby exploiting economies of scale. But one should recall that, although the potential gains from liberalization are increased in some cases, in others, where industries with economies of scale contract following liberalization, there is now scope for losses. Rodrik (1992a) reviews both the theoretical arguments and the empirical evidence supporting the claim that trade liberalization tends to enhance technical efficiency and concludes that there is little support for this claim from either. Second, protection encourages socially unproductive resource-use in lobbying and other rent-seeking activities. Indeed some argue that an important characteristic of commitment to a free trade regime is that it prevents the introduction of policy-induced distortions. Third, protection can change market conduct, introducing distortions in the process. Quota protection converts a single domestic producer in a small country from a price-taker to a monopolist, for example. Allowing competition through trade may be the best anti-monopoly policy available. Fourth, protection may induce inefficiencies by inducing changes in the characteristics or quality of the goods produced and traded. Finally, protection may induce "tariff-jumping" foreign investment which, by further substituting for the already suboptimal volume of imports, may further lower welfare.

One factor likely to be important is the effect of trade policy on an economy's access to new goods and to the full range of goods available on international markets. Romer (1994a) emphasizes that the standard assumption of a fixed range of goods keeps us from studying how trade policy may prevent or facilitate the introduction of new types of products and production techniques from abroad. This can be particularly important for developing countries, since products embodying the latest technical advances are initially produced in developed countries with developing countries gaining access through imports. The welfare costs of missing products are likely to be large, since the full consumer surplus is being sacrificed. In Romer's view, the surpluses generated because the producer of a new good is unable to extract the full consumer surplus it provides "...form the basis for the wage gains that we associate with development" (1994a, 30). Romer further argues that the true costs of trade restrictions in developing countries come not from their static reallocation effects on already existing activities, but from "...the stifling effect distortions have on the adoption of new technologies, the provision of new types of services, the exploitation of new productive activities, and on imports of new types of capital goods and produced inputs" (1994a, 25). Expanding estimates of the costs and benefits of trade liberalization to capture these benefits is clearly an important task for future applied research.

The debate over trade reform in developing countries has generated a considerable literature. The general case for trade liberalization in developing countries can be found in Dornbusch (1992), Michaely et al. (1991), and Thomas et al. (1991). More sceptical views, emphasizing the problems in implementation and the lack of clear empirical support, are Rodrik (1992), Greenaway and Morrissey (1993), and Greenaway (1993). The mechanics of reform—timing, sequencing, comprehensiveness, and speed—are discussed in Falvey and Kim (1992).

Trade Liberalization and Growth in Per Capita Real Income

This section is concerned with the role of trade policy in influencing the long-run per capita growth rate. The literature examining the relationship between trade and growth is extensive, and surveys and references are provided in Findlay (1984, 1995) and Bardhan (1995).

Discussion of trade and growth within the standard trade model tended to focus on the effects of growth on trade. This was perhaps not unnatural in models where the steady-state rate of growth was largely independent of trade (or any other) policy. There have been attempts to relate trade policy and factor accumulation, however (for example, Corden 1971, Baldwin 1992). Where factors such as (physical and human) capital are accumulated, their steady-state levels are determined endogenously, and trade policy can affect these levels. Trade liberalization raises real income which may lead to an increase in desired saving or education and hence capital accumulation. But trade liberalization also changes relative product prices, and hence the return(s) to capital (through the Stolper-Samuelson theorem). If trade liberalization raises capital's return, the induced capital formation will raise output by more than static estimates of the gains from trade would predict. Since capital accumulation takes time, this effect will appear as a short-term to medium-term rise in the growth rate. Whether such accumulation involves welfare gains, losses, or is welfare-neutral, depends on whether the social return to capital is above, below, or equal to its private return.

In the neoclassical growth model, growth in output per capita is explained by the accumulation of capital and by exogenous technical progress. When confronted with the data for developed economies, the significant empirical implication of this model is the importance of technical progress in explaining this growth, and the correspondingly small share of growth attributable to capital accumulation. If technical progress is treated as exogenous, the major source of growth is left unexplained. When the same exercise is performed for developing countries, the technical progress residual appears to be less important. It may even have been negligible for some of the fastest-growing East Asian NIEs (Young 1994). An important objective of recent developments in growth theory has been to make technical progress endogenous.

There are two other areas in which this recent literature attempts to extend the neoclassical model (Romer 1994b). First, with regard to explaining differences in the levels and growth rates of per capita incomes across countries, Lucas (1988) observed that, when differences in technology and international factor mobility are excluded, the standard model predicts a strong tendency to equality in income levels and growth rates (the "convergence" hypothesis). This tendency would be reinforced by any international factor mobility. Lucas concludes that technology seems to be the one factor that has the potential to account for wide differences in income levels and growth rates, and is critical of the neoclassical model for treating technological progress as an exogenous parameter. Second, expanding the scope of growth models to include imperfect market structures is particularly important once models are extended to explicitly include technological advances as the output of resource using research and development (R&D) activities. These advances are nonrival inputs into production, but are not pure public goods in that the discoverer can control access for some period of time during which monopoly rents can be obtained.

Developments in endogenous growth theory over the last decade have identified a variety of potential sources of steady-state growth (Hammond and Rodriguez-Clare 1993, Grossman and Helpman 1991b). For the purposes of this discussion, which is concerned with trade policy implications, it is useful to group these sources into three categories: physical capital accumulation, human capital accumulation, and investments in R&D.

Physical Capital Accumulation

Physical capital (including infrastructure) accumulation can be a source of long-run growth, if technology is such that capital's marginal product remains above the discount rate and investment continues to remain profitable. In the standard two-factor model this was prevented by the assumption (one of the Inada conditions) that the marginal product of capital became infinitely small as the capital-to-labor ratio became infinitely large. Growth in the capital-to-labor ratio eventually removed the incentive for investment beyond that necessary to maintain capital per worker. If, instead, there is a strictly positive lower bound on the marginal product of capital, then physical capital accumulation can lead to steady-state growth in income per capita. This may simply be a characteristic of the aggregate production function. Alternatively, it may result from some externality associated with capital accumulation that offsets any tendency to diminishing returns to capital. Investments in public intermediate inputs or infrastructure that enhance private sector productivity can generate the same outcome (Barro 1990, Findlay 1995).

The policy implications of this structure are relatively straightforward. If capital accumulation generates a positive externality, then the market solution will involve a suboptimal level of such accumulation. Policies that increase investment will therefore raise welfare and the growth rate. In a trading context, border interventions that raise the cost of capital goods and other goods complementary to investment would have a negative impact on growth in addition to the standard static distortions they introduce. A complete description of the effects of trade policy on the modernization of the capital stock may require consideration of vintage-capital growth models (Bardhan 1995), but evidence consistent with the notion that correct pricing of capital goods may indeed have a significantly positive impact on growth was presented above.

Human Capital Accumulation

Although individuals have finite lives, human capital accumulation can generate long-run growth if it results in spillovers or externalities that raise the productivity of future generations. This is the approach used by Lucas (1988), who argues that, since technology is the knowledge of particular people, to explain technical progress we need to investigate the ways in which individuals acquire knowledge, either as a result of explicit choice or as a by-product of other activities, and the implications of this for productivity. In this context, human capital can be viewed as being acquired in two ways—through formal schooling, or as a by-product of production through "learning by doing".

Schooling

Lucas (1988) adds individual human capital accumulation to the standard model by introducing an explicit schooling activity. This approach is extended in Stokey (1991), whose model is discussed here. Suppose individuals acquire human capital by investing time in schooling when they are young, and that the level of human capital they achieve depends on both the time in school and the existing "social stock of knowledge", which determines the "effectiveness" of schooling. Private investment in schooling then generates an externality by increasing the social stock of knowledge, which increases the effectiveness of time spent in schooling by later generations. Individuals have finite lives, so this externality is the only source of steady-state growth. This puts the emphasis on the quality of schooling, rather than its quantity, as a source of growth. The representative individuals of each generation have higher levels of human capital than previous generations. On the production side, there is imperfect substitution between workers of different levels of human capital. In particular, suppose high quality goods (where high quality goods have preferred attributes to low quality goods) can only be produced by highly skilled workers (who can also produce goods with lower skill requirements). As the social stock of knowledge accumulates, output growth consists of dropping lower quality goods from production and adding higher quality goods.

When extended to a trading world, a country's comparative advantage in this model is determined by its stock of labor of different skill levels. Since growth is a by-product of schooling, our interest is in how trade affects the incentives for human capital acquisition in this form. Consider the introduction of free trade between a small economy which has the same preferences and technology as the large rest of the world, but different initial stocks of knowledge. Suppose that the knowledge externality does not spill over international boundaries. The opening up of trade at relative prices different from the small country's autarky prices, presents opportunities for the standard (static) gains from trade. Since trade alters prices and wages in the small country, it also alters the returns on investments in human capital. This may strengthen or weaken the incentives for human capital accumulation. If the small country is sufficiently backward relative to the rest of the world, as seems the most likely scenario for a developing country, then free trade lowers the relative prices of goods produced by highly skilled labor and hence reduces the returns to investment in skills. The outcome is that the small country falls even further behind in terms of skill levels. The implication is that trade links with larger, more advanced countries may result in a reduction in the growth rate of a small developing economy. Whether the small country is made better or worse off depends on whether the static gains from trade are greater or smaller than the loss from slower growth.

The presence of the externality associated with schooling in this model means that competitive equilibria are inefficient (and there may be multiple equilibria). Private individuals undertake less than the socially optimal amount of schooling. In a closed economy, the obvious policy response is to encourage (by subsidization) more of this externality-

generating activity. In an open economy, the appropriate response depends on both the extent of internationalization of the externality and the
size of the country contemplating action. Consider the two extreme cases:
(i) If this externality is completely international, the effectiveness of
schooling is the same in all countries and depends on the world stock of
human capital. Small countries have no incentive to subsidize schooling
(since they have a negligible impact on this stock), and the incentive for
large countries to subsidize is attenuated by free-rider problems. Conversely, it is clearly not in the interest of a small country to adopt policies
that limit an externality which raises the productivity of domestic factors.
The same need not be true for some large countries, however. One can
speculate that there may be circumstances under which a large country
might attempt to limit its "export" of this externality as an "nth" best
means of improving its terms of trade. (ii) If this externality is completely
local, then a subsidy on schooling will raise welfare and each country has
the incentive to provide it. The magnitude of the optimal subsidy would
differ in trade from autarky, but provided the subsidy is appropriately
adjusted, free trade should not lead to a welfare deterioration. Any role for
trade interventions here is then purely a second-best role. Since schooling
provides a positive externality, small interventions that lead to an increase in the incentives for schooling will be welfare-improving. The
growth rate will also increase in this context.

The most plausible case will be somewhere between these two extremes. The extent of schooling spillovers will depend, separately, on the
per capita human capital levels of both the domestic and foreign populations (at least when the latter is higher). Again subsidization is the appropriate intervention for the domestically generated externality. For a small
developing country potentially able to benefit from the higher human
capital level in the rest of the world, an important policy consideration is
the links through which the foreign externality might be transferred to the
domestic market. Unfortunately, our knowledge of this externality is as
limited as it is of most others. But since we are considering an externality
that is supposedly associated with a formal schooling activity, it would
seem inadvisable to restrict international trade in the inputs to that activity. Access to foreign educational materials and foreign educators,
broadly interpreted, should not be restricted. There is of course no suggestion that all educational activities necessarily result in these externalities, and one can imagine that some governments might also be concerned with the impact of foreign knowledge on the local culture.

Learning by Doing

An alternative form of human capital acquisition is through on-the-job training or learning by doing. Lucas (1988) adapts the Ricardian trade model to allow output per worker in any particular activity to increase with the effort devoted to that activity, but with the rate of increase differing across industries. In a two-good trading world composed of many small countries, each country specializes in the good in which it has a comparative advantage. With learning by doing, this comparative advantage grows through time, so there is a tendency for the pattern of trade to be locked in place with rates of growth variable across countries but stable within each country. The terms of trade are likely to be turning against the exporters of the goods with the higher rate of learning, however, so we could observe some countries switching production into goods with lower rates of learning by doing.

Findlay (1995) takes the standard two-factor trade model with a finite number of goods, and assumes that the rate of learning by doing across products is positively related to their capital intensities. This means an economy's growth rate is positively related to its capital-to-labor ratio (and hence its saving propensity). In a two-country model, trade accelerates growth in the more capital-abundant country and reduces growth in the other country, though the latter is compensated by continually improving terms of trade. For a small country, trade policy can increase the rate of growth by shifting resources into more capital-intensive sectors.

One deficiency of the learning by doing models discussed so far is the tendency for learning by doing to simply reinforce the initial pattern of comparative advantage, thereby "locking in" the trade pattern. In practice, we do observe significant changes in the composition of trade, particularly over long periods of time. Stokey (1988) provides a version of this model which emphasizes growth through the introduction of new goods (product innovation) rather than process innovation on a fixed set of goods. Suppose there is a continuum of potentially producible goods, but only a limited subset are produced in each period. Over time the set of produced goods changes, with higher quality goods entering and lower quality goods leaving. Driving this change is learning by doing, which takes the form that the input requirements for production of any good by any firm in any period depend on the economy's cumulative experience in the production of all goods in all previous periods. Learning therefore displays complete spillovers among firms and may display spillovers among goods. These spillovers are needed if learning by doing is to do more than just reinforce the existing pattern of production. Within any period, production costs increase smoothly with the quality of the good. Through time, production costs fall as a result of the learning by doing spillovers, and the assumption that forward (i.e., up the quality ladder) learning by doing spillovers are stronger than backward spillovers is required to ensure that new, higher quality goods are introduced. Since learning spills over completely and without lag to other firms, no firm has an incentive to suffer losses to accelerate learning. The measured rate of growth is always positive, but may be increasing, decreasing, or constant over time.

Studies of productivity growth (for example, Argote and Epple 1990) show learning by doing in any particular activity occurs at a declining rate and eventually ceases, so that learning by doing in a fixed set of activities could not be an engine of growth. Sustained growth requires the continuous introduction of new goods, with diminishing returns to learning by doing in each separately, but with the human capital acquired from learning in the old activities somehow being inherited in the production of the new. The approach just considered achieves this through biased spillovers that induce the replacement of old goods by new. A model where steady state growth is generated by learning by doing bounded on each good is developed by Young (1991). This model incorporates two important characteristics implied by an analysis of technical progress at the industry level. The first is the existence of strong diminishing returns in the learning by doing process, which can be viewed as the "working out" of the productive potential of new technologies. Over time learning by doing slows, and perhaps ultimately stops. "This would explain why, despite considerable economic activity, learning by doing did not lead to sustained economic growth prior to the modern era" (Young 1991, 372). The second is the spillover effect in the development of knowledge across industries. Important innovations tend to have wider applications than to the product or industry from which they originate. The process of development of the new goods themselves is ignored, however. Blueprints of all future technologies are available at any point in time, but an economy must pass through a certain amount of production experience before the costs of production of advanced goods fall to acceptable levels. A continuum of potentially producible goods exists, but at any point in time only a finite number are actually produced. The bound on learning by doing in any good is taken as exogenous, but learning by doing exhibits spillovers across goods and these are in the public domain. Activity in neighboring goods contributes positive spillovers. At any point in time, learning by doing is exhausted in a subset of goods but continues in others. There are no spillovers from activities where learning by doing is exhausted. Growth involves production of a changing basket of goods, with both the quality and variety of goods consumed increasing. Production takes place under perfect competition since the spillovers from learning by doing are not appropriable.

Assuming no international diffusion of knowledge, the effect of trade on a country's growth rate in this framework will depend on whether the country has a static comparative advantage in the goods where learning by doing is exhausted or in the goods where learning by doing is continuing. Obviously trade will improve intertemporal welfare where it accelerates technical improvement and growth. Even where trade slows growth, a country may still obtain a welfare improvement through improvements in real income over time. While unbounded learning by doing tends to reinforce existing patterns of comparative advantage and yield fairly static trade patterns, bounded learning by doing gives a realistic evolving trade pattern. Consider trade between two countries. In autarky each is producing a particular set of goods, and suppose that when free trade is opened up, the set in one country (the advanced country) is centered above that of the other (the developing country). A range of possible equilibria can then emerge. In terms of technical progress, the advanced country experiences dynamic gains from trade, and the developing country experiences dynamic losses. The keenest competition between them is in the range where the advanced country has exhausted learning by doing but the developing country is still experiencing learning by doing. This competition drives resources into learning by doing industries in the advanced country and out of learning by doing industries in the developing country. Thus the developing country's specialization according to comparative advantage, while statically optimal, has detrimental effects on its rate of technical progress. If the advanced country is large enough, this technical gap may increase without bound. Trade need not therefore accelerate the growth of income in all trading partners. In a multicountry trading world, this model offers the prospect that, in equilibrium, countries may locate on the rungs of a product-quality ladder. Each country, other than those at the ends, is being pushed down by trade with the country above, and being pushed up by trade with the country below. Upward progress occurs in the steady state, with each country hot on the heels of that above it.

The implications of learning by doing for trade policy can be analyzed in the same way as for schooling. Again we have an externality. Production today reduces the costs of production tomorrow, but the latter is a public good and is not taken into account by agents today. This externality may be confined within the production of individual goods, or it may spill over into the production of technologically "neighboring" goods. Either way, the market equilibrium is not efficient, but this time the externality is not tied to a particular identifiable activity. Suppose there are no spillovers. When agents make their production decisions in line with static comparative advantage, they do not take into account potential future cost reductions. An appropriate intervention is one that puts the correct value on current production (i.e., valuing both current utility and future cost reductions). Given our ex ante ignorance of the potential extent of learning by doing in any activity, such interventions, which involve "picking winners", are both difficult and risky. Perhaps the risk is less for later producers, but the characteristics of learning by doing may vary across countries for a given product. If the characteristics of learning by doing are predictable, we are faced with the standard infant industry problem, and border intervention is very much a second-best response. If there are spillovers, then the same analysis applies as for schooling, except that it may be even more difficult to identify the appropriate activity to subsidize.

Lucas (1993) observes that learning by doing spillovers are consistent with a positive relationship between openness and rapid productivity growth. For rapid growth we need a rapid turnover in goods produced, which is difficult under an IS strategy that ties domestic production to the slowly changing domestic consumption mix. Bardhan (1995) suggests that this framework may also explain why a policy of protecting infant export industries, as opposed to protecting infant import-substitute industries, is sometimes more growth-promoting in the long run. In the former case, the opportunities for learning by doing spillovers into newer and more sophisticated goods are wider than when the potential beneficiaries are restricted to the home market. It has also been suggested that exporting firms may be more willing to share knowledge than import-substituting firms, given the more direct rivalry among local firms catering for the domestic market.

One expects the extent of automatic international spillovers to be limited in this case. Most of the learning by doing benefits are likely to spill over between firms, and the international mobility of skilled labor may be the vehicle of their international transmission. Still it is important that domestic producers have full access to information on the likely benefits from learning by doing. If these benefits can be transferred through foreign commercial contacts, the hiring of foreign consultants, or foreign direct investment, then this externality should be kept in mind when border interventions are considered.

Investments in Research and Development

The Neo-Schumpeterian approach begins from the premise that most technical progress is the outcome of resource-using activities undertaken by profit-seeking firms and entrepreneurs. To model growth one must therefore explicitly model the process of technological advance as the outcome of the R&D activities of firms motivated by the possibility of monopoly profits (Romer 1990, Grossman and Helpman 1991b, 1994). In these models, sustained growth is achieved through spillovers from the output of current R&D to subsequent investments in R&D. The productivity of employees in R&D depends on the general level of scientific, engineering, and industrial knowledge in the country. Because current R&D activities on new goods increase this stock of knowledge as a by-product, they also increase the productivity of R&D for subsequent innovators.

A framework that includes both externalities and imperfect competition can explain a wider range of observations, but only at some cost in terms of increased complexity. The Grossman and Helpman (1991b) model, whose trade implications have been investigated by the authors, has the following general features. An R&D sector where innovators invest resources (factors) in the hope of discovering ways to produce new, higher quality intermediate inputs (the model can alternatively be formulated in terms of discoveries of final outputs or capital goods). These discoveries can be patented, and the innovator can sell the patent to competitive intermediate producers or produce the corresponding intermediate itself. Either way, if innovators are to recover their R&D outlays, the intermediate outputs must sell at prices above unit production costs. Thus the sales and profits of firms offering the various types or generations of each intermediate input are determined by oligopolistic competition. But some R&D generates knowledge that has wider applicability than can be patented for; and, even with the patent restrictions, subsequent innovators have the opportunity to study all that has gone before. These externalities imply a continuous increase in productivity in the R&D sector. Innovators finance their activities from the savings of firms and households. The value of these innovating firms on asset markets depends on the expected discounted value of their profits, taking into account the expected evolution of technology in the industry. The intermediate inputs produced as a result of the innovators' activities are combined with other factors to produce final goods (which can be used for consumption or investment in physical capital). The economy experiences sustained growth through the continuous introduction of new improved intermediate inputs that raise the productivity of resources in the production of the final output. The costs and benefits of R&D determine the rate of long-term growth. In any particular intermediate-producing industry, growth may be uneven and stochastic, but as long as the number of these industries is large, in aggregate the economy grows at a steady rate. Final goods are produced and sold in competitive markets. Finally, factor markets clear at returns for which the demands for factors by innovators, intermediate goods producers and final goods producers equal the corresponding supplies.

This model has two features which suggest that the market outcome may not be an efficient one. First, since innovators are rewarded from monopoly profits, the price of intermediate inputs exceeds their marginal production costs. This leads to substitution of other inputs for intermediates in the production of final output. Second, innovators cannot capture the full surplus generated by their efforts (consumer surplus and R&D externalities), which suggests that the market will provide insufficient incentives for innovation. This need not be the case, however, because included in the private expected profit calculations of innovators may be some profits that are redistributed from existing producers (this outcome is formally the same whether new intermediates simply add to the range of those available or displace existing, now obsolescent, intermediates). This profit redistribution effect can lead to excessive use of resources in R&D and insufficient use of resources in production with existing technologies. Of course, some innovations may be complementary to their predecessors and add to their rents. The important point is that the issue of whether the market outcome results in too much or too little innovation relative to the social optimum is ambiguous. Further, even where this ambiguity can be resolved, care must be taken in the use of policies (particularly second-best policies) to achieve the optimum (Grossman and Helpman 1994). If the market equilibrium leads to below-optimal technical progress, then a subsidy to R&D will raise the rate of technical progress. The alternative policy of a subsidy on sales of intermediate products also provides an increase in the expected return to a successful innovator. But by distorting the intermediate market, this subsidy affects the demands for factors in both the intermediate-producing and final goods (intermediate-using) sectors. Depending on relative factor intensities, the net result may be to raise the cost of factors (scientists and engineers for example) used in innovation, and this indirect, general equilibrium effect might even be strong enough to offset the expected return increase, thereby reducing growth.

When it comes to discussing the implications of this framework for trade and trade policy, there are a large number of possibilities that might be considered. Potentially up to three layers of trade can be involved—patents, intermediates, and final goods. At any point in time, there is a distribution in comparative advantage across countries in all these layers. The actual trade pattern will also be influenced by the nature of the oligopolistic competition in the intermediate markets. Over time, comparative advantage may change, depending on factor accumulation and the extent to which R&D spillovers flow across national boundaries.

There are forces leading toward higher growth rates with increased international integration (Rivera-Batiz and Romer 1991). Exposure to international competition should reduce redundancy in R&D. In a closed market, a successful innovator need only innovate with respect to that market. But innovation for the world market must be globally original. Increased openness is also likely to provide innovators in any country with some access to the larger global pool of technological knowledge. Further, by expanding the size of the potential market, increased linkages with the international economy may expand the incentives for innovation. But whether increased openness impacts positively or negatively on a particular country's growth rate depends on how successful domestic innovators are in competition with foreign innovators. This competition depends on whether technological spillovers are national or international, and who has the comparative advantage in the R&D activity.

If innovators worldwide have equal access to the global knowledge base, then past innovation in any particular country has no implications for the long-run pattern of international trade. Countries will trade in line with relative resource endowments. This could lead some countries to specialize in the production of standard final products, where productivity change is low or nonexistent. Output growth rates will be correspondingly low or nonexistent. If technological spillovers are national, then comparative advantage in innovation depends on both relative resource endowments and the economy's knowledge stock. Here then is the potential for an initial technological lead in an industry, however generated, to be sustained. On the other hand, innovators in a country with a small knowledge base may find it increasingly difficult to compete. Trade liberalization, leading to a shift in resources in line with static comparative advantage, can reduce the growth rate (Grossman and Helpman 1991b, chapter 9). Again one should note that output growth rates do not measure welfare. There are the usual gains from specialization according to comparative advantage, and while GDP may grow more slowly than otherwise, the present discounted value of the economy's consumption stream may be higher. The relative prices of those final goods with the highest rates of productivity improvement will be falling.

As noted above, analyzing the trade policy implications of this type of framework is complicated by the number and range of potential sources of externalities and distortions. So let us concentrate on issues most likely to be of interest to developing countries. As a number of authors have noted (Bardhan 1995, Findlay 1995, Pack 1994), developing countries do not undertake much R&D. Even the NIEs undertook relatively little R&D before the 1980s, and their R&D is still mainly directed toward adaptation of existing technologies. Their comparative advantage is not in this area. Instead, the developing countries efforts are directed towards *imitation* of technologies used in the advanced countries rather than true *innovation*. But the Grossman and Helpman model can easily be adapted to deal with innovation by firms in the "North" and subsequent imitation by firms in the "South" (Grossman and Helpman 1994). Even though technology may appear to be available "off the shelf", resources are still required to adapt it to local conditions and to learn how to use it. Bell et al. (1984) note that the relatively slow productivity growth of "infant industries" seems to reflect a lack of effort to acquire and use the capabilities necessary for continuous technical change. These capabilities require the explicit allocation of resources and do not arise from experience alone. The rate of imitation will depend on the same type of considerations as determine the rate of innovation, though with perhaps a smaller role for uncertainty. The expected return on imitation will depend on the economy's institutions, property-rights regime, and pricing structure in the same way.

One question investigated by Grossman and Helpman (1991b) is whether the possibility of imitation will reduce the net incentives for Northern firms to innovate. While subsequent imitation directly reduces the return from any particular innovation, the general movement of production abroad as a result of imitation releases resources in the North, causing factor price changes which may lower the costs of innovation. The net result may be a shorter term as a monopolist, but a higher rate of profit during this period. Imitation might therefore increase or reduce the return to innovation.

One form of imitation would be the movement of production to the South by the Northern producer or patent holder. If relative resource endowments are such that the North has a comparative advantage in R&D but the South has the comparative advantage in intermediate production (or if transport costs are sufficiently large), then foreign direct investment or the international licensing of patents may occur. In this case, the innovator also controls (to some degree) the imitator. For this to be successful, innovators' patent rights (or trade secrets) must be protected in the South. Transferring the technology will still involve resource costs. The question of whether imitation in this form brings any of the externalities (for subsequent imitation) claimed for innovation is unresolved. But there is little evidence to suggest that any technological externalities generated by IS-induced foreign direct investment have been significant.

If the intermediate inputs can be traded, then not having an R&D sector does not prevent a trading economy from getting some of the productivity gains from innovation, namely those through increased factor productivity in its final goods sectors. If some intermediates are nontraded, then either they must be produced domestically or substituted for by other inputs where they are not essential. Technical progress then requires either domestic innovation or domestic imitation. The latter can be through a commercial contract with the foreign innovator (through foreign direct investment or licensing), or an independent imitation by a domestic entrepreneur. However this takes place, its efficiency depends on domestic productivity in the R&D sector, and here we return to the importance of spillovers. In particular, which international links are likely to provide a channel for the international transmission of R&D spillovers.

Grossman and Helpman (1991) examine a variant of their model in which the stock of domestic R&D knowledge can be increased two ways: as an externality from local R&D, as before, and now, in addition, through interaction with agents in the rest of the world. Grossman and Helpman (1991, 520) argue that "...While knowledge can be acquired from the international community through channels that have nothing to do with business relations, it seems reasonable to suppose that the extent of the spillovers between two countries will increase with the volume of their bilateral trade." Three possible steady-state growth paths emerge in this model, and in the case Grossman and Helpman choose to focus on, trade liberalization reduces two dynamic distortions in this economy. First, it encourages international interactions, which have positive spillover benefits for the economy's stock of knowledge capital. Second, it raises the incentive for local R&D, which generates a similar positive externality. Trade liberalization therefore raises welfare and in fact it is optimal to subsidize trade to some degree.

If there is something to this notion that trading relationships are also a channel for technology spillovers, then it is clear that developing countries potentially have a lot to gain. They can draw in this way on the large stock of knowledge in the developed world. The externalities in the other direction are likely to be much less important (Pack 1994). Diffusion of technological know-how occurs through foreign direct investment, licensing, consultants, and informal knowledge transfers. Each of these modes of transfer may be facilitated by international trade. Once one attempts to draw out the policy implications of this result for a particular developing country, however, things are less clear-cut. It seems unlikely that this externality is present in all trade flows, but rather in some trade flows with some advanced countries. Which advanced countries will depend on the source of comparative advantage in R&D, but human capital-abundant advanced countries appear likely candidates. This raises a range of unresolved issues. Are externalities only transmitted through trade in high-technology products with high-technology innovators? Or can a country also learn from subsequent imitators? Which arm of trade carries the benefits, imports or exports? Pack (1994) notes that for countries that undertake R&D, much of the resulting knowledge is embodied in equipment. For nonproducers, imported equipment may improve their average technology level. But there is little theoretical basis for arguing that externalities, as opposed to improved productivity in the purchasing firm, are generated by the use of foreign-produced equipment. Imports can be reverse engineered, but this need only happen a few times for any product. Exports provide feedback from foreign purchasers, but again this learning process eventually ceases for any product. In summary the case for a general trade subsidy on these grounds seems very weak. The case for limiting interference in the general flow of goods and services is much stronger.

Evidence

Empirical verification of the propositions generated by endogenous growth theory is necessary if they are to be taken seriously by policymakers. Backus et al. (1992) explicitly test four of the variables identified as important for growth by these models (learning by doing, schooling, R&D, and "specialized inputs"), by relating growth rates in GDP per capita and output per worker in manufacturing to scale and intensity (per capita) measures for each of these variables. The outcomes can be summarized as follows:

- Both GDP and the total manufacturing output can be used as potentially relevant measures of scale to test the hypothesis that countries with larger industries grow faster because of externalities associated with learning by doing. While there is little evidence of scale effects in determining the growth of GDP per capita, there is significant evidence of scale effects in output per worker in manufacturing. This confirms the widely held view that learning by doing is largely a phenomenon of the manufacturing sector.
- Data on numbers of students and teachers are used to construct scale and intensity indices for human capital stocks. There is some evidence that intensity of human capital is related to growth in GDP per capita, but little evidence of a scale effect.
- Numbers of scientists, engineers, and technicians, and total expenditures on R&D, are used as measures of inputs into R&D. There is little evidence of scale or intensity effects for GDP growth, but significant evidence of a relation between growth of manufacturing productivity and scale of inputs in R&D.
- If technological advances are embodied in traded specialized inputs, this allows a small country to grow as fast as a large one. Backus et al. note the problems of relating the notions of differen-

tiation used in the theory to the fixed product categories employed in collecting trade data. They resort to using indicators of specialized inputs based on measures of intra-industry trade. There is evidence that both GDP growth and productivity growth in manufacturing are positively related to these measures of trade in differentiated products.

In total, this evidence provides support, although admittedly rather weak or indirect support, for each of the growth models considered above. But it is clear that the externalities identified by the theory are likely to be confined to some sectors, particularly manufacturing. This is supported by the results in Helleiner (1986), who found no significant links between export growth and output growth for poor countries whose economies are dominated by agriculture. Indeed, as noted above, the effects are not even likely to be uniform across the manufacturing sector. This suggests that, ultimately, multisector growth models will be needed to explain cross-country differences in the rate of growth in GDP per capita.

Summary

Externalities of different types formed the foundation for sustained long-term growth in each of the models considered above. It is important to note that, while they have been modelled separately, these potential sources of growth are not mutually exclusive. In fact, they are expected to interact and build on each other. For example, a country's ability to take advantage of learning by doing and to innovate or imitate will very likely depend on its stock of human capital. The learning by doing models are based on the existence of blueprints for a continuum of potential new products. Yet these blueprints have to be developed somewhere, presumably through the R&D activities of profit-driven innovators. The neo-Schumpeterian models, on the other hand, assume that the full productive potential of any new technology is realized at the moment of invention. This neglects the many instances of product improvement and cost reduction that originate in suggestions coming from production workers, process engineers, and customers (Solow 1994). "Empirically there is evidence that the actualisation of the productive potential of existing technologies may lead to productivity increases several orders of magnitude greater than those associated with the original technical innovations" (Young 1991, 375).

The presence of externalities yields a presumption that the market outcome will not provide the socially optimal rate of growth. Although border interventions will be second-best policies for dealing with these domestic externalities, border interventions do provide some of the few policy instruments readily available to all developing countries. There is evidence that distorting the prices of capital equipment and intermediate goods can be detrimental to growth. This may explain why countries that pursued the full IS strategy of industrialization generally have such a poor growth record. The first, or "easy", stage of IS is the replacement of imports of nondurable consumer goods and their principal direct inputs. Most developing countries (the obvious exception being Hong Kong) have used trade policy to attempt at least this first stage. Extending IS beyond this takes us into the production of intermediate products and durable producer and consumer goods, which also draws heavily on the output of other industries. The evidence reported above supports the view that it is this second stage that is detrimental to growth. Countries that switched to an EP strategy (e.g., Republic of Korea and Taipei,China) have a better growth record than those that continued with IS policies (e.g., Argentina, Brazil, and Mexico).

The notion that a skilled and educated population generates externalities for the schooling of its children is plausible. Schooling at most levels is subsidized to some degree in all countries. Whether the level of subsidization provided is greater or lower than that necessary to achieve the optimal level of schooling is arguable. While trade policy can influence the schooling decision, it seems a very indirect instrument for this task. The by-product distortions created by its use for this purpose could easily outweigh any benefits. But clearly the presence of this externality, and the possibility that it can be transmitted internationally, should be recalled in debates over the desirability of protecting local suppliers of educational and training inputs. Although it has yet to be modelled in this way, one should also bear in mind that education is a tradeable service.

The efforts of developing countries in R&D activities will continue to concentrate on imitation rather than innovation. In innovating countries, government subsidies might be used to promote the externality-providing R&D activities, although there are obvious problems in identifying exactly which activities these are (Shaw 1992). Does imitation provide the same type of externalities? Even if it does, the difficulties in identifying the relevant imitative activities to be subsidized seem enormous. The notion of countries lying on a technology or quality ladder may provide some clues as to where the externalities are likely to arise. Imitation will focus on those imports likely to be a country's next exports. The spillovers will be from the latest generation of exports to the next generation of exports. Trade policies that penalize new exporters, or discourage imports that potentially can be imitated, will reduce these externalities.

In developing countries, learning by doing is linked to the production of new products and hence to imitation. The use of trade interventions to promote learning by doing is a strategy that involves picking winners and is no more likely to be successful in this case than it has been elsewhere in the promotion of infant industries. But if assistance is to be provided to new industries, it should be temporary, general, and not confined to production for the domestic market.

There is strong evidence, particularly from multicountry case studies, that the more outward-oriented economies (those economies in which incentives for production are not biased in favor of the domestic market) have had the stronger growth performances. Exactly why this is the case, and whether it also applies to a country's steady state rate of growth, remain debated issues. A range of propositions attempting to explain this evidence was noted, but tests of them have been suggestive at best.

Recent developments in trade theory suggest that the static resource misallocation costs associated with protectionist policies may be much higher than is conventionally estimated. Trade liberalization is likely to do more than simply shift an economy to a more appropriate position on its production possibilty frontier. The range of products produced and traded, the speed with which new products are introduced into the economy, the characteristics of the products traded, the degree of domestic competition, and the extent of directly unproductive lobbying and rent-seeking, are all influenced by the trade regime. These developments may partly explain why more open economies have performed better than expected.

Developments in endogenous growth theory have also provided a clearer picture of the potential relationships between trade and growth in the long run. In particular they have identified plausible cases where trade liberalization will reduce a developed country's growth rate. Authors are always careful to note that growth and welfare are not the same, and that the adverse welfare consequences of this reduction in the growth rate may be more than compensated for by the benefits of reallocating resources in accordance with static comparative advantage and the terms of trade improvements that are likely to occur for those countries exporting products with low rates of technical progress. While this is a very important point, one cannot help but wonder how convincing it will sound to policymakers in developing countries. It brings to mind an earlier debate that still haunts the literature over whether developing countries faced a long-term decline in their terms of trade. Although there have been difficulties in determining much of a trend one way or the other in the data, one would not be surprised if policymakers were very concerned that trade liberalization might reduce the rate of growth of output, and that they were not comforted by promised improvements in the terms of trade.

Some government action in support of growth therefore seems inevitable. In principle, one could devise a set of government interventions that would move the economy to its optimal growth rate. Whether these policies could ever be applied in practice is another matter. By their very nature, externalities are difficult to measure, and while the evidence from cross-section regressions may provide clues as to their whereabouts, this will not be accurate enough for policy purposes. Trade policy has the potential for influencing an economy's long-run growth path. But trade policies are also clearly second best for this purpose. General concerns over the possible growth-inhibiting effects of trade reform could combine with the political influence of those vested interests that benefit from the existing trade interventions to prevent trade liberalization in some instances. Still, all the evidence suggests that open economies grow more rapidly. Until such time as the more recent propositions on growth have been adequately verified, the basic role for trade policy would seem to be one of keeping open the channels through which international spillovers might flow.

Acknowledgment

The author thanks Mohamed Ariff, Y. Iwasaki, and M. G. Quibria for comments and suggestions.

References

Anderson, J. E., and J. P. Neary, 1994. "Measuring the Restrictiveness of Trade Policy." *World Bank Economic Review* 8(2):151-69.

Argote, L., and D. Epple, 1990. "Learning Curves in Manufacturing." *Science* 247(23 February):920-24.

Backus, D. K., P. J. Kehoe, and T. J. Kehoe, 1992. "In Search of Scale Effects In Trade and Growth." *Journal of Economic Theory* 58(2):377-409.

Balassa, B., ed., 1982. *Development Strategies in Semi-industrial Economies.* Baltimore: Johns Hopkins University Press.

Balassa, B., 1985. "Exports, Policy Choices and Economic Growth in Developing Countries after the 1973 Oil Shock." *Journal of Development Economics* 18(2):23-35.

Baldwin, R., 1992. "Measurable Dynamic Gains from Trade." *Journal of Political Economy* 100(1):162-74.

Bardhan, P., 1995. "The Implications of New Growth Theory for Trade and Development: An Overview." In M. G.Quibria, ed., *Critical Issues in Asian Development: Theories, Experiences and Policies.* Hong Kong: Oxford University Press for the Asian Development Bank.

Barro, R. J., 1990. "Government Spending in a Simple Model of Endogenous Growth" *Journal of Political Economy* 98(5):S103-25.

———, 1991. "Economic Growth in a Cross-Section of Countries." *Quarterly Journal of Economics* 106(2):407-43.

Barro, R. J., and J-W Lee, 1993. "Losers and Winners in Economic Growth." Proceedings of the World Bank Annual Conference on Development Economics. Supplement to the World Bank Economic Review and the World Bank Research Observer. World Bank, Washington, D. C.

Bell, M., B. Ross-Larson, and L. E. Westphal, 1984. "Assessing the Performance of Infant Industries." *Journal of Development Economics* 16:101-28.

Bhagwati, J. N., 1978. *Anatomy and Consequences of Exchange Control Regimes.* Cambridge: Ballinger.

Burgess, R., and N. Stern, 1993. "Taxation and Development." *Journal of Economic Literature* 31(2):762-830.

Corden, W. M., 1971."The Effects of Trade on the Rate of Growth." In J. Bhagwati et al., eds., *Trade, Balance of Payments and Growth.* Amsterdam: North-Holland.

Dollar, D., 1992. "Outward-Oriented Developing Countries Really Do Grow More Rapidly: Evidence from 95 LDCs, 1976-1985." *Economic Development and Cultural Change* 40:523-44.

Dornbusch, R., 1992. "The Case for Trade Liberalisation in Developing Countries." *Journal of Economic Perspectives* 6(1):69-85.

Dowrick, S., 1994. "Openness and Growth." In P. Lowe and J. Dwyer, eds., *International Integration of the Australian Economy.* Sydney: Reserve Bank of Australia.

Easterly, W., 1993. "How Much Do Distortions Affect Growth?" *Journal of Monetary Economics* 32(2):187-212.

Easterly, W., M. Kremer, L. Pritchett, and L. H. Summers, 1993. "Good Policy or Good Luck?: Country Growth Performance and Temporary Shocks." *Journal of Monetary Economics* 32(3):459-83.

Edwards, S., 1993. "Openness, Trade Liberalization, and Growth in Developing Countries." *Journal of Economic Literature* 31(3):1358-93.

Esfahani, H. S., 1991. "Exports, Imports, and Economic Growth in Semi-Industrialised Countries." *Journal of Development Economics* 35(1):93-116.

Falvey, R., and C-D. Kim, 1992. "Timing and Sequencing Issues in Trade Liberalisation." *Economic Journal* 102 (July):908-24.

Feder, G., 1982. "On Exports and Economic Growth." *Journal of Development Economics* 12(1/2):59-73.

Feenstra, R. C., 1992. "How Costly is Protectionism?" *Journal of Economic Perspectives* 6(3):159-78.

Findlay, R., 1984. "Growth and Development in Trade Models." In R. W. Jones, and P. B. Kenen, eds., *Handbook of International Economics.* Vol. I. Amsterdam: North-Holland.

———, 1995. "Recent Advances in Trade and Growth Theory." In M. G. Quibria, ed., *Critical Issues in Asian Development: Theories, Experiences* and Policies. Hong Kong: Oxford University Press for the Asian Development Bank.

Greenaway, D., 1993. "Liberalising Foreign Trade Through Rose Tinted Glasses." Economic Journal 103(January):208-23.

Greenaway, D., and O. Morrissey, 1993. "Structural Adjustment and Liberalisation in Developing Countries: What Have We Learned?" Kyklos 46(2):241-61.

Greenaway, D., and D. Sapsford, 1994. "What Does Liberalisation Do for Exports and Growth." Weltwirtschaftliches Archiv 130(1):152-74.

Grossman, G. M., and E. Helpman, 1991a. "Trade, Knowledge Spillovers, and Growth." European Economic Review 35(3):26.

————, 1991b. Innovation and Growth in the Global Economy. Cambridge: MIT Press.

————, 1994. "Endogenous Innovation in the Theory of Growth." Journal of Economic Perspectives 8(1):23-44.

Hammond, P. J., and A. Rodriguez-Clare, 1993. "On Endogenizing Long-Run Growth." Scandanavian Journal of Economics 95(4):391-425.

Heitger, B., 1987. "Import Protection and Export Performance: Their Impact on Economic Growth." Weltwirtschaftliches Archiv. 123(2):249-61.

Helleiner, G. K., 1986. "Outward Orientation, Import Instability and African Economic Growth: An Empirical Investigation." In S. Lall and F. Stewart eds ., Theory and Reality in Development: Essays in Honour of Paul Streeten. London: Macmillan.

Helliwell, J. F., 1992. "Trade and Technical Progress." Working Paper No. 4226. National Bureau of Economic Research, Cambridge, Massachusetts.

Krueger, A. O., 1978. Foreign Trade Regimes and Economic Development. Cambridge: Ballinger.

Lee, J- W., 1993. "International Trade, Distortions, and Long-Run Economic Growth." IMF Staff Papers No. 40. International Monetary Fund, Washington, D. C.

Levine R., and D. Renelt, 1991. "Cross-Country Studies of Growth and Policy." Staff Working Paper 608. World Bank, Washington, D.C.

————, 1992. "A Sensitivity Analysis of Cross-Country Growth Regressions." American Economic Review 82(4):942-63.

Little, I. M. D., 1982. Economic Development: Theory, Policy and International Relations. New York: Basic Books.

Lucas, R. E., 1988. "On the Mechanics of Economic Development." Journal of Monetary Economics 22(1):3-42.

————, 1993. "Making a Miracle." Econometrica 61(2):251-72.

Michaely, M., D. Papageorgiou, and A. Choksi, 1991. Liberalising Foreign Trade: Volume 7 — Lessons of Experience in the Developing World. Oxford: Basil Blackwell.

Nishimizu, M., and J. M. Page, 1991. "Trade Policy, Market Orientation, and Productivity Change in Industry." In J. de Melo and A. Sapir, eds., Trade Theory and Eonomic Reform: North, South, and East. Oxford: Basil Blackwell.

Pack, H., 1994. "Endogenous Growth Theory: Intellectual Appeal and Empirical Shortcomings." *Journal of Economic Perspectives* 8(1):55-72.

Rivera-Batiz, L. A., and P. Romer, 1991. "Economic Integration and Endogenous Growth." *Quarterly Journal of Economics* 106(2):531-55.

Rodrik, D., 1992a. "Closing the Productivity Gap: Does Trade Liberalisation Really Help?" In G. K. Helleiner, ed., *Trade Policy, Industrialization and Development: New Perspectives.* Oxford: Clarendon Press.

———, 1992b. "The Limits of Trade Policy Reform in Developing Countries." *Journal of Economic Perspectives* 6(1):87-105.

Romer, P., 1990. "Endogenous Technical Change." *Journal of Political Economy* 98(5): S71-102.

———, 1994a. "New Goods, Old Theory, and the Welfare Costs of Trade Restrictions." *Journal of Development Economics* 43(1):5-38.

———, 1994b. "The Origins of Endogenous Growth." *Journal of Economic Perspectives* 8(1):3-22.

Shaw, G. K., 1992. "Policy Implications of Endogenous Growth Theory." *Economic Journal* 102:611-21.

Solow, R. M., 1994. "Perspectives on Growth Theory." *Journal of Economic Perspectives* 8(1):45-54.

Stokey, N. L., 1988. "Learning by Doing and the Introduction of New Goods." *Journal of Political Economy* 96(4):701-17.

———, 1991. "Human Capital, Product Quality and Growth." *Quarterly Journal of Economics* 106:587-616.

Taylor, L., 1991. "Economic Openness: Problems to the Century's End." In T. Banuri, ed., *Economic Liberalization: No Panacea.* Oxford: Clarendon Press.

Thomas V., J. Nash and Associates, 1991. *Best Practices in Trade Policy Reform.* Oxford: Oxford University Press for the World Bank.

Tybout, J. R., 1992. "Linking Trade and Productivity: New Research Directions." *The World Bank Economic Review* 6(2):189-211.

Young, A., 1991. "Learning by Doing and the Dynamic Effects of International Trade." *Quarterly Journal of Economics* 106(2):369-405.

———, 1993. "Lessons from the East Asian NICs: A Contrarian View." Working Paper No. 4482. National Bureau of Economic Research, Cambridge, Massachusetts.

———, 1994. "The Tyranny of Numbers: Confronting the Statistical Realities of the East Asian Growth Experience." Working Paper No. 4680. National Bureau of Economic Research, Cambridge, Massachusetts.

Chapter 8

The Uruguay Round
and Asian Developing Economies

T. N. Srinivasan

After nearly eight years of long and contentious debate, the Uruguay Round of Multilateral Trade Negotiations, launched in Punta del Este, Uruguay, in September 1986, was successfully concluded with the signing of the Final Act embodying its results on 15 April 1994 at Marrakesh, Morocco, by ministers representing 124 governments and the European community. One of the most important results is the decision to establish the World Trade Organization (WTO). It came into existence formally in January 1995, replacing and subsuming the General Agreement on Tariffs and Trade (GATT) with the ratification of the Final Act by the required number of countries. To appreciate the significance of this event, it is worth recalling the history of the GATT.[1] The Bretton Woods Conference of 1944 that led to the establishment of the International Monetary Fund and the World Bank recognized the need for a comparable institution for trade. In February 1946, at its very first meeting, the Economic and Social Council of the United Nations called for a conference to draft a charter for such an institution, to be called the International Trade Organization (ITO). The United States published a suggested draft charter and a preparatory committee was formed to discuss the draft. The preparatory committee met four times, first in London in 1946 and last in Havana, Cuba, in 1948.

At its third and principal meeting in Geneva in October 1947, besides preparing a charter for the ITO, the committee also negotiated a multilateral agreement to reduce tariffs reciprocally as well as a set of rules and obligations (the so-called "General Clauses") regarding tariff reductions. The multilateral agreement and the General Clauses constituted the General Agreement on Tariffs and Trade—the GATT. The GATT was to be merely a multilateral treaty and not an organization, but the draft of its clauses reflected the expectation that it would operate under the umbrella of the ITO when the ITO came into being.

The US negotiators in the preparatory committee in 1945 were operating under an extension of the power granted to the President by Congress to negotiate reciprocal reductions of tariffs and other barriers to trade with other countries. It was made clear to the US negotiators that this power did not extend to negotiating an agreement to enter an international organization. They then redrafted the general GATT clauses to eliminate any suggestion of an organization so that multilateral decisions under GATT were to be taken by the "Contracting Parties" acting jointly rather than by an "organization".

The charter of the ITO as negotiated at the Havana conference was submitted to the US Congress for approval in 1948, but in that year's election, while Truman, a Democrat, won the presidency, Republicans won control of Congress. With wartime urgency for creating new multilateral institutions fading away, and in the face of Republican opposition, the US Executive announced that it would no longer seek approval of the ITO at the end of 1950. This ended any chance of the ITO coming into being. However, with continued interest in implementing the agreed schedule of tariff reductions, the GATT, through its Protocol of Provisional Application, came to be applied as a treaty application under international law. Although the GATT was not an organization and its existence was provisional, it not only succeeded in reducing tariffs and other barriers to trade through several rounds of multilateral trade negotiations sponsored by it, but also maintained a continuing commitment (despite deviations) by the major contracting parties to a liberal world trading order. The latest round, the Uruguay Round, the longest and most contentious but also with the largest number of participants including many developing countries for the first time, has not only consolidated and extended the achievements of the earlier rounds, but has also brought the WTO into being.

At the signing of the Final Act, the ministers also agreed to set up a preparatory committee for the WTO with four subcommittees, Budget, Finance and Administration; Institutional, Procedural and Legal Matters; Trade and Environment; and Services. The last has three negotiating groups, on maritime transport, movement of natural persons, and basic telecommunications. A fourth on financial services is under consideration.

According to the press summary issued by the Information and Media Relations Division of the GATT (1994, 5), the WTO is

> a single institutional framework encompassing the GATT,
> as modified by the Uruguay Round, all agreements and
> arrangements concluded under its auspices and the com-

plete results of the Uruguay Round. Its structure will be headed by a Ministerial Conference meeting at least once every two years. A General Council will be established to oversee the operation of the Agreement and ministerial decisions on a regular basis. This General Council will it- self act as a Dispute Settlement Body and a Trade Policy Review Mechanism, which will concern themselves with the full range of trade issues covered by the WTO, and will also establish subsidiary bodies such as a Goods Council, a Services Council and a TRIPs Council. The WTO frame- work will ensure a "single undertaking approach" to the results of the Uruguay Round—thus, membership in the WTO will entail accepting all the results of the Round without exception. The WTO will also manage the plurilat- eral arrangements not covered by the Uruguay Round (Trade in Civil Aircraft, Government Procurement, Dairy Products and Bovine Meat).

The structure of the WTO is shown in Figure 8.1. The value of a single institutional framework can hardly be overemphasized.

The Final Act includes several agreements that go far beyond the GATT of 1947 as subsequently amended. These include agreements on: Agriculture, Sanitary and Phytosanitary measures, Textiles and Clothing, Technical Barriers to Trade, Trade-Related Investment Measures (TRIMS), Anti-Dumping, Customs Valuation, Preshipment Inspection, Rules of Origin, Import Licensing Procedures, Subsidies and Countervailing Meas- ures, Safeguards, Trade in Services, Trade-Related Intellectual Property Rights (TRIPS) including Trade in Counterfeit Goods, Dispute Settlement Mechanism, Trade Policy Review Mechanism, and Government Procure- ment. To bring about greater coherence in global economic policy making and to achieve expansion of trade, sustainable growth and development, and the timely correction of external imbalances, the WTO is called upon to develop its cooperation with the Bretton Woods institutions. The Final Act includes, unfortunately in my view, a commitment to implement the 1979 decisions of the GATT contracting parties on Differential and More Favorable Treatment relating to least developed countries. It also allows a slower pace of reduction of their trade barriers and a longer period of im- plementation for all developing countries with respect to those obligations from which they are not exempted. I would argue that, contrary to widely held belief, such special and differential treatment is not in the best interests of developing countries: these either eliminate altogether or delay

Figure 8.1
Structure of the WTO

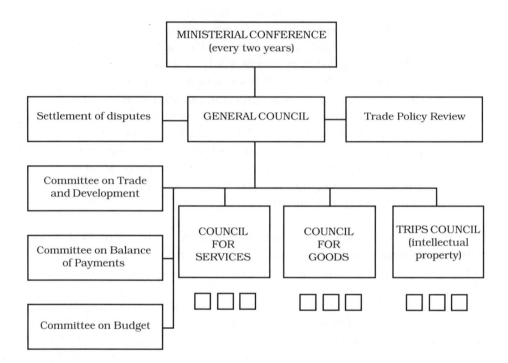

☐ Committees set up to administer the various arrangements

Source: GATT *Focus* (1994).

the benefits that developing countries could reap with rapid and full integration into the world economy.

The Final Act is over 450 pages long and contains "28 agreements and appended to by some 26,000 pages of national tariff and services schedules" (GATT Focus 1994, 1). The document, and particularly the passages in legal language, are not exactly transparent. It is virtually impossible to provide a comprehensive assessment of the likely impact of such a complex agreement on the Asian developing economies (ADEs) or for that matter any other set of economies. However, according to the analysis of the GATT Secretariat (1994, 6),

- Estimates of the increase in world income from the liberalization of trade in goods range from a low of $109 billion to a high of $510 billion in 2005 (the end of the implementation period), depending on which version of the economic model is used. The view of the GATT Secretariat is that the assumptions underlying the $510 billion figure more closely approximate the real world economy.

- The upper range assumptions yield estimated annual income gains of $122 billion for the United States, $164 billion for the European Communities, $27 billion for Japan and $116 billion for developing and transition economies as a group.

- Estimates of the increase in the volume of world trade in goods range from 9 to 24 percent once the liberalization has been fully implemented; in terms of actual 1992 trade flows, the gains would range from $244 billion to $668 billion (since trade in 2005 would have been larger than trade in 1992 in any case, the actual value increases due to the Round are very likely to be larger).

- All versions of the model estimate that the percentage increase in the exports and imports of the developing and transition economies as a group will be 50 percent above the average increase for the world as a whole.

The same document suggests that even the high estimate of a $510 billion increase in global income is an understatement of the likely actual gains from the Uruguay Round for three reasons. First, the estimate ignores dynamic effects. Second, the avoidance of a large loss that would have been the inevitable consequence of the failure of the Round should be counted as part of the gains from the Round. Third, the gains arising from other aspects of the final act besides liberalization of trade in goods are ignored.

The estimates of the global and regional gains in real income by other researchers are more modest and also span a wide range. Francois et al. (1995) estimate them to be in the range of $125-251 billion, and Harrison et al. (1995) place them in the range of $52-113 billion. Brown et al. (1995) put the figures at $205 billion.

Market access will expand and become more secure with the implementation of the Final Act. Among the important actions in this regard are (GATT Secretariat 1994, 6-7):

- Developed countries have agreed to reduce their tariffs on industrial goods from an average of 6.3 percent to 3.8 percent, a 40 percent reduction.
- The proportion of industrial products which enter the developed country markets under MFN zero duties will more than double, from 20 to 44 percent ... the proportion of imports into developed countries from all sources that encounter tariffs above 15 percent will decline from 7 to 5 percent, and from 9 to 5 percent for imports from developing economies.
- Minimum market access commitments on agricultural products subject to tariffication will create market opportunities for, among other products, 1.8 million tons of coarse grains, 1.1 million tons of rice, 807,000 tons of wheat and 729,000 tons of dairy products.
- Other reforms in agriculture include a 36 percent reduction in export subsidies, from $22.5 billion to $14.5 billion (of which one-half is accounted for by the European Union), and a decline of 18 percent, from $197 billion to $162 billion in domestic support to agricultural products.
- In the case of industrial products, the percentage of *bound* tariff lines has risen from 78 to 99 percent for developed countries, from 21 to 73 percent for developing economies, and from 73 to 98 percent for transition economies—results that provide a substantially higher degree of market security for traders and investors.
- While the overall level of protection of agricultural products in most developed countries will remain well above the level of protection of industrial products, agricultural trade has been put squarely on the path of liberalization.
- Following the first multilateral negotiation of its kind, most developed countries have made market access commitments on the great majority of the most important trade services—the main exceptions being telecommunications and maritime transport, which are both the subject of ongoing negotiations, and the audiovisual sector.

In what follows, I discuss the implications of those parts of the Final Act that are likely to be of primary interest from the perspective of most, if not all, ADEs. These relate to agriculture, services, textiles and clothing, and trade-related intellectual property rights (TRIPS) and investment measures (TRIMS). Also, the understanding in the Final Act of the interpretation of GATT Article XXIV relating to customs unions (CU) and free trade areas (FTA) appears to ease the requirements for "GATT-compatibility" of any future CU or FTA such as an expanded ASEAN, or a South Asian preferential trading arrangement. Besides the actual provisions in the Final Act, there are two other areas in which future decisions in the WTO might have significant consequences for ADEs. These are the use of trade policy measures to achieve environmental goals, and the linking of market access to performance in nontrade-related areas such as labor standards and human rights. I discuss these as well.

In the next section, I turn to liberalization of agricultural trade. The following sections consider textiles and clothing, and the proposed preferential trading arrangements in Asia in the post-Uruguay Round global trading system. I then take a critical look at the demand for harmonization of domestic policies for protecting the environment as a precondition for free trade, and linking market access to labor standards. The Uruguay Round results on Nontariff measures are then summarized, and the paper concludes with brief remarks on Services, TRIMS, and TRIPS.

Agricultural Trade Liberalization

Almost all governments in developed as well as developing countries have massively intervened, and continue to do so, in agricultural production, consumption, and trade. Long ago GATT (1979, 7) pointed out that:

> When GATT rules were originally drafted in the 1940s, they were intended to apply to trade in agricultural and industrial products alike. Things have worked out differently however. Agriculture has been virtually excluded from the broad sweep of trade liberalization and insulated from the normal disciplines of market forces and international competition....

According to Parikh et al. (1988), agricultural trade until the end of the 1960s was conducted by either completely bypassing GATT rules or by obtaining exemptions and waivers from their applications. The Kennedy Round (1963-1967) of multilateral trade negotiations did not accomplish much on agricultural trade, primarily because of the conflict between efficient agricultural producers such as the US, which wanted liberalization of trade, and the less efficient European Community, which preferred to manage agricultural trade through commodity agreements in order to protect its agriculture and raise farm incomes. During the Tokyo Round, there was some progress with liberalization of trade in a number of products and an agreement was reached on dairy products and bovine meat. There was a compromise on subsidies though its application to agriculture was rather general. In sum, until the Uruguay Round, agricultural trade was largely outside the GATT framework. (For a history of agriculture in the GATT see Hathaway 1987).

The agreement on agriculture under the Uruguay Round is claimed to "provide a framework for the long-term reform of agricultural trade and domestic policies over the years to come. It makes a decisive move toward the objective of increased market orientation in agricultural trade. The rules governing agricultural trade are strengthened which will lead to improved predictability and stability for importing and exporting countries alike" (Information and Media Relations Division 1994, 8). It encourages the use of less trade-distorting domestic support measures, although countries are allowed some flexibility in implementing the change, albeit under rather stringent conditions.

The most important component of the agreement ostensibly is the requirement that all nontariff border measures be replaced by tariffs that initially provide the same level of protection. Tariffs resulting from this "tariffication" process and other agricultural tariffs are to be reduced over a period of six (ten) years by an average of 36 percent (24 percent) in the case of developed (developing) countries, with minimum reductions required under each tariff line. The tariffication is subject to the maintenance of existing market access opportunities. However, under a "special treatment" clause, a country is allowed to maintain import restrictions until the end of the implementation period under certain carefully and strictly defined circumstances. Developing countries are afforded special and differential treatment, in effect exempting them from the commitment to liberalize with respect to any agricultural product that is a predominant staple in their traditional diet.

Unfortunately, in actual implementation the process of tariffication has resulted in tariff bindings that are much above the prevailing average levels in many cases. Two countries, Japan and the Republic of Korea, have even succeeded in negotiating a delay in tariffication of their very high barriers to rice imports. A few egregious examples of base ad valorem equivalent tariffs (BT) in percentage terms from which the Uruguay Round reductions may take place and their actual average (AA) during 1986–1988 are as follows:

A. Developed Countries

	Rice		Wheat		Coarse Grains		Sugar		Dairy	
	AA	BT	AA	BT	AA	BT	AA	BT	AA	BT
European Union	153.0	360.5	103.0	155.6	133.0	134.4	234.0	297.0	177.0	289.0
United States	1.0	5.0	20.0	6.0	4.0	8.0	131.0	197.0	132.0	144.0
Japan	500.0	*	651.0	239.6	679.0	233.1	184.0	126.1	501.0	489.0

B. Developing Countries

	Rice		Wheat		Coarse Grains		Sugar		Dairy	
	AA	BT	AA	BT	AA	BT	AA	BT	AA	BT
Mexico	6.8	50.0	-1.0	74.0	73.0	174.0	-57.7	173.0	-3.0	66.0
Colombia	4.0	210.0	20.0	138.0	14.0	221.0	25.3	130.0	...	150.0
Korea, Rep. of	213.8	*	...	10.9	421.3	450.0	...	23.7	103.4	220.0
Bangladesh	45.0	200.0	...	200.0	...	200.0	...	200.0		
India			1.8	100.0			...	75.0		
Indonesia	8.8	180.0	...	30.0	6.0	70.0	87.0	110.0		
Thailand	1.0	58.0	...	64.0	...	81.0	...	104.0		
Nigeria	74.9	230.0	249.0	230.0	250.2	230.0	31.7	230.0		

* Tariffication delayed

... data not available

Source: Hathaway and Ingco (1995, Tables 2a and 2b).

If countries choose to apply these bindings and phase their Uruguay Round reductions from them, then paradoxically agricultural protection will increase rather than decrease in the immediate future. Hopefully this will not come about.

Domestic support measures with no or only a minimal impact on trade (the so-called "green box" policies) need not be reduced. In particular, income support to agricultural producers that is "decoupled" from production could continue. Research, disease control, infrastructure, and food security policies are among the "green box" policies. Other policies, such as direct payments to limit production and those that encourage agricultural and rural development, are also excluded from the purview of reduction commitments as long as they do not in all account for more than five (ten) percent of the value of production in the case of developed (developing) countries. Nonexcluded support has to be reduced by 20 (13.3) percent by developed (developing) countries during the implementation period. As in tariffication, there appear to be loopholes in the implementation of reductions in domestic support measures. The main farm programs of the US and the European Union (EU) are exempted, and recently Japan increased its direct payments to farmers. Of course, the least developed countries are not required to make any reduction. Direct export subsidies by developed (developing) countries are to be reduced over six (ten) years to a level 36 (24) percent below the 1986-1990 base period level, and the quantity of subsidized exports by 21 (14) percent. It would appear that these commitments are likely to be most liberalizing since they are much harder to evade. Once again, least developed countries are exempted.

While the formally agreed upon liberalization is indeed substantial, with high levels of bound or base level tariffs resulting from the tariffication process, fairly long implementation periods, and with exemptions (albeit under special circumstances) permitted and with many (albeit minimally) trade-distorting policies allowed to continue, it is hard to judge the short-term to medium-term impact of liberalization. As such I draw on several model-based simulations of the likely long-term impact of liberalization. Most of these simulations consider only liberalization of direct interventions in agricultural trade. However, as Krueger et al. (1988) have shown, the protection or liberalization of agriculture in developing countries arising from indirect measures (such as exchange rate overvaluation and protection of industry) is much stronger than those arising from direct measures. However, the liberalization of nonagricultural trade envisaged under the Final Act will reduce indirect distortion of agricultural trade to some extent.

There have been many studies estimating the effects of liberalizing agricultural trade. Some studies (Parikh et al. 1988 and those reported in Goldin and Knudsen 1990) were done prior to the completion of the Uruguay Round. Others (e.g., Brandão and Martin 1993) were based on the extent of liberalization in the draft of the Uruguay Round agreement (proposed by Arthur Dunkel, the then Director General of GATT) rather than the actual offers and commitments in the Final Act as signed. Table 8.1 presents the broad orders of magnitude of the impact of the liberalization assessed by the most recent studies that translate the various components of the schedules of bindings, offers, and commitments into reductions in trade barriers as specified in their models. These studies include Brown et al. (1995), Francois et al. (1995), Goldin and Mensbrugghe (1995), and Harrison et al. (1995). Their models differ in many respects: levels of aggregation with respect to consumers, commodities and countries, parameter estimates including in particular their actual or implied elasticities of supply, demand or substitution in production or consumption, assumptions regarding scale economies and market structure, their base periods etc. I will not discuss the models since even to describe each model meaningfully, let alone their differences and the relative strengths and weaknesses, will require a lot of space. However, there is no alternative methodology that I know of, other than some type of economywide and global modeling exercise, for assessing the overall effect of simultaneous change in the trade policies of several countries. As such, although the absolute magnitudes of the changes in production, consumption, trade, and welfare are noncomparable across studies, the changes relative to some normalizing magnitudes such as gross domestic product (GDP) or their magnitudes in a base scenario of no change in policies are likely to be comparable. The results reported in Table 8.1 are to be assessed with these caveats in mind. The striking feature of Table 8.1 is the relatively small effect of liberalization, perhaps reflecting the fact that once "dirty tariffication" and exemptions are taken into account, the extent of liberalization is modest. Although there are some changes of sign across models of the effects on particular countries or regions, almost all the estimates for Africa are negative, though not large.

From the perspective of Asian developing economies, the existing quantitative restrictions (for example, in India and other South Asian economies) on agricultural trade and domestic support measures (e.g., subsidies on fertilizers, irrigation, credit, etc.) could be subject to the phase-out provisions of the Final Act. As noted earlier, the "special treatment" clause allows any country under certain conditions to maintain import restrictions up to the end of the ten-year implementation period and the "special and differential" treatment applicable to developing countries. But even without these loopholes, many countries have bound their tariffs at very high levels. Under these circumstances few, if any, of the ADEs are likely to be required to make any substantial changes in their interventions in agricultural production and trade under the Final Act. Of course, there is nothing in it to rule out such changes should some countries wish to make them in their own interest, indeed they should be encouraged to do so.

Table 8.1. **Welfare (Real Income) Effects of Liberalization of Agricultural Trade**

Country/Region	Brown et al. (1995) $billion[1]	Francois et al. (1995) (% of GDP)2	Goldin and Mensbrugghe (1995) (% of GDP)[3]	Harrison et al. (1995)[4] ($ billion)
I. Developed Countries				
Australia and New Zealand	-0.197	(0.17, 0.27)	(0.0, 0.6)	(1.082, 1.709)
Canada	-0.514	(0.11, 0.21)	(-0.2, 0.4)	(0.244, 0.280)
European Union	-0.899	(0.01, 0.12)	(0.1, 1.9)	(16.236, 8.194)
Japan	12.290	(-0.03, -0.01)	(0.2, 1.6)	(6.632, 7.757)
US		(-0.01, -0.01)	(0.0, 0.2)	(2.248, 4.372)
II. Asian Developing Countries				
China, People's Rep. of		(0.03, 0.09)	(-0.1, -0.2)	(-0.533, -0.530)
India			(0.0, 0.8)	
Indonesia			(0.1, 0.5)	(0.016, 0.115)
Rep. of Korea				(2.646, 2.927)
Malaysia				(0.356, 0.792)
Philippines				(0.116, 0.258)
Taipei,China				(0.117, -0.045)
Thailand				(0.541, 1.049)
Asian NICs	0.199			
East Asia				
South Asia		(-0.10, 0.05)		(0.222, 0.263)
Low Income Asia		(-0.10, -0.05)	(0.0, 0.4)	
Upper Income Asia			(0.8, 4.9)	
III. Other Regions				
Sub-Saharan Africa				(-0.103, -0.059)
Africa		(-0.73, 1.79)	(-0.5, -0.2)	
Latin America		(0.02, 0.19)	(-0.3, 0.4)	
IV. World		(0.02, 0.04)		(34.824, 9.498)

Notes:

[1] European Union includes also Norway and Switzerland. Asian Newly Industrializing Countries (NICs) include Hong Kong, Republic of Korea, Singapore, and Taipei,China.

[2] The interval covers the range of estimated welfare effects in six variants, three each for constant returns to scale and perfect competition and for increasing returns to scale and imperfect competition models. Within each model the variants cover the case of no change in capital stock and two cases of endogenous changes in capital stock, one brought about by fixed savings rates, and the other by endogenously changing savings rates.

[3] The interval covers the range of estimates from six scenarios that vary in the base level tariffs from which the Uruguay Round reductions take place, whether or not inputs subsidies are included and so on. Africa in this column excludes Nigeria and South Africa and Latin America excludes Brazil and Mexico.

[4] The interval covers the two estimates from the base model and the steady state version of the base model. Except for the European Union, steady effects were always larger.

Textiles and Clothing

This is perhaps the most important sector from the perspective of developing economies in general and poorer ADEs in particular. The percentage share of merchandise exports accounted for by textiles and clothing for the ADEs in 1992 was as follows (World Bank 1994a, Table 8.15): Nepal 85, Bangladesh 72, India 25, Pakistan 69, Sri Lanka 52, Indonesia 18, Philippines 10, Malaysia 6, Republic of Korea 20, Singapore 5, Hong Kong 40. As is by now well known, what started out in 1961 as a short-term agreement mainly to restrain the growth of Japanese exports of cotton textiles soon became a long-term agreement, and by 1974 expanded to include trade in textiles and clothing made with other fibers (natural and man–made). Thus it became the Multifibre Arrangement (MFA) under which each exporting country gets and administers a bilaterally agreed quota of exports to each market. The current MFA IV expires at the end of 1994. Over time the MFA has become increasingly restrictive.

Under the Final Act, MFA will be eliminated in three stages over a period of ten years from January 1, 1995. During each stage, annual growth in the import quotas on those products that are still under restraint will be increased by no less than 16 percent per year over MFA IV in Stage 1 (until 1998), by no less than 25 percent over Stage 1 in Stage 2 (1998-2001), and finally by no less than 27 percent over Stage 2 in Stage 3 (2002-2004). As soon as the agreement comes into force, products which accounted for not less than 16 percent of 1990 imports will be integrated into the GATT. At the beginning of Stage 2 (Stage 3) a further 17 percent (18 percent) will be integrated. All the remaining products will be integrated on January 1, 2005. At each of the first three stages, products are to be chosen from each of the following categories: tops and yarns, fabrics, made-up textile products, and clothing. Although the phase-out of the MFA is backloaded (in fact, products accounting for as much as 49 percent of the value of 1990 imports could still be under quota restrictions as of the end of the ten-year period, i.e., on December 31, 2004), the growth in quotas during the transition period will not only yield substantial benefits but will also make lobbying harder for interest groups opposed to the abolition of the MFA. They will have to lobby for an extension of the quota system of MFA and for a slowdown in the growth of quotas, a difficult task.[2] The transitional safe-guard mechanism that is part of the agreement could be invoked (albeit under restrictive conditions) to slow down the phase-out even further. However, quotas imposed under these safeguards have to be terminated by January 1, 2005. As such they could not be used to extend the MFA. Even with these caveats taken into account, substantial opportunities for increasing textiles and clothing exports for poorer ADEs, particularly from South Asia, are likely to arise in the coming decade.

A number of studies on the restrictive effects of the MFA on exporters and on welfare of consumers in individual countries and the likely consequences of its phase out are available (Cline 1990, De Melo and Tarr 1990, Francois et al. 1995, Goto 1989, Harrison et al. 1995, Hertel et al. 1995, Hufbauer and Elliott 1994, Trela and Whalley 1990). The most recent of these estimates are shown in Table 8.2. As is to be expected, the estimates from different models differ both in magnitude and sometimes in sign. Yet they agree in projecting a substantial gain for the US and the EU. Among developing countries, the People's Republic of China and South Asia gain by most estimates. Africa and Latin America stand to lose by all estimates.

Srinivasan and Canonero (1993b) project a substantial increase in trade in textiles and clothing for the South Asian economies once it is liberalized. Their projections are based on their parameter estimates from a gravity model of bilateral trade flows during 1968–1991. The expected increase in clothing exports as a percentage of total bilateral trade of selected South Asian countries consequent to liberalization by major partners in the industrial world are as follows:

Trading Partners	Bangladesh	India	Nepal	Pakistan	Sri Lanka
US	5.7	9.8	4.1	10.2	1.8
EU	10.4	20.1	86.0	22.3	3.6
Japan	0.9	1.3	0.5	8.7	1.6

Although these figures are impressive, caution is needed in interpreting them since the existing quotas under the MFA permit exports also from countries that are not internationally competitive. With its phase-out, a very competitive export market will emerge. Unless poorer Asian exporters can compete in cost as well as quality, they might not be able to maintain, let alone increase, their share in growing world export markets.

Table 8.2. **Welfare Effects of Liberalization of Trade
in Textiles and Apparel**

Country/Region	Francois et al. (1995) (% of GDP)[1]	Harrison et al. (1995) ($ billion)[2]	Hertel et al. (1995) (% of GDP)
I. Developed Countries			
EU	(0.14, 0.36)	(6.173, 6.417)	0.32
Japan	(-0.06, 0.10)	(-0.370, -0.239)	0.03
US	(0.17, 0.41)	(6.838, 7.436)	0.29
Canada	(-0.08, 0.18)	(0.601, 0.605)	
II. Asian Developing Countries			
China, People's Rep. of	(1.20, 5.17)	(-0.433, 0.098)	0.42
East Asia	(-0.18, 3.67)	(-1.481, -1.156)	
Hong Kong			
Indonesia		(-0.002, 0.276)	1.10
Malaysia		(-0.121, 0.009)	-0.63
Philippines		(-0.167, -0.046)	-0.18
Singapore		(-0.264, -0.256)	
South Asia	(0.85, 4.77)	(-0.451, 0.250)	0.35
Taipei,China		(-0.436, -0.322)	
Thailand		(-0.150, 0.176)	0.32
III. Other Regions			
Latin America	(-0.05, 0.24)	(-0.556, -0.498)	-0.27
Sub-Saharan Africa		(-0.179, -0.103)	-0.24
Africa	(-0.06, 0.24)		
IV. World	(0.12 0.56)	(7.728, 9.889)	0.59

Notes:
    [1] The interval covers the range of estimated welfare effects in six variants, three each for constant returns to scale and perfect competition and for increasing returns to scale and imperfect competition models. Within each model the variants cover the case of no change in capital stock and two cases of endogenous changes in capital stock, one brought about by fixed savings rates, and the other by endogenously changing savings rates.
    [2] The interval covers the range of estimates from six scenarios that vary in the base level tariffs from which the Uruguay Round reductions take place, whether or not input subsidies are included and so on.

Preferential Trading Arrangements in the Post-Uruguay Round Trading System: South and East Asia[3]

In spite of the many failed attempts at regional integration and preferential trading arrangements (RIA and PTA respectively), regionalism became popular again in the late 1980s, even as the Uruguay Round negotiations were under way. The most celebrated and recent of the regional agreements is the North American Free Trade Agreement (NAFTA) between Canada, Mexico, and the US, signed in 1992 and approved by the legislatures of all three countries by the end of 1993. It superseded and was preceded by the Canada-US Free Trade Agreement of 1989. Mercosur, an agreement between Argentina, Brazil, Paraguay, and Uruguay to form a common market, was signed in 1991. The Asia Pacific Economic Cooperation (APEC) was formed in 1989 as a consultative body dealing with such issues as harmonization of customs data and exchange of information on marine pollution and so on. Although the report of an Eminent Persons Group presented at its 1993 summit meeting called for APEC to become an Asian Pacific Economic Community and to take specific steps toward the establishment of an ASEAN Free Trade Area, the members then appeared to be deeply divided about the nature and degree of future cooperation. Yet there was a clamor to join APEC—Mexico, Chile, and Papua New Guinea had already applied for membership and India, Pakistan, Macao, Sri Lanka, Russia, Ecuador, and Peru had expressed an interest in applying (Financial Times 1993). At its 1994 summit meeting, it was decided that members will trade freely with each other by 2020.

Many scholars and organizations (including GATT and the World Bank) have written on and held conferences on the recent increase in popularity of regionalism (Anderson and Blackhurst 1993, Bliss 1994, De Melo and Panagariya 1993, Hufbauer and Schott 1994, and Lawrence 1994, to mention just a few). Anderson and Blackhurst (1993) attribute the popularity as induced in part by two events. The first was the admission of Greece, Portugal, and Spain into the European Community and the agreement to remove all internal barriers on the movement of goods, services, capital, and labor by 1992. The second was the conclusion of the Canada-US Free Trade Agreement of 1989. Although the two events were largely independent of each other and had little to do with the failure to conclude the Uruguay Round by December 1990 as originally envisaged, Anderson and Blackhurst suggest, plausibly, that the rest of the world saw the two events and the difficulties of concluding the Uruguay Round negotiations as indicating that the future of the multilateral and liberal framework of GATT was uncertain. This led them to seek membership in the existing or newly established PTAs.

Whalley (1993, 352) also attributes a key role, among factors explaining the enthusiasm for PTAs, to the "search for safe-haven trade agreements by smaller countries who now, more than ever before, wish to secure markets of large neighboring trading partners because of the fear of higher trade barriers in the future." Besides this fear on the part of small countries, Whalley also sees a strategic motive on the part of some large countries which, by threatening to negotiate, or actually negotiating, regional arrangements, may be able to force other reluctant large powers to make concessions multilaterally which they are apparently unwilling to make in the Uruguay Round negotiations. Since growth of trade between neighboring countries in recent times has exceeded that of global trade, Whalley suggests that regional PTAs are now being viewed more positively as accelerating further the already dynamic portion of world trade. Perroni and Whalley (1994) confirm with numerical simulations from their general equilibrium trade model of tariff retaliation that recent regional trade agreements are indeed safe-haven or insurance arrangements sought by smaller countries who have paid premiums in the form of non-trade concessions to large countries (e.g., side agreements signed by Mexico with respect to labor and environment as part of NAFTA mainly to mollify opponents of NAFTA in the US). They find that the value of such agreements to large countries rises as the risk of global trade conflict rises, since the enhanced risk will naturally lead to larger premiums extractable from smaller countries. At the noncooperative Nash Equilibrium of a tariff war, they estimate the real income losses compared to a 1986 status quo to be 6 percent for the global economy, 11 percent for the developing countries and the rest of the world, 26 percent for Canada, and 32 percent for Europe outside the EU. Only the US and EU gain real income, of 41 percent and 4 percent respectively. Viewed in this light, the recent proliferation of PTAs is a serious threat to the global trading system.

Bhagwati, a committed warrior in the cause of a multilateral process of trade liberalization, raises a number of searching questions as to the compatibility of the liberal-multilateral-nondiscriminatory framework for the world trading system with discriminatory PTAs in his critical overview of regionalism and multilateralism (Bhagwati 1993). In particular, he asks whether the immediate impact of preferential trading blocs is to reduce rather than increase world welfare and, regardless of the immediate effect, whether a dynamic time-path of expansion of regional blocs will get the world closer to the goal of multilateral free trade for all than multilateralism as the process of trade negotiation will.

To ensure a negative response to his first question, Bhagwati would minimize the potential world welfare, reducing the immediate effects of trading blocs by replacing the existing Article XXIV of the GATT on PTAs by ruling out all PTAs other than customs unions and insisting that the common external tariff of any customs union on any item be the lowest tariff of any union member on that item prior to the union. While recognizing the practical problems of its implementation, Bhagwati also endorses a simple aggregative test proposed by McMillan (1991) for the admissibility of a customs union or a PTA, "does the bloc result in less trade between member countries and outsider countries?" This test is based on balancing the classic Vinerian benefits of trade creation against the costs of trade diversion.

On Bhagwati's second question, there is very little[4] by way of analytical and empirical results in the literature other than the well-known proposition of Kemp and Wan (1976) that a common external tariff could be found that makes at least some residents of a customs union better off while not hurting any citizen of nonmembers, as compared to the pre-union situation. Thus, the Kemp-Wan proposition shows the existence of a dynamic path toward multilateral free trade for all through customs unions that is monotonically increasing in world welfare. But there is no reason to believe that such a path would in fact be followed. Bhagwati finds unpersuasive the argument that regionalism is a quicker, more efficient, and more certain process toward multilateral free trade for all. While judging the recent revival of regionalism to be unfortunate, he nonetheless recognizes that only time will tell whether regionalism has been a benign or a malign force.

I noted above that the enthusiasm for regionalism in part reflected uncertainty about the conclusion of the Uruguay Round. Since this uncertainty has disappeared with the signing of the Final Act, is it time to pronounce "Regionalism is dead and long live the new World Trade Organisation!"? A recent paper of the World Bank (1994b) suggests that it is premature to pronounce the death of regionalism. The reason is that the "new regionalism" is qualitatively different from earlier cycles of regional integration. It envisages deep integration going beyond conventional trade arrangements and addresses not only trade in goods, but also the liberalization of trade in services, movements of labor and capital, the harmonization of regulatory regimes, and the coordination of domestic policies that influence international competitiveness.

Even though the mere fact that the "new regionalism" covers many more issues than the earlier ones is not in itself a strong argument in its favor, policymakers appear to believe it to be so. This suggests that regionalism is unlikely to fade away. It is therefore worth examining whether particular regional arrangements within Asia, such as South Asian or East Asian or even Pan Asian preferential trading arrangements, make sense. Further, there are three special features of a possible South Asian integration which the voluminous literature on economic integration has not adequately analyzed. First, the large economy of India could be viewed as a common market of its many states. This in turn means that, in the formation of the market, potential international trade with neighbors could have been diverted to internal trade among states, since transport costs (as a proportion of price) on internal trade could be significantly less than the tariff rates applicable to international trade.

Clearly, regional integration could then replace internal trade in the large country with international trade. For example, with integration, trade flows between the southern states (Tamilnadu and Kerala, for example) of India and Sri Lanka, the eastern states (Assam, Bihar, and West Bengal) and Bangladesh, northwestern states (Haryana, Punjab, and Rajasthan) and Pakistan and so on, could exceed significantly the pre-integration trade flows between the relevant pairs of countries. Second, trade among neighbors could easily include trade in goods and services (e.g., electricity) that are usually treated as nontraded. For example, between Bangladesh, India, and Nepal, such trade could be potentially significant. Third, in the pre-integration situation with significant trade barriers of differing intensity, illegal trade between neighbors usually flourishes. If the internal barriers of the neighbors differ substantially, then it is also possible that goods from the rest of the world enter the low barrier country legally and then are smuggled into the high barrier neighbor. Clearly regional integration by eliminating trade barriers among neighbors would substantially reduce the incentives for illegal trade flows. These three reasons alone suggest that an extension of the existing analytical literature on regional integration is desirable in considering such integration of South Asia. Srinivasan and Canonero (1993a) formulate a bare-bones analytical model intended to capture the first two effects.

It is difficult to anticipate the impact on a potential South Asian bloc (whose structure could range all the way from some loose preferential trading arrangement to full economic integration) of other actual and potential blocs with yet to be decided structures. An attempt has been made (Srinivasan and Canonero 1993b) to assess such impacts, however imprecise they might be, using a gravity-type quantitative model explaining bilateral trade flows among South Asian countries and the rest of the world, grouped into relevant countries and regions. Srinivasan (1994a) summarizes the results of numerical simulations from the theoretical models and projections from empirical models of Srinivasan and Canonero (1993a, 1993b). Effects of preferential trade liberalization to the full extent (i.e., eliminating all tariff barriers among partners) as well as a more limited multilateral liberalization of about 25 percent reduction in all tariffs, are projected. The latter is meant to capture the effect of the Uruguay Round reduction.

Their estimates of the expected increase in trade with complete liberalization on a preferential basis are very large, in fact too large to be totally credible. However, these should not be viewed as forecasts but only as indicating the broad orders of magnitude of potential increases.[5] It is clear that the greatest proportional increase expected in bilateral trade would come from regional integration. The countries in the region all have higher tariffs than other countries and therefore a larger impact from reduction in their tariffs should be expected. For example, trade between Bangladesh and other South Asian countries is expected to increase by 9.5 times, and almost the same is the case for Pakistan (8.9). For Sri Lanka, the expected proportional increase is about 10.3 times, for India 12.8 times, while for Nepal this increase is even higher, at 17.2 times. However, given the initial trade pattern of these countries, regional integration leads to a greater increase in trade for Bangladesh and Nepal than for the other South Asian countries.

For the two small economies of Bangladesh and Nepal, regional integration seems to be the most powerful preferential arrangement for trade creation. The values of expected increases in trade are incredible. Bangladesh's new trade with the region would account for $4.6 billion, exceeding its actual total trade of $3.8 billion by 17 percent, and accounting for a whopping 21.1 percent of its GNP.

In the case of Nepal, the trade expected to be created in the region is around $1.7 billion. Though this is smaller than that for Bangladesh, it is no less impressive considering the (economic) size of Nepal. The new trade would be almost three times the actual total trade of Nepal and 58.5 percent of its GNP.

The effects of regional integration on the large economies in the region, India or Pakistan, are naturally very different from those of Bangladesh and Nepal. For India and Pakistan, regional integration is important, but their much larger trade with the EU and US makes integration with the latter more attractive. Both countries would achieve the greatest impact on their trade by integrating their economies with the EU, for India, bilateral trade would increase by twice its actual total trade, while for Pakistan the corresponding figure is around 0.95. Translating these effects into US dollars, new bilateral trade between India and the EU would amount to $85 billion, representing 30 percent of India's GNP. For Pakistan, these figures would be $13 billion and 30 percent.

There is significant trade expansion from a modest nonpreferential 25 percent reduction in tariffs on all commodities by all countries (this is meant to represent, in an aggregate sense, the expected reduction in various tariff and nontariff barriers once the Uruguay Round agreement is fully enforced). For example, for India, total trade with the US and Canada increases by 9.4 percent of its 1990-1991 value, with East Asia by 8.2 percent and the rest of the world by 20.5 percent. On the other hand, for the land-locked and smallest economy, Nepal, the gain in trade volume is largest (14.3 percent) with the rest of the world trade, with its neighbors in South Asia being a close second at 12.9 percent—trade with the EU and East Asia expands by approximately equal amounts of 10.5 percent and 10.7 percent, respectively.

Used with appropriate caution and awareness of their limitations, the simulations from the two theoretical models of Srinivasan and Canonero (1993a) do have a few policy implications for South Asian countries. Given the substantial transport costs associated with internal trade within the large countries of the region, and also with trade between each of the countries of the region and their major trading partners outside the region, preferential liberalization of trade within the region could lead to a significant increase in intraregional trade that would be beneficial to all partners. However, even larger gains could be achieved by liberalizing trade with all partners. The second model also suggests that removal of trade barriers within the region (preferentially or on a most-favoured nation basis) could generate trade in goods and services, the demand for which is currently being entirely met by domestic supply in each country. Since some of these would be infrastructure services (e.g., power), whose production involves scale economies (not modeled) and whose limited and erratic supply inhibits efficient production of other goods, a more rational investment, production, and trade pattern could lead not only to a once-and-for-all improvement in efficiency of production of all goods and services, but also a more rapid growth. The growth-enhancing effect could be significant, with the prospect of supplying to a larger market following trade liberalization attracting direct foreign investment into infrastructure sectors.

The following main conclusions based on the findings of the empirical study of Srinivasan and Canonero (1993b) should stimulate further consideration of options for regionalism in South Asia.

- Unilateral trade liberalization still promises substantial gains. The continuation of unilateral trade liberalization efforts by each of the South Asian countries would indeed yield substantial benefits. From a strategic perspective, however, it might be easier to increase its momentum if liberalization is part of a coordinated effort in all of South Asia, with liberalized access being extended to the rest of the world on a most-favored nation principle.
- Potential gains in intraregional South Asia trade are substantial. The low transport costs between countries in the subcontinent come into play once tariffs begin to be reduced. The simulations suggest some orders of magnitude. If all tariffs on intra-South Asia trade are removed, total trade increases by between 3 percent of GDP (India) and 59 percent of GDP (Nepal) — and in between for the other countries. For more modest tariff reductions, say 50 percent, trade increases by between 1 percent of GDP for

India and 9 percent of GDP for Nepal. The increases are much larger, in proportional terms, for the smaller countries (Nepal, Sri Lanka, and Bangladesh, in declining order of gains) than for the larger countries (Pakistan and India, again in declining order of benefits).

- Potential gains in trade for South Asia—across the Big Three trading blocs—are greatest with the EU but for the South Asia region as a whole, analysis based on historical data suggests that a tie-up with the EU would be more beneficial than with either NAFTA or with an East Asian group.
- A strategic tie-up with East Asia may be even more beneficial. Giving more weight to the recent growth of trade between South and East Asia and recognizing that East Asia is the fastest growing region of the world, preliminary analysis and qualitative judgments suggest that a strategic tie-up with an East Asian group is likely to be more beneficial. Such a tie-up might be more consistent with today's realpolitik, because the EU continues to seek ways to accommodate regionalism with Eastern Europe and the states of the former Soviet Union.
- South Asia may do better by approaching one (or more) of the Big Three as a group.[6] The relative gains to individual South Asian countries from linking up with the Big Three vary considerably. For Sri Lanka, Nepal, and Bangladesh the potential gains are similar across the Big Three, and indeed are dominated by those in an intra-South Asian grouping. But for India and Pakistan, the historical dominance of the EU and the prospective benefits of a link with an East Asian group are clearly more beneficial. This suggests that the subcontinent may do better if it approaches one (or more) of the Big Three as a group.

None of the above conclusions imply that regionalism is a first-best approach. Indeed, it is in the interest of South Asia as well as developing countries as a whole that the global trading system is multilateral. Any regional arrangement that weakens the WTO-based trading order is against their long-term interests.

Turning now to East Asia, Panagariya (1993, 43) on the whole takes a pessimistic view of regionalism. His pessimism,

> follows, inter alia, from low or negative gains in the case of sub-regional groupings such as the ASEAN, insurmountable external and internal barriers to effective integration in the case of an Asia wide discriminatory bloc, and ad-

verse terms of trade effects in the case of nondiscrimina-
tory regionalism. In the ultimate, if regionalism is to be
pursued, it is perhaps the last option which holds most
promise. This option has the limitation that it may not offer large opportunities for liberalization and, if it does, the
terms of trade effects of East Asia will be adverse. Yet, it
has the advantage of promoting a more liberal and open
world trading system the gains from which will far outweigh
the losses due to adverse terms of trade effects.

Taken together, the findings of Srinivasan (1994a) and Panagariya
(1993) suggest that the benefits for ADEs from unilateral liberalization on
a most-favored-nation basis are likely to be much higher than those from
regional integration. However, it should be kept in mind that neither study
takes into full account aspects of the new regionalism referred to earlier.

Trade and the Environment[7]
The potency of the contention that fair trade or level playing fields
constitute a precondition for free trade and that, therefore, harmonization
of domestic policies across trading countries is necessary before free
trade can be embraced to advantage, should not be underestimated today. It is nowhere more manifest, and compelling in its policy appeal,
than in the area of environmental standards.

Both the general view that cross-country intra-industry (CCII)
harmonization of environmental standards is required if free trade is to be
implemented, and the specific proposals currently in vogue to implement
this view, are therefore in need of analytical scrutiny.[8] In reviewing and
assessing the demands for CCII harmonization of environmental standards, it is customary to make a distinction of analytical importance between (i) environmental problems that are intrinsically domestic in nature; and (ii) those that are intrinsically international in nature because
they inherently involve "physical" spillovers across national borders.

Thus, if India pollutes a lake that is wholly within its borders, that
is an intrinsically domestic question. If, however, she pollutes a river that
flows into Bangladesh, that is an intrinsically international question. So
are the well-known problems of acid rain, ozone layer depletion, and
global warming. These latter, intrinsically international problems of the
environment raise questions that interface with the trade questions both
in common and in different ways from the former, intrinsically domestic
problems.

It has become commonplace among some environmentalists to
assert that this distinction is of no consequence because domestic envi-

ronmental problems are increasingly seen to have transnational impacts. Science has shown, for instance, that aerosol sprays are not just an environmental nuisance where used; they endanger the planet. But the fact that science seems occasionally to turn local (and partial-equilibrium) environmental impacts into transnational (and general-equilibrium) impacts, is no proof that the former are an empty set. We should not be deterred therefore from using this important conceptual distinction.

It would seem, at first glance, that at least the domestic environmental problems should be matters best left by governments to domestic solutions and within domestic jurisdiction (although transnational, global "educational" and lobbying activities by environmental nongovernmental organizations are compatible with this solution). If a country's preferred environmental choices and solutions (by way of setting pollution standards and taxes) to domestic questions are different from those of another, why should anyone object to the conduct of free trade between the two on the ground that such differences are incompatible with the case for (gains from) free trade? Yet the fact is that they do, and the objections are directed, not merely at free trade, but also at the institutional safeguards and practices, such as the GATT, which are designed to ensure the proper functioning of an open, multilateral trading system that embodies the principles of free trade. These objections mainly take four forms:

- *Unfair Trade.* If you do something different, and especially if you do what appears to be less, concerning the environment than I do in the same industry or sector, this will be considered to be tantamount to lack of "level playing fields" and therefore amounts to "unfair trade" on your part. Free trade, according to this doctrine, is then unacceptable as it requires, as a precondition, "fair trade".

- *Losing Higher Standards.* Then again, the flip side of the "fair trade" argument is the environmentalists' fear that if free trade occurs with countries having "lower" environmental standards, no matter what the justification is for this situation, the effect will be to lower their own standards. This will follow from the political pressure brought to bear on governments to lower standards to ensure the survival of their industry. An associated argument is that capital will move to countries with lower standards, so that countries will engage in a "race to the bottom", each winding up with lower standards than desired because standards are lowered to attract capital from each other.

- *Conflicting Ethical Preferences.* Environmentalists also want at times to impose their ethical preferences, considered "morally superior", on other nations. Free trade in products that offend one's moral sense (either in themselves, or because of the way in which they are produced as in the use of purse nets in catching tuna or the leghold traps in hunting for fur) is then considered objectionable because either trade in such products should be withheld so as to induce or coerce acceptance of such preferences, or such trade should be abandoned, even if it has no effective consequence and might even hurt only oneself, simply because "one should have no truck with the devil".[9] The former argument presumes higher morality on one's behalf, which should be spread to other nations with lower morality (and with corresponding lack of standards/laws therefore to reflect the higher morality). The latter argument seeks no such morally imperial outreach; it simply wants no part in complicity with lower morality elsewhere via participating in gainful free trade with nations guilty of tolerating such lower morality. In either case, the diversity of standards is considered then to be incompatible with the pursuit of free trade.

- *Institutional Vulnerability of High Standards to Countries with Low Standards Fearing Protectionism.* Then, finally, the environmentalists fear that they will lose their high standards, not because market forces under free trade bias the domestic political equilibrium in favor of lower standards or generate a race to the bottom,[10] but because the current "institutional arrangements", at the GATT in particular, enable the low standards countries to object to, and threaten, the high standards in other countries by claiming protectionist intent or consequences, for instance.[11]

Thus, just consider why the first argument concerning the unfair trade of lower CCII standards elsewhere has become such a politically salient issue today. It should suffice to note here that the fear is that competition will be greater if a rival abroad faces lower burdens of environmental regulations, and hence the argument follows that this competitive advantage enjoyed by foreign rivals is illegitimate and must be countervailed, much like dumping or subsidization is, or must be eliminated at the source.

Thus, Senator Boren introduced legislation in the US Congress to countervail the "social dumping" allegedly resulting from lower standards abroad, proposing such a measure on the grounds that some US manufacturers, such as the US carbon and steel alloy industry, spend as much as 250 percent more on environmental controls as a percentage of gross domestic product than do other countries. He saw in this difference an unfair advantage enjoyed by other nations exploiting the environment and public health for economic gain (Boren 1991).

Environmental diversity is, contrary to these assertions, perfectly legitimate, it can arise not merely because the environment is differently valued between countries in the sense that the utility function defined on consumption and pollution abatement is not identical and homothetic, but also because of differences in endowments and technology across countries. In fact, even with homothetic preferences income matters: at the same cost of abatement relative to consumption, a country with ten times the income of another will spend ten times as much on abatement. Forcing the poor country to spend as much on abatement will reduce its welfare substantially. Hence, the common presumption driving harmonization and (alternatively) "social-dumping"-countervailing demands, that others with different CCII standards are illegitimately and unfairly reducing their costs, is untenable.

Nonetheless, these demands are part of a general shift to demands to harmonize a great, and possibly increasing, number of domestic policies: in labor standards, in technology policy, etc. With industries everywhere increasingly open to competition, thanks precisely to the postwar success in dismantling trade barriers, with multinationals spreading technology freely across countries through direct investments, and with capital more free than ever to move across countries, producers now face the prospect that their competitive advantage is fragile and that more industries than ever before are "footloose". There is therefore much more sensitivity to any advantage that rivals abroad may enjoy in world competition, and a propensity therefore to look over their shoulders to find reasons why their advantage is "unfair".

Finally, the demands for CCII harmonization are fed also by the feared adverse effects of free trade and capital flows on the real wages of workers: an issue that became important in the last presidential election in the US. The Clinton campaign focused not only on the failure of the Bush administration to revive the economy, it also made much of the so-called "structural" problem, which is defined by the stagnation of real wages for unskilled workers during the 1980s. At least one of the candidates for explaining this phenomenon has been the integration of the world economy and the consequent competition with poor countries with abundant unskilled labor. While the empirical relevance of this explanation is doubtful, it has powerful appeal. The attempts at globalizing the higher environmental and labor standards, with the latter coming uncomfortably close to attempts at also raising wages in the industrial sectors of the poor countries on human-rights and labor-rights grounds (see the next section), can be seen in fact as indirect ways of trying to reduce the perceived threat to real wages for the unskilled in rich countries from free trade with (and capital outflows to) the poor countries.

If the argument about the adverse effect of trade on wages of the unskilled is really bought, we are back to the old concerns that free trade with poor countries will truly act like free immigration from them: free immigration would directly depress workers' wages, free trade would do so indirectly. These arguments are based on the two justly celebrated theorems of international trade, Samuelson's Factor Price Equalization Theorem and the Stolper-Samuelson Theorem. If the strong assumptions on which the theorems rest do not hold, as is likely to be the case empirically, real wages of unskilled labor could rise when free trade is opened with a country with abundant unskilled labor (Bhagwati and Dehejia 1994). On the other hand, Leamer (1994) claims that some of the empirical estimates of the relative effects of technological change, increased trade, and technical change on US labor markets, are apparently computed in ways that are in direct conflict with the Stolper-Samuelson Theorem. Leamer cites a number of such studies and criticizes the authors for having misunderstood the two theorems and suggests that no firm conclusions can be drawn about the effects of trade without firmly linking theory and empirics.

Given the controversy among scholars, it is not surprising that public sentiment that free trade with poor countries will increasingly depress rich countries' real wages is growing. This is very likely eventually to lead to not just palliatives like the imposition of harmonized environmental and labor standards, but also to attempts at restricting capital outflows (synonymous in politics with "losing jobs") by way of direct foreign investment and other policy demands on them. We witness increasing attempts at encouraging population control in these countries: the prominent US role in the United Nations Conference on Population in Cairo in September 1994 may be explained, at least in part, in this fashion.

It can be shown (Bhagwati and Srinivasan 1995) that the arguments in favor of free trade and diversity of environmental standards across countries are essentially robust. This follows from a straightforward extension of the proposition that, under standard assumptions ensuring perfect competition in all relevant markets, free trade is globally Pareto optimal. Introduction of environmental externalities (domestic or international) necessitates the use of appropriate taxes, subsidies, and transfers to internalize the externality, but does not call for a departure from free trade to achieve a globally Pareto optimal outcome. Still some policy problems do arise in the context of transborder externalities.

Transborder externalities are generally more complex in character than those that arise with purely domestic pollution, and more compelling as well. It may be useful, from a policy viewpoint, to distinguish between two cases: a special case where the problem is simplified by assuming a single country that pollutes the other, raising questions of response such as the use of trade barriers by the other; and a general case where the problem is truly global in character. A good example of the former is US transmission of acid rain to Canada; an excellent example of the latter is global warming, to which many countries contribute while all are affected by it (though each in different degrees, and not all negatively).

The case of one-way transmission of pollution between two countries is helpful because it illustrates in a simple way the problem raised by transborder externalities concerning the use of second-best trade instruments by the injured country when the offending country does not implement a first-best solution and uses its jurisdictional autonomy in the spirit of malign neglect. The principal question then is whether a country that is being damaged by pollution from another has the right to impose a trade restraint to affect the exports, and hence production, and hence the pollution, of the other country.

Thus, suppose that the US is transmitting acid rain to Canada, thanks to sulphur dioxide produced because electricity generation in the US uses fossil fuel (whereas the Canadian industry uses cleaner, hydroelectric processes). If the US refuses to tax her electricity producers for the sulphur dioxide pollution they generate, or refuses to compensate Canada for the damage that is inflicted by the acid rain transmitted to Canada by wind drift, then should Canada have the right to tax her import of US electricity (if any), or of other US exports that are produced using the electricity that generates acid rain?

Modifying the GATT rules to explicitly allow for such a possibility arguably makes sense as a second-best solution, since the offending party (the US in the example) refuses to undertake a first-best solution, provided the usual caveats about satisfying science tests etc. are taken into account. That also seemed to be the position taken in some early and unofficial thinking by the GATT Secretariat.

The problem, of course, is that this type of trade remedy is generally likely to be so weak for problems like acid rain that one may ask, "Is it worth modifying the GATT/WTO to legitimize such trade actions?" Thus, take the example of acid rain itself. The generation of acid rain in the US, a fraction of which comes across to Canada, is geographically concentrated, of course, at the border, whereas the Canadian import tariff on US products produced with electricity would affect all electricity generation in the US; moreover, the effect on sulphur dioxide generation would be indirect, not direct through a tax on the process of electricity production itself; then again, only a fraction of the acid rain generation effect would get into the transmission. The tariff instrument would then be extremely weak and the Canadian gain from its use in reducing the loss from the acid rain would be outweighed by the reduced gains from trade, i.e., the gains from importing cheaper products from the US. Even apart from this consideration, once a trade policy remedy is contemplated for an environmental problem, it will be advocated for other problems such as alleged human rights violations, endangered species, threats to biodiversity, etc. This danger of sliding down a slippery slope is real.

The chief policy questions concerning trade policy when global pollution problems are involved instead, as with ozone layer depletion and global warming, take a different turn related to the cooperative-solution-oriented multilateral treaties that are sought to address them. They are essentially tied into noncompliance ("defection") by members and "free riding" by nonmembers. Because any action by a member of a treaty relates to targeted actions (such as reducing chlorofluorocarbons or carbon dioxide emissions) that are a public good (in particular, that the benefits are nonexcludable, so that if I incur the cost and do something, I cannot exclude you from benefiting from it), the use of trade sanctions to secure and enforce compliance automatically turns up on the agenda.

At the same time, the problem is compounded because the agreement itself has to be legitimate in the eyes of those accused of free riding or noncompliance. Before those pejorative epithets are applied and punishment prescribed in the form of trade sanctions legitimated at the GATT/WTO, these nations have to be satisfied that the agreement being pressed on them is efficient and, especially, that it is equitable in burden-sharing. Otherwise, nothing prevents the politically powerful (i.e., the rich nations) from devising a treaty that puts an inequitable burden on the politically weak (i.e., the poor nations) and then using the cloak of a "multilateral" agreement and a new GATT/WTO legitimacy to impose that burden with the aid of trade sanctions with a clear conscience, invoking the white man's burden to secure the white man's gain.

This is why the policy demand, often made, to alter the GATT/WTO to legitimate trade sanctions on contracting parties who remain outside a treaty, whenever a plurilateral treaty on a global environmental problem dictates it, is unlikely to be accepted by the poor nations without safeguards to prevent unjust impositions. The spokesmen of the poor countries have been more or less explicit on this issue, with justification. These concerns have been recognized by the rich nations. Thus, at the Rio Conference in 1992, the Framework Convention on Climate Change set explicit goals under which several rich nations agreed to emission level-reduction targets (returning, more or less, to 1990 levels), whereas the commitments of the poor countries were contingent on the rich nations footing the bill.

Ultimately, burden-sharing by different formulas related to past emissions, current income, current population etc. are inherently arbitrary; they also distribute burdens without regard to efficiency. Economists will argue for burden-sharing dictated by cost minimization across countries, for the earth as a whole: if Brazilian rain forests must be saved to minimize the cost of a targeted reduction in carbon dioxide emissions in the world, while the US keeps guzzling gas because it is too expensive to cut that down, then so be it. But then this efficient "cooperative" solution must not leave Brazil footing the bill. Efficient solutions, with compensation and equitable distribution of the gains, make economic sense.

A step toward them is the idea of having a market in permits again, at the world level: no country may emit carbon dioxide without having bought the necessary permit from a worldwide quota. That would ensure efficiency, whereas the distribution of the proceeds from the sold permits would require a decision reflecting some multilaterally agreed ethical or equity criteria (e.g., the proceeds may be used for refugee resettlement, United Nations peace–keeping operations, aid dispensed to poor nations by the United Nations Development Programme, the World Health Organization fight against the Acquired Immuno-Deficiency Syndrome [AIDS] disease, etc.).[12] This type of agreement would have the legitimacy that could then provide the legitimacy in turn for a GATT/WTO rule that permits the use of trade sanctions against free riders.

Trade and Labor Standards[13]

The linkage between international labor standards (or worker rights) and international trade and investment came to the fore in international discussions during 1994, though its origins go a long way back to the Treaty of Versailles and, later to the Havana Charter of 1948 for the ITO (Charnovitz 1986, 1987). The issue was elevated to the international agenda on January 11, 1994, at the European Union Headquarters in Brussels, Belgium, when President Clinton stated, "While we continue to tear down anticompetitive practices and other barriers to trade, we simply have to ensure that our economic policies also protect the environment and the well-being of workers."

The Final Act came within a whisker of not being signed with the demand of the US, France, and others for the inclusion of international labor standards that had not been part of the agreed text. The attempts to link international trade with observance of "fair and humane conditions of labor for men, women and children" goes back, as noted above, to the Treaty of Versailles that led to the establishment of the International Labour Organization (ILO). Periodically, various US administrations, Democrat and Republican, have proposed the inclusion of a labor standards article in GATT, unsuccessfully as it turned out, during several rounds of multilateral trade negotiations. Thus the latest demand for formal inclusion of labor standards in the mandate of the WTO is not a surprise except in its timing, namely, that it was raised after the painful and lengthy negotiations had been completed, almost holding the negotiated agreement hostage. The agreement was signed, but not without an understanding that the topic of labor standards could be discussed by the preparatory committee for the WTO. Of course, the facts that the demand has been raised repeatedly and that an understanding to discuss it has been arrived at do not necessarily make it legitimate.

The US Labor Secretary Robert Reich (1994, 1) defined the issue of labor standards as "the weight that internal workplace practices should have in external economic relations" and argued that "as economies become increasingly interwoven with each other, we must either actively accept some share of responsibility for how our economic partners conduct their affairs, or else passively accept complicity". This led him to plead for a middle ground between what he termed the two extreme positions of treating labor standards as a purely domestic matter for a country and of no concern for its trading partners, and trading only with those partners who have similar labor laws and standards, wage rates, and political institutions.

Seeking a middle ground between extremes may seem eminently reasonable prima facie, but in the present context this is not necessarily the case. First of all, a humanitarian concern about the working conditions of laborers in other countries does not imply that it is best expressed through the imposition of unilateral conditionalities on trade relations with such countries, or through enunciation of codes of acceptable labor standards as part of the multilateral framework governing international trade. Indeed, if the citizens and workers of a country with "higher" labor standards than those prevailing in another country are genuinely concerned about the welfare of the workers of the latter, then they could well urge their own government to lift any restrictions on immigration of such workers so that they are able to enjoy higher labor standards prevailing in the country of immigration, rather than attempt to raise the lower labor standards of the country of emigration through trade sanctions. One could go further and invoke Rawls (1993), who views freedom of movement and freedom of choice of occupation as essential primary goods equivalent to other basic rights and liberties, the entitlement to which is not open to political debate and allocation through the political process. While Rawls was writing about these freedoms in the context of constitutional essentials of a just society, implicit in the very expression of humanitarian concerns about others must be a view of the whole human race as one society. As such, a natural extension of Rawls in a view of human race as a single society would treat freedom of movement of humans across artificial political boundaries as a basic human right. Of course, none of the proponents of linking trade relations with observance of labor standards even raise the issue of free movement of labor across countries. In all fairness, one should add that opposition to immigration of workers from poorer countries is not unique to the developed countries—for example, in India there is opposition to alleged illegal immigration of Bangladeshi workers.

Even if free movement of labor as a way of raising labor standards everywhere is politically unthinkable, there is yet another way of expressing humanitarian concerns, namely, through income transfers to workers (not to their governments) in poor countries so that the supply price (broadly defined to include labor standards) of their (and their children's) labor is raised. Once again, enthusiasm for foreign aid of any kind in most rich countries (with the possible exception of the Dutch, Scandinavians, and other Northern European do-gooders) is nonexistent.

Long ago, Professor Jan Tinbergen, a winner of the Nobel Memorial Prize in economics, wrote about the correspondence between objectives and instruments of policy. He argued that, in general, there must be at least as many instruments of policy as there are objectives, and that in achieving any objective, that policy instrument which has the most direct impact on that objective is most likely, though not always, to do so at the least social cost. Thus, for example, objectives of policy cover economic, political, military, and humanitarian goals, some of which might be systemic, e.g., the framework of rules and codes governing international trade. Policy instruments would of course include economic, political, and military, many of which could be exercised unilaterally or multilaterally. While in principle economic instruments could be and have been used to attain political and military objectives (e.g., the use of trade sanctions), and vice versa, it is fair to say that, first of all, specialization rather than linkage has been the rule in the creation of agencies to formulate and enforce rules governing the exercise of economic, political, and military policies. Indeed, specialization has been pushed further within each of these categories. Thus, GATT, the United Nations Conference on Trade and Development (UNCTAD), etc. were created as agencies specializing in issues relating to international trade; the World Bank and the International Monetary Fund were designed to deal respectively with financing long-term development and short-term stabilization. The Universal Postal Union covered postal and other matters of international communication, Berne and Paris conventions addressed some aspects of intellectual property rights, and the ILO deals with labor issues.

Clearly such specialization makes eminent sense. Loading one specialized agency with matters that fall within the purview of another, rather than ensuring consistency of actions of both through mutual consultation where appropriate, is not conducive to addressing them efficiently. Unfortunately, the US has taken the lead in demanding precisely such a loading or, should I say, overloading, of the WTO by bringing the so-called trade-related intellectual property rights and investment measures and labor and environmental standards within its purview. Second, there is ample evidence that the use of trade policy instruments for achieving nontrade-related objectives has not been very effective, claims such as "Trade Policy in Foreign Policy" (Cooper 1972) notwithstanding. For example, the analysis of Hufbauer and Schott (1983, 1990) amply demonstrates that trade and economic sanctions are effective only under very special circumstances. Clearly there are costs to both imposers and victims of sanctions.

Freeman (1994) discusses ways in which citizens of one country could express their concerns about any features of the process of production (working conditions included) in countries of origin of imports through their own actions in the market rather than through their governments. By not buying the products of a firm (or a state or a country) that does not observe what consumers view as acceptable standards, be they with respect to working conditions or with respect to the environment or whatever, they can send a clear and effective signal to the firm to force it to choose between observing standards and retaining the market or losing the market altogether. Market forces could themselves generate the information needed to distinguish the nonobserving firms from observing ones as long as the consumers refuse to buy that product (or all products from a country) if they suspect that it (or some products from that country) is being produced under unacceptable conditions. In such a case, producers (or countries) who maintain acceptable standards will have an incentive to invest in signalling (in a credible way) to the consumers that they in fact do so, and thus distinguish themselves from those that do not. Freeman's point that those who argue for governmentally imposed standards and punishment (through withholding of trading privileges, for example) are really afraid that other consumers might not share their concerns about standards and might be willing to trade violation of standards off against the cost of the product, is well taken. But then, if the concerns for particular standards are not universal, the argument for state action is considerably weakened. Further, nonuniversality in this sense implies that standards could legitimately vary across countries without calling for action by one country against another for enforcement of its standards on the other. Even if there are universal standards, their enforcement would naturally call for multilateral action and not unilateral action.

Are there any aspects of labor standards that might conceivably attract universal support? Proscription of slave or prison labor or labor of children below a certain age and the recognition of right of association of workers for collective bargaining might arguably attract such support. Slaves and prisoners do not voluntarily supply their labor and as such proscription of coercive exploitation of prisoners or the practice of slavery might enjoy universal support. In fact, GATT already allows signatories to take action against importation of products produced by prisoners.

The issue is not so clear in the case of child labor. Very young children certainly do not have the capacity to decide whether to work or not, and thus their employment has an element of involuntariness associated with it. However, as long as it is a socially accepted norm that parents decide for their young children, barring the cases of child abuse, it might be reasonable to presume that the parents do take into account the interests of their children as well as themselves. The parents would allow their children to be employed only if family welfare is enhanced by the use of children's time in such employment. Thus proscription of such labor, if strictly enforced without compensation, would lower family welfare among those who are already desperately poor. Carried to the extreme, it might worsen the already terrible phenomenon of infanticide, particularly female infanticide, that is seen in very poor countries.

The issue of freedom of association and formation of labor unions is also not as simple and straightforward as it might appear. Even in the US where this freedom is assured by law, its exercise in practice is not unfettered. Instances of resistance on the part of employers to the unionization of their workers are not rare. Whether such a freedom should be deemed a primary good in the Rawlsian sense is arguable. If it is not, in a participatory democracy, the freely elected legislative bodies could choose not to confer such freedom by law for sound reasons. In any case, even in societies where the right to form unions is legally enshrined, it is rarely absolute: some categories of workers, such as public servants, are precluded by law from exercising the rights (e.g., the right to strike) granted to others. It is amusing to contemplate where a "results-oriented" policy based on measuring the extent of freedom of association by the proportion of workers unionized might lead: Japan, with a higher rate of unionization than the US, might argue that, despite its laws, "invisible" barriers keep US workers from unionizing and hence progress toward reduction of these barriers would come about only if the US is forced to set numerical targets for unionization.[14] Until 1994, the US Congress had exempted itself from the application of many labor laws, including occupational safety regulations it imposes on others in the US, while some of its members were vociferously demanding imposition of such laws on other countries.

The presumption that unions promote democratic values is contradicted by the nondemocratic procedures in the internal management of many unions. The notorious history of the Teamsters Union in the US comes to mind as an example. In some poor developing countries, such as India, labor laws imitative of those in industrialized countries, and not in consonance with Indian labor market realities, have long been on the statute books. With the overwhelming majority of the labor force still engaged in agriculture, and with self-employment (as cultivators, artisans, or producers in the informal sector) being the dominant mode of employment, labor unions (organized as labor wings of each political party) operate only in the so-called organized sector consisting of large-scale manufacturing and services, including the public sector. Their membership constitutes a tiny proportion of the total labor force, an island of labor aristocracy in a sea of poorer unorganized wage workers and self-employed. Far from being a dynamic force for progress and egalitarian growth, these unions, representing bastions of restrictive work practices and whose members receive wages, salaries, privileges, and perquisites that bear no relation to productivity, are major stumbling blocks to economic reforms, liberalization, and privatization that would benefit the large majority. It would indeed be a tragedy if other poor countries, which have not enacted imitative labor laws under which an obstreperous labor aristocracy could emerge, are to be required to enact such laws under a threat of losing their trading rights.

The EU and the US have linked the granting of concessionary tariff treatment (under the generalized system of preferences, or GSP as they are known) of imports from developing countries to meeting labor standards. The GSP are no more, and according to some, are worse, than crumbs from a rich man's table. The developing countries would be far better off under a liberal trading system than under one in which they get special and differential treatment in return for their acquiescing in the illiberal trade policies of the rich. By attaching undue significance to GSP and other measures of special and differential treatment, the developing countries have opened themselves to being pressured into imposing unsustainably high labor and environmental standards.

It is no coincidence that the cry for linking trade and observance of labor and environmental standards is shrillest in developed countries and at the present time. After all, unemployment has been growing and real wages have been stagnant in many of these countries in a period where global economic integration has been growing and when competition from some dynamic less developed countries has been intensifying as well. It is not surprising to see the ancient but crude pauper-labor arguments reappear, but now couched in lofty and idealistic terms of "fair" labor standards.

Several studies have in fact shown that, allowing for productivity differences, labor is not much cheaper in many of the developing countries and, in any case, differences in unit labor costs and in costs of meeting environmental regulations do not appear to be the driving forces in the locational decisions of multinational corporations. One would be forgiven, therefore, if one attributes crass protectionist motives, rather than genuine humanitarian concerns about working conditions of foreign labor, to many who seek to link trade with labor standards. Charnovitz (1994), one of the few sober and analytically oriented among the proponents of "a code of basic labor standards that can serve as a floor for international commerce", recognizes that "the potential for protectionist abuse (of linkage of trade privileges with labor standards) is obvious." Not only would such linkage be used for gaining protection, but also enunciating basic labor standards and monitoring their observance would become yet another avenue for "managed trade".

The demand for linkage between trading rights and observance of standards with respect to environment and labor would seem to arise largely from protectionist motives. If conceded and incorporated into the charter of the WTO, it can only disrupt healthy growth in international trade along the lines of comparative advantage, and retard the development of poor countries, and thereby their progress toward a better life for their workers and their families. Monitoring the observance of standards could lead to managed trade and intrusion into the domestic political processes of other countries. Indeed, Reich (1994, 4) appears to suggest precisely such an intrusion when he says, "If a country lacks democratic institutions and fails to disseminate the benefits of growth, other countries might justifiably conclude that low labor standards are due not to poverty itself, but to political choices that distort development and warp the economy's structure."

It is in the vital interest of most of the poor ADEs that no linkage whatsoever between trade privileges and achievement of nontrade objectives is included in the charter of the WTO. At its 1994 meetings, the Sub-Committee on Trade and Environment established at the signing of the Final Act discussed, inter alia, issues relating to trade-distorting policies and environmental degradation, the contribution that elimination of such policies could make for environmental improvement, and the special problems of poor countries in meeting environmental standards imposed on their exports. One hopes that a rigid linkage between trade policy measures and nontrade objectives is not advocated by its successor committee under the WTO. But if linkage cannot be avoided, they should insist that the three principles stated by Reich (1994), viz. interventions, if called for, should be multilateral; there should be a menu of potential responses to perceived labor standards abuses; and, finally, pragmatism, rather than dogmatism, should govern the decisions whether to intervene and if so, how.

Nontariff Measures

It is widely held that in the Kennedy and Tokyo Rounds, the reductions in tariff barriers on products of major export interest to developing countries were lower than the average for all products. Besides, the escalation in tariffs in industrialized countries with the level of a product's processing also acts as a constraint on the export of processed rather than raw products from developing countries. Apart from tariffs, the nontariff measures in the Organisation for Economic Co-operation and Development (OECD) are considered to be even more detrimental than tariffs to the interests of exports from developing countries.

Low and Yeats (1994, 2) seek to determine "how far the Uruguay Round, when its results are fully implemented, will change the level, nature and incidence of OECD countries' nontariff measures on developing countries' exports". The major changes in nontariff measures brought about in the Uruguay Round relate to "tariffication" in agriculture, the abolition of the MFA, and the elimination of voluntary export restraints, though all of these changes will not happen instantaneously with the WTO coming into existence. Low and Yeats find that the Uruguay Round changes will dramatically reduce the incidence of nontariff measures on developed country exports, with the share of their non-oil exports subject to nontariff measures falling from 18 percent to about 4 percent. Tables 4 and 5 of their paper (not reproduced here) provide the details of this dramatic change across regions and countries. They rightly caution that it is likely that industrial country producers will demand new measures to insulate them from import competition from developing countries arising from the dramatic reduction in nontariff measures. They suggest that safeguards and antidumpings are the most likely new such measures. As noted above, safeguards could be invoked, albeit under restrictive conditions, to restrain imports.

In his comprehensive discussion of all safeguard provisions in GATT, Finger (1995) notes that while antidumping was a minor instrument when GATT was negotiated in 1947, it has been used with increasing frequency in the last two decades. According to him, the efforts during the Uruguay Round negotiation to restrict the use of antidumping measures met with little success. The Final Act certainly sets public notice and transparency requirements and a five-year sunset clause on antidumping actions. But Finger suggests that these are not as far reaching as they may seem. First, as long as GATT panels continue to treat procedural errors in antidumping actions merely to call for rectification of errors or to recalculate antidumping duties rather than remove them, stricter procedural requirements such as transparency and public notice are unlikely to deter protectionist use of antidumping. And the sunset clause has little bite since there is virtually no limit to the number of times an antidumping duty can be reviewed and extended.

Since antidumping enforcement is based on national antidumping laws and, as is well known, producer interests are usually concentrated while consumer interests are diffused in most nations, Finger argues that producers will treat protection through antidumping action as an entitlement in domestic politics. They will lobby at home for national antidumping laws that make it easier to prove dumping and initiate antidumping action. During the negotiations of the Uruguay Round, the same lobbyists were active in Geneva, seeking to influence the contents of antidumping clauses in GATT. Finger suggests that in the pitched battle between victims and users of antidumping during these negotiations, the bone of contention was the extent of antidumping that the Final Act would permit, rather than finding ways of distinguishing socially justifiable from unjustifiable dumping. Since the determination of social justification will necessarily involve going beyond import-competing interests to include consumer-user interests, it is unlikely such weighing of all affected interests will become part of national law, let alone GATT law.

Services, TRIMS, and TRIPS

Trade in services (defined as nonfactor services in the balance of payments minus government transactions plus labor income) grew at an annual average rate of 8.3 percent between 1980 and 1992, a rate faster than merchandise trade (Hoekman 1995). Although the share of developing countries in service trade declined during the same period, it is still over 10 percent. The objective of the General Agreement on Trade in Services (GATS) is to establish a multilateral framework that is analogous to that for trade in goods. However, evaluating the extent of liberalization of trade in services envisaged in the agreement, offers, and commitments received thus far, and their effects, is difficult in comparison to trade in goods. The reason is that there is no equivalent of a tariff as a barrier to market access in services. The significant barriers arise from the bewildering variety of applicable domestic laws and regulations. In addition, the available data on trade in services are incomplete, unreliable, and noncomparable across countries and over time. Apparently only cross-border service transactions within foreign-owned firms are covered, with their domestic sales left out of the data altogether.

A comprehensive discussion of many of the conceptual and practical issues involved in liberalizing service trade is available in UNCTAD (1993). According to this document, ADEs accounted for 7.1 percent of world trade in commercial services in 1990, 7.3 percent in shipment, 6.7 percent in passenger and other transport, 7.9 percent in travel, 6.2 percent in labor and property income, and 3.0 percent in other services. The share of merchandise exports of the ADEs was 7.5 percent in 1990. Thus services trade recorded in the balance of payments data are quite important for the ADEs. Of the 40 leading exporters of commercial services in the world, ten were Asian: Singapore (rank 12); Hong Kong (14); Republic of Korea (19); Taipei,China (21); Thailand (22); Turkey (23); Malaysia (31); India (32); the Philippines (33); and Saudi Arabia (39). Among 40 leading importers, eleven were Asia: Taipei,China (14); Saudi Arabia (17); Republic of Korea (19); Hong Kong (22); Singapore (23); Thailand (25); Malaysia (26); India (27); Indonesia (28); People's Republic of China (32); and Kuwait (34).

Hoekman (1995) provides an in-depth assessment of GATS. According to him, GATS applies to measures that affect the consumption of services in a member country that originate in other member countries. It covers all modes of supply, viz. cross-border supply without physical movement of consumer or supplier, supply involving the movement of consumer to the country of supplier, services sold in one member country by legal entities with a commercial presence in that country but originating in another member country, and services requiring temporary migration of "natural" persons. The agreement consists of a set of general concepts; principles and rules of applicability across the board; specific commitments on national treatment and market access applicable to those sectors or subsectors listed in a members' schedule subject to any qualifications or conditions; an understanding of possible future negotiations to liberalize service trade further; and a set of attachments including annexes listing specific sectoral commitments and ministerial decisions relating to the implementation of GATS.

It is clear that, although the core principles of GATS, viz. most-favored-nation (MFN) and national treatments apply generally in GATS, they are heavily qualified. First, on entry into force of GATS each member can exempt any service from the application of MFN and further exemptions can be sought through the normal waiver procedure. Second, national treatment applies to only those sectors and subsectors listed in a member's schedule, and even then, only in so far as existing measures are not exempted. With diversity among members in their GDP levels, the share of tradeable services in their GDP, and the sectoral and subsectoral commitments, exemptions etc., it is not a simple matter to calculate the extent of coverage of the MFN and national treatment commitments across country groups. At one extreme, if one were to use the magnitude of commitments where no restrictions apply to both market access and national treatment as a measure of how close GATS will take its members to free trade, Hoekman's estimates are not very encouraging. Eighteen high-income countries, including OECD with EU counted as one, Singapore, Hong Kong, and the Republic of Korea, placed no restrictions on market access only on 30.5 percent of the services established by the Group of Negotiations on Service (GNS). The corresponding figure for all other countries (including most developing countries) was far less, 6.7 percent. With respect to national treatment, the figures were not much higher, with HIC percentage being 35.3 and that of all other countries 8.5 percent. Hoekman's calculations of sectoral commitments adjusted for mode of supply, proportion of service sectors from liberalization, and sector's weight in GDP, result in the following percentage of commitments relative to the total number in the GNS list.

	High-Income Countries	Developing Countries
Market Access	48.5	11.4
National Treatment	53.0	12.6

These are far lower than the corresponding figures for goods trade. Brown et al. (1995) estimate the real income gains from liberalization in services to be $39 billion for Europe, $37 billion for the US, $22 billion for Japan, $9 billion for Canada, $5 billion for Australia and New Zealand, and $24 billion for the rest of the world. Together these amount to a global total of $136 billion, which is more than half their estimate of the gain from liberalization of all trade including agriculture, manufactures, and services.

Hoekman notes that market access commitments by OECD countries in services (as they are in manufacturing) tend to be more restrictive with respect to services in which developing countries have an actual or potential comparative advantage, such as services intensive in labor (skilled and unskilled) but which would require a temporary permit for workers to be able to sell their services in importing countries. Developing countries should certainly press for removal of such restrictions in future negotiations under the WTO, Hoekman is certainly right in his assertion that most of the immediate potential gains for them would arise in further liberalization of access to their own service markets. He is also right in drawing attention to several disquieting, though easily addressed, features of the GATS, particularly its allowing members not to bind the status quo in many sectors. Hopefully members will muster enough political courage to push forward toward free trade in services in their future negotiations.

Evaluating TRIMS and TRIPS involves difficulties similar to those applicable to services. Both were "new" issues that, at the time of the Punta del Este declaration, were seen as requiring the discipline of a multilateral framework. The Final Act affects domestic rules and regulations in those areas and formally extends the core principles of GATT, i.e., MFN and national treatment to these issues as well. As in the case of GATS, this extension is neither complete nor absolute. It can be argued, as Braga (1995) does, that in a static perspective, TRIPS is an exercise in rent transfer from South to North and its implementation would require significant reforms of the intellectual property regimes of developing countries. Braga suggests that the relatively long implementation period allowed for developing countries will attenuate this loss. However, the dynamic gain from TRIPS could be significant if the recent "new" growth and development literature is to be believed. According to this literature, the driving force of sustained growth is accumulation of "knowledge" capital, through domestic research, import, and imitation where appropriate. In models with spillover effects, knowledge created anywhere has potentially beneficial effects everywhere. To the extent subscribing to TRIPS (and to TRIMS, since foreign direct investment is a means of technology transfer) makes accumulation of knowledge capital more rapid, it will be beneficial to all developing countries. Many of the ADEs, with their relatively better endowment of skills and knowledge capital as compared to the rest of the developing world, are likely to reap a significant share of the benefits. Also, adhering to the provisions of the agreement on TRIMS and TRIPS will make investment in ADEs more attractive to foreigners. Whether the likely short-run adverse effects in terms of price rises in sectors such as pharmaceuticals etc. are quantitatively significant is not easy to discern.

Low and Subramanian (1995) find that the TRIMS negotiations produced an outcome more modest than was hoped for at Punta del Este. This outcome, in their view, largely reaffirmed certain pre-existing disciplines. Nonetheless, establishing international rules such as TRIMS for investment strengthens the opportunities for members to benefit from international specialization, as GATT did for trade in goods. However, whether the rules should be extended to domestic competition policy, and in particular whether such policies should be harmonized, are debatable issues. Some of the arguments offered earlier in defense of diversity of environmental standards could be applied with appropriate modification to competition policies as well. Since many of the restrictions that developing (and some developed) countries place on foreign investors (such as local content requirements) make sense, if at all, only in a second-best environment, their elimination under TRIMS should be beneficial. Low and Subramanian rightly characterize the failure of TRIMS to address export performance requirements as the most serious. It is to be hoped, once again, as in the case of GATS, future negotiations would expand TRIMS and TRIPS in the direction of further liberalization.

To conclude, now that the WTO is in place, the implementation of the liberalizing measures of the Final Act should gather momentum. Their full implementation should yield significant benefits in terms of global opportunities for trade, investment, and technical progress. Asian developing economies should avail of these emerging opportunities. Indeed, by foregoing special and differential treatment, binding their tariffs, entering into other commitments on an equal basis with other participants, and by eliminating restrictive regulations that have outlived their utility, ADEs would be able to increase the credibility of their ongoing economic reform processes. They should, however, resist the extension and application of trade policy instruments through the WTO to achieve objectives that do not involve trade. Such objectives, where legitimate, should be pursued in more appropriate fora.

Acknowledgment

The author wishes to thank Anne Krueger, Philip Levy, Will Martin, M. G. Quibria, and the three discussants, Nurul Islam, Narhari Rao, and Yeong-Yuh Chiang for their valuable comments on an earlier draft. Of course, none of them is responsible for the views expressed here.

Notes

1. I am drawing heavily on Jackson (1992) for this brief history of the GATT.

2. I thank Will Martin for drawing my attention to these aspects of quota growth.

3. This section draws from Srinivasan (1994a).

4. Levy (1995) examines whether incentives for multilateral trade liberalization are blunted by the possibility of concluding regional trade agreements in a political economy model of trade policy determination. More precisely, he considers two periods, during the second of which an opportunity for multilateral liberalization arises, and asks whether two countries concluding bilateral trade agreements in the first period will retain any interest in multilateral liberalization in the second period. In a standard Hechscher-Ohlin-Samuelson model with median voter politics, the answer is in the affirmative since the only effect of trade liberalization, bilateral or

multilateral, is the Stolper-Samuelson effect on factor prices induced by terms of trade changes. However, if the model is of the differentiated-product-monopolistic competition type, there is an additional effect to consider, namely, the expansion of the varieties of the product available for consumption with trade liberalization. In such a model, concluding a bilateral agreement in the first period might result in the two countries losing interest in multilateral liberalization in the second period. For example, consider two countries identical in factor endowments to each other but differing from those in the rest of the world. Opening up of trade between them clearly has only a variety expansion effect and would be beneficial. But opening up of their trade with the rest of the world has both effects which could go in opposite directions. If the negative Stolper-Samuelson effect more than offsets the variety expansion effect, clearly the two countries could not be interested in expanding their trade bloc multilaterally.

5. Using a partial equilibrium model (i.e., assuming that terms of trade and incomes do not change as liberalization takes place) and values of trade elasticities found in the literature, Canonero (1994) estimated the expected net trade expansion following the formation of a South Asian and other PTAs. These estimates, as is to be expected, are considerably smaller.

6. Will Martin pointed out to me that the present "request-offer" system of negotiations in the multilateral trading system worked well as long as there was a small group of large traders. But with many diverse (in terms of relative economic size) countries in the system the discipline imposed by negotiating from an initial "request-offer" is weakened since a size imbalance between two countries limits the scope of reducing each other's protection through reciprocal reductions. Martin cites the excessively high bindings from the agricultural tariffication process as an example of this phenomenon. Only because a trading partner took the trouble to negotiate, India brought down its high initial ceilings to lower levels. Clearly forming groups reduces size imbalances and makes it more likely that negotiations among groups of similar size will lead to significant reductions in trade barriers.

7. This section is based on Bhagwati and Srinivasan (1995).

8. CCII means harmonization of standards within the same industry across different trading countries.

9. The suspension of trade generally, i.e., the use of trade "sanctions" (to promote human rights, for instance) is a related but different issue.

10. As in the second argument above.

11. The difficulties posed by GATT, and now the WTO, for the environmentalists extend to GATT law, i.e., Dispute Settlement Panel findings, in regard to the ethical-preference issue as well.

12. Will Martin in his comments on an earlier draft suggested that the Coase Theorem can be used as the conceptual basis for trading permits. The theorem implies that under any given distribution of rents from permits, efficiency is achieved and, as such, an agreement on the distribution of rents deemed "fair" is also consistent with efficiency of the distribution of pollution outcomes. Thus trade and other sanctions then merely "support" this agreement by threats of punishment for violations.

13. This section is based on Srinivasan (1994b).

14. I owe this illustration to Will Martin.

References

Anderson, K., and R. Blackhurst, eds., 1993. *Regional Integration and the Global Trading System.* New York: Harvester/Wheatsheaf.

Bhagwati, J., 1993. "Regionalism and Multilateralism: An Overview." In J. De Melo and A. Panagariya, eds., *New Dimensions in Regional Integration.* Cambridge: Cambridge University Press.

Bhagwati, J., and V. H. Dehejia, 1994. "Freer Trade and Wages of the Unskilled—Is Marx Striking Again?" In J. Bhagwati and M. H. Kosters, eds., *Trade and Wages—Leveling Wages Down?* Washington, D. C.: AEI Press.

Bhagwati, J., and T. N. Srinivasan, 1995. "Trade and Environment: Does Environmental Diversity Detract from the Case for Free Trade?" Economic Growth Center, Yale University. Processed.

Bliss, C., 1994. *Economic Theory and Policy for Trading Blocks.* New York: Manchester University Press.

Boren, D. L., 1991. International Pollution Deterrence Act of 1991. Statement of Senator David L. Boren, Senate Finance Committee, October 25, 1991.

Braga, C. A. P., 1995. "Trade-Related Intellectual Property Issues." Paper presented at the World Bank Conference on the Uruguay Round and the Developing Economies, January 26-27, 1995.

Brandão, A., and W. Martin, 1993. "Implications of Agricultural Trade Liberalization for the Developing Countries." *Agricultural Economics* 8:313-43.

Brown, D., et al., 1995. "Computational Analysis of Goods and Services Liberalization in the Uruguay Round." Paper presented at the World Bank Conference on the Uruguay Round and the Developing Economies, January 26-27, 1995,

Canonero, G., 1994. "Preferential Trade Arrangements: Partial Equilibrium Estimates for South Asian Countries." World Bank, Washington, D. C. Processed.

Charnovitz, S., 1986. "Fair Labor Standards and International Trade." *Journal of World Trade Law* 20:61-78.

_____, 1987. "The Influence of International Labour Standards on the World Trade Regime: A Historical Review." *International Labour Review* 126:565-84.

_____, 1994. "Promoting World Labor Rules." *The Journal of Commerce* (April).

Cline, W., 1990. *The Future of World Trade in Textiles and Apparel.* Washington, D. C.: Institute for International Economics.

Cooper, R., 1972. "Trade Policy is Foreign Policy." *Foreign Policy* 9 (Winter):18-36.

De Melo, J., and A. Panagariya, 1993. "Introduction." In J. de Melo and A. Panagariya, eds., *New Dimensions in Regional Integration.* Cambridge: Cambridge University Press.

De Melo, J. and D. G. Tarr, 1990. "Welfare Costs of U. S. Quotas in Textiles, Steel and Autos." Discussion Paper No. 401. Centre for Economic Policy Research, London.

Financial Times, 1993. November 15, page 15.

Finger J. M., 1995. "Legalized Backsliding: Safeguarding Provisions in the GATT." Paper presented at the World Bank Conference on the Uruguay Round and the Developing Economies, January 26-27, 1995.

Francois, J., B. McDonalde, and H. Nordström, 1995. "Assessing the Uruguay Round." Paper presented at the World Bank Conference on the Uruguay Round and the Developing Economies, January 26-27, 1995.

Freeman, R., 1994. "A Hard-Headed Look at Labor Standards." In *International Labor Standards and Global Economic Integration: Proceedings of a Symposium.* Washington, D. C.: U.S. Department of Labor.

GATT, 1979. *Report on Multilateral Trade Negotiations.* Geneva: GATT Secretariat.

GATT Focus, 1994. Newsletter No. 107, May.

GATT Secretariat, 1994. "Market Access for Goods and Services: Overview of the Results." In *The Results of the Uruguay Round of Multilateral Trade Negotiations.* Geneva: GATT.

Goldin, I., and O. Knudsen, eds., 1990. *Agricultural Trade Liberalization: Implications for the Developing Countries.* Paris/Washington, D. C.: OECD/World Bank.

Goldin, I., and D. van der Mensbrugghe, 1995. "Uruguay Round Reforms: Emphasizing Agricultural Reforms." Paper presented at the World Bank Conference on the Uruguay Round and the Developing Economies, January 26-27, 1995.

Goto, J., 1989. "The Multifibre Arrangement and Its Effects on Developing Countries." *The World Bank Research Observer* 5(2):203-27.

Harrison, G., T. Rutherford, and D. G. Tarr, 1995. "Quantifying the Uruguay Round." Paper presented at the World Bank Conference on the Uruguay Round and the Developing Economies, January 26-27, 1995.

Hathaway, D., 1987. *Agriculture and the GATT: Rewriting the Rules.* Washington, D. C.: Institute for International Economics.

Hathaway, D., and M. Ingco, 1995. "Agricultural Liberalization and the Uruguay Round." Paper presented at the World Bank Conference on the Uruguay Round and the Developing Economies, January 26-27, 1995.

Hertel, W. M., K. Yanagishima, and B. Dimaranan, 1995. "Liberalizing Manufactures Trade in a Changing World Economy." Paper presented at the World Bank Conference on the Uruguay Round and the Developing Economies, January 26-27, 1995.

Hoekman, B., 1995. "Tentative First Steps: an Assessment of the Uruguay Round Agreement on Services." Paper presented at the World Bank Conference on the Uruguay Round and the Developing Economies, January 26-27, 1995.

Hufbauer, G., and K. Elliott, 1994. *Measuring the Costs of Protection in the United States.* Washington, D. C.: Institute for International Economics.

Hufbauer, G., and J. Schott, 1983. *Economic Sanctions of Foreign Policy Goals, Policy Analysis in International Economics 6.* Washington, D.C.: Institute for International Economics.

_____, 1990. *Economic Sanctions Reconsidered.* Vols. 1 and 2. Washington, D.C.: Institute for International Economics.

_____, 1994. *Western Hemisphere Economic Integration.* Washington, D. C.: Institute for International Economics.

Information and Media Relations Division, 1994. *News of the Uruguay Round.* Newsletter NUR 084, 5 April. GATT, Geneva.

Jackson, J., 1992. *The World Trading System.* Cambridge: MIT Press.

Kemp, M., and H. Wan, Jr., 1976. "An Elementary Proposition Concerning the Formation of Trade Unions." *Journal of International Economics* 6(1):95-8.

Krueger, A., M. Schiff, and A. Valdes, 1988. "Agricultural Incentives in Developing Countries: Measuring the Effect of Sectoral and Economy-wide Policies." *World Bank Economic Review* 2(3):255-72.

Lawrence, R. 1994. *Regionalism, Multilateralism and Deeper Integration.* Washington, D. C. : Brookings Institution.

Leamer, E., 1994. "Trade, Wages and Revolving Door Ideas." National Bureau of Economic Research Working Paper No. 4716. Processed.

Levy, P., 1995. "Free Trade Agreements and Inter-bloc Tariffs." Economic Growth Center, Yale University. Processed.

Low, P., and A. Subramanian, 1995. "TRIMS in the Uruguay Round: An Unfinished Business?" Paper presented at the World Bank Conference on the Uruguay Round and the Developing Economies, January 26-27, 1995.

Low, P., and A. Yeats, 1994. "Nontariff Measures and Developing Countries: Has the Uruguay Round Leveled the Playing Field?" Policy Research Working Paper 1353. World Bank, Washington, D. C.

McMillan, J., 1991. "Do Trade Blocs Foster Open Trade?" University of California at San Diego. Processed.

Panagariya, A., 1993. "Should East Asia Go Regional? No and Maybe." World Bank. Processed.

Parikh, K., et al., 1988. *Towards Free Trade in Agriculture.* Massachusetts: Kluwer Academic Publishers.

Perroni, C., and J. Whalley, 1994. "The New Regionalism: Trade Liberalization or Insurance?" Paper presented at the Universities Research Conference on International Trade Rules and Institutions, December 4, 1993, NBER, Cambridge, Masachusetts.

Rawls, J., 1993. *Political Liberalism.* New York: Columbia University Press.

Reich, R., 1994. "Keynote Address." In *International Labor Standards and Global Economic Integration: Proceedings of a Symposium.* Washington, D. C.: U.S. Department of Labor.

Srinivasan, T. N., 1994a. "Regional Trading Arrangements and Beyond: Exploring Some Options for South Asia Theory, Empirics and Policy." Report No. IDP-142. South Asia Regional Discussion Paper Series. World Bank, Washington, D. C. Processed.

_____, 1994b. "International Labor Standards Once Again!" *International Labor Standards and Global Economic Integration: Proceedings of a Symposium.* Bureau of International Labor Affairs, U.S. Department of Labor.

Srinivasan, T. N., and G. Canonero, 1993a. "Liberalization of Trade Among Neighbors: Two Illustrative Models and Simulations." South Asia Region Discussion Paper Series. Supplement II to Report No. IDP 142. World Bank, Washington, D. C.

_____, 1993b. "Preferential Trade Arrangements: Estimating the Effects on South Asia Countries." South Asia Region Discussion Paper Series. Supplement III to Report No. IDP 142. World Bank, Washington, D.C.

Trela, I., and J. Whalley, 1990. "Global Effects of Developed Country Trade Restrictions on Textiles and Apparel." *Economic Journal* 100 (December):1190-205.

UNCTAD, 1993. *Liberalizing International Transactions in Services: A Handbook.* New York and Geneva: United Nations.

Whalley, J., 1993. "Regional Trade Arrangements in North America: CUSTA and NAFTA." In J. de Melo and A. Panagariya, eds., *New Dimensions in Regional Integration.* Cambridge: University Press.

World Bank, 1994a. *World Development Report.* New York: Oxford University Press.

_____, 1994b. "Consequences of Trading Blocs." World Bank, Washington, D.C. Processed.

Chapter 9

The Role of Cross-Border Division of Labor and Investment in Promoting Trade: Two Case Studies from East Asia

Motoshige Itoh and Jun Shibata

The East Asian economy has experienced very rapid economic growth during the last two decades. Trade and investment between East Asian economies and the rest of the world have expanded rapidly. More importantly, intra-Asian trade and investment have also experienced rapid growth. Various patterns of trade can be observed, such as cross-border trade of intermediate goods within multinational companies, development imports (goods produced to order exclusively for retail firms in other countries), and export of goods produced by multinational subsidiaries to their headquarters.

It is important to understand the economic mechanism that lies behind this intraregional trade to have a clear picture of the pattern of regional economic development in East Asia. There were no formal trade agreements to promote trade and investment in this region. However, the Asia-Pacific Economic Cooperation (APEC) may begin to play a role through the formalization of free trade and investment agreements in the near future. The North American Free Trade Area (NAFTA) and the European Union (EU) may have had some indirect effects on the region, but these effects were very small. Trade and investment in the region were promoted by unilateral liberalization actions by each country and some bilateral negotiation between industrial countries such as the United States and Japan and the developing countries. In this paper, we focus our attention on the pattern of intraregional division of labor, and discuss how it is related to changes in the domestic economic structure of an industrial country in the region, namely Japan.

Domestic structural change in Japan has had a significant effect on the pattern of direct investment, intraregional trade, and intraregional division of labor. This relationship is not one-directional. Just as changes in the Japanese domestic economic structure affect the pattern of trade and investment, developments in intraregional trade and investment affect economic changes in Japan. Although this paper is restricted to the domestic economic structure of Japan, a similar analysis should be done to help understand the relationship between the domestic economic structures of developing economies and the pattern of trade and investment.

Cross-border division of labor in the East Asian region has various patterns. In this paper, we discuss two important cases, electronics and textile-apparel products, based on our previous studies (1995). Detailed pictures of recent developments in these industries will aid understanding of the relationship between intraregional trade and investment and the structure of the domestic economy. Although a macroeconomic picture of regional development is desirable, this study is restricted to an industry-level micro analysis.

Although there have been no formal regional arrangements in the past, this may soon change. At the 1994 APEC meeting in Jakarta, it was announced that the countries in APEC had agreed to establish some kind of regional agreement on trade and investment liberalization within a specified period of time. If APEC is going to develop a more formal free trade agreement, then more attention should be given to the effects of such regional arrangements on each economy. It should also be noted that some subregional arrangements are emerging, such as the Association of Southeast Asean Nations (ASEAN) Free Trade Area (AFTA), which are pursuing free trade agreements. The pattern of liberalization in the region, which up to now has been basically a result of unilateral liberalization, may change as a result of these developments, and regional negotiation and agreements may have more influence.

This paper reviews recent developments in trade and investment in this region. It discusses how foreign direct investment affects the pattern of economic development using electronics as an example, and how changes in domestic economic structure affect the pattern of trade using textile-apparel products as an example. The final section discusses regionalism and its implications for developing economies in the East Asian region.

The Patterns of Trade and Investment in Asian Countries

There is no doubt that the most important driving forces behind the rapid economic growth of the East Asian economies have been direct investments and the growth of exports in the region. The rate of economic growth in East Asian countries has far exceeded that of other regions, including the Organisation for Economic Co-operation and Development (OECD) countries, over the last decade. The growth rate of exports was higher than the growth rate of output, a typical pattern of export-led growth.

Table 9.1 shows the trade matrix of the world in 1970, 1980, and 1990. The amount of exports from Asian Newly Industrializing Economies (NIEs) expanded 43.7 times between 1970 to 1990, and that from ASEAN countries by 22.4 times in the same period. The world average for export expansion from 1970 to 1990 was 10.7. Table 9.1 also confirms the increase in trade between Asian NIEs and ASEAN countries.

East Asian countries followed import substitution policies before they liberalized their domestic markets. Quotas were imposed on imports, inward direct investment was restricted, and important industries were brought under government control. These restrictions were intended to nurture domestic industries. However, these policies did not promote economic development, just as in many other developing economies in the world. Domestic markets were too small to provide sufficient demand, protection policies allowed domestic firms to operate in less competitive environments, and they had little incentive to improve efficiency or reduce costs.[1]

The development strategies in Southeast Asian countries changed greatly in the 1970s, and the People's Republic of China (PRC) followed a similar process of liberalization in the 1980s. Tables 9.2 and 9.3 summarize the liberalization processes in Thailand and PRC, showing the gradual process of import liberalization, promotion of foreign direct investment, and the use of various kinds of export promotion policy measures. As the case study of the electronics industry below will show, the promotion of foreign direct investment by East Asian countries coincided with structural changes in industrial countries such as Japan. Thus the liberalization policies were very successful in attracting investment from industrial countries.

Direct investment from industrial countries promoted division of labor between developing and industrial countries in Asia. Trade patterns have taken various forms. Some machinery parts and intermediate goods are exported from Japan to subsidiaries in other countries, and some machinery parts and intermediate goods are purchased from domestic firms in developing countries. Assembled goods are not only exported to Japan and sold in the host country, but are also exported to other countries in the region. Reflecting this locational choice, intraregional trade in intermediate goods and final goods between developing countries in the region has increased. Intraindustry trade has also expanded, as well as intrafirm trade.

Table 9.1. **Trade Matrix** (US$ million)

		Japan	U.S.	NIEs[a]	ASEAN[b]	Singapore	World
Japan	70		6.015	2.219	1.818	423	19.318
	80		31.649	15.248	12.981	3.869	129.542
	90		91.120	46.487	31.979	10.739	287.678
	(90/70)		(15.1)	(21.0)	(17.6)	(25.4)	(14.9)
U.S.A.	70	4.569		1.255	1.077	230	42.590
	80	20.457		11.142	8.679	2.943	212.887
	90	48.586		33.740	18.802	8.019	393.113
	(90/70)	(10.6)		(26.9)	(17.5)	(34.8)	(9.2)
NIEs	70	628	1.857		351	149	4.778
	80	6.114	16.562		4.887	1.673	56.969
	90	25.548	60.512		16.793	6.423	208.996
	(90/70)	(40.7)	(32.6)		(47.9)	(43.2)	(43.7)
ASEAN	70	1.378	1.077	371		587	6.065
	80	17.829	11.298	4.900		5.573	66.517
	90	25.838	27.657	14.329		9.539	135.771
	(90/70)	(18.7)	(25.7)	(38.6)		(16.3)	(22.4)
Singapore	70	118	172	87	330		1.554
	80	1.560	2.464	2.005	4.962		19.375
	90	4.457	11.031	5.979	11.653		51.655
	(90/70)	(37.7)	(64.0)	(68.8)	(35.4)		(33.2)
World	70	18.881	39.952	6.416	7.258	2.461	312.001
	80	139.892	250.280	63.918	63.317	24.003	1.993.312
	90	235.307	517.093	205.055	158.489	60.203	3.332.100
	(90/70)	(12.5)	(12.9)	(32.0)	(21.8)	(24.5)	(10.7)

[a] NIEs include Hong Kong; Republic of Korea; and Taipei,China
[b] ASEAN includes Brunei Darussalam, Indonesia, Malaysia, Philippines, and Thailand
Source: International Monetary Fund, *Direction of Trade Statistics.*

Table 9.2

Process of Liberalization, Thailand

1960	"law for the promotion of industrial investment"
	- reduction of tariff on imports of raw materials for export products
1968	restriction of foreign direct investment in export-oriented industries, heavy industries, and process industries which use domestic resources
1972	"new law for the promotion of industrial investment" (revision of 1960)
	- preferable treatment for export industries
	- abolition of tariff reduction for raw materials (1972)
1973	special tax treatment for investments in regional areas
1977	revision of "new law for the promotion of industrial investment" (1972)
	- reduction of corporate tax or revenue tax for export industries
1978	"restriction of imports"
	- prohibition of imports (18 items), high tariffs (151 items)
	set up of "investment promotion areas"
	- exemption from taxation on revenue for 5 years
	- tax reduction on investment of infrastructure for 10 years
	special treatment of taxation for export firms
	prohibition of new set-up or expansion of automobile assembly lines (1993)
1983	revision of "law for the promotion of industrial investment" (1977)
	- more attractive tax incentive for foreign capital
1984	special treatment for the electronics industry
1985	plan for the domestic production of motor vehicles
	- technology transfer through foreign direct investment
1986	revision of "law for the promotion of industrial investment" (1983)
	- permission of 100% foreign capital for export industry
	- decrease of the mandated export rate for export-oriented industry
	plan for the domestic production of automobile engines
1988	special treatment for investments related to parts industry
1989	relaxation of the mandated export rate for electronics firms with more than 75 percent domestic capital
1990	transition to IMF code 8 country
	preferential treatment to regional areas
	reduction of tariffs on machinery
	abolition of the special exemption of import taxation on machinery for foreign firms
1992	CEPT scheme (mutual preferential tariffs)
	expansion of the "preferential treatment to regional area" (1990)
	deregulation of foreign currency exchange
1993	expansion of preferential tax treatment for investment in poorly developed areas

Table 9.3
Process of Liberalization, People's Republic of China
(1,000 US$)

1978	permission for foreign direct investment in PRC
1979	legislation of "Joint Venture Law"
	- legal treatment about the foreign direct investment in PRC
1980	delegation of permission for foreign direct investment in Kangtong and Fukken prefecture
	setting up of "special economic areas" (4 areas)
1983	introduction of special treatment for foreign capital firms
	- exemption from taxation on imports of raw material and production facilities
	- decrease of prescribed export rate
1984	delegation of permission for foreign direct investment to another 14 cities with harbors
	permission for domestic sales of products for foreign firms under certain conditions
1986	"guidelines for the promotion of foreign direct investment in China"
	- promotion of export-oriented industry
	- exemption from taxation on corporate profit
	- exemption from taxation on transfer to the home country
	- exemption from taxation on the uniform tax on exports
	- promotion of technology transfer
	set up of Shanghai foreign currency trade center
	- priority treatment for export-oriented firms
	"foreign firm law"
	- formal permission for 100 percent shareholding by foreigners
	"the 7th 5-year economic plan"
	- making "special economic areas" export centers
	- expansion of infrastructure
1988	abolition of regulations on the hiring policy of foreign firms
1989	"priority industry policy"
	- promotion of heavy industries or export-oriented industries
1990	revision of "Joint Venture Law" (1979)
	- promotion of bigger foreign direct investment
1991	set up of "bonded areas"
	- exemption from tariffs
	- promotion of processing trade
1992	liberalization of foreign capital to tertiary industry
	set up of "economic development areas" and "bonded areas" in inland areas

The case studies below show how the change in trade patterns from simple trade of primary and finished goods to intermediate goods and intrafirm trade has allowed East Asian producers better access to other markets. The expansion of intermediate goods trade, intraindustry trade, and intrafirm trade was often triggered by the aggressiveness of Japanese firms in utilizing intraregional division of labor.

Cross-border Division of Labor in the East Asian Region: The Japanese Electronics Industry

Foreign direct investment in Asian countries played an important role in promoting economic growth and exports in the region. The relationship between direct investment and the pattern of economic growth is demonstrated in this case study of the Japanese electronics industry, based on Itoh and Shibata (1995). Direct investment and cross-border division of labor among Asian countries are very active in the electronics industry, and this industry is a good example for studying the relation between direct investment and international trade.

Table 9.4 shows the pattern of distribution of foreign affiliates of the Japanese electronics industry in Asian countries. About 59 percent of the affiliates are located in East Asia, and about 70 percent of employment is in this region. This table shows the importance of East Asia for the Japanese electronics industry. The number of affiliates and employees in the region increased substantially in the latter half of the 1980s and in the 1990s.

The rapid appreciation of the yen promoted the shift of production locations out of Japan, and East Asia attracted a large portion of foreign direct investment from Japan for this industry.[2] The yen appreciated from about US$1 = Y240 in 1985 to US$1 = Y100 in 1994. The exchange rate of the yen relative to other Asian countries changed in a similar way. Reflecting this appreciation of the yen, per capita gross domestic product (GDP) in Japan in dollar terms increased from about US$11,000 in 1985 to about US$30,000 in 1993, roughly a three-fold increase during the last ten years, most of which was due to the appreciation of the yen. This drastic increase in per capita income implies two things: the relative increase in labor costs in Japan, and the expansion of the Japanese market. The former made domestic producers in Japan less competitive relative to foreign producers, and thus promoted further direct investment outflow from Japan. The latter induced more imports of goods into Japan.

Table 9.4

Number of Affiliates and Employees of
Local Subsidiaries of the Japanese Electric and Electronics Industry

Host Country	Total Number of Corporations	%	Total Number of Employees	%
Republic of Korea	61	11	31,831	8
Taipei,China	90	17	48,631	12
Hong Kong	24	4	32,534	8
Singapore	71	13	38,290	10
Thailand	68	12	49,704	12
Malaysia	132	14	118,222	30
Philippines	19	3	24,485	6
Indonesia	21	4	11,139	3
PRC	59	11	42,865	11
Asia Total	545	100	397,701	100
World Total (except Japan)	924	59	570,167	70

Source: Electronic Industries Association of Japan, *The Overseas Corporations' List.*

The active foreign direct investment from Japan to East Asian countries and the resulting increase in production by subsidiaries substantially affected the pattern of trade in this industry. Increased production in the host countries caused sales in the host country, in third countries in Asia, and in Japan to increase. Although we do not have good data indicating trade patterns of subsidiaries, a survey conducted by the Ministry of International Trade and Industry may be useful to see the pattern of trade in this industry and how it changed in the past. Figure 9.1 shows one result of this survey, comparing the place the products of subsidiaries are sold for four types of products: automobiles, automobile parts, electronics (final products), and electronic parts, in 1984 and 1992.

The comparison of electronic products and parts on the one hand, with automobiles and automobile parts on the other hand is interesting. More than 90 percent of automobiles produced in Asian countries were sold in the host countries, while only 45 percent of electronic products were sold in the host countries. This difference between the two industries became even more marked from 1984 to 1993. The high share of the host country as the place automobiles were sold is a reflection of severe

Figure 9.1
**Contents of Sales by / Parts Supply
for Asia Affiliates of Japanese Firms**

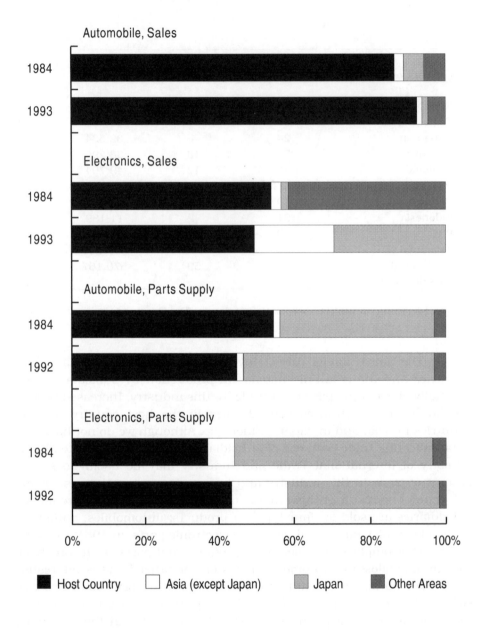

Source: MITI, *Foreign Operations of Japanese Firms.*

import restriction policies in importing countries and large transaction costs.

As for electric machinery, the share of host countries and the rest of the world (non-Asian region) decreased between 1985 and 1992, and the share of Japan and other Asian countries substantially increased. For electronic parts, the share of host countries as well as that of other Asian countries increased between 1985 and 1992. This pattern of change in the direction of trade reflects the following type of cross-border division of labor discussed below.

There was a rapid increase in Japan's imports of home electronic appliances from Asian subsidiaries. The change in the labor costs we mentioned above is the most important change behind these trends. For example, Japan imported about 3.7 million color television sets in 1993, and exported only 3.3 million sets in the same year. More than 95 percent of imports came from East Asian countries: 44.8 per cent from NIEs, 43.2 percent from ASEAN countries, and 8.4 percent from PRC. Although some of these figures include imports from Korean producers under original equipment manufacturing (OEM) arrangements, quite a large portion of these imports are from the subsidiaries of Japanese firms in Asia.

Third countries in Asia are also becoming important markets for the products of subsidiaries. Due to economies of scale in production, most of the products are not produced in all countries.[3] Electronics companies choose the location strategically and export from there to other Asian countries. The rapid increase in intra-Asian trade of electric machinery indicates that exports from local affiliates are now replacing exports from Japan.

Note that intra-Asian trade of electronic parts also increased, and this increase is based on the same mechanism as the increase in intra-Asian trade of electric machinery. In the case of electronic parts, the share of the host country increased. This reflects the fact that there was a large amount of direct investment by parts suppliers following the direct investment by assemblers. Thus, subsidiaries in Asian countries purchase increasing amounts of parts from other subsidiaries in the same country.

The increasing share of intra-Asian trade in the electronics industry indicates that cross-border division of labor is influenced by the location strategy of Japanese companies as well as the companies in other industrial countries. These companies see the East Asian region as one large region, and allocate their products from production centers. This pattern of cross-border division of labor increased intra-Asian trade.

The pattern of electric parts trade is more complicated than that of assembled goods. Often two or more countries are involved in the production of some parts. A typical example is the integrated circuit (IC) board used for items such as personal computers. We once visited a factory in Japan that produced IC boards for small portable computers. Central processing units were imported from the United States, memory chips were imported from Korean firms, and other materials imported from Taipei,China and other Asian countries. Final assembling of these parts was conducted in the Japanese factory. According to the engineer we interviewed, the assembly process (including several complicated production steps) was so sophisticated that only his factory in Japan could manage it. The IC boards, which were still intermediate goods, were exported to several other countries for final assembly. Thus the pattern of this particular part is very complicated.

Note that the pattern of trade mentioned above can also be seen in trade data between Asian countries and Japan. Table 9.5 shows trade (both exports and imports) of electric machinery and electronic parts between Malaysia and Japan in 1985 and 1993. On the export side (from Malaysia to Japan), we observe a drastic increase in the exports of electric machinery, in particular audiovisual equipment. On the import side (to Malaysia from Japan), we observe a substantial increase in semiconductors and audiovisual parts. Thus, such high-technology electric parts such as IC boards and audiovisual parts are increasingly exported from Japan following increasing outputs of assembled goods by local affiliates in Malaysia, while products such as color television sets are increasingly exported from Malaysia to Japan.

Electric machinery, in particular home electric appliances, are now becoming important exportable goods for East Asian countries, while the high-technology parts used for these industries are exported from Japan to these factories. The share of home electric appliances in the total domestic production of electric and electronic products in Japan decreased from about 28 percent in 1984 to about 14 percent in 1993.

Due to the technical characteristics of the electronics industry, the industry has a very complicated pattern of division of labor, with many firms involved. Before it became international, the Japanese electronics industry was characterized by intimate and complicated networks of firms located in narrow regions in Japan. The internationalization of assembly promoted the internationalization of this pattern of division of labor, and now labor is spread all over the Asian region. The large volume of intraregional trade of intermediate goods and parts suggests this cross-border pattern of division of labor.

Table 9.5
Exports from Japan to Malaysia, Vice Versa
(1,000 US$)

Exports from Japan to Malaysia	1985	1993
Electric machinery	561,744	3,679,827
Electric power control equipment	82,503	60,599
Audiovisual apparatus	129,499	685,268
television receiver & video monitor	14,479	22,207
radio receiver	27,464	9,331
parts of AV apparatus	32,334	601,945
Domestic electrical equipment	26,675	25,536
refrigerators	6,007	1,823
electric washing machines	8,513	6,820
parts of electric domestic equipment	...	7,264
Semiconductors & IC	69,958	1,507,324

Exports from Malaysia to Japan	1985	1993
Electric machinery	55,446	1,022,131
Electric power control equipment	585	154,749
Audiovisual apparatus	12	405,023
television receiver & video monitor	...	119,407
radio receiver	...	133,363
parts of AV apparatus	...	58,301
Domestic electrical equipment	4	25,945
refrigerators	...	10
electric washing machines	...	3,146
parts of electric domestic equipment	...	3,458
Semiconductors & IC	42,764	216,667

... means data not available.
Source: JETRO (Japan External Trade Organization).

Note that this internationalization of the division of labor by Japanese firms was accelerated by the entry of foreign products into Japan. Typical is the case of the personal computer. In the last few years, American personal computers have made aggressive advances into the Japanese market. Facing severe competition from American products, Japanese personal computer producers found they had a cost disadvantage: while American producers fully utilized inexpensive Asian parts, Japanese producers depended more on expensive Japanese parts. So, Japanese producers began to shift aggressively from local parts to less expensive imported parts. Foreign direct investment to Asian countries coincided with this expansion in imports of parts.

Table 9.4 shows about 400,000 workers are employed by Asian subsidiaries of Japanese electronic companies. This number suggests that the magnitude of the activities of electronic companies in this region is quite large. Note that there are also many local indigenous firms as well as subsidiaries of companies from other countries, such as Republic of Korea; Taipei,China; and the United States, involved in this division of labor.

Structural Changes in the Distribution System in Importing Countries and Asian Trade: Textiles and Apparel

Structural change in the domestic economy of importing countries is crucial for increase in imports. Without it, imports cannot be expected to increase greatly. This general principle is true for East Asian economies where trade is an important driving force for economic growth.

The case of textiles and apparel is very interesting for several reasons (Itoh 1991, 1993). Firstly, textile and apparel products are important exportable products for developing economies. The industry is quite labor-intensive and heavy investment is not required for start-up. Secondly, a substantial structural change in the distribution system in Japan was observed during the process of expanding imports of textiles and apparel from Asian countries. Note that Japan is unique as an importer of textiles and apparel because it does not apply quotas based on the multifiber arrangement (MFA).[4] In spite of the absence of formal trade barriers, the pace of expansion of imports of textile and apparel products in Japan was slow before 1985 as compared with other industrial countries, and this can be considered to result from the slow pace of restructuring of the domestic distribution system. Thirdly, in textile and apparel products, we can observe various kinds of interesting cross-border division of labor, where several countries are involved in the production process. This is due to the technological characteristics of the textile and apparel industry, where production processes can be easily separated into several independent steps, and each step can be organized in different locations under different management.

The structure of the traditional distribution of apparel products in Japan can be characterized as a system of small-volume, wide-variety retailers. By small volume, we mean that each retailer sells only a small volume of each product, and by wide variety, we mean that each retailer sells a large variety of goods in one shop. The department store, the major channel for apparel products in Japan, is a typical example of this small-volume, wide-variety distribution. It sells a wide variety of products in a few shops, and it does not have a chain system.[5] With this kind of system, retail stores depend on various services of wholesalers and manufacturers.[6] Thus, a consignment arrangement is quite common for the sales of apparel products in Japan. Small local retail stores are also heavily dependent on the services of wholesalers and manufacturers and rarely take the initiative for developing new channels of imported products.

One of the distinguishing characteristics of the Japanese retail market in the past was the fact that the share of family-run small-scale retail stores was very high. Textile products were not exceptional in this respect. There were a large number of shops all around the nation. Naturally, these shops depended heavily on various services by wholesalers and manufacturers. Thus, these small stores were obedient to the channel strategy and price structures set by wholesalers and manufacturers.

Small-volume, wide-variety distribution is not suitable for active imports of inexpensive Asian textile products. In order to import inexpensive Asian products profitably, the imported products should be sold in large volumes.[7] The fact that the import penetration ratio of apparel products in Japan was low before 1985, in spite of Japan's policy of not using MFA quotas, may be explained by the fact that the structure of the Japanese domestic distribution system did not allow active imports from Asian countries.

The drastic structural change in the domestic distribution system in Japan changed the picture of textile and apparel imports considerably. Due to various factors such as deregulation and motorization, various types of chain stores are emerging rapidly.[8] Chain stores usually have more than 100 shop outlets, sometimes as many as 500 shop outlets. They specialize in a limited number of products, sometimes only store-brand products. In this sense, their strategy is characterized as large-volume and limited-variety distribution. The large volume of sales allows them to take advantage of large-lot imports from Asian countries. It is no wonder that these chain stores are much more aggressive in using imported products from Asian countries than the traditional channels such as department stores.[9]

Note also that there is a partial shift in the position of channel leader from manufacturer/wholesaler to retailer in some areas of the apparel industry.[10] The market for men's suits is a good example. In this market, department stores and apparel firms have been the channel leaders for a long time. A large portion of consumers purchased men's suits at department stores. As mentioned before, department stores depend heavily on apparel firms. Large apparel firms producing men's suits in Japan play the role of manufacturer as well as wholesaler. The majority of men's suits sold in department stores are under consignment. Thus, prices are set by the apparel firms and the major risk is taken by them.

Newly emerged chain stores selling men's suits in suburban locations take a very different approach. They rarely depend on consignment arrangements with apparel firms, but take the risk of purchasing products from manufacturers. This commitment enables these chain stores to determine the prices themselves, unlike department stores. In this new channel, the chain store retailers, not the apparel firms, are the channel leader. Various factors, such as motorization, yen appreciation (thus cheaper import costs), and economic recession promoted the expansion of the share of this new channel. This shift of channel leader from manufacturers and wholesalers to retail stores has been observed in many areas, not only in apparel but also in many other consumer goods. Large chain stores are key players in this channel leader shift. This change in channel leaders is an important factor in promoting imports.

The share of imports in the total domestic consumption of apparel products (in terms of quantity)[11] increased from 45 percent in 1989 to 65 percent in 1993. There is a two-way causal relationship between the structural change in the domestic distribution system and import expansion: the increase in the share of imported apparel was triggered by the change in the domestic distribution system, and the change in the distribution system was promoted by increasing opportunities for utilizing inexpensive imported products.

In textiles and apparel, just as in electronic products, various kinds of cross-border division of labor can be observed. Figure 9.2 illustrates three typical cases. For men's suits made with wool, most of the fabrics used in Asian factories (for the products sold in Japan) are sent from Japan and final products are returned to Japan for retail sales. Yarn used for the fabrics is often imported from Asian countries to Japan. In this case, the sewing process is the most labor-intensive and technologically simple, thus, quite a large portion of the sewing is now delegated to foreign countries such as PRC. However, weaving (including finishing processes) requires delicate technical skills for products such as those sold in Japan. Thus, most of the fabrics used for men's suits sold in Japan are either produced in Japan or imported from Europe.

In the case of synthetic fiber products, large Japanese chemical companies invested actively in countries such as Malaysia and Indonesia, and these local affiliates not only have the spinning process, but also the weaving process. Hence, direct investment has been an important driving force for the deepening of cross-border division of labor in this industry.

For cotton products, the process of division of labor is often more complicated than other cases and often more than three countries are involved in producing one product. For example, the production of boys' trousers by one retail chain store in Japan is as follows (see Figure 9.2):

Figure 9.2
Some Patterns of Cross-Border Division of Labor in Textile Products

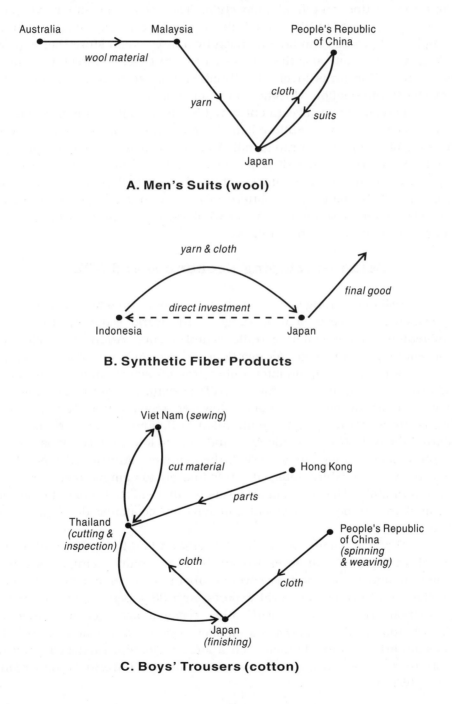

A. Men's Suits (wool)

B. Synthetic Fiber Products

C. Boys' Trousers (cotton)

Cotton fabrics are purchased from PRC and dyed and pressed in Japan. Accessories are purchased in Hong Kong and a local factory in Thailand does the cutting and final inspection. The most labor-intensive part, sewing, takes place in Viet Nam. This may be an extreme case, but such a complicated process can only be used by a large chain store that can sell a large volume. Note also that in this particular case, no direct investment is involved. The firms involved in producing these trousers do not have any ownership relation with the retail store chain.

Foreign direct investment is not as important for textiles and apparel as for electronics. Still we can observe various forms of cross-border division of labor and intraregional trade both in intermediate and final goods. Furthermore, the direction of trade is not only from developing countries to industrial countries, but also from Japan to developing countries. This complicated pattern of trade is often triggered by active behavior of Japanese retail stores or wholesalers to utilize the inexpensive labor force in other Asian countries.

Asian Developing Economies and APEC

Regional arrangements such as customs unions and free trade agreements now cover a wide range of the world economy. Under the proliferation of regional free trade arrangements, Asian economies are now entering a new stage. As mentioned above, Asian economic development was promoted by unilateral liberalization action under the General Agreement on Tariffs and Trade (GATT) system, and no formal regional free trade arrangement was made. However, regional free trade arrangements are now attracting more attention in this region. ASEAN countries started the ASEAN Free Trade Area and plan to lower international tariffs. In the Indonesian meeting of APEC, the member countries discussed the possibility of abolishing internal tariffs and quotas among member countries until 2020. The question arises as to what effects this kind of formal regional free trade arrangement will have on economic development in Asia.

The Asia Pacific Economic Cooperation is different from other regional arrangements in several respects. First, many countries are participating and a wide area is covered: about 52.5 percent of world production, 41.7 percent of world exports, and 38.4 percent of the world's population. This contrasts with other regional arrangements such as NAFTA and the EU, as well as smaller regional free trade areas. The question arises as to whether such a large regional arrangement can do more than a global arrangement such as the GATT-World Trade Organization (WTO).

Second, countries participating in APEC have very different economic structures and backgrounds from each other. The difference includes not only the wide range of per capita income—from high-income countries such as Japan and the United States to low-income countries such as PRC—but also differences in economic system, for instance capitalism in the United States versus a strong government-controlled system in PRC. This heterogeneity of the member countries in APEC contrasts with the EU, where member countries have common historical backgrounds and some similarity. In the case of NAFTA, where the income difference of the United States and Mexico is quite large, the difference is still smaller. Also, NAFTA is dominated by the United States, whose shares of production and trade in this region are quite large.

Due to these characteristics, a regional free trade arrangement is more difficult to pursue in APEC than in other regions. Unilateral liberalization action by member countries under the GATT-WTO system is considered to be more appropriate by some member countries. According to this view, each country has more of a free hand for the pace and the process of liberalization without having a formal regional free trade agreement. Severe competition to attract foreign direct investment among the countries in this region will promote liberalization actions by each country.

In contrast to the above view, there are several reasons for believing that having a formal regional arrangement in this region is beneficial for further economic development. First, it should be noted that there is no reason for the liberalization process to continue further without having any formal arrangement. In spite of the rapid liberalization process in East Asian countries, the developing countries in this region still keep many protectionist measures. Liberalization usually proceeds in areas where it is politically less difficult. Thus, formal international commitment may be necessary to promote further liberalization in politically difficult areas.

The position of Mexico in NAFTA is useful for considering the implications of a formal regional free trade agreement in the Asian region. Mexico, which achieved high economic growth by liberalization policies, was successful in attracting capital inflow from abroad. For Mexico to sustain this trend of inward direct investment and increasing flow of trade, it is necessary to make its free trade policy stance a credible long-run position. However, mere announcement by the present government of its commitment to such a strategy is not enough to make such a commitment credible. To make the free trade and investment position internationally credible, some kind of international arrangement is useful. To be a member of NAFTA is a good opportunity for Mexico to make its free trade position credible. By this credibility, it can attract more capital flow not only from the United States and Canada, but also from other parts of the world.[12] Similar arguments can be made for Asian countries. It is certainly very useful for Asian countries to make their free trade policy position credible for attracting capital inflow and expanding trade. Although unilateral action under the GATT-WTO system is one way for such commitment, a regional arrangement can provide an alternative and stronger signal of commitment.

A second reason for a free trade arrangement is the regional agglomeration discussed above. Division of labor often covers more than two countries in the region, and a concerted liberalization process by the countries involved in the division of labor is certainly very useful. There are externalities among member countries. As we discussed briefly in the case of electronics, intraregional trade of parts and assembled goods allows firms to enjoy economies of scale.

Third, we can expect an investment incentive mechanism to result from a formal free trade arrangement. Here we should note that trade and investment liberalization not only has the usual effects of promoting trade and investment by removing trade and investment barriers, but also has a strong incentive on domestic firms to prepare for competition with foreign firms. The latter mechanism is something like the following: when the domestic firms know that trade and investment will be liberalized in a certain period, they will prepare for the liberalization. Liberalization (removal of quotas, reduction of tariffs, and more liberal inward investment policy) implies severe competition with foreign firms for domestic producers. It also implies more opportunity for cooperation with foreign firms.

The effects of protection policies on the behavior of domestic firms are quite different, depending on whether the protection policies are temporary or not.[13] If domestic firms recognize that protection policy measures will be removed in the near future, they will feel strong competitive pressure and prepare for the future competition by investing actively. However, if protection policy measures are expected to exist for a long time, domestic firms have less incentive to invest because competitive pressure is much weaker.

Here, the commitment by the government to the timing of liberalization is crucial. It is a typical example of a "dynamic inconsistency" problem (for example, Kydland and Prescott 1977). The mechanism of the problem is as follows. Even if the government announces the liberalization process in advance, the government may not be able to follow the process if it faces slow domestic adjustment. When the domestic firms recognize this, they may not have a strong incentive to incur high costs in preparing for liberalization: they recognize that the liberalization process will be postponed if they are not prepared for it. In this circumstance, credible commitment to the liberalization process is necessary to give domestic firms incentive for investment. The government, whose future behavior is affected strongly by the position of domestic firms, is not able to make a credible commitment to liberalization. External arrangements such as a free trade agreement under APEC can thus be an instrument to give credible commitment to this liberalization process.[14]

Fourth, under a regional liberalization arrangement, we can expect some kind of competition for liberalization. Competition for inviting foreign investment among Asian countries promoted liberalization in these countries. This kind of competition for liberalization will be promoted if coordinated liberalization rules make trade and investment barriers of neighboring countries lower.

In this paper we have presented two brief case studies concerning the pattern of cross-border division of labor in the East Asian region. In the case of the electronics industry, foreign direct investment from Japan played an important role in promoting cross-border division of labor and intraregional trade, while in the case of the textiles and apparel industry, direct investment was not much involved. In both cases, the drastic structural change in the domestic economy in Japan had crucial effects on the changing pattern of trade between Japan and East Asian developing economies.

The pattern of trade in this region changed substantially: previously, exports of primary goods from developing countries and exports of finished goods from Japan were the basic trade pattern, but such types of trade as intrafirm trade, intraindustry trade, and trade of intermediate goods are increasing. Expansion of intermediate goods trade implies that cross-border division of labor has deepened, and deepening of cross-border division of labor has given producers in Asian developing economies better access to the Japanese market. In fact, as indicated by our case studies, much of the intrafirm trade and intermediate goods trade were triggered by the aggressive behavior of Japanese firms to utilize inexpensive labor in Asian countries.

The rapid economic development in East Asia was driven by active foreign direct investment and expanding trade in this region. Cross-border division of labor, not only at the level of finished goods, but also, and more importantly, at the level of intermediate goods, is behind these trends of investment and trade. It is obvious that this active trade and investment could not have been realized without the East Asian countries' liberalization policies.

East Asian countries have changed their trade policy stance from protectionistic import substitution to more liberal export promotion. They have also introduced various measures to attract foreign capital inflow. These policy changes were the result of voluntary action by these countries, and no formal free trade agreement existed in this region before.

However, the situation seems to be changing as a result of recent developments in APEC. Although no formal agreement regarding the possibility of a free trade arrangement in this region under APEC has been reached, there is more discussion now about the possibility of such a formal arrangement, and the possible effects of the agreement on economic development in the region. It is still too early to make any conclusive judgment on this issue, but it deserves serious attention.

Notes

1. There are not many countries which succeeded in economic development by import substitution policy. Japan may be one exceptional case. However, even in Japan, protection policy did not work to weaken competitive pressure on domestic producers, for Japan's entry to the GATT system did not allow Japan to enjoy permanent protection policy. Thus, domestic producers actively invested in order to prepare for the entry of foreign goods. On this point, see Komiya and Itoh (1988).

2. For example, the total number of employees in Matsushita's local affiliates in Malaysia was about 4,500 in 1985, while it increased to about 20,000 in 1993. We can observe this kind of rapid increase in the number of employees for any major electronics company in any East Asian country.

3. Thus, for Matsushita, Malaysia was the center for producing color televisions in Asia other than Japan, although the People's Republic of China is going to be another center in the near future due to its large domestic market.

4. Very recently, however, the position of the Japanese government changed and the government established the rule to utilize quotas based on MFA.

5. The numbers of branches of department store companies are at most 30 and usually around 10, and the sizes of branches are different depending on the size of demand at the place where branches are located. Thus, it is impossible to centralize the procurement system.

6. In Japan, apparel producers usually function as both wholesalers and manufacturers.

7. For example, suppose that retail stores can save 500 yen (about 5 dollars) for each unit of import as compared with domestic production. If retailers import only 1,000 volume, the net saving is only 500,000 yen (5,000 dollars), while if a trader imports 100,000 volume, it can save 50,000,000 yen (500,000 dollars). Note that American retailers are in a much better position to enjoy this kind of scale economy. As an example, compare the largest retailer in the United States, Walmart, and the largest retailer in Japan, Daiei. The total sales of Walmart are about three times as large as that of Daiei, while the total number of shop outlets of Walmart is almost ten times as large

as that of Daiei. Roughly speaking, Walmart has about 3,000 shop outlets, while Daiei has about 350 shop outlets. If both import 300,000 units of T-shirts, Walmart must sell 100 units per shop outlet, while Daiei must sell 860 units per shop. The story might be different if wholesalers import. By selling to many retailers, wholesalers can import products in large volumes. However in Japan, the sizes of most wholesalers are small and their import business is not very active.

8. Japan is now in the process of rapid restructuring of the distribution system. This phenomenon is called *kakaku hakai* (price destruction). There are several factors generating this structural change, among which such factors as deregulation by the government, change in the relative price of foreign goods due to yen appreciation, and increasing use of cars for shopping in the last 15 years are most important.

9. Perhaps the best example of this is the case of men's suits. Department stores, which heavily depended on the domestic distribution channel, sell either domestically produced suits or very expensive European suits. They were the dominant channel leader in the distribution of men's suits until the middle of the 1980s. However, so called "roadside stores", or chain stores specializing in men's suits and located along major roads in the suburbs, were expanding their share based on a very aggressive pricing strategy and now have about 50 percent share (in terms of the number of suits) of the market. Roadside stores utilize sewing factories in the PRC and in the Republic of Korea. Note that roadside stores usually have more than 100 shop outlets; the largest one has about 500 shop outlets. Thus, they can sell a large volume of the same suits. On the other hand, the department stores, which depend so heavily on consignment arrangement of domestic manufacturers, cannot utilize Asian production facilities.

10. Note that major apparel manufacturers in Japan are actively involved in wholesale activities as well as some retail activities. We thus use the expression manufacturer/wholesaler.

11. The data is based on Textile Statistics Annuals (Seni Tokei Nenpo) and covers only outerwear such as suits, coats, jackets, trousers, skirts, and shirts.

12. However, recent experience of capital outflow from Mexico taught us NAFTA was not enough to attract sufficient capital to Mexico.

13. Matsuyama and Itoh (1985) analyze this mechanism by using a duopolistic investment race game a la Spence (1978). According to the model, a domestic firm and a foreign firm are competing for investment. Under free trade each firm maximizes the pace of investment in order to reach long-term Stackelberg position. However, if protection is expected to continue for a long time, the domestic firm will slow down the pace of investment, since it does not face competitive pressure from the foreign firm. However, when protection measures are expected to be removed soon, the domestic firm will prepare for it by pacing up investment.

14. The liberalization process of Japan in the 1950s and in the 1960s had a similar effect. Japan committed to the liberalization process by becoming a full member of GATT. By this commitment, domestic firms had less room for asking the government to retard the process of liberalization.

References

Itoh, M., 1991. "The Japanese Distribution System and Access to the Japanese Market." In P. Krugman, ed., *Trade with Japan: Has the Door Opened Widely?* Chicago: University of Chicago Press.

Itoh, M., and K. Hatanaka, 1993. "Access to the Japanese Market by Asian Countries: A Case Study of the Wool Textile Industry." In T. Ito and A.O. Kruger, eds. *Trade and Protectionism.* Chicago: University of Chicago Press.

Itoh, M., and J. Shibata, 1995. "Cross Border Division of Labor in Electric and Electronic Industry." In K. Y. Chen and P. Drysdale, eds. *Corporate Links and Foreign Direct Investment in Asia and the Pacific.* Pymble: Harper Educational.

Kydland, F. E., and E. C. Prescott, 1977. "Rules Rather Than Discretion: The Inconsistency of Optimal Plans." *Journal of Political Economy* 85: 473–91.

Komiya, R., and M. Itoh, 1988. "Japan's International Trade and Trade Policy, 1955–84." In T. Inoguchi and D. Okimoto, eds., *The Political Economy of Japan, Vol. 2: The Changing International Context.* Stanford: Stanford University Press.

Matsuyama, K., and M. Itoh, 1985. "Protection Policy in a Dynamic Oligopoly Market." Discussion Paper. Faculty of Economics, University of Tokyo.

Spence, A. M., 1979. "Investment Strategy and Growth in a New Market." *Bell Journal of Economics* 10:1–19.

Chapter 10

Reflections on Agricultural Development, Population Growth, and the Environment

Marc Nerlove

Freres humains qui après nous vivez
N'ayes les cuers contre nous endurcis ...
Mais priez Dieu que tous nous vueille absoudre.

François Villon (1431-c.1463)

Approximately 80 percent of the world's 5.7 billion people live in countries in which 50 percent or more of the economically active population is engaged in agriculture (estimates based on World Bank and International Labour Organisation data). These countries are overwhelmingly poor, with low per capita gross national product (GNP) and high rates of population growth. Of these 5.7 billion people, 3.4 billion live in Asia, 2.2 billion of them in the People's Republic of China and India alone. Although the worst problems of population growth and environmental degradation are to be found in sub-Saharan Africa, what happens in Asia is of overwhelming importance because of the sheer numbers involved.

According to United Nations and World Bank projections (1992 and 1994), the world population may double between now and 2100, reaching 11.2 billion in the most probable scenario, with a rapid fertility decline in areas currently experiencing high rates of population growth. Or population may more than triple, reaching 19.2 billion, if the so-called demographic transition begins late in areas where it has not yet occurred, or proceeds more slowly than expected in those areas where it is already taking place. In either case, more than half the world population is expected to be Asian, and more than half of these Indian or Chinese. It is expected that this increase in world population will be accompanied by rapid urbanization: by 2025, more than half the people in the world are expected to be living in urban areas. Catastrophe might overtake us, of course, for example, a world pandemic of AIDS might kill most of us off. But it would be unduly pessimistic and, indeed, foolhardy to count on it.

In the past, remarkable increases in agricultural productivity have sustained the large population growth in Asia; little new land has been brought under cultivation since the 1950s. Rates of growth of food production have exceeded rates of growth of population largely because of agricultural modernization, which consists of use of modern inputs such as irrigation and chemical fertilizers, pesticides and herbicides, and improved varieties of major food crops (Jha et al. 1993). As existing technology and modern inputs are increasingly used, however, and as agriculture in Asia and worldwide becomes increasingly modern, a renewal of the agricultural extension that characterized North America in the 19th century and Latin America in the 20th may be required to sustain further population growth. Such extension will require, as it has in the past, new technology, new inputs, and capital formation to permit production on lands, or in the sea, which were not hitherto considered suitable for agriculture.[1]

Such increasing population and urbanization will clearly put a good deal of pressure on natural resources and the environment, and will pose especially severe problems for agriculture, which must expand into increasingly fragile environments and intensify and modernize in ways that may greatly affect air, water, and soil quality, and stocks of fish, timber, and other renewable resources in order to feed a much larger population. (Exhaustible, nonrenewable resources present a somewhat different problem; so far technological progress has prevented prices from rising in real terms.) During the past 30 years or so, the output of food and fiber have more than kept pace with a growing world population overall, although severe problems of distribution remain. Grains, for example, account for more than 80 percent of food crops consumed in developing countries directly and, of course, for a substantial part of total food consumption in developed countries indirectly through conversion into animal products. The average rate of growth of grain output over the last 30 years has been around 2 percent, more than enough to match world demand, and grain prices have actually fallen and are expected to continue to fall for the next 20 to 25 years. Much of this progress has occured in Asian countries, particularly in the production of rice. Dire predictions of worldwide famine have not materialized, although there is plenty of hunger and malnutrition around, and famines, such as have occurred in Somalia and are now occurring elsewhere in Africa, still result from war and civil disruption. Low and falling world prices, however, do not mean that poor people in poor countries will automatically have access to food and will not have to continue to produce much of what they themselves consume, nor is the predicted overall world abundance for the next generation any ground for complacency in the long run.

There have been three "agricultural revolutions" in the history of mankind. Each has permitted and been followed by a vast increase in population. The first was the "discovery" of agriculture, 12,000 to 10,000 B.C. in the Old World, and 10,000 to 8,000 B.C. in the New (Cohen 1977, Sauer 1969). The second "revolution" occurred primarily in Western Europe in the 17th century and consisted of the adoption of agricultural techniques developed principally in the Low Countries, and the adoption of New World crops such as potato and maize. These techniques and crops not only made productive agriculture possible on poorly drained soils, and greatly enhanced productivity of existing crops through new crop rotations and expansion of animal husbandry, but also permitted far more calories to be produced by the same land and labor inputs. Some authors hold that these changes in agriculture not only permitted a great increase in European population but were also a prime factor in the Industrial Revolution, which began in England in the mid-18th century (Bairoch 1976, Grigg 1980; for a contrary view see Livi-Bacci 1991). In more recent years, the so-called "Green Revolution", meaning the introduction of new, high-yielding varieties (HYV) of major food crops, principally maize, wheat, and rice, in the agricultural sectors of developing countries, has resulted in huge increases in food production worldwide and in many fundamental changes in agriculture and agriculture-related industries everywhere, including in developed countries. Indeed, the current world food "glut" and falling world prices of grain that are expected to continue well into the next century are a product of the Green Revolution and the agricultural modernization and extension that are part of it.

In the next section, I discuss the second agricultural revolution in some detail, since I believe it was the cause of the demographic transition in Western Europe. Its story has many lessons for developing countries today, although there are important differences between what happened in Western Europe in the 17th century and what is happening and has happened since the end of World War II.

The development and spread of HYVs (hybrid corn in the US in the 1920s and 1930s and dwarf varieties of wheat and rice in the less developed countries in the 1960s and 1970s) are the result of considerable research and development, carried out in developed countries, developing countries, and, especially, in international research institutes and by private seed firms, state enterprises, and publicly supported institutes. While many HYVs are hybrids, which suffer severe reductions in yields or in other desirable properties when reproduced from saved seed, many are open-pollinated improved varieties that do not immediately suffer such reductions. The seed industry and continuing research and development (R&D) are thus an essential part of the Green Revolution, but the implications for public versus private support of R&D differ depending on the biological basis of the innovation. In essence, all improved varieties function partly through making more efficient use of water and nutrients supplied in the form of inorganic fertilizers, and in part by increased resistence to pests and improved structural properties that may permit mechanization. By implication, therefore, the Green Revolution involves not only biological innovation, supported by both public and private R&D, but many other institutional and economic changes: agricultural modernization, development of markets, transport, irrigation, and other infrastructure, and the growth of industries supplying modern inputs and seeds. The demographic impact of the Green Revolution in Asia, and to some extent in other developing countries, may be seen as a parallel to the second agricultural revolution in Europe in the 17th and 18th centuries, leading to the demographic transition there in the 19th and early 20th centuries.

While further progression of the Green Revolution and concomitant agricultural modernization and development may be expected to continue, such developments are not likely to result in such dramatic increases in food supplies in the future without further extension of agriculture into environmentally fragile areas and into areas inhospitable to traditional agriculture. Whether modern biotechnology involving novel approaches to cell and tissue culture and genetic manipulation of biological material will provide the basis for a fourth agricultural revolution is problematic and uncertain. But what is certain is that, without further intensification of agricultural production, agricultural modernization, and expansion of agriculture into other areas, a growing world population will not continue to be supported at tolerable levels of nutrition and quality of life. Such expansion, intensification, and modernization will not occur without considerable research effort and investment and will involve severe pressures on environmental and renewable resources. Whether future generations will indeed be happy to be alive, that is, whether a substantially larger population can be sustained on this planet at an acceptable quality of life, will depend largely on measures we undertake now and over the next century.

To guide discussions of this issue and policies designed to bequeath a tolerable world to our progeny in the mid-21st century and beyond, it is important to understand the process of agricultural modernization and its environmental impact, the relation of such modernization to demographic change (in particular, the nature and sources of the demographic transition), and, finally, the effects of environmental change on both population growth and agricultural modernization and extension. In the remainder of this essay, I propose to take up these matters. First, I shall discuss the nature and sources of the demographic transition, focusing on the one that followed the second agricultural revolution in Europe. I then describe the changing role of agriculture in the process of general economic development and show that, even as it shrinks relative to the economy as a whole, agriculture must become more efficient at a rate faster than both the nonagricultural sector and the rate of growth of population if general economic growth is not to be choked off. Next, I take up the nature of traditional agriculture and the process of agricultural modernization and its relation to both environmental and demographic change. Finally, I deal with the way in which the use of renewable resources, including the environment, impacts on both population change and agriculture.

Central to my argument is the view that fertility is essentially endogenous, in the sense that parents decide how many children to have in order to maximize their own satisfactions, including the love and altruism they may bear toward their offspring, subject to whatever economic, social, and environmental constraints they may face. The implication of this view is twofold: first, population change, whatever its momentum, is essentially endogenous to the process of economic growth and development, and depends on parents' decisions and on factors affecting morbidity and mortality, some of which are themselves related to parental choices. There is nothing inevitable about continued population growth in the long run. Second, the view that the present generation effectively determines who and how many shall exist in future generations has profound moral and ethical implications for the weight these generations should have in choices that will affect their well-being and the constraints under which they will live. However, such moral issues are beyond the scope of this essay.

Population Change, Endogenous Fertility, and the Demographic Transition

Malthus's Theory of Demographic Change

For most of human history, birth rates and death rates have fluctuated roughly in tandem, so that the population itself remained stable or grew only slowly. With the development of agriculture some 12,000 years ago, it is believed that both birth and death rates increased substantially, and that there was some acceleration in the rate of growth of population (Coale 1974). A second major change occurred in Western Europe following what I describe as "the second agricultural revolution" above. This was a remarkable fall in death rates followed only slowly by a fall in birth rates, so that population literally exploded. In the 18th and 19th centuries, the population excess was relieved by the vast migrations of Europeans to the new lands of the Western Hemisphere and Oceania. It was against this backdrop that Malthus (1798, 1830) wrote.

Malthus's theory of population and growth is well-known: passion between the sexes, unless checked by human misery, leads to a continual growth in population. Positive checks to population growth include "...war, disease, hunger, and whatever... contributes to shorten the duration of human life." (1798, 23). Preventative checks include abstinence from sexual relations, continence within marriage, and/or delay of marriage. But Malthus thought that even the preventative checks would fail to operate to any great extent in the absence of the incentives forced on mankind by increasing misery. As long as living conditions did not deteriorate greatly, population would grow exponentially. Since, however, Malthus believed that food supplies and ultimately the means to human welfare more generally could only grow linearly, he predicted population growth with increasing immiserization until equilibrium was reached for a large population living under the most abysmal conditions.

That Malthus's dire prediction has not yet been realized is the result of many factors. First, in Western Europe and later in Eastern Europe, North America, and Japan, as death rates (particularly infant and child mortality rates) fell, birth rates ultimately came down as well, although with a substantial lag. Second, agricultural productivity increased substantially and new lands were opened up, reducing population pressure in older settled areas and making more food and other resources available to support a growing world population. In the 20th century, modern medical advances and public health investments have reduced death rates in many parts of the world, and a similar pattern of falling birth rates, agricultural extension and intensification, and general economic growth has followed (Africa is a notable exception). The pattern of falling death rates followed after a lag by falling birth rates has been called the "demographic transition" (a definitive treatment is Chesnais 1992; see also Beaver 1975, Caldwell 1982). But, to date, a rigorous theory about whether and how this demographic pattern might be linked to economic growth has proven elusive.

In this connection, it is important to make a distinction between endogenous population change and endogenous fertility. Models can be constructed in which there is a relation between economic and other factors and the size, composition, and changes in population, but in which no decision making mechanism is presupposed. Purely biological models of animal populations in which food supplies or predator population limit the size of the population in question are of this character. The Malthusian theory comes close to this paradigm.

A Theory of the Demographic Transition in Western Europe

In contrast to biological models, recent developments in population and family economics suggest many causal paths between the economic environment and human family formation and fertility decisions, including the possibility that mortality may be influenced by families' decisions on the investments in human capital they will make in their children, in the form of health and nutrition, and by their fertility decisions. In particular, recent economic theories of fertility focus on explicit family decision making models in which optimal fertility choices are made in a utility-maximizing framework. This is what I have called elsewhere as new home economics, but perhaps is more accurately referred to as endogenous fertility (see Nerlove et al. 1987 for a survey). Fertility is, of course, only one component of population change. In a closed population without migration, demographic composition and mortality also play a role over which families may have little control.

The transformation of agriculture in Western Europe that preceded and accompanied the Industrial Revolution and subsequent demographic changes that occurred were closely related to one another.

The changes in agricultural technique, principally those connected with water control and drainage originating in the Low Countries, and the introduction and diffusion of New World crops in Western Europe, especially the potato, are described in some detail by Bairoch (1976), Slicher van Bath (1977) and Grigg (1980, 145-234). I argue that the better health and nutrition that these changes made possible was not only responsible for the initial explosion of population that accompanied the Industrial Revolution but, ultimately, also for the decline in fertility that followed, i.e., for the "demographic transition".

The Industrial Revolution was, first and foremost, an agricultural revolution that permitted and fostered an unprecedented development of industry and mining in those countries where it occurred. At the beginning of the 18th century in England, and in other industrial nations in modern times, 75-80 percent of the population was engaged in agriculture. In this respect, these nations were similar to many third world, developing countries of today. Between 1600 and 1800, a definite break occurred in the evolution of the conditions of agricultural production. This period in England is characterized by a marked rise in labor productivity in agriculture and an absence of either famines or less extreme food shortages. By 1750, England was exporting 13 percent of domestic food production (Bairoch 1976, 459).

The upsurge in agricultural productivity began first in England (1690-1700), followed by France (1750-1760) and the US (1760-1770). Switzerland, Germany, and Denmark soon followed suit (1780-1800). Austria, Italy, and Sweden (1820-1830), and Russia and Spain (1860-1870) did not experience the same growth until the 19th century.

The majority of the technical innovations in agriculture that characterized the first stages of the second agricultural revolution originated in the Low Countries of Flanders and Brabant (modern day Netherlands and Belgium) and consisted of the accelerated application, in relatively sparsely populated areas, of techniques of crop rotation, animal husbandry and, especially, drainage and water control. These techniques developed to cope with an increasingly high density population and water-logged soils in these areas (Grigg 1980). The circumstances of soil and climate and a growing population created incentives for the development of new technology, which in turn permitted further population growth, the development of an export surplus, a trading economy, and urbanization.[2] It is remarkable that such wealth and abundance as realized by the Dutch and Flemish could have been achieved in such unfavorable conditions.[3] In addition, the discovery of the New World at the beginning of the 16th century and beginnings of European settlement there led to the introduction of many new crops in Europe, especially the potato in Northern Europe and maize in Southern Europe. The major innovations of the second agricultural revolution were as follows:

- Gradual elimination of fallow land and its replacement by continuous rotation of crops, in which fodder and leguminous crops replenished nitrogen content and prevented exhaustion of soils, in turn permitting expansion of livestock and lavish manuring of fields. The celebrated enclosures, which eliminated common lands and reorganized the system of land ownership, played a major role in these developments.

- The introduction and diffusion of new food crops, which permitted far more calories to be produced on the available land with less labor and capital. The major New World crops which appeared in Europe in this period and were later introduced by Europeans in Africa and Asia, where some subsequently became even more important staples than in Europe, were potato, maize, sweet potato, peanut, manioc, all kinds of beans, pepper, squash, tobacco, and tomato. Though European in origin, turnip, peas, and lentils played a major role in the new crop rotations that greatly enhanced agricultural productivity during the Second Agricultural Revolution. No significant livestock animals originated in the New World. The introduction of new crops is an example of the phenomenon of technological diffusion, which has characterized the third agricultural, or green, revolution in the 20th century (see Foster and Cordell 1992, Viola and Margolis 1991).

- Improvement of traditional farm implements, especially the plough, which replaced the hoe, and the scythe, which replaced the sickle, and the development of new implements.
- Improved selection of seed and breeding animals.
- Extension and improvement of arable land, especially by drainage and water control.
- Increased use of horses for farm work, replacing the more inefficient oxen as draft animals.

There was a close connection between agricultural and industrial development. Indeed, the low level of agricultural development had been an obstacle to general economic development in Europe. Movement of labor from farms to towns and to nonfarming occupations required increases in productivity to sustain the new entrants to the nonfarm labor force. A richer, more affluent agricultural sector provided the first markets for the new industrial goods. High transport costs, especially for bulky foodstuffs, kept markets local and population close to food supplies. Falling transport costs not only widened national markets, but also made the opening of new and agriculturally productive lands in North and South America and Oceania possible.[4]

Agriculture provided a major impetus for the development of the iron and steel industry, which laid the foundation for industrialization more generally in England, and agricultural development was arguably even more significant than the building of railroads, which is the conventional explanation. Moreover, the effects of agricultural development were realized at a much earlier date. In the case of ploughs and other implements, wooden parts were replaced by iron. Elimination of fallow land increased the need for ploughing. Tools for land clearance, such as axes, saws, and other tools, were of iron or steel. The wider use of horses in transport and draft and the practice of shoeing them greatly increased the demand for iron. Bairoch (1976, 491) suggests that horseshoes accounted for 15 percent of iron consumption in England in 1760.

Increasing demand for smelted iron products, especially in agriculture, depleted forests and led to the substitution of coal for charcoal in smelting and the eventual development of blast furnaces. Economies of scale inherent in the new technology and in the wider market for iron products led to falling prices that further stimulated demand in other sectors, especially in textiles, which became increasingly a town product. Hitherto, textiles had been produced in rural areas as a cottage industry, helpful in balancing the seasonal labor demand in agriculture. Much of the capital and entrepreneurship involved in the development of the textile industry in England came from the wealthier agricultural classes.

Bairoch (1976, 498) writes, "...agriculture not only set free food resources and workers needed for that big adventure that was the industrial revolution; it not only made possible or even fostered the demographic revolution and generated the birth of the modern textile and iron industries; but it also provided in the early stages a large part of the capital and entrepreneurs that animated the motive sectors of that revolution."

Exactly what role did agricultural development and the resulting increase in food supplies play in the extraordinary demographic changes that began in Western Europe in this period and continue to unfold in the modern era? Fogel (1994) has shown that the improvements in human nutrition that resulted were fundamental in reducing mortality and morbidity and in increasing energy levels and productivity of labor. It is clear that the effects of the second agricultural revolution were initially both demographically and economically destabilizing. In the first place, falling death rates, particularly infant and child mortality, led to massive and explosive increases in European population (McKeown 1976). These developments, in turn, led to the outpouring of the European population, the European settlement of the New World, and the opening of new and productive lands, which, because of improvements in ocean transport, further augmented food supplies and improved nutrition of the Europeans who remained. I argue further that these changes were ultimately responsible for the achievement of a new population equilibrium through demographic transition.

Recent developments in population and family economics suggest many causal paths between the economic environment and human family formation and fertility decisions, including the possibility that mortality may be influenced by families' decisions on the investments in human capital they will make in their children, in the form of health and nutrition, and by their fertility decisions. In particular, recent economic theories of fertility focus on explicit family decision making models in which optimal fertility choices are made in a utility-maximizing framework (see Nerlove et al. 1987 for a survey). Fertility is, of course, only one component of population change. In a closed population without migration, demographic composition and mortality also play a role over which families may arguably have little control.

The problem of explaining the demographic transition within the framework of endogenous fertility is to show how family decisions with respect to fertility, investment in the human capital of their children and their bequests to them in other forms of capital, and other variables interact over time to determine the size of the population, the stocks of capital, both human and physical, and the well-being of successive generations, and then to deduce the demographic transition as a possible outcome of these interactions. An attempt at such an explanation is contained in Nerlove (1974) and further elaborated in Nerlove and Raut (1995).

Good nutrition and health care increase children's chances of survival and may also affect their ability to absorb future investments in intellectual capital. To the extent that such investments increase life span, particularly the span of years over which a person can be economically active, such an increase in quality will raise the return to investments in human capital, which sons and daughters may later wish to make in themselves. To the extent that better health and nutrition result in a reduction in child mortality, they increase the satisfaction accruing to parents from other forms of investment, which also raise child quality, for the returns to these investments may then be expected to be enjoyed over a longer period of time. Better health and nutrition lower the costs of further investments in human capital relative to those in other forms of capital and increase the returns therefrom. In his monumental study of the origins of the modern family, Stone (1977) comes to much the same conclusion, although from an entirely different direction.[5]

Of course, parents have many reasons for having children. Not only do children serve as a source of support in old age in poor countries and of emotional sustenance in better-off times and places, but children are also valued for their own sake, because parents love them and perhaps see them as extensions of themselves beyond the grave. In strictly economic terms, all of these boil down to the presence, with positive marginal parental utility, of children's utilities in the utility function of the family to which they belong. In consequence, parents, unless they themselves are very poor, may desire to bequeath a stock of capital to their children. Since the stock of capital, material and intangible, human and nonhuman, is growing per capita in most economies today (sub-Saharan Africa is an exception), one must assume that parents desire to pass along more than that which they received from their parents, or that institutions in the economy function in such a way as to induce this outcome.

As long as the rates of return to investments in human capital remain above, or fall more slowly than, the rates of return to investments in other forms of capital, parents will be induced to bequeath a greater part in the form of human capital. Thus the tendency toward increasing quality of children will be intensified by the bequest motive. But, as rates of return tend to equality over time, parents tend to bequeath less in the form of human capital and more in the form of financial and physical capital. In equilibrium, rates of return will be the same. Nonetheless, as long as they differ, parents will invest in those assets yielding the highest rates of return, and as long as investment in human capital occurs, substitution will occur in favor of fewer children of higher quality and perhaps eventually against both quality and quantity of children in favor of commodities and knowledge. There is considerable evidence that an increasing proportion of total capital formation in this century has occurred in the form of human capital (Schultz 1961, 1971, 1973), which suggests that we may be far from the point at which such substitution begins to take place against children, quality, and quantity combined.

Thus my theory is that what happened sometime in the 19th and early 20th centuries in the West was that the second agricultural revolution sparked off a cumulative movement away from an unstable equilibrium between population and natural resources. This reduced infant and child mortality and set off a cumulative process of investment in better health and nutrition and in public health, leading to a surge in economic growth and population, but eventually resulting in substitution of quality in the form of further human capital investments for numbers of children.

Relevance to Developing Countries Today

In contrast to what occurred in Western Europe, demographic changes in developing countries today are driven by the diffusion of modern medical knowledge and public health technology. Moreover, techniques of population control and contraception are much better understood and more widely available than in earlier times. The role of agricultural development has been quite different. The extraordinary improvements in agricultural technology and the modernization of traditional agriculture in much of the world permitted population to grow in response to falling death rates as the forces behind the demographic transition came into play. The rapid rate at which these changes ensued, in contrast to the earlier European transition, was surely due in part to the more readily available technology of contraception and population control, but also, I believe, to processes associated with agricultural modernization itself, which I discuss in the next section. Yet the basic theory outlined above, if correct, has implications for future demographic developments, since the occurrence of the demographic transition in the areas of the world where it has not yet occurred, and its continuance in those areas where it is now under way, depends, if these conjectures are valid, on the existence of opportunities for, and absence of obstacles to, further investments in human capital. Such opportunities depend, in turn, on continued agricultural development at a pace sufficient not only to feed and clothe a growing population but also to offset technical progress in the nonagricultural sector to a degree sufficient to prevent the terms of trade from turning too much in agriculture's favor.

Depletion of environmental resources, which may result from population and general economic growth and the agricultural development which must take place to support such growth, may impact on endogenous fertility decisions in a variety of ways, some resulting in fertility decline and a slower rate of population growth, others in an increase (Nerlove 1991, 1993). These are discussed below. To anticipate: environmental degradation and resource depletion, by increasing morbidity and mortality, may make numbers of children more attractive than investment in them and thus act perversely to increase population growth until such growth is checked by mortality or by parents' own misery. On the other hand, such depletion and degradation may reduce the productivity of physical capital and existing technology and enhance the return to investment in knowledge and human capital, thus reinforcing the fertility decline and reducing the rate of population growth. The interactions between stocks of human and physical capital and renewable natural and environmental resources and the factors that determine population, particularly those factors that determine families' fertility and investment decisions, are poorly understood. (An attempt to provide a framework for an analysis of these interactions is given in Nerlove and Raut 1995.)

Role of Agriculture and Agricultural Productivity in General Economic Growth

More than thirty years ago, when T. W. Schultz wrote his famous *Transforming Traditional Agriculture* (1964), agriculture worldwide could overwhelmingly be characterized as traditional. Today, it is in the throes of becoming modern. Indeed, the third agricultural revolution, for all its biological basis, is essentially agricultural modernization. As the world becomes richer, per capita demand for food, fiber, and other agricultural products declines relative to the demand for nonagricultural products, but total demand increases inexorably with population growth. Since the elasticity of per capita demand for agricultural products is typically less than one and falling as incomes rise, it is apparent that the rate of increase in agricultural demand will come to be dominated by population growth, provided the terms of trade do not turn too much in favor of agriculture (i.e., the prices of agricultural products rise greatly relative to nonagricultural products). A greater proportion of total output will be in the form of nonagricultural goods and services, and this changing structure of demand has generally been accompanied in the past by a falling proportion of the economically active fraction of the population engaged in agriculture and by extensive urbanization. In very poor economies today, the agricultural sector is dominant, with 80 percent of the labor force and close to 50 percent of GDP. In highly developed, industrialized economies such as the United States, the fraction of the labor force directly engaged in agriculture is under three percent. But as Timmer (1988, 292) notes: "When directly related input and output industries and marketing activities are included, 'agribusiness' seldom declines to less than 20 percent of any country's economy. Hence the sector remains the largest single 'industry' in absolute size even in rich countries." To accommodate both general economic development and population growth, agriculture must grow rapidly even as it declines in relative importance. It has done so, in instances of successful economic development, by large increases in total factor productivity and by becoming increasingly integrated, on both input and output sides, with the nonagricultural economy.

Demand for Agricultural Products

In this section, I develop a simple framework for the sectoral shifts in demand which occur during the process of growth. I show how rising real per capita incomes and growing population affect the demand for food and other agricultural products in absolute terms, and the size of the agricultural sector relative to the nonagricultural sector of the growing economy. More importantly, I show how these effects depend on the terms of trade between the agricultural and nonagricultural sectors of the economy and on the price and income elasticities of the demand for agricultural products. The terms of trade between agriculture and nonagriculture depend on the conditions of agricultural supply and agricultural development, a theme which I have developed extensively elsewhere. In the next subsection, I will briefly summarize the main conclusion of a more detailed analysis which shows that total factor productivity in agriculture must grow rapidly if the process of general economic development is not to be choked off.

Let:

Y = the total income or product of an economy = total expenditure on goods and services. I will identify Y also as the total income of individuals in this society that is available to spend on goods and services, including investment,

qX = total expenditures on food and other agricultural products, denominated in units of manufactures and other nonagricultural products, where q = the price of food etc. relative to these other products (in my subsequent discussion of Jorgenson's [1961] model, I will use $p = 1/q$ rather than q, i.e., the terms of trade between agriculture and nonagriculture),

N = population,

y = Y/N = per capita income, and

x = X/N = the per capita demand for food and other agricultural products, which I assume to be a function of the relative price of agricultural and nonagricultural products:

$$x = f(q,y).$$

$$\xi = -\frac{\partial \log x}{\partial \log q} = \text{the price elasticity of demand.}$$

(1)

$$\eta = \frac{\partial \log x}{\partial \log y} = \text{the income elasticity of demand.}$$

S = qX/Y = the share of food and agricultural products in the total output of the economy.

Now

$$S = \frac{qX}{Y} = \frac{qxN}{yN} = \frac{qx}{y}.$$

(2)

Taking logs and differentiating with respect to time, I obtain

$$\frac{\dot{S}}{S} = \frac{d \log q}{dt} + \frac{d \log x}{d \log q}\frac{d \log q}{dt} + \frac{d \log x}{d \log y}\frac{d \log y}{dt} - \frac{d \log y}{dt}$$

$$= (1-\xi)\frac{\dot{q}}{q} - (1-\eta)\frac{\dot{y}}{y}$$

(3)

Equation (3) shows how the share of agriculture in the economy as a whole depends on the rates of change of the relative price of agricultural and nonagricultural products and per capita income. If the total output of the economy is growing faster than population, per capita income will be growing at a rate

$$\frac{\dot{y}}{y} = \frac{\dot{Y}}{Y} - \frac{\dot{N}}{N}$$

(4)

The formula for the absolute growth of demand for agricultural products corresponding to (3) is

$$\frac{\dot{X}}{X} = -\xi\frac{\dot{q}}{q} + \eta\frac{\dot{y}}{y} + \frac{\dot{N}}{N}$$ (5)

Price elasticities of the demand for food and other agricultural products are generally thought to be low; this means that the first term in (3) may be quite close to the rate of increase in q, so that the terms of trade in favor of agriculture, relative prices of agricultural commodities, do not have to rise much to offset the effects of rising per capita incomes, which are in any case attenuated by the "fact" reflected in Engel's Law (1857): Expenditures on food decline as a proportion of total expenditures as the latter increase (i.e., holding prices constant and ignoring the relation of savings to income, $0 < \eta < 1$).

Thus (3) shows that the declining relative importance of agriculture in the process of general economic development depends crucially on the terms of trade between agriculture and the rest of the economy.

On the other hand, because ξ can be assumed to be small and because η has been found empirically to average about 0.5 (Houthakker 1957), the absolute level of agricultural demand is dominated by the growth in real per capita incomes and by population growth. For many developing countries, the former is low and the latter relatively high.

The Supply of Agricultural Products

To see what happens to the terms of trade between agriculture and industry in the course of general economic development, we have to look at what happens to agriculture. It is this aspect of development that is addressed in the models of dual economic growth of Jorgenson (1961) and Lewis (1954). Here, I will only summarize the main conclusions of an analysis I have presented elswhere (Nerlove 1994b).

Let p be the ratio between the price of manufactures and the price of agricultural products, taking the latter as the numeraire, i.e. the reciprocal of q above. In these terms,

$$\frac{\dot{p}}{p} > 0$$

represents a turning of the terms of trade against agriculture (favorable to

general economic development), while $$\frac{\dot{p}}{p} < 0$$

represents a turning in favor of agriculture (unfavorable to general economic development). Let:

α = the rate of growth of total factor productivity in agriculture;

λ = the rate of growth of total factor productivity in the nonagricultural sector;

1-β = the elasticity of output with respect to labor input in agriculture;

1-σ = the elasticity of output with respect to labor input in the nonagricultural sector; and

ε = the rate of growth of population.

In Nerlove (1994), I show that

$$\frac{\dot{p}}{p} = \alpha - \lambda\left(\frac{1-\beta}{1-\sigma}\right) - \varepsilon$$

(6)

which is positive or negative according as

$$\alpha - \lambda\left(\frac{1-\beta}{1-\sigma}\right)\begin{Bmatrix}>\\<\end{Bmatrix}\varepsilon$$

Thus the terms of trade between agriculture and industry turn against agriculture or in favor of agriculture according to whether

The rate of technical change in agriculture - (the rate of technical change in industry) x (the elasticity of output with respect to labor input in agriculture / the elasticity of output with respect to labor input in manufacturing)

is greater or less than the rate of population growth.

A reasonable approximation to the adjustment, $(1-\beta)/(1-\sigma)$, to the rate of technical change in industry would be to take the ratio of the share of labor in total output in the two sectors. This would presumably be less than one, but perhaps not too much less.

The importance of the terms of trade to the process of general economic development is not to be found in Jorgenson and Lewis, for they do not really describe the process by which labor and other resources move out of the agricultural sector and into the nonagricultural sector. They assume that the wage in agriculture is always a fraction of the industrial wage sufficient to induce movement of labor from agriculture to industry. But clearly the real returns to factors of production in the nonagricultural sector depend on the prices of agricultural products relative to nonagricultural products. If the former rise relative to the latter, real returns in the nonagricultural sector will fall relative to real returns in agriculture, and the movement of labor and other resources out of agriculture will be impeded or even choked off and the process of general economic development will be slowed or halted. Thus, improving agricultural efficiency, technical change in agriculture, and agricultural modernization are integral parts of the process of general economic development. High rates of improvement in total factor productivity in agriculture relative to rates in industry and relative to the general rate of population growth can prevent or impede the turning of the terms of trade between agriculture and industry in favor of agriculture, a turn that might otherwise slow or choke off the process of general economic development.

The development of the agricultural sector and the improvements in total factor productivity necessary to general economic growth depend on continuation of agricultural modernization, which is a process of transition from traditional agriculture to modern agriculture and, in modern times, a product of agricultural research and investments in agricultural infrastructure. What traditional agriculture is and how the process of modernization occurs are the subjects of the next section.

Traditional Agriculture, Agricultural Modernization and Expansion: Process, Demographics, and Environmental Impacts

Schultz's Characterization of Traditional Agriculture

In his famous characterization of traditional agriculture, Schultz (1964) described it as efficient, in equilibrium, but very poor: a situation in which the marginal productivity of physical capital might be high, but in which the rate of return to net new investment in both physical and human capital was close to zero, in part because people living on the margin have extremely high rates of time preference, but also because an economy in which there has been little change for a long time, and which is therefore in static equilibrium, has already adjusted stocks of both forms of capital to equilibrium levels so that there is little or no incentive to net investment which would change those levels. Moreover, since it is largely the process of change that gives human capital its value, and since high mortality and low expectations of length of life reduce rates of return to investments that are embodied in individual human beings, human capital is particularly affected.

The view that traditional agriculture may be poor but is nonetheless characterized by efficient use of the resources available implies that, if factors of production are withdrawn from the agricultural sector in order to fuel the growth of the nonagricultural sectors of a developing economy, agricultural output will fall, choking off further growth and development. Why then is traditional agriculture so poor and why does it appear so stagnant? A part of the explanation is the lack of modern or effective technology. But this is not the whole story, for it remains to be explained why there is so little investment in the discovery and development of more effective technology in a traditional context. This is what Schultz attempts to explain and, in so doing, to lay the foundation for a theory of how agriculture is, or can be, transformed from traditional to modern.

Schultz (1964, 3-4) puts the problem as follows: "The man who farms as his forefathers did cannot produce much food no matter how rich the land or how hard he works. The farmer who has access to land and knows how to use what science knows about soils, plants, animals, and machines can produce an abundance of food though the land be poor. Nor need he work nearly so hard and long. He can produce so much that his brothers and some of his neighbors will move to town to earn their living. Enough farm products can be produced without them. The knowledge that makes this transformation possible is a form of capital whenever it is an integral part of the material inputs farmers use and whenever it is part of their skills and what they know.... Farming based wholly upon the kinds of factors of production that have been used by farmers for generations can be called traditional agriculture.... How to transform traditional agriculture, which is niggardly, into a highly productive sector of the economy is the central problem.... Basically this transformation is dependent upon investing in agriculture." Under what circumstances will the kind of investment needed to effect the agricultural transformation, as this process is called, be forthcoming endogenously in a developing economy, and under what circumstances must outside forces, exogenous to the agricultural sector, come into play?

The view that Schultz seeks to counter is stated by him in rather stark terms (1964, 8): "...the opportunity for growth from agriculture is among the least attractive of the sources of growth; agriculture can provide a substantial part of the capital that is required to mount industrialization in poor countries; it can also provide an unlimited supply of labor for industry; it can provide much labor at zero opportunity costs because a considerable part of the labor force in agriculture is redundant in the sense that its marginal productivity is zero; farmers are not responsive to normal economic incentives but instead often respond perversely, with the implication that the supply curve of farm products is backward sloping; and large farms are required in order to produce farm products at minimum costs."

In contrast, Schultz (p.16) proposes that: "...the agricultural sector in a large class of poor countries is relatively efficient in using the factors of production at its disposal.... Farm people who have lived for generations with essentially the same resources tend to approximate the economic equilibrium of the stationary state. When the productive arts remain virtually constant over many years, farm people know from long experience what their own effort can get out of land and equipment. In allocating the resources at their disposal, in choosing a combination of crops, in deciding on how and when to cultivate, plant, water, and harvest, and with what combination of tools to use with draft animals and simple field equipment—these choices will embody a fine regard for marginal costs and returns. These farm people also know from experience the value of their household production possibilities; in allocating their own time along with material goods within the domain of the household, they too are finely attuned to marginal costs and returns. Furthermore, children acquire the skills that are worthwhile from their parents as children have for generations under circumstances where formal schooling has little economic value."

Schultz (1964, Ch. 6) spends a great deal of effort arguing that the costs of the income streams yielded by net new investments in traditional

forms of capital in traditional agriculture are very high in terms of foregone consumption. The rate of time preference in traditional societies is
high. This is because people are very poor; the value of current consumption is high relative to future consumption when it spells the difference
between life or death for people "living on the edge".

The implications of allocative efficiency, stationary equilibrium,
and high rates of time preference in traditional agriculture are responsible for the apparent stagnant quality of traditional agriculture and low or
zero rates of investment in physical and human capital and knowledge. In
the technical appendix to this section, I present a simple model of investment in a traditional society in stationary equilibrium, which illustrates the following propositions:

- Given the state of agricultural knowledge and the relative scarcities of each quality of each factor of production, factors are allocated efficiently in the sense that all are fully employed up to the
  point at which their marginal value products (shadow prices in
  modern terminology) are equal in every use. It follows that agricultural output cannot be increased by reallocating factors of production.

  Think of every factor of production as the flow of services
  from a stock of capital available to society at the beginning of each
  period: this may be the human population with skills and knowledge, tools, buildings, ditches, fences and other physical capital,
  land and its qualities, or the stock of general knowledge. The flows
  of services from these stocks yield a flow of output or gross income during the period (according to some production function)
  but are wholly or partially used up in the process. Tools wear out,
  ditches silt up, seed germinates and is transformed. Thus, in order to maintain the stocks of capital and corresponding flows of
  services in the next period, some current output must be devoted
  to replenishing them, that is, some potential consumption must
  be foregone. The aggregate of consumption foregone in order to
  maintain stocks of capital is depreciation. Similarly, human beings die and must be replaced by children, the rearing of whom is
  not costless. The difference between gross income and the amount
  of output available to society for consumption if capital stocks are
  to be maintained is net income. In a society in stationary equilibrium, stocks are just maintained and are the same at the beginning of every period; consumption each period is equal to net income. In order to augment any stock of capital and its associated
  flow of services, some additional consumption would have to be

foregone; the difference between net income and consumption is net new investment. Gross investment is the sum of net new investment and depreciation.

- Traditional agriculture is in a state of stationary equilibrium, that is, given the state of knowledge and relative factor scarcities, farmers not only have no incentive to change the allocation of factors, they have little incentive to invest in augmenting the supply of any factor. Any incremental increase in any factor of production will bring only a return equal to its shadow price, which is in common with every other factor. If the stock of agricultural knowledge embodied in farm people is regarded as a factor of production like other material factors, it too has a shadow price equal to all others and, in equilibrium, its shadow price represents the return to its incremental augmentation.[6] The implication of optimal allocation in traditional agriculture is that we might as well think of a single factor of production, which is the flow of services yielded by the stock of a single type of capital.

  Human beings represent a profound complication in the analysis when fertility is endogenous, since they are both a produced factor of production and the ultimate consumers of output. In the following exposition of Schultz's characterization of traditional agriculture, I shall neglect this complication by assuming that population is exogenously determined and constant from one generation to the next. The simplification of a single type of capital and a single factor of production is then possible without loss of significant generality.

- Because the traditional agricultural sector is in equilibrium, the demand for investment in the stock of capital, which includes human capital and knowledge, is essentially a replacement demand. The marginal product of a factor of production, which is best thought of as the marginal product of the flow of services yielded by a corresponding capital stock, may be large or small, but the expected returns from net new investment in that stock must be very small relative to the community's rate of time preference, i.e., the equilibrium rate at which the possibility of additional future consumption is traded off against the reality of present consumption, by the representative individual.[7] In traditional agriculture, the expected returns from net new investment are low relative to the costs, in terms of foregone consumption, of making such investments, and the rate of time preference is high. In stationary equilibrium, there is no net new investment.[8] Consequently, traditional agriculture appears stagnant.

The implication of Schultz's analysis for the modernization of traditional agriculture is that something exogenous must happen to disturb the equilibrium of traditional agriculture. That something could be the discovery of new technology and knowledge, or new opportunities for net investment, which would yield greater possibilities for future consumption than can be realized by investing in traditional factors of production and knowledge. Or it could be a response to population growth a la Boserup (1965, 1981, 1990).[9]

A general formal analysis of these propositions is difficult because consumption and income streams, as well as costs, may vary over time, and because time preference is not simple to characterize in a multiperiod context. Stationarity helps to simplify matters a great deal because it means that each pair of periods is like any other pair and population is unchanging. In the technical appendix to this subsection, I give an analysis of the stationary case, in which some additional simplifying assumptions are introduced.

An Apparent Asian Contradiction to Schultz's Theory of Traditional Agriculture

Agricultural Involution in Java

In 1830, the population of Java (the central, and even today overwhelmingly the most populous, part of Indonesia) was estimated to be about 7 million (Geertz 1963). In 1992, the population of Indonesia as a whole was estimated to be 184 million, of whom nearly 60 percent, i.e., about 108 million, are estimated to live on the island of Java, despite the great efforts of the Indonesian government to promote settlement in the outer islands. This represents a somewhat more than 15-fold increase over 160 years, or about five generations. (Contrast this growth with that projected by the World Bank [1994] and the UN [1992] that, even in the best case scenario, the world population is likely to more than double in the coming five generations.) Even in 1900, the population of Java is estimated to have been more than 28 million, or a four-fold increase in a little more than two generations (Geertz 1963, 69).

The persistence of traditional agriculture in the context of rapid population growth on the island of Java during the 19th and early 20th centuries represents a challenge to the characterization of traditional agriculture presented in the previous section. Table 10.1 reproduces Geertz's (1963, 69) estimates of the population of Java from 1830 to 1900, and reports recent estimates of Java's population from the Indonesian Central Bureau of Statistics.

Table 10.1
Population Estimates in the Island of Java

Year	Population (millions)
1830	7
1840	8.7
1850	9.6
1860	12.7
1870	16.2
1880	19.5
1890	23.6
1900	28.4
1961	63.0
1971	76.1
1980	91.3
1985	99.9
1990	107.6

Sources: 1830-1900: Geertz (1963, 69). 1961-1990: Indonesian Central Bureau of Statistics, Census Reports (1961,1971,1980, 1990).

How such a huge growth in population occurred with little change in traditional agricultural technique, major social, cultural or institutional change, or substantial out-migration, requires an explanation that significantly modifies Schultz's view of how agriculture is transformed from traditional to modern. Geertz (1963) offers such an explanation. Part lies in the peculiar nature of the Dutch colonial administration in Indonesia during the 19th and 20th centuries until ended by the Japanese occupation in 1942, followed by independence in August 1950. But a major part of the explanation has to do with the nature of the rice plant and its unique ability to grow under flooded conditions. This story has been a major source for the theory of economic dualism.

Indonesian Background
The Indonesian archipelago consists of more than 13,000 islands strewn across an expanse of 3,200 miles of sea, of which about 3,000 are large enough to be inhabited. The largest of these are Sumatra, Kalimantan (Borneo) occupied jointly with the Malaysian provinces of Sabah and Sarawak and the Kingdom of Brunei, the central island of Java, Sulawesi

(Celebes), and Irian, occupied jointly with Papua New Guinea. Most of the population is concentrated on the island of Java, but, since independence, there has been a conscious policy to induce, sometimes by force, migration to the "outer islands", as all of Indonesia apart from Java and Bali is called. All of the islands lie within the tropical zone, but the surrounding seas exert a moderating influence on the climate, so that variables like topography, altitude, and rainfall produce greater variations in "microclimates" than do seasons or latitude. Most of the archipelago lies within the equatorial "everwet" zone, where no month passes without several inches of rainfall. Most of the islands get much more than this from the monsoon, November through April. Topography and vegetation are extremely varied, ranging from quite high and rugged mountains to gently sloping alluvial plains. The entire region is actively volcanic and has many rich soils characteristic of such activity.

The islands of the Indonesian archipelago have a long history of varied civilizations and art, but our part of the story begins with the arrival of the Portuguese in 1509 and the spices they brought back to Western Europe, which formed the basis of a flourishing trade. The Portuguese, except for a few locations such as East Timor, were driven out by the British, who were eventually supplanted by the Dutch. The latter organized the Netherlands East India Company in 1602, which not only monopolized the spice trade, but also established sugar, tobacco, indigo (a dye stuff), and especially coffee, on Java and Sumatra. The East India Company went bankrupt in 1799 and the Dutch government assumed control of the Indies in 1800. There was a brief period of British control from 1811 to 1816, under Thomas Stamford Raffles (1781-1826),[10] who introduced a system of land taxes that was adopted by the Dutch when the Indies were restored to them by the treaties signed at the Congress of Vienna (1814-1815). In 1829, Johannes van den Bosch, later Governor-General, proposed a system of taxes based on those that Raffles had introduced, in which payment was to be made not in rice nor in cash but in labor corvées to be used on Dutch plantations or estates, and/or in using some of the community's land to grow crops for export. This was called the *Cultuurstelsel* in Dutch, properly translated as "cultivation system"; note that Geertz uses the phrase "culture system" because of its more common use in the English language literature on Indonesia. I will refer to it as the System.

The System, which was operated through indigenous rulers in a way that did not disturb local social and cultural institutions, provided for one third of the land devoted to rice terraces in Java, for example, to be devoted to export crops, principally sugar. Coffee, pepper, tobacco, spices, and later rubber, were first grown on estates or plantations, later by small holders in upland areas or on the outer islands where rice was not, or could not be, grown. It evolved in a way that permitted an export sector, which was in effect a part of the Dutch economy, to coexist with a traditional rice-based economy on Java, and deepened and stabilized the differentiation between the economies of the outer islands and Java. According to Geertz (1963, 53): "...it prevented the effects on Javanese peasantry and gentry alike of an enormously deeper Western penetration into their life from leading to autochthonous [indigenous, native] agricultural modernization at the point it could most easily have occurred."[11] It led to what the Dutch economist Boeke (1910, 1953) was to term economic dualism, which despite significant conceptual differences with the theory of dual economies, had a major impact on development economics in this connection (Kanbur and McIntosh 1987).

Rice

A good summary of the characteristics and development of rice culture and its historical spread throughout Asia is contained in Bray (1986). Barker, et al. (1985) emphasize developments since World War II, especially the research and development that led to the HYVs and their introduction in the mid-1960s. In this subsection, I discuss traditional wet rice culture and the ability of this mode of production to absorb increasing amounts of factors other than land, principally labor and capital improvements produced by labor, without any great decline in the marginal productivity of labor, and thus to sustain an increasing large population in a limited space.

Rice is not an aquatic plant but a grass like wheat, barley, rye, oats, sorghum, or millet. Its unique characteristics, however, make it possible to grow the plant in a highly productive manner in flooded fields. There are also varieties of rice that can be grown on dry land and steep hillsides, but the yields of these varieties are considerably below those of rice grown in flooded fields. In Malay and the languages spoken throughout the Indonesian archipelago, the flooded fields are called *sawah*, but the term is used by various authors, including myself, to refer to the whole manner of highly intensive traditional agriculture typified by wet rice cultivation in Java.[12] Most rice grown in Asia is wet rice (about 5/6ths of the world total); the little dry land rice grown is typically grown on steep hillsides or in the outer islands of Indonesia under long-fallow, slash-and-burn traditional, or swidden, conditions. Weeds and nitrogen fertilization are much greater problems in dry rice cultivation than in *sawah*. Wet rice is started in "trays" and then is transplanted to very wet but not flooded soil. The field, surrounded by a bund, or low dike, is gradually flooded as the stems of the rice become high enough to permit respiration. Wet rice varieties are characterized by tall, stiff stalks (although there are some floating varieties) and a unique physiological system of respiration (Grist 1975). Gently circulating water provides nutrients, and the anaerobic conditions at soil level prevent weed growth. (Geertz [1963], rather poetically likens the rice terrace to a gigantic aquarium).[13] "Rice fields come in an astonishing and ingenious variety, from dizzying flights of terraces perched high up on mountainsides, to dyked fields reclaimed from marshes or the shores of the sea" (Bray 1986, 29). To obtain high yields in wet rice cultivation, it is necessary to control the depth and timing of water very precisely: "A rice field should ideally be carefully leveled so that the depth of water is uniform, and in the absence of modern engineering this severely restricts field size" (Bray 1986, 29). Taken together, these characteristics imply increasing intensification of wet rice cultivation on fragmented holdings as population expands. Because of the high costs of investment in terms of foregone consumption in traditional agriculture, noted above, expansion of the area of wet rice cultivation might be expected to take place very slowly, if at all, under population pressure unless an outside source of technology and/or investment resources were present. As we shall see shortly, the Dutch, who are after all masters of hydraulic engineering, water control, and land reclamation, provided just such a source of know-how and other resources to expand *sawah* and to reduce swidden and uncultivated areas in Java and the other parts of the Indonesian archipelago they controlled.

Rice has other characteristics that suit it to the intensification of traditional agriculture under population pressure:

- First, rice has a high yield-to-seed ratio. "Wheat, barley and rye, the staple cereals of Northern Europe, bear heads with relatively few grains, say between 20 and 90; each plant will normally develop four or five tillers,[14] giving a possible maximum of 400 or so grains per plant in all.... Theoretically, then, each seed grain could produce 400 offspring. In reality, given the physiology of the plant and inefficient sowing techniques like broadcasting, in Europe up to the seventeenth or eighteenth century the ratio of crop to seed grain averaged no more than 4:1 or 3:1, of which, of course a high proportion had to be set aside as seed for the next crop.... A single panicle[15] of rice may contain up to 500 grains although 75 to 150 is more usual, and a well-watered plant on fertile soil can produce up to 50 tillers.... Yield to seed ratios of 100:1 can be obtained using even such simple techniques as those practiced in parts of Malaysia...." (Bray 1986, 15).

- Second, rice has high yields per unit land relative to other grains, with the exception of maize. In 1981-1982, the world rice harvest was over 400 million tons from 145 million hectares, whereas, in the same crop year, 450 million tons of wheat were harvested from 230 million hectares (Bray 1986). Thus the per hectare world yield of rice is 40 percent higher than that of wheat. (This says nothing about calories per hectare; potato and cassava dominate here.) High output per unit of land in wet rice cultivation is partly accounted for by multicropping; two and even three crops can be obtained per year, either additional crops of rice or other crops.[16] The practice of transplanting also frees up the land for other uses since a crop of transplanted rice occupies the field for as little as two to three months (Bray 1986).
- Third, rice comes in many different varieties and flavors. This makes it possible to diversify risk and to stagger input requirements, principally labor and water, so as to utilize resources more efficiently. The most important difference among rice varieties is the ripening period, which may vary between 90 and 260 days (Bray 1986, 18). Although the yields for the longer maturing varieties are typically larger than for the shorter, the variation in growing period makes rice more adaptable to a variety of climates and regimes of cultivation.
- Finally, the techniques of rice farming lend themselves to selection. It is by this most ancient process that domestication of plants and animals occurred in the first place, and it remains the principal means by which traditional farmers improve technology.

The conclusion is that wet rice cultivation offers, among all the possibilities for sustaining life through agriculture, the greatest potential on a limited area of land. Provided water is abundant and can be controlled and distributed, great intensification can be achieved through increased use of human labor alone, without great decreases in the marginal productivity of labor. Given fairly minimal capital investment in water control, itself requiring mostly human labor to put in place, the marginal product of labor in rice production need fall hardly at all. This means that a traditional agriculture based on wet rice culture can respond to population pressure without fundamentally altering technique, that is, by what Geertz calls agricultural involution. Of course, this need not happen: failure to increase output would put an end to population growth; or, what is perhaps more usual is a kind of Boserupian response to population pressure, in which the equilibrium of traditional agriculture is destabilized and a new equilibrium characterized by a different type of agriculture is ultimately attained.

Agricultural Involution in Java: How Did It Happen?

The main elements of the explanation of how population grew so much and agriculture nonetheless remained traditional are now in place. It remains to examine the characteristics of the Dutch colonial administration after 1830 and how it contributed to the process. The best description I know is contained in two chapters of Geertz (1963, 47-123), here, I will try to summarize what he says:

When the Dutch came to Indonesia, they found in Java a heartland with an already fairly dense population sustained by *sawah*; on the outer islands there were only small tribes of swidden farmers. "...What the Dutch were essentially concerned to do, from 1619 to 1942, was to pry agricultural products out of the archipelago, and particularly out of Java, which were salable on world markets without changing fundamentally the structure of the indigenous economy" (Geertz , 47). The *Cultuurstelsel* described above was essentially the means for doing this from the beginning of the 19th century, after the collapse of the Netherlands East Indies Company. The Dutch established large-scale, well-capitalized rationally organized estate or plantation agriculture, " ...which by 1900 accounted for 90 percent by value of Indonesia's exports... [and which] was essentially not part, save in a merely spatial or geographic sense, of the Indonesian economy at all, but of the Dutch." There were indeed two economies on the island of Java: the Dutch estate sector (enclave), which produced primarily sugar and coffee for export in the 19th century; and the traditional *sawah* economy. Later in the 20th century, the Dutch expanded to other crops and to the outer islands, which required other modes of exploitation. Coffee was largely grown on the hillsides that were not used for wet rice culture, but sugarcane thrived in the areas most suitable for wet rice culture, indeed in rotation with rice in the terraces themselves. Much of it, in fact, was cultivated on the *sawah* itself under the land tax remission provisions of the System (p. 55). Moreover, both crops, especially sugar, required considerable labor input, which was also supplied under the remission provisions of the System.[17] Geertz, (p. 88), for example, reports a one-third/ one-third/ one-third distribution of *sawah*/ sugarcane/ dry crops in 1900.

The System also meshed well with traditional Javanese culture and social organization. Geertz (p. 9) states that the terraces "...are closely integrated with the modes of work organization, forms of village structure, and processes of social stratification." A vivid description of how the Dutch "inserted" their export crop enclave into the traditional communal system of Javanese rice culture and controlled the local population and enforced the System, which gave them a continuous flow of labor and use of suitable land, all through the indigenous rulers, is contained in the novel by Multatuli (1861). Moreover, in contrast to the kind of dual economic development which Lewis and others argue characterizes many third world countries today, in which a stagnant traditional agriculture and a growing population lead to urban/industrial growth and mass migration to the cities, there was essentially no urban/industrial sector to which the Javanese could migrate. Because increasing rice production required more and more labor, the population could not be removed from the agricultural sector except part-time as the Dutch managed to do. With a little expansion of area and better water control, which the Dutch helped provide, the traditional wet rice agricultural sector was able to absorb a huge increase in population with little diminution in the marginal product of labor.

Geertz (1963) outlines the steps by which greater efficiency in cultivation was attained almost entirely through intensification: (1) pregermination; (2) transplanting; (3) more thorough land preparation; (4) fastidious planting and weeding; (5) razor blade harvesting (see the picture in Bray [1986, 21] of such a knife and the discussion of why its use increases output so substantially); (6) double cropping; (7) more exact regulation of terrace flooding; and (8) addition of more fields, especially at the edges of volcanoes.

But the Dutch did not take all and give back nothing in return (granted that what they gave the Javanese was for the benefit of the Dutch themselves). Geertz reports that, between 1880 and 1939, the Dutch invested 250 million guilders in irrigation and flood control facilities (Geertz, p. 145). Of course, we do not know how much this amounted to in terms of current dollars or in relation to the size of the Dutch economy, but there is no doubt that Dutch investments in land reclamation along the coast, irrigation facilities in the interior, and extensive development of transportation infrastructure permitted and facilitated *sawah* expansion, which of course benefited the Dutch export enclave as well as the Javanese. Moreover, Dutch political control by imposing a *Pax Neerlandica* stifled the internecine tribal warfare, which earlier took a heavy toll on crops and ultimately population, and in this sense was partly responsible for the increase in population that occurred.

Thus the growth in population from 1830 did not kick off a transition from traditional agriculture, or mass migration, or a Malthusian disaster by destabilizing the Schultzian equilibrium of traditional agriculture. Rather it led to a process of intensification within the traditional sector, a process Geertz calls agricultural involution. The Indonesian story requires some modification in Schultz's characterization of traditional agriculture in the stationary state. It is possible under certain circumstances for traditional agriculture to exist in a dynamic setting, at least for a time, as it did in the Dutch East Indies from the beginning of the 19th century until the Japanese occupation of the archipelago in 1942. But the circumstances in which this occurred were rather special and depended on the particular and somewhat peculiar characteristics of wet rice culture and the Dutch colonial administration. The "miracle" of Indonesian agricultural development in this period was that it permitted massive population growth on Java without extensive change in cultural or social institutions or emigration. It may serve, in this respect, as a somewhat pessimistic prognosis for the shape of our world to come.

Agricultural Modernization[18]

In his work, Schultz focuses on how the economy moves from a state of traditional agriculture to a state of modern agriculture. He terms this process the agricultural transformation. In the United States, for example, the transformation, although it began in the 19th century following the Civil War, did not reach full fruition until the development and spread of hybrid corn in the 1930s and 1940s and the remarkable fall in the cost of nitrogen fertilizer that occurred in the 1950s and 1960s, which resulted in a significant increase in the optimal amount of such fertilizer that could be applied to a variety of crops. In their recent paper disputing Hayami and Ruttan's (1985) interpretation of US agricultural development in the 19th century in terms of induced innovation, Olmstead and Rhode (1993) point out that the former's interpretation in terms of massive mechanization in response to labor scarcity and land abundance simply does not accord with observed trends in factor prices, pattern of settlement, changing crop patterns, evidence on the role of biological research and innovation, and infrastructure development in permitting the settlement and productive farming of previously sparsely settled and marginal areas. Indeed, long before the development and spread of hybrid corn, biological innovation, as opposed to mechanical innovation, was a major factor in US agricultural development. A similar pattern has been repeated in the second half of the 20th century in Brazil, in which biological innovation and infrastructure investments have opened up new lands to productive agriculture, particularly the *cerrado* in central Brazil, where high concentrations of aluminum hydroxide and acid soils had heretofore precluded economically viable agriculture with traditional crop varieties. The innovation, and the research upon which it is based, occurs largely outside the traditional agricultural sector, often in the public sector, and generally not in response to relative factor scarcities or trends in factor prices, but rather to perceptions of profits to be made or to enhancement of the general welfare.[19] The development of industries outside agriculture, and of infrastructure which ties nonagricultural and agricultural sectors together, is crucial to the interaction between technology and resource allocation decisions which characterize the process of agricultural modernization, intensification, and extension. But they are not the whole story.

The following generalizations concerning the process of agricultural modernization, drawn from my work on the Zona da Mata (Minas Gerais, Brazil), are germane to my discussion (Nerlove 1988):

- Information and education facilitate modernization. The use of modern inputs requires that farmers be aware of their existence and know their properties in order to compare the distribution of returns under various technological alternatives. The accuracy or quality of a farmer's knowledge depends on his source of information and on his level of education. Basic literacy is, of course, a fundamental prerequisite, but education more generally improves a farmer's ability to collect and use information and to adjust to changes in prices, markets, and technology.

- Market imperfections impede modernization. The presence of market imperfections reduces incentives to adopt new technology and new inputs, and to extend agriculture into previously unprofitable areas. Potential sources of market imperfections are varied. In input markets, prices charged to farmers may vary according to farm size and location in a way not reflecting marketing or transport costs, or there may be nonprice supply constraints. Use of modern inputs may require complementary inputs, such as labor or use of machinery in land preparation, which constitute an indivisible input. If rental markets for agricultural machinery exist, both large and small farmers will be able to adopt, but these markets often do not exist. In output markets, prices paid for food by farmers may be higher than prices received, leading farmers to grow food crops that may be much less responsive to modern inputs than cash crops. Farmers may obtain different prices from their crops depending on where they sell them: farmers who sell only in local markets may get lower prices, thus reducing the profitability of modern inputs.

- Farm tenure and property rights in land diversely affect the modernization process. There has been continuing discussion especially of the role of share tenancy in reducing the pace of agricultural modernization (Bhaduri 1973, Braverman and Stiglitz 1986, Newbery 1975, Scandizzo 1979). While much of the theoretical discussion has not led to clear-cut conclusions, it is plausible that, if a sharecropper has to bear all the costs of inputs and give the landowner a share of the output, the expected return required to trigger adoption of new technology or modern inputs will be higher than for owners, *ceteris paribus*. The weight of empirical evidence suggests that, in transitional agriculture, tenants are less prone to modernize than are land owners but that contractual arrangements are all-important; given the right contractual arrangements, land owners may themselves lead the pace of modernization by, for example, providing modern inputs to their tenants. The widespread prevalence of land leasing, share tenancy, and share leasing in highly modern US agriculture suggests that legal and social institutions that permit sophisticated and diverse contractual arrangements, especially clear title to land, may be more important than how farmers gain access to land, by ownership or otherwise.[20]

• The natural environment shapes the extent and direction of modernization. Yields obtained with each technology differ across farms and even within the same farm from plot to plot. Some land may be close to a river or a stream, some land may be flat, other land steeply sloped. Soils differ considerably, often even for plots rather close together, and past decisions (which crops were grown, and which inputs and tillage practices were used) also affect present soil characteristics. Livestock quality and numbers are affected in both the short and long term by the nature of natural pasture and the suitability of land for growing feed crops. Yet while the course and pace of agricultural modernization is greatly affected by environmental factors, modernization increasingly breaks down the dependence of agriculture on environmental factors: irrigation and water control alleviate dependence on climate and weather. Chemical fertilizers and additives, and novel or improved tillage practices, free agriculture to a greater or lesser degree from its dependence on soil structure and composition, and on topography. Chemical or biological pesticides and improved, resistant varieties reduce damage and losses from weeds, pests, and disease. Antibiotics and hormones, as well as improved breeds and breeding practices, feeds and feed supplements, enhance livestock productivity and free production and location decisions from dependence on the availability of natural pasture. Together with biological innovation, improved technology and inputs increasingly free agriculture from location specificity and environmental dependence and permit extension to hitherto unsuitable and environmentally fragile areas. At the same time, modernization itself impacts powerfully on the environment.

- Cash constraints limit farmers' ability to use modern inputs. Using modern inputs often involves switching from on-farm-produced inputs to market-supplied (factory-produced) inputs. Farmers need greater cash resources to use modern rather than traditional inputs. Where output and capital markets are not well developed, farmers face a cash constraint that impedes their access to new technology. The availability of cash depends on how much of his production a farmer sells, what he produces, how much credit can be obtained, and whether other sources of income are available (e.g., from off-farm employment). Increasing population density, urbanization, and improvements in infrastructure improve the functioning of labor markets in rural areas and enhance agricultural commercialization and the integration of agriculture and rural life into the national economy, and thus improve cash flows. Together with the development and greater efficiency of financial institutions serving the agricultural sector, these changes promote modernization and increase its pace. At the same time, these very changes diminish the availability of land for agriculture and create pollution and other environmental problems with serious consequences for agricultural development.

- The product mix changes in the course of modernization and plays a role in it. Although the mixture of crop and livestock products is an endogenous variable affected differently by several factors mentioned above, it is exceptionally important in determining the diffusion of new technology and new inputs. Particularly in developing countries, few agricultural sectors and few individual agricultural establishments are monocultural. Most farmers the world over produce a variety of crop and livestock products. Because new technology affects different products in profoundly different ways, the mix of crop and livestock products is a major factor in the determination of how new technology and inputs will spread and is, in turn, itself changed greatly by the use of modern techniques and inputs. In addition, as marketing, storage, and transportation infrastructure improve, increased specialization, regionally and among farms, occurs to take advantage of differing comparative advantages of soils, climate, and topography. Such specialization makes modern agriculture more efficient but leaves it more vulnerable to pests, epidemics, and other results of diminished biodiversity. In the long run, five generations or so, very large increases in the world's population, as well as the expansion and intensification of agriculture, will very likely reduce the animal-product component of agricultural production and result in other major changes in the composition of agricultural output. Increased specialization will require a higher level of compensatory use of supplementary inputs and increased attention to biological threats.

- Finally, infrastructure and the availability of complementary inputs are essential in the process of modernization. As suggested earlier, the availability of marketing, storage, and transportation infrastructure almost certainly plays a key role in agricultural modernization because such infrastructure permits commercialization of agriculture. Another way of saying this is that the transition from subsistence-oriented to market-oriented agriculture generates cash flows which, in turn, are essential to the use of modern technology and the purchase of modern inputs from the nonagricultural sector, and which enable farmers to use the extensive credit programs and newly developed financial institutions that are characteristic of public support of agricultural development. Beyond this, however, the availability of certain kinds of complementary inputs similar to infrastructure, such as irrigation and water control, and rural electrification, may greatly influence the profitability of using new technology and modern inputs. Indeed, the whole question of energy use in agriculture and of new energy technology and novel energy sources provides yet another point of departure for relating agricultural development to environmental change. Not only does increased specialization leave agriculture more vulnerable to biological threats, as mentioned above, but the increased use of modern inputs and irrigation may also impact unfavorably on the environment.

A large number of economywide, environmental, and demographic factors interact in the process of agricultural modernization. Research, both basic and applied, is an essential component of the process, and both public and international involvement in this aspect especially, as well as in the development of infrastructure and institutions, is crucial. Agricultural modernization will not and cannot take place without continuing research and social interventions at both the national and international level. New knowledge is essential to permit the extension of agriculture, its intensification through the use of new inputs, and its sustainability in the long run. Demographic changes, including but not limited to population growth, such as changes in infant and child mortality, adolescent and adult morbidity, and in labor markets and institutions, are intertwined in the process. Both directly and through these demographic interactions, agricultural development both influences and is influenced by environmental change, by possibly irreversible effects on renewable resources, and by the depletion of exhaustible resources.

Population and the Environment: Economic and Demographic Interactions

A Simple Model of the Relation between Size of the Human Population and Environmental and Other Natural Resources

Few issues, it is safe to say, excite as much interest and concern in contemporary economics as those related to environment and to un-priced resources of all kinds. At bottom, many long-term environmental problems, whether they derive from the use of modern agricultural technology or extension of agriculture into environmentally fragile areas to augment food production, or from pollution due to rapid urbanization and industrialization, or from too rapid exploitation of exhaustible energy and other natural resources, stem ultimately from the pressure of human population and human desires for subsistence if not greater levels of creature comforts. In the preceding sections of this essay, I have outlined the requirements for agricultural development and modernization that must take place if projected increases in the world's population are to be accommodated at levels of living and quality of life that will make people happy to be alive. But population growth does not occur in a vacuum. It is the joint effect of decisions parents make with respect to the number of children they bring into the world, of mortality and morbidity due both to exogenous factors and to investments parents, individually and socially, make in the health and nutrition of their offspring, of the stocks of human and physical capital and knowledge which each generation bequeaths to the next and which serve as means of production, together with the labor and stocks of depletable and renewable resources which remain or can be regenerated. "Besides the torch of life itself, the material wealth of the world, a technological system of vast and increasing intricacy and the habituations which fit men for social life must in some manner be carried forward to new individuals born devoid of all of these things as older individuals pass out" (Knight 1921, 375).

General economic growth and capital formation can do much to ameliorate the adverse effects of population growth on environmental and other resources. Moreover, urbanization and concentration of population can ease the pressure of population on land and other resources necessary to agriculture. But industrialization, which is not synonymous with economic growth by any means, and urbanization are also important sources of environmental degradation.

In Nerlove (1991, 1993), I lay out a framework for the formal analysis of the relation beween endogenous population change and the general state of the environment. In this analysis, I abstract from the problems associated with general economic growth and urbanization and, more importantly, I do not consider the effects of capital formation on the relation between the size of the human population and the natural re-source base. The simplified model I present can be viewed as a model of how agricultural extension and intensification resulting from the growth of human population may affect the environment in which humans live and procreate, and which in turn may affect humans' desires for progeny. My principal finding in the papers cited is that a favorable outcome is possible only when parents are altruistic toward their children, and thus toward future generations, and when possibilities exist for investments in human and physical capital and knowledge to mitigate unfavorable effects of population growth and enhance the quality of life of future generations. The principal points are as follows:

- Population pressure affects environmental quality by natural re-source depletion, by pollution, and by forcing people to live under environmentally adverse circumstances. Population density also affects the costs of transport, communication, and infrastructure in ways that may enhance the efficiency of agricultural and other production of goods and services and increase the pace of agricul-tural development and modernization.
- Environmental degradation and resource depletion affect the out-put of the economy and thus the immediate well-being of indi-viduals. They also affect infant and child mortality, maternal mortality, and adult mortality and morbidity. More significantly, these factors affect agricultural productivity and the comparative advantages of different crop and livestock products. To the extent that children are productive assets for their parents, the benefits of having them may be affected.
- Mortality and morbidity, especially child and infant mortality, af-fect survival probabilities and the costs of births, the costs and benefits of surviving children, and the returns to investments in human and physical capital. Of course, mortality directly affects the rate of population growth.
- Survival probabilities, the costs of births, and the costs and benefits of surviving children affect household decisions and

choices with respect to fertility and investment in human and physical capital.

- Fertility affects the rate of growth of population.
- Investment in human and physical capital may affect household decisions in subsequent generations, and may mitigate the effects of population pressure on environmental degradation and resource depletion.

The Prognosis for a Stable Equilibrium at a High Level of Environmental Quality and Abundant Natural Resources per Capita

In Nerlove (1991, 1993), I assumed that population pressure affects the environment adversely, and focused on how environmental quality affects the expected discounted benefits of having children and therefore families' fertility decisions. I neglected both the consequences of environmental degradation and resource depletion for investment in human and physical capital and in new knowledge, and the effects of such investments, in turn, on environmental quality, output of goods and services and well-being, mortality and morbidity, and families' fertility decisions. The pessimistic conclusions provide some insight into how the factors which I neglected by assumption might mitigate, modify, or reverse the bleak outcome which followed. The principal conclusion was that the possibility for a stable equilibrium between population and environment were quite limited in the absence of significant investment in human and physical capital:

- An equilibrium between population and environmental quality may not even exist short of human extinction.
- If equilibrium exists, there may be several equilibria, some of which may be stable, in the sense that a small perturbation results in a dynamic process leading to a return to the equilibrium, and some of which may be unstable, in the sense that a small displacement may lead to further movement away from the point of balance.
- In the case of multiple equilibria, these may be of two types:

  Type I: A low level of population and a high level of environmental quality and well-being.

  Type II: A large population associated with serious environmental deterioration and a low level of well-being.

- A stable equilibrium is possible only if: (a) environmental quality is dynamically stable in the absence of population change, and (b) fertility and/or the net rate of population growth is reduced by environmental degradation and resource depletion.

On the basis of some simple arguments with respect to infant and child mortality, the desire for surviving children, and the comparative advantages of children and adults in traditional or transitional agriculture, I concluded that, in the absence of substantial agricultural modernization, general economic development, and significant returns to investment in human capital, fertility would generally be reduced by further environmental degradation and resource depletion only at already low levels of environmental quality, and increased rather than decreased by deterioration from relatively good conditions. Consequently,

- a stable Type I equilibrium, with a small population and a high level of environmental quality, is generally unlikely in the absence of social intervention, and

- such intervention in the form of per capita taxes on children and lump-sum subsidies to parents could achieve and maintain a Type I equilibrium.

I also argued, however, that, although every generation is better off at a Type I equilibrium, in which both present and future generations enjoy a better environment and higher per capita consumption, in the absence of parental altruism and significant returns to investments in their children's human capital or to investments in physical capital in terms of the income streams available to future generations, the present generation is unambiguously worse off than had no social intervention taken place. Therefore,

- members of the present generation have no incentive to prevent movement toward a potentially stable Type II equilibrium with a large population, a low level of per capita well-being, and a deteriorated environment and depleted resource base, or, worse, toward eventual human extinction.

Finally, I argued that altruism toward future generations is not, in itself, enough to reverse this conclusion. Love is not enough because, in the absence of significant opportunities to invest in their children's human capital or to bequeath productive physical capital to the next generation, parental altruism always leads, *ceteris paribus,* to a higher birth rate than when parents' motives are purely selfish. Consequently,

- a precondition for a demographic transition to occur and for the achievement of a stable Type I equilibrium is, generally speaking, parental altruism coupled with high perceived rates of return to investment in human and physical capital and new knowledge. Such high rates of return are more likely under conditions of a high level of economic development and modern agriculture than in a traditional agricultural setting.

However, especially when parents are altruistic, failure to price environmental resources appropriately leads parents, under general circumstances, to overestimate their children's, and children's children's, etc., future welfare and thus to misperceive the benefits of having additional children. Without a clear understanding, however, of the effects of unpriced or inappropriately priced environmental resources on rates of return to investment in human and physical capital, one cannot necessarily conclude that the fertility, and the net rate of population growth will therefore be higher. In any event, a clear case can be made from the standpoint of the present generation for the correct pricing of environmental and other natural resources.

The Role of Agricultural Modernization

What then is the role of agricultural development and modernization? First, it is obvious that, without increases in agricultural productivity and the extension of agriculture, a larger population cannot be supported at tolerable levels of well-being. Insufficient agricultural development would lead to destitution and immiserization and, until mortality caught up with increased fertility, to a high rate of population growth and low rates of investment in human and physical capital. On the other hand, together with industrialization and urbanization, agricultural intensification and extension is a prime source of environmental degradation and resource depletion. Agricultural modernization is a principal path by which population growth puts pressure on the environment.

Is agricultural modernization facilitated or impeded by a larger population? Up to a point, it can be argued that a larger, more densely settled population facilitates agricultural development by making transport, communications, and infrastructure less costly and agriculture more efficient (Boserup 1965, Simon 1977, Nerlove and Sadka 1991). Urbanization and industrialization are essential to the process of agricultural modernization and to the maintenance of modern agriculture. To the extent that urbanization and industrialization are fostered by population growth, such growth promotes agricultural development. Ultimately, of course, continued population growth and consequent increases in population densities, environmental degradation, and resource depletion will reduce agricultural productivity.

What will life be like two generations from now in the mid-21st century, and five generations from now in the mid-22nd century? Will our great-great-great grandchildren curse us for having given them life and existence and the world we have left them? This is the stuff science fiction is made of. But I am dealing here not with fantasy but with hard reality and the choices that we, of the present generation, must make.

Even in the best-case scenario, the world will be a much more crowded place, with population densities approaching those in Bangladesh, Java, or Holland today. Human diets will probably have to change quite a lot, incorporating fewer animal products and far more of vegetable origin. But the quality of life, health, and longevity need not thereby be reduced. Denser settlement should facilitate increased human contact and a higher level of cultural amenities. A high level of investment in human capital and a large stock of physical capital should make it possible for the world's population to lead productive and materially comfortable lives.

But stabilizing the world population at 12 billion is far different from stabilizing it at 25-30 billion—or not stabilizing it at all except through rising death rates. Unless opportunities for parents to invest in the human capital of their children are maintained, or opened up in areas where they are now limited, and rates of return to such investments are kept up by both social and private investments in new knowledge and in health and nutrition, declines in fertility and net rates of population growth will not occur, or not occur at a rapid enough pace to stabilize the world's population at two to two-and-a-half times the present level.

Agricultural development and modernization are essential to the occurrence and pace of the demographic transition; to the final outcome, i. e., the process by which population stability is finally achieved; and to the state of the world and quality of life; as well as the size of the population when it is achieved. Current complacency, which is a consequence of the world food glut and forecasts of falling real food prices over the next 30 years, should not blind us either to the severe distributional problems in the short term, nor to the long-term need for investment in agricultural research and infrastructure to support essential intensification, extension, and modernization.

Acknowledgment

This paper draws on an earlier paper, "Le developpement de l'agriculture, la croissance de la population et l'environnement", presented at the Société Canadienne de Science Économique, Ottawa, 19 May 1994. I thank Anke Meyer, Marcel Dagenais, my colleagues Bruce Gardner and Ramón Lopez, M. G. Quibria, and participants at the Third ADB Conference on Development Economics, especially Frank Harrigan, Hun Kim, and Sarfraz Khan Qureshi, for helpful comments and discussion.

This research was supported by the Maryland Agricultural Experiment Station; MAES Paper No. 9077/A7756.

Appendix

Let K_0, K_1, K_2, K_3, ... be the stocks of capital available to society in the current and subsequent periods. In each period, the stock K yields a flow of services that can be transformed into output = gross income y by the function

$$y_n = f(K_n), n = 0,1,2,... \tag{A1}$$

Let the cost, in terms of foregone consumption in the current period, of augmenting the stock of capital by one unit be I_0, and let the depreciation of the stock between period 0 and period 1 be d_0. If the stock of capital is just maintained between the two periods, consumption can be equal to net income, i.e., gross income minus depreciation:

$$c_0 = y_0 - d_0 \tag{A2}$$

whereas, if the capital stock is augmented by one unit in the next period, consumption can be only

$$c_0^* = y_0 - d_0 - I_0 \tag{A3}$$

The difference between the two values, I_0, is foregone consumption. If the new stock of capital is maintained at K_1 gross income will be y_1 in all subsequent periods but depreciation will increase to d_1 so that potential consumption in the next and all subsequent periods will be only

$$c_1 = y_1 - d_1 \tag{A4}$$

But c_1 is certainly larger than c_0—otherwise what's the point?

Let me now assume that a representative individual's utility in this society for his consumption and that of all his progeny and himself in future periods, that is, the consumption stream, $c_0, c_1, c_2, ...$, is characterized by an additively separable, recursive utility function, such that today's utility of the stream is

$$V(c_0, c_1, c_2 ...) = U(c_0) + \rho V(c_1, c_2, c_3, ...), \text{ where } 0 \leq \rho \leq 1 \tag{A5}$$

It is well-known that this formulation is equivalent to

$$V(c_0, c_1, ...) = \sum_0^\infty \rho^n U(c_n) \tag{A6}$$

Time preference in this formulation is measured by how much present consumption an individual is willing to give up in order to get a little bit more in the future and retain the same utility level

Reflections on Agricultural Development, Population Growth, and the Environment

$$dV = 0 = \rho^n U'(c_n)dc_n + \rho^{n+1}U'(c_{n+1})dc_{n+1}$$

that is,

$$-\frac{dc_n}{dc_{n+1}} = \rho\frac{U'(c_{n+1})}{U'(c_n)} = r$$

where, under stationary conditions, r is a constant >0 but <1, since $0 < \rho < 1$, and assuming diminishing marginal utility of consumption. r will be smaller the greater the rate at which the future is discounted, that is, the smaller ρ, and the faster the marginal utility of consumption is diminishing. The smaller r, the greater the rate of time preference, that is the greater the preference for present versus future consumption.

Now let us consider the utility of the representative member of society for these two consumption streams: c_0 forever versus c_0-I_0 then c_1 ever after. We will also need a measure of the utility of the stream $c_1, c_1, c_1, \ldots$ forever:

$$V_0 = V(c_0, \ldots) = \sum_0^\infty \rho^n U(c_0) = \frac{U(c_0)}{1-\rho}$$

$$V_1 = V(c_1, \ldots) = \frac{U(c_1)}{1-\rho}$$

$$V* = U(c_0 - I_0) + \rho\sum_0^\infty \rho^n U(c_1) = U(c_0 - I_0) + \rho V_1$$

Now if I_0 is small relative to c_0, but not necessarily small relative to c_1-c_0,

$$U(c_0 - I_0) \cong U(c_0) - U'(c_0)I_0$$

so that

$$V* - V = \rho[V_1 - V_0] - U'(c_0)I_0 \tag{A7}$$

which is greater than, equal to, or less than zero, depending on whether

$$r\left[\frac{V_1 - V_0}{U'(c_1)}\right] \tag{A8}$$

is greater than, equal to, or less than I_0. It follows that the gain in utility for the representative member of society is likely to be negative when I_0 is large relative to the difference in the utilities of the consumption streams c_1, ... versus c_0, ... , respectively, when the rate of time preference is great (r is small), and the larger the single-period marginal utility of consumption relative to the difference V_1-V_2.

Notes

1. Expansion of agriculture on the Great Plains of North America required, and was facilitated by, a great deal of innovation, not only mechanical but also biological (see Olmstead and Rhode 1993, Cochrane 1993).

2. Grigg (1980, 160) disagrees with this assessment. He writes, "In the first place the prosperity of the country as a whole was due not to any great advance in the agricultural sector, but to the growth of trade and industry. This, together with the expansion of the fishing industry, allowed the relatively successful absorption of those who left the countryside for the towns." But this is a typical result of agricultural development. Improvements in agricultural productivity both facilitate and promote the movement of factors of production out of agriculture, regardless of the origin of these improvements.

3. For an account of the cultural and artistic consequences that followed from the new technology see Schama (1988).

4. See Nerlove and Sadka (1991) for a discussion of the role of falling transport costs in agricultural and, more generally economic, development.

5. Stone (1977, 81-82) writes: Before the decline in mortality "...so many infants died that they could only be regarded as expendable; ...the family itself was a loose association of transients, constantly broken up by death of parents or children or the early departure of children from home. It is impossible to stress too heavily the impermanence of the Early Modern family, whether from the point of view of husbands or wives, or parents and children. None could reasonably expect to remain together for very long, a fact which affected all human relationships. Death was a part of life, and was realistically treated as such .... the relative lack of concern for small infants was closely tied to their poor expectation of survival...." In other words, as long as infant and child mortality and maternal mortality remained high there was no point in investing much love, care, or tangible resources in children or spouses. The reciprocal bonds of affection and concern of husbands and wives and of parents and children are products of the enhanced chances of survival which were in part a consequence of the better nutrition resulting from the second agricultural revolution. And these effects were cumulative.

6. The difference between skills and knowledge embodied in the human agent and other forms of knowledge and stocks of physical capital is that the rate of return to embodied human capital is very sensitive to the expectation of life. Moreover, such embodied human capital needs constantly to be replaced as each generation gives way to the next; the vessels in which it is stored must be constantly replenished as well.

7. Knowledge and skills, whether embodied or not, obviously represent a special category of capital in this respect, since the returns to a quantum

jump in the stock of such capital are inherently unknowable by those potential investors who must decide whether to augment such a stock rather than
merely replace it. This is a general proposition about equilibria characterized
by local optima: There may be a far better position for individuals in the economy at some distance, but, in the absence of a destabilizing shock, the superior position will not be attained because of the myopia of optimizing agents in
the economy.

8. That net new investment is essentially a disequilibrium phenomenon
was first cogently put, to the best of my knowledge, by Haavelmo (1960).

9. Also see Cohen (1977) for a detailed account of the archaeological evidence for Boserup's hypothesis that population growth provides the impetus
for agricultural progress.

10. Better known for founding Singapore.

11. A good description of how this worked is contained in Multatuli
(1861).

12. The term *paddy* refers not to the fields themselves but to the rice
plants that have been transplanted there, and is often used to refer to the
obtained output of unhusked rice. It is also of Malay origin.

13. That land is in reality a created factor of production, rather than
some unique irreproducible resource, was emphasized years ago by Schultz
(1953, 125-45).

14. Tillering is the growth of multiple shoots around the main stem of the
plant and is characteristic of grasses.

15. From Latin *panicula* = tuft, referring to the seed-bearing shoot of the
plant.

16. In Buck (1965), a traditional rice culture is described in which the
harvested fields are reflooded and used for aquaculture.

17. Sugar production from cane is carried out in a central mill with very
little labor (modern sugar mills operate with almost no labor, like oil refiner-
ies) and with little need for inputs other than cane, but to operate efficiently
they require a continuous flow of raw material. This can be accomplished in
the humid tropics provided suitable land and a continuous supply of labor for
cultivation and harvesting can be obtained (see Mintz 1985). Geertz (1963, 55)
states that sugarcane culture requires a discontinuous flow of labor that
meshes well with the more continuous demands of coffee culture on the hillsides, but this all depends on how the crops of sugar are staggered. In any
case the two crops together can produce an almost continuous demand for
labor, which could also be supplied under the remission provisions of the
System.

To give a rough idea of the importance of these two crops:

Year	Percent of NEI Exports	
	Sugar	Coffee
1830	36	13
1870	43	45

18. This subsection draws on Nerlove (1988).

19. There is a large and growing literature on the nature and institutional basis of agricultural research, which is not possible to summarize here. I have found the papers in the recent volume edited by Anderson (1994) to be particularly instructive. For an earlier, comprehensive account see Pinstrup-Anderson (1982). Tribe's recent book (1994) focuses on the relation between agricultural development and research and the environment, particularly on how agricultural research may permit sustainable extension and intensification of agriculture.

20. In the US, widespread leasing is in part a response to the demographic changes which accompany agricultural modernization (see Nerlove 1994a , 19-22).

References

Anderson, J. R., 1994. *Agricultural Technology: Policy Issues for the International Community.* Wallingford: CAB International.

Bairoch, P., 1976. "Agriculture and the Industrial Revolution, 1700-1914." In C. M. Cipolla, ed., *The Fontana Economic History of Europe,* Vol. 3. London: Harvester Press, Ltd.

Barker, R., R. W. Herdt, and B. Rose, 1985. *The Rice Economy of Asia.* Washington, D. C.: Resources for the Future.

Beaver, S. E., 1975. *Demographic Transition Theory Reinterpreted: An Application to Recent Natality Trends in Latin America.* Lexington: Lexington Books.

Bhaduri, A., 1973. "Agricultural Backwardness under Semi-Feudalism." *Economic Journal* 83: 120-37.

Boeke, J. H., 1953. *Economics and Economic Policy of Dual Societies as Exemplified by Indonesia.* New York: Institute of Pacific Relations.

Boserup, E., 1965. *The Conditions of Agricultural Growth.* Chicago: Aldine Publishing Co.

——, 1981. *Population and Technological Change.* Chicago: University of Chicago Press.

——, 1990. *Economic and Demographic Relationships in Development.* Baltimore: The Johns Hopkins University Press.

Braverman, A., and J.E. Stiglitz, 1986. "Landlords, Tenants and Technological Innovations." *Journal of Development Economics* 23:313-32.

Bray, F., 1986. *The Rice Economies: Technology and Development in Asian Societies.* Oxford: Basil Blackwell.

Buck, P. S., 1965. *The Good Earth.* New York: John Day.

Caldwell, J. C., 1982. *Theory of Fertility Decline.* New York: Academic Press.

Chesnais, J-C., 1992. *The Demographic Transition: Stages, Patterns, and Economic Implications.* Oxford: Clarendon Press.

Coale, A. J., 1974. "The History of the Human Population." *Scientific American.* Reprinted in *The Human Population,* a Scientific American Book. San Francisco: W. H. Freeman.

Cochrane, W. W., 1993. *The Development of American Agriculture: A Historical Analysis*. 2nd ed. Minneapolis: University of Minnesota Press.

Cohen, M. N., 1977. *The Food Crisis in Prehistory: Overpopulation and the Origins of Agriculture*. New Haven: Yale University Press.

Engel, E., 1857. "Die Productions-und Consumptionsverhältnisse des Königreichs Sachsen." Originally in *Zeitschrift des Statistischen Bureaus des Königlichen Sächsischen Ministerium des Inneren*, 8-9 (November 22, 1857). Reprinted in *Bulletin de l'Institut International de Statistique* 9 (1895).

Fogel, R. W., 1994. "Economic Growth, Population Theory, and Physiology: The Bearing of Long-term Processes on the Making of Economic Policy." *American Economic Review* 84: 369-95.

Foster, N., and L. S. Cordell, eds., 1992. *Chilies to Chocolate: Food the Americas Gave the World*. Tucson: University of Arizona Press.

Geertz. C., 1963. *Agricultural Involution: The Process of Ecological Change in Indonesia*. Berkeley: University of California Press.

Grigg, D. B., 1980. *Population Growth and Agrarian Change: An Historical Perspective*. New York: Cambridge University Press.

Grist, D. H., 1975. *Rice*, 5th ed. London: Longman.

Haavelmo, T., 1960. *A Study in the Theory of Investment*. Chicago: University of Chicago Press.

Hayami, Y., and V. W. Ruttan, 1985. *Agricultural Development: An International Perspective*, 2nd ed., revised and enlarged. Baltimore: The Johns Hopkins University Press.

Houthakker, H. S., 1957. "An International Comparison of Household Expenditure Patterns, Commemorating the Centenary of Engel's Law." *Econometrica* 25:532-51.

Jha, S. C., A. B. Deolalikar, and E. M. Pernia, 1993. "Population Growth and Economic Development Revisited with Reference to Asia." *Asian Development Review* 11:1-46.

Jorgenson, D. W., 1961. "The Development of the Dual Economy." *Economic Journal* 71:309-34.

Kanbur, R., and J. McIntosh, 1987. "Dual Economies." In Eatwell et al., eds., *The New Palgrave Dictionary of Economics*. New York: Stockton Press.

Knight, F. H., 1921. *Risk, Uncertainty and Profit*. Boston: Houghton Mifflin Co.

Lewis, W. A., 1954. "Economic Development with Unlimited Supplies of Labour." *Manchester School of Economics and Social Studies* 22:139-91.

Livi-Bacci, M., 1991. *Population and Nutrition: An Essay on European Demographic History*. New York: Cambridge University Press.

Malthus, T. R., 1798. *An Essay on the Principle of Population*, London: In J. Johnson and Donald Winch, eds., *Cambridge Texts in the History of Political Thought*. Cambridge: Cambridge University Press.

———, 1830. *A Summary View of the Principle of Population*. London: John Murray.

McKeown, T., 1976. *The Modern Rise of Population.* New York: Academic Press.

Mintz, S., 1985. *Sweetness and Power: The Place of Sugar in Modern History.* New York: Viking.

Multatuli (pseudonym of Edward Dekker, 1820-1887), 1986. *Max Havelaar, of de koffieveilingen der Nederlandsche Handel-Maatschappij.* Rotterdam: A.D. Donker [1958]. English translation by Roy Edwards. Amherst: University of Massachusetts Press [1982].

Nerlove, M., 1974. "Household and Economy: Toward a New Theory of Population and Economic Growth." *Journal of Political Economy* 82:S200-18.

———, 1988. "Modernizing Traditional Agriculture." Occasional Paper No. 16. International Center for Economic Growth, San Francisco.

———, 1991. "Population and the Environment: A Parable of Firewood and Other Tales." *American Journal of Agricultural Economics* 73:1334-57.

———, 1993. "Procreation, Fishing and Hunting: Problems in the Economics of Renewable Resources and Dynamic Planar Systems." *American Journal of Agricultural Economics* 75:59-71.

———, 1994a. "Reflections on the Economic Organization of Agriculture: Traditional, Modern and Transitional." In J. J. Laffont, ed., *Agricultural Markets: Mechanisms, Failures, Regulations.* Amsterdam: North-Holland. Forthcoming.

———, 1994b. "The Role of Agriculture in General Economic Development: A Reinterpretation of Jorgenson and Lewis." Department of Agricultural and Resource Economics, University of Maryland. Unpublished manuscript.

Nerlove, M., A. Razin, and E. Sadka, 1987. *Household and Economy: Welfare Economics of Endogenous Fertility.* New York: Academic Press.

Nerlove, M., and L. K. Raut, 1995. "Growth Models with Endogenous Population: A General Framework." In M. R. Rosenzweig and O. Stark, *Handbook of Population and Family Economics.* New York: Elsevier Science Publications. Forthcoming.

Nerlove, M., and E. Sadka, 1991. "Von Thuenen's Model of the Dual Economy." *Zeitschrift fuer Nationaloekonomie / Journal of Economics* 54:97-123.

Newbery, D. M. G., 1975. "Tenurial Obstacles to Innovation." *Journal of Development Studies* 2:63-77.

Olmstead, A. L., and P. Rhode, 1993. "Induced Innovation in American Agriculture: A Reconsideration." *Journal Political Economy* 101:100-18.

Pinstrup-Andersen, P., 1982. *Agricultural Research and Technology in Economic Development.* New York and London: Longman.

Sauer, C. O., 1969. *Seeds, Spades, Hearths and Herds: The Domestication of Animals and Foodstuffs,* 2nd ed. Cambridge: The MIT Press.

Scandizzo, P. L., 1979. "Implications of Sharecropping for Technology Design in Northeast Brazil." In A. Valdes, G.M. Scobie, and J.L. Dillon, eds.,

Economics and Design of Small Farmer Technology. Ames: Iowa State
  University Press.

Schama, S., 1988. *The Embarrassment of Riches: An Interpretation of Dutch
  Culture in the Golden Age.* Berkeley: University of California Press.

Schultz, T. W., 1953. *The Economic Organization of Agriculture.* New York:
  McGraw-Hill.

————, 1961. "Education and Economic Growth." In N. B. Henry, ed., *Social
  Forces Influencing American Education.* Chicago: University of
  Chicago Press.

————, 1964. *Transforming Traditional Agriculture.* New Haven: Yale
  University Press.

————, 1971. *Investment in Human Capital.* New York: Free Press.

————, 1973. "Explanation and Interpretations of the Increasing Value of
  Human Time." Woody Thompson Lecture, Midwest Economics
  Association, Chicago, April 15.

Simon, J. L., 1977. *Economics of Population Growth.* Princeton: Princeton
  University Press.

Slicher van Bath, B. H., 1977. "Agriculture in the Vital Revolution." In *The
  Cambridge Economic History of Europe*, Vol. V. Cambridge: Cambridge
  University Press.

Stone, L., 1977. *The Family, Sex and Marriage in England, 1500-1800.* New
  York: Harper and Row.

Timmer, C. P., 1988. "The Agricultural Transformation." In H. Chenery and
  T. N. Srinivasan, eds., *Handbook of Development Economics*, Vol. I.
  New York: Elsevier Science Publications.

Tribe, D., 1994. *Feeding and Greening the World: The Role of International
  Agricultural Research.* Wallingford: CAB International.

United Nations, 1992. *Long-Range World Population Projections: Two
  Centuries of Population Growth, 1950-2150.* New York: United Nations
  Department of International Economic and Social Affairs.

Viola, H. J., and C. Margolis, 1991. *Seeds of Change.* Washington, D. C.:
  Smithsonian Institute Press.

World Bank, 1992. *World Development Report: Development and the
  Environment.* New York: Oxford University Press.

————, 1994. *World Tables 1994* data on diskette. Prepared by the World
  Bank International Economics Department.

Chapter 11

Population and Economic Development

M. Ali Khan

Population and economic development are broad and amorphous subjects, and the relationship between them can be charted in many possible ways. One way is to examine the impact of population growth rates on various selected indices of economic development: poverty, environment, human capital accumulation, income distribution, sustainable economic growth, rural-urban migration, health, and nutrition. An alternative is to take economic development as the "independent variable", and to examine its impact on various selected indices of population: completed family size, desired fertility, mortality and morbidity, age at marriage, birth intervals, son preference, and others. Either way, once these relationships are conceptually and empirically isolated, they govern the further development of theory and empirical work, and also offer prescriptions for policy.

However, concepts and theorems come with a history of their own, and it is frequently the case that one gets insight into a particular concept or a particular index by going back to the motivations that prompted it. What were the questions to which a particular theorem furnished an answer? To what other theorems and concepts did it relate, both at the time that it was formulated and at the time that it was applied? Are there breaks and discontinuities in the language of its formulation? Or does it show up in an essentially recycled form from one period to the next? Are there different conceptual levels at which it can be read and understood? The point is that once one moves from the world of mathematics to that of demography and economics, questions of the context of a particular theorem become as important as the analytical truth that it manifests. More succinctly, meaning and context, or interpretation and understanding, of a particular relationship can no longer be divorced.

The reason for this is simply that problems of policy, pertaining as they do to the "real world", have an unfortunate aspect of presenting themselves in ways that do not conform to current disciplinary boundaries. There is a persistence in the way that bracketed considerations keep coming up to assert their relevance and question their exclusion. That such exclusions are inherent in the very act of theorizing and in the way that disciplinary boundaries have been cut at a particular point in time is well understood; what is not equally emphasized is that it is around them that the discredited view of yesterday becomes the orthodox scientific view of today. Put another way, what currently counts as theory within a discipline is really a form of practice embodying all the conventions and compromises that have been reached to proceed with the analysis. It is fruitful therefore to take a somewhat longer interpretive view, and go behind the current consensus.

This paper examines the extent to which current understandings of population and economic development have their roots in older debates. I want to see how "support of population planning" has been understood and implemented over the last 50 years, and whether the literature of this period yields some broad and general prescriptions that can be valorized under the heading of a universally valid science. The basic thrust of this essay will only be sharpened if I uncover discontinuities and reformulations of previous formulations even in this limited a perspective of intellectual history. An added advantage of focusing on the last half-century is that I can treat the vocabulary and the literature under a more or less unified rubric. The more analytical the context within which these questions are posed and investigated, the less the ever-present danger of an anachronistic reading of the past in terms of the present.[1]

A concept that has played a key role in the relationship between population and economic development over the last half-century is that of the demographic transition. I trace its evolution, and identify its two particular moments as essentially hinging on the speed with which economic variables are seen to have an impact on population variables. I focus on what Szereter calls the orthodox position[2]—population as the dependent "variable," and economic development as the independent and explanatory "variable"—and in two subsequent sections, I turn to a fuller development of this position, the so-called Columbia-Chicago approach to fertility, and its elaboration by Easterlin and his co-workers. Next, I present an application of this framework to an investigation of the socioeconomic determinants of tastes and follow it by looking at a more literal application to normative issues concerning optimal population levels for society as a whole. In their focus on tastes and preferences, these directions turn to variables that necessarily evolve slowly over time; and in their treatment of population as falling within the domain of direct policy and design, they sharpen the proactive stance of the founders. The last substantive section sets out Sen's recasting of the issues in terms of the override and voluntary approaches to population policy. I conclude the essay by summarizing the main findings that emerge from my inquiry.

The Theory of Demographic Transition

Szereter (1991, 659) writes, "Demographic transition has been confusingly invoked at different times by different authors—or even by the same author at different times—as theory ('the' demographic transition), historical model, predictive model, or mere descriptive term."[3] This notwithstanding, an originary moment can be identified in two classic articles authored by Davis (1945) and Notestein (1945). The theory in its canonical or classical form was born in these two articles after World War II.[4]

The structure of the classical theory can best be appreciated by drawing an analogy with another conception that was to come 15 years later, Rostow's theory of take-off into sustained growth. As is well known, this theory involved five distinct stages: "the traditional society, the preconditions for take-off, the take-off, the drive to maturity, and the age of high mass consumption" (Rostow 1990). Demographic transition theory in its original form also classified all societies, but by a threefold rather than a fivefold categorization.[5] The three distinct stages are labeled pre-industrial agrarian, transitional growth, and incipient decline.

"The first stage pertained to agrarian societies with high and static fertility. Such societies had high vital rates, with the high fertility rate being a response to the high mortality rate."[6] The high growth potential is that of population rather than of economic indices. However, with global interdependence, such societies could not continue on an autarchic static trajectory, and were subject to inevitable pressures toward industrialization, and, what was then seen as synonymous, toward modernization. It is these pressures that were seen to push a pre-industrial agrarian society into the second stage of the typology.

As the society moves from a pre-industrial to a post-industrial state, fertility levels remain the same as before, whereas mortality levels decline. In this second stage of transitional growth, "fertility [is] much less responsive to the process of modernization, [and its levels] change only gradually and in response to the strongest stimulation" (Notestein 1945, 39-40). In this stage, fertility levels do not change by "making modern contraception available to populations that have not utilized the folkway methods at their disposal" (Notestein and Stix 1940, as quoted in Hodgson 1988, 543). As Hodgson makes clear, the conception of the second stage is very much influenced by the fact that the "timing and extent of Western fertility decline had not been related to advances in contraceptive technology", and that the spread of contraception itself had "taken place in a hostile environment, with established governments and religions expressing strong opposition" (see Hodgson 1988, 542).[7]

> If the role of woman be that of wife and mother, with no vital functions taking her from home and family, and with important values realizable only in and through a large family, large families follow as a matter of course (Beebe 1942, as quoted in Hodgson 1988, 543).

Thus, the second stage makes explicit the view that mortality levels "respond more quickly to the modernization process than do fertility levels" (Hodgson 1983, 8).[8]

The full effects of modernization become evident only in the third stage of evolution identified by the theory. The period of fast transitional growth has worked itself out, and "the social aim of perpetuating the family [gives] way progressively to that of promoting the health, education[9] and material welfare of the individual child; family limitation became widespread; and the end of the [second] period of growth came in sight."[10] Notestein emphasizes that "large families [became] a progressively difficult and expensive undertaking; expensive and difficult for a population increasingly freed from older taboos and increasingly willing to solve its problems rather than to accept them" (see Notestein 1945, 40-41).[11] A low level of fertility was the demographic trait indicating movement into a final stage of demographic development, "incipient decline" (Hodgson 1983, 9). The society now has a high growth potential, but this time, of economic variables, rather than those of population.

It is important to note the theory's "anti-imperial, decolonizing diagnosis and its liberalizing and democratizing prognosis"[12] (see Szereter 1991, 666). The second stage involves a differential effect of modernization with more of an emphasis given to mortality than to fertility. Once the theory is given a universal dimension, the existence of colonialism is seen to further accentuate this differential effect. The authors emphasize what Thompson refers to as "Malthusian dilemma of all colonialism"; simply that "where traditional societies experienced colonial domination, an attenuated, one-sided modernization experience produced mortality decline, population growth, but no fertility decline. Because, in promoting their colonies as markets for their industrial goods, mother countries prevented or failed to foster industrialization, fertility remained high."[13] There was a distinction, in Hodgson's terms (Hodgson 1983, 13), between attenuated modernization and comprehensive modernization.[14] Political autonomy and the establishment of a market economy took on an important dimension.

> If a period of peace, order, and a rapidly rising production
> were to be accompanied by a thorough and balanced mod-
> ernization, ... [with] urbanization, industrialization, rising
> levels of living, popular education, and popular participation
> in political life, the same forces that eventually induced a
> declining fertility in the West would probably come into play
> (Notestein 1945, 52).

One cannot help being impressed with the broad interdisciplinary range
of these remarks, and the theoretical conception from which they ema-
nate. Economic development is seen within an enlarged political and socioeconomic rubric, and it is this, along with all of the changes that it
brings in its wake, rather than a narrow concern with contraceptive efficacy, that lowers fertility and through it, population growth.

In summary, the theory of demographic transition, not unlike
Rostow's theory of take-off into sustained growth, or Marx's earlier theory
of economic development, has strong universalistic underpinnings. All
populations can be placed in a single continuum of demographic development,[15] albeit one with three well-identified thresholds. A necessary
consequence of the theory is that the dampening of population growth,
based on declines in both mortality and fertility, is an inevitable consequence of industrialization, and hence of economic development. It is
worth underscoring that by giving a broad scope to the economic variables, the authors allowed for considerable heterogeneity of views as regards their impact. It was precisely around this heterogeneity that the
orthodox or revisionist position developed, which I now turn to.

The Change in Demographic Transition Theory

I have dated the canonical version of the theory of demographic
transition to the mid-1940s (e.g., Szereter 1991) and well within a decade,
one can locate a changed theory.[16] Even though the evolution was not discontinuous, what the theory evolved into was qualitatively very different
from the form in which it originated. This new version of the theory, the
so-called orthodox form, gained wide acceptance and applicability, and it
can be clearly sighted by a variety of benchmarks.

The classical version of the theory focused on "the whole process
of modernization", and thereby also drew its anticolonial implication. It
saw fertility as culturally embedded and therefore the problems of population and of economic backwardness not amenable to "simple, cheap or
easy solutions". It saw fertility and mortality as dependent variables only
in the specific sense that they would respond to a society's progress along

the trajectory of modernization. It was economic development that had to be worked on; and its indices were to be the independent variables.

> Demographic variables were dependent variables, determined by social structural factors.
> Demographic change was a consequence of socioeconomic change (see Hodgson 1983, 13).
> There must be a will to reduce fertility. If our own history means anything, it means that this comes gradually and in response to broad changes in living conditions. Birth control as an isolated movement—and inexpensive panacea—has small chance for success (Notestein 1940 as cited by Hodgson 1983, 11, 20).[17]

By 1950, the dependent variable had become independent, and population growth came to be seen as the stumbling block to economic development. Hodgson (1983, 13) remarks that by 1955, "Notestein was viewing demographic trends as independent variables, as determinants of economic trends; rapid population growth [as] a cause of continued underdevelopment; fertility ... as a variable that had to be lowered by policy interventions." By 1950, Davis had posed the question "Can industrialization of the underdeveloped areas be achieved in face of their population problem?"

> Population growth had become an independent variable in Davis's thinking and economic change a dependent one (Hodgson 1983, 16).[18]

An alternative way to view this change in the theory is through the terminology of demand and supply. The canonical version of the theory, in its emphasis on a broad socioeconomic and cultural backdrop, drew attention to desires, intentions, and motivations. As such, it can be distinguished from the later noncanonical and proactive version that solely emphasized the provision and supply of contraceptive information and methods. "If new birth control technologies could be developed, and if governments would use the means at their disposal to construct effective family planning programs," Davis contended [in 1953], "the results may prove astounding to the skeptics" (see Hodgson 1983, 18). As we shall see below, this changed emphasis from demand to supply, albeit interpreted in a manner broader than the purely economic, is still with us and of direct relevance to current debates.

Another productive index of comparison between the two versions is one grounded in epistemological considerations. In a 1948 document authored by Notestein (Balfour et al. 1949),[19] there is a conceptual distinction between "the *first-order* deeply embedded forces that maintained large-scale *inter*-national differences in overall fertility levels between different cultures, and ... a finer set of "second-order" *intra*-national factors that might produce observable and manipulable variation in fertility behavior within a single cultural regime" (Szereter 1991, 673). The distinction is made operational by being phrased in terms of nations,[20] but this is by no means necessary to it. The basic point is that the speed of response and of adjustment of fertility levels differs across empirically identifiable groups, be they classified on national, racial, ethnic, or even on more general socioeconomic grounds. Whereas the first-order factors are slow to change, the same cannot be said of the second-order ones; these factors operate within the group and can be directly manipulated to influence fertility.

> It should be possible to modify reproductive behavior to some extent without fundamental changes in other components of the culture. No social system, however coercive, maintains absolute homogeneity of behavior. The limits within which variation of fertility is restricted by the culture and economy are rather broad (Balfour et al. 1949, 113, 117).

With the introduction of second-order variables, the proactive stance of the noncanonical version of the theory is a necessary consequence. Whereas the canonical version delineated what would happen, the positive theory so to speak,[21] the noncanonical version was normative in tone and emphasized what ought to happen. Once the evolution was understood, and the second-order variables were identified as the provision of contraceptive technologies, it became incumbent to hurry history along the desirable direction.[22]

> Fertility control is not a substitute for other ameliorative effort; instead it is a means that will assist in making the ameliorative effort successful—indeed it may turn out to be a necessary condition for such success. The East, unlike the West, cannot afford to await the automatic processes of social change, incident to urbanization and industrialization, in order to complete its transition to an efficient system of population replacement (Balfour et al. 1949, 118).

The only reservation was that the attempts at control be not, in the 1953 words of Davis, "half-hearted" and confined to "middle-class birth control methods". If they are accompanied by "propaganda and education, there is no inherent reason why peasant agrarian populations cannot adopt the customs of fertility control, in advance of and to the advantage of modern economic development (Davis 1953 as quoted by Hodgson 1983, 18)." Once fertility is assumed to be changeable even for agrarian societies, one can appreciate the extent to which we have travelled away from the canonical version of the theory to the noncanonical one.[23]

Another possible criterion to distinguish between the two theories is to fall back on Davis's (1951) dichotomy between the direct and the indirect approaches. The indirect approach focuses on the lowering of socio-economic barriers, as emphasized by the original version of the theory. As emphasized above, this would be slow and difficult.[24] The direct approach involves "all-out governmental campaign backed by every economic inducement, educational device, and technical assistance to diffuse contraception (see Davis 1950, 17)." As Hodgson (1983, 17) documents, the crucial shift was in Davis's perception that the "political impediments to government sponsorship of effective birth control programs were a greater threat to the success of the direct approach than were the sociological barriers."

In my discussion so far, I have not touched on what may possibly be the single most important *desideratum* for the comparison between the two theories. This is the prominence given to the individual in the second theory. The canonical form is phrased in terms of societies with only an oblique reference to individuals. It sees "the thoughts, feelings, and actions of individuals in the specific context of their social environment", and what Ricoeur calls a special history.

> Special histories take as their theme abstract aspects of culture such as technology, art, science, religion, which lack continuous existence and which are linked together only through the initiative of the historian who is responsible for defining what counts as art, as science, as religion (see Ricoeur 1984, 195).

It is precisely the societal discontinuities distinguishing the three stages that make the theory of demographic transition a special history as well. Society is seen "as one great individual, analogous to the individuals who make it up" (Ricoeur 1984, 195, 198).[25] In the words of Samuelson (1958, 480-481),

> Certain patterns of thought appropriate to a single mind become appropriate, even though we reject the notion of a group mind. Society *acts as if* it were maximizing certain

functions, [and] we can predict the effect upon equilibrium of specified exogenous disturbances.

In the proactive version of the theory, on the other hand, the individual is explicitly brought to the fore and made responsible for his or her actions. In the words of Notestein, individuals "may be counted upon to be interested in understanding the nature of situations that present problems in terms of their own values and to seek solutions of such problems" (as quoted by Hodgson 1983, 13). Szereter (1991, 669) sees this as a "transposition in the basic terms of reference [and] a startling and dramatic conceptual *volte-face*". The peasant was seen, if not as a full-fledged *homo economicus*, certainly one who was not irrational. In a 1955 paper, Davis argued that "the peasant, though poor and illiterate, was not "stupid", and one who may easily connect ... [with the fact that he was] no longer living under conditions in which a high birth rate had utility."[26]

Thus, in summary, the transition between the two theories of demographic transition hinged on dependent versus independent variables, demand versus supply, first-order versus second-order variables, positive versus normative criteria, understanding versus control, history versus prediction, and social versus individual categorizations. It is, in particular, the category of the individual with unbounded rationality that found fuller articulation in the work of Becker and his followers.

The Chicago-Columbia Framework

The words of Keynes (1937, 518) are illuminating as an introduction to the Chicago-Columbia approach to the economics of fertility:

> An ingredient in the complacency of the nineteenth century [was] that, in their philosophical reflections on human behavior, they accepted an extraordinary contraption of the Benthamite School, by which all possible consequences of alternative courses of action were supposed to have attached to them, first a number expressing their comparative advantage, and secondly another number expressing the probability of their following from the course of action in question; so that multiplying together the numbers attached to all the possible consequences of a given action and adding the results, we could discover what to do. In this way, a mythical system of probable knowledge was employed to reduce the future to the same calculable status as the present. No one has ever acted on this theory. But even today I believe that

our thought is sometimes influenced by such pseudo-rationalistic notions.

Keynes's views notwithstanding, there has been an imposing volume of work[27] stemming from Becker's (1960) observation that the Hicksian theory of the consumer can be fruitfully applied to a family's decisions concerning its size. More that 55 years after Keynes's remarks, Becker (1993, 396) writes:

> The point of departure of my work on the family is the assumption that when men and women decide to marry, or have children, or divorce, they attempt to raise their welfare by comparing benefits and costs.

More specifically, the distinguishing characteristic of the research program is its reduction of fertility to be within the calculus of individual choice, depending both on the prices of marketed commodities, and on the shadow prices of nonmarketed commodities, especially time.[28] It is the latter dependence that constitutes the essential innovation of the theory (see Becker 1965, Lancaster 1966, Muth 1966).[29]

One possible way of understanding the household production model is to view it from the angle of the pure theory of international trade. In its standard development, such a theory is formulated for a "small" economy with international prices and factor endowments given as exogenous parameters, and output levels and the "shadow prices" of these endowments as the unknowns to be determined. Outputs are internationally marketed, factors are internationally nonmarketed, technology is assumed to exhibit constant returns to scale and nonjointness in production, and the "preferences of the economy" are summarized by a utility function of the "representative consumer". Now, if one thinks of the household instead of the economy, and the household's nonmarketed inputs, including possibly the working time of a nonworking wife, instead of factor endowments, the analogy is complete. Indeed, one has the Muellbauer-Pollak-Wachter analogue to the factor-price equalization theorem:

> The shadow prices of the nonmarketed commodities are independent of the commodity bundle consumed if and only if the household technology exhibits constant returns to scale and no joint production.[30]

Once the shadow prices are shown to be independent of the actions of the household, the Becker-Lancaster-Muth household production theory can be reduced to the standard Hicksian theory of the consumer, and the comparative static propositions of the latter straightforwardly applied. Children have now been "commodified", and children of different qualities can be seen as different commodities with different prices. It is precisely this "commodification" that adherents of the approach find fruitful, and that draws criticism and controversy from its opponents. Duesenberry's (1960) statement constitutes even now a good summary statement of the opposition.

> I submit ... that most couples would consider they have a very narrow range of choice ... [regarding] the number of children and expenditures per child. I suggest that there is no one in this room ... who considers himself free to choose either two children who go to university or four children who stop their education after high school (Duesenberry 1960 as quoted by Khan and Sirageldin 1979, 524).

In terms of the two versions of the theory of demographic transition, Duesenberry's statement calls attention to sociological and cultural norms that cannot be captured by economic variables, and thereby questions both "commodification" as well as the proactive and orthodox version of the theory that underlies it. Under the methodology of positive economics, however, the descriptive validity of the household consumer is never in question, and the sole test of a construct rests on how well it stands up to the data. At this point, a concurrent development was to have a major role in the empirical implementation of the Chicago-Columbia approach. Following a survey of Indian peasantry in 1950, surveys of knowledge, attitudes, and practice with regard to family planning (KAP surveys) became commonplace[31] in the 1950s and 1960s. Without going into their methodological underpinnings (e.g., Hauser 1967, Marino 1971, Pritchett 1994a), these surveys furnished a rich data source on which Duesenberry's assertion, and more generally the entire fertility framework, could presumably be tested.

Indeed, Malthus had already proposed a "simple model in which aggregate economic and demographic change were tied together by a reproductive behavior at the family level" (see Birdsall 1988, 486).[32] This was a model of a stationary level of income and population. Higher than subsistence incomes lowered the age at marriage, increased the number of marriages and births, and thereby the levels of population and labor supply. This in turn, given diminishing returns to land, lowered labor productivity and hence labor incomes back to their subsistence levels.

Malthus's conclusion that fertility would rise and fall as incomes increased and decreased was contradicted by the
large decline in birth rates after some countries became industrialized during the latter part of the nineteenth century and
the early part of this century (see Becker 1993, 396-397).

The point is that Becker sees Malthus as a precursor, but one who neglected the value of time. It is this that allows him to apply the vocabulary
of international specialization to the household. "Given such a large gain
from specialization within a marriage, only a *little* discrimination against
women or *small* biological differences in child rearing skills would cause
the division of labor between household and market tasks to be strongly
and systematically related to gender" (Becker 1993, 397-398). Furthermore, once the problem is seen through the lens of standard consumer
theory, an obvious "puzzle" emerges as a consequence of the stylized fact
that fertility falls with a rise in income. This is simply whether children,
or children's services in Lancaster's version, constitute inferior commodities and exhibit negative income effects.[33] Once the wife's value of time, as
proxied by her education or by her wage rate, is included in the picture,
income has a positive effect on fertility.[34]

The resolution of the puzzle by the conception of children as non-
inferior consumption commodities is of interest to those who unhesitat-
ingly subscribe to the Chicago-Columbia approach and to the commodification that it entails. A more interesting question, however, is why the
findings captured the imagination of a more general audience. The answer, it seems to me, is twofold. They undercut the canonical version of
the theory of demographic transition, and simultaneously reinforce the
orthodox version. If economic development is identified by income growth,
then negative income effects strengthen the voices that argue for economic development and for leaving population alone. The analysis establishes income as the relevant and efficacious independent variable. This is
no longer true once we have positive income effects. Now one cannot leave
everything to income growth alone—it requires supplementation, if not by
family planning efforts, then certainly by an increased focus on education
and especially if the latter is conceived, as by Davis, in terms of influence
and propaganda.[35] On the other hand, with its emphasis on the rationality
of the individual household, the Chicago-Columbia approach dovetailed
into the emphases of the later Notestein and Davis that I discussed above.
Thus, the conclusion that rationality at the ground level of individual decision making leads *ceterus paribus* to the demand for children rising
with income, was a satisfying one from the viewpoint of the orthodox version of the theory of demographic transition.

The problem with any empirical finding is that it is fraught with interpretation of how the empirical measures correspond to the theoretical variables. What does one mean by income? What does one mean by sufficiently good proxies? At what point do the deficiencies of the database prove fatal for the entire exercise? Is the confidence in the implementation of the *ceterus paribus* phrase warranted? Are there precise tests for justifying this confidence? Even on bypassing these questions as stultifyingly abstract, and remaining with the concrete categories at hand, it is far from clear that, when all is said and done, children are normal commodities universally. In her survey, Birdsall (1988, 516) refers to thresholds, both of space and time,[36] above which children are an inferior commodity. Indeed, one can argue that to tie the Chicago-Columbia approach either to income effects or to the Muellbauer-Pollak-Wachter theorem, is not really to appreciate the novelty of its contribution.

> The economic approach had been refined during the past two hundred years. It now assumes that individuals maximize their utility from basic preferences that do not change rapidly over time, and that the behavior of different individuals is coordinated by explicit and implicit markets.... The economic approach is not restricted to material goods and wants to markets with monetary transactions, and *conceptually* does not distinguish between major and minor decisions or between "emotional" and other decisions. Indeed, I assert that the economic approach provides a framework applicable to all human behavior—to all types of decisions and to persons from all walks of life. My intention [is] to present a comprehensive analysis that is applicable, at least in part, to families in the past as well as in the present, in primitive as well as modern societies, and in Eastern and Western cultures (Becker 1981, 3).[37]

The point is that Becker goes into the microfoundations or the mechanisms underlying the assertions of the theory of demographic transition in either incarnation. The universality evident in the above statement draws its force from the fact that the theory generates empirically refutable hypotheses, with existing data sets being the backdrop against which both of the words empirical and refutability are to be understood. Apart from this qualification, the work of Becker-Tomes is a testimony to how the theory itself does not ride in any essential way on the Muellbauer-Pollak-Wachter theorem (Khan 1979). These observations aside, however, it is interesting that in his Nobel lecture, Becker does not focus extensively on family size but on issues confronting a given, already constituted family.[38] Nerlove's words written about 15 years after Becker's 1960 observation are a fitting conclusion to this section.

> The four main elements of the theoretical structure of the new home economics ... are incapable of yielding a series of well-defined implications about the main problems of household behavior with which we are concerned. It is only a framework within which to think about these problems (Nerlove 1974, 210).

Easterlin's Elaboration and Interpretation

The work of Easterlin and his collaborators combines the "economists' demand-oriented analysis with demographer's modelling of the supply of children (Birdsall 1988, section 4.1.2)." This synthesis model[39] shares with the Chicago-Columbia framework the emphasis on "commodification" of children and on seeing fertility decisions as outcomes of individual maximization problems. Where it further elaborates that framework is in its particularization of the household technology— the inclusion of birth and death functions, for example—as well as in its explicit recognition of the dependence of individual preferences on demographic variables such as "frequency of intercourse ... length of time over which contraception is practiced and its intensity, infant mortality ... and a vector of 'practices' or social norms, such as lactation or breastfeeding, appropriate age at marriage, [and an] appropriate period of postpartum abstinence" (Birdsall 1988, 506).[40]

Birdsall (1988) structures her discussion of the microfoundations of fertility determinants as a contestation between the household "demand" model and the synthesis model. However, if we depart from Birdsall's specific formulation of the household "demand" model, and ground it somewhat more generally along the lines emphasized by Becker and Nerlove, Easterlin's model emerges as a special case of their framework, and a particular elaboration of its basic insights. Children, or children services, are produced in the household, and it is difficult to see how a detailed specification of the household technology precludes the variables which Easterlin specifically includes. Indeed, it could be argued that the strength of the Chicago-Columbia framework is precisely its weakness; in its generality and lack of specification as to whether a particular variable pertains to the household technology or to household preferences or to both, it is entirely eclectic on how a particular statistical relationship is to be interpreted.

Where Easterlin's work departs from the Chicago-Columbia approach is in its threefold classification of fertility into natural, desired and optimal components. Natural fertility refers to outcomes in which no conscious decisions are taken to control fertility, whereas desired fertility is the number of children the couple would like to have in a society where contraception is costless. Finally, optimal fertility levels are those that obtain when couples maximize their preferences with all constraints, including those relating to costs of contraception, taken into account. These are contraceptual categories, and in the additional a priori information that they bring to bear on the Chicago-Columbia approach, they moderate some of its more universal pretensions. Easterlin and his coworkers emphasize that natural levels of fertility differ across societies depending on different socioeconomic and cultural norms, and that varying levels of each of the indices can be used, by themselves or in conjunction, to contextualize different individual maximization problems. Thus, different phases or stages can be distinguished according to whether: (i) desired fertility exceeds natural fertility; (ii) desired fertility is less than natural fertility but no contraception is used; (iii) desired fertility is less than natural fertility, and actual fertility is regulated to some extent and falls between desired and natural fertility; (iv) actual fertility equals desired fertility, and fertility is perfectly regulated. It is in this added structure, and specific concretization, rather than a somewhat straightforward inclusion of demographic variables, that Easterlin's approach attains its defining characteristic and comes into its own.

Indeed, when presented this way, Easterlin's model can also be seen as a more detailed elaboration of the theory of demographic transition. The first phase is really the agrarian pre-industrial society of the canonical theory, whereas the last phase is that of "incipient decline", when fertility levels are responsive to the forces of modernization and to individual choice. The third phase is one where there are unwanted or excess births, and an unmet need for contraception.[41] Even though individual maximization problems are considered, they are differentiated along social lines and by criteria pertaining to a collectivity as a whole. Indeed, in more recent developments of the theory, Easterlin et al. (1980) explicitly incorporate the dependence of individual preferences on the measures of fertility and consumption of previous generations. This emphasis on the endogeneity of preferences also allows one to locate the difference between Becker and Easterlin along analytical lines on which I have been silent so far—those that emphasize externalities and in so doing allow an opening to Nash equilibria and other solution concepts of modern game theory.

However, how is one to decide which particular phase a particular society falls into? Ideally, it is the data that ought to determine whether supply considerations predominate, or whether fertility is completely regulated and the Chicago-Columbia categories are operative. It is far from clear that this ideal situation obtains. A good example is Birdsall's discussion of a variable not seen to be particularly clouded with interpretative difficulties.

> Female education above about four years ... bears one of the strongest and most consistent negative relationships to fertility. Its negative effect is consistent with the price of time effect postulated in the household model, with a "taste" effect ... postulated in the synthesis model, and with an efficiency effect, operating through a woman's improved efficiency in the use of contraception. Female education is also associated with a higher age at marriage, and may well have some intangible effect on a woman's ability to plan and on her taste for non-familial activities. Distinguishing empirically among the postulated mechanisms is difficult (Birdsall 1988, 514).[42]

This raises what appears to be a universal difficulty; namely the inability of existing databases to distinguish between different theories, or even different phases or periodizations within the same theory. The issue is not what a particular statistic says in terms of other statistics—that may be entirely noncontroversial; what is a source of controversy is the interpretation that is given to the relationship. As Poovey (1993) points out, these are figures of arithmetic and one has to go into more detail into the reality they measure and portray. Pritchett puts the identical point this way:

> Fertility rates and contraceptive use are strongly negatively associated across countries, across households and across time. Hence, it is easy to conclude that variations in contraceptive access *cause* variations in fertility. The temptation to infer causation from association is strong, even overwhelming (Pritchett 1994a, 39).

The point is that to get a handle on the data, one has to use the vocabulary of a particular framework, and whereas the data can possibly be used to distinguish among various hypotheses phrased in terms of that particular vocabulary, it cannot adjudicate on the vocabulary itself. As Solow (1994, 53) puts it, "Any particular metaphor can impose a bias on subsequent trains of thought." Both versions of the household model commodify children, and see them as being determined by the calculus of cost-benefit analysis, but in the empirical testing, the variables are so inextricably intertwined as to lack enough discriminatory power. Birdsall remarks how a positive effect of income on fertility is consistent with an income effect, with a supply effect, and with a socioeconomic effect stemming from the propensities of "small" farmers. Moving over to mortality, she identifies a biological as well as a behavioral effect, but notes that even if a response is pinned down as a behavioral one, there is a question whether it is "hoarding" behavior, presumably in Bangladesh, or "replacement" behavior, as in Malaysia (Birdsall 1988, 516, 518, 519).

This inability of data to distinguish between frameworks is further underscored by its inability to formalize the conceptual variables themselves. The nature of the enterprise calls for finding adequate proxies, and the question of adequacy cannot itself be put to the test.

> With a few exceptions, census and household surveys collect no information on the exogenous "prices" critical to the models: e.g., the price of child quality (i.e., price of schooling, health care, child care providers other than parents, food); the price of child quantity or cost of fertility regulation (i.e., access to and cost of conceptive methods); the price of parental time (i.e., expected wage rates for men and women) (Birdsall 1988, 513).[43]

The point is that the ambiguity in the translation between the conceptual and the empirical can only be attenuated, never removed. What is a reasonable proxy for the price of child quality in the Chicago-Columbia framework can equally reasonably be considered a proxy for an entirely different variable in a different framework, say a socioeconomic norm or an index of modernization. There is slippage and overdetermination in that a particular statistical measure may be a measure of several conceptual variables at the same time. Thus, Pritchett links the effect of changes in contraceptive supply to "other considerations, such as child and maternal health, the timing of first births, and the prevention of sexually transmitted diseases", and concludes that "measuring the cost of avoiding a birth or the costs of a child is very difficult, both conceptually and empirically, and both of these estimates are subject to wide margins of errors" (Pritchett 1994a, 24, 39). Elsewhere, Birdsall writes, "Lack of good information on change of the 'price' of family planning (i.e., in the availability and quality of information or services) meant that until about a decade ago it was difficult to resolve the debate about the relative importance to fertility decline of the supply of family planning services vs. the "demand" factors—increasing education, falling infant mortality and so on. More recently, however, such information has accumulated, especially at the national level ... and at the community level; and though *this and other such measures remain controversial due to measurement problems*, they have permitted analyses ... taking into account both supply and demand factors" (Birdsall 1988, 520). [44] My point is simply that this controversy cannot be eliminated, and that there is a certain inevitability to it.

This inability of data to validate interpretations and thereby distinguish among competing theories is underscored by the fact that existing databases are themselves socially constructed. This is simply a statement of the fact that data is collected by institutions with objectives of their own, and that sample survey questionaires can hardly be designed in a way that is innocent of any theoretical schema.

> Archives constitute the documentary stock of an institution. It is the specific activity of this institution that produces them, gathers them and conserves them. And the deposit thereby constituted is an authorized deposit through some stipulation added to the one that sets up the entity for which the archives are "archives" (see Ricoeur 1988, 117). [45]

Of course, as emphasized by the so-called covering law model (see Ricoeur 1984, 111-120), one can formulate precise, and empirically expressed, hypotheses that test for the biases introduced by institutional objectives and/or those introduced in the process of data collection. This is to engage in what Ricoeur (1984, 112) terms the first order of discourse and has its own ambiguities and conceptual and empirical compromises. In a more positive vein, I am simply arguing for econometric subtlety being matched by an equal sophistication about the databases on which it is exercised.

In summary, Easterlin's work, in attempting a synthesis between the demographic, sociological, and economic approaches, provides a vocabulary that insists on disciplinary crossovers, and thereby prevents univalent and literal readings of the Chicago-Columbia framework. I now turn to another interpretation and use of such a framework.

The Turn to Desired Fertility

In the 1950 survey above, Indian female respondents were asked how many living children a woman of 40 should have. In the modal preference for two or three children, Davis (1950, 17) saw "a desire among Indian peasants for small families", and concluded that the "pattern of lower fertility thus appears to be incipient". The work reported in this subsection can be traced to Davis's emphasis on desired fertility, and his consequent extrapolation to completed fertility.

The difficulty with the Chicago-Columbia framework in explaining completed family size is that each couple's life cycle is reduced to one period. Given the restraints and parameters pertaining to this period, utility-maximizing couples make decisions that are adhered to for the whole period. The common preferences and the technology of the household remain unchanged, and there is no room for the incorporation of additional information and for responding to previous decisions. In her discussion of the conceptual limitations of "fertility models", Birdsall (1988, 509-512) emphasizes the absence of sequential decision making, as well as questions relating to maximization, agency, and marginality. She does not question the "commodification" of children, but singles out utility maximization and the degree of rationality that it presupposes. "The critique is that an increasing degree of rationality in society as a whole is ignored as a possible explanator of fertility decline. For example, a decline in the influence of religion could reduce fertility even in the absence of price changes."[46] The other two limitations are the "family" utility function, and the fact that "economic models of fertility appear more effective in explaining the broad sweep of fertility in explaining changes at the margin than in explaining the broad sweep of fertrility change over time."[47] Khan and Sirageldin (1977) introduce their study along three different directions: a shift from "completed family size" as the dependent variable to "desired additional fertility", an emphasis on son preference, and a distinction between wives' and husbands' responses. They focus on the question, Do you want any (more) children? This simple question, with its emphasis on the you and the now, and with its minimal demands on literacy and numeracy, leads the investigation of fertility away from completed family size to desired additional fertility.[48] What has to be singled out in this and subsequent work is its emphasis on sequential decision making. The estimated model can be summarized as

$$AC = f \text{ (boys, girls, demographic variables, socioeconomic variables)}$$

where AC takes the values of unity or zero depending on whether a respondent wants any more children; demographic variables refer to the respondent's age, age at marriage, and infant mortality; and socioeconomic variables refer to indices of income and assets on the economic side, and those of education, nuclearization, contraceptive use, and urbanization on the social side.

The statistical analysis is based on cross-section KAP data from Bangladesh, Egypt, and Pakistan at different periods of time.[49] The diversity of time and space is attenuated by the conceptual simplicity of the variable *AC* being investigated. Without going into details, I want to focus attention on two considerations: first, the inclusion of the current (which is to say at the time of interview) number of living boys and girls as explanatory variables; and second, the division of the sample between husbands and wives. The differential importance of current family size along gender lines for desired additional fertility is one possible quantification of "son preference", while different individual equations for wives and husbands furnish a methodology for quantifying "interspousal communication".[50] Indeed, the basic analysis suggests several other lines of inquiry: simultaneous equation models in which the wife's and the husband's desired additional fertility are treated as endogenous variables;[51] a supplementation of the dichotomous variable by information as to the number of additional boys and girls desired by the husband and the wife;[52] and measurement of "fatalistic attitudes" as revealed by respondents who refused to give information as to desired fertility—the so-called "up-to-God" response.[53]

The interesting question, however, turns on the interpretation of these findings. Do they say anything about the particular stage that Bangladeshi, Pakistani, and Egyptian societies are at in terms of the canonical theory of demographic transition? Looking at Pakistan alone, does the differential in the results over a 20-year period, especially as it pertains to the provincial levels, say anything about the approach to the third stage of incipient decline? Alternatively, can one extend the "commodification" to treat boys and girls as distinct commodities with their own implicit prices, and thereby not only see the outcomes as a direct validation of the Chicago-Columbia model, but also as predicting an increased derived demand for service ensuring the more desirable commodity, males?[54] Yet again, the results can be interpreted along with Easterlin as pertaining to endogenous tastes and as a reflection of socioeconomic norms. Khan and Malik (1994) do not interpret them in this way:

> To the extent that our results identify son-preference as a critical explanatory variable in desired fertility, they emphasize to that extent differences in tastes, and deemphasize economic variables which apply to a single representative agent.

However, rather than pursue interpretations along lines that are by now standard, I turn to a bolder move in the recent literature. This reverts to Davis and sees desired fertility, additional or completed, as a reasonable proxy for actual fertility.[55] Indeed, the assertion is put forward in a somewhat less understated way:

> The analysis ... demonstrated that the "desired children" view of fertility is valid. Analyses purporting to demonstrate the dominant importance of the provision of family planning services are typically based on analytical errors. We show that to a striking extent the answer to why actual fertility differs across countries is that desired fertility differs. The level of contraceptive use, measure of contraceptive availability (such as "unmet need"), and family planning effort have little impact on fertility after controlling for fertility desires. The key question is to what extent fertility desires are determined by economic influences and to what extent by social and cultural forces (Pritchett 1994b).

Pritchett (1994a) puts into play two views: the "family planning gap" view versus the "desired children" view. The former has a parallel to Davis's direct method, but whereas Davis saw desired fertility as very much a part of his larger proactive stance, buffering it by the canonical theory and opposing it to indirect sociological barriers, Pritchett ties down desired fertility to the Chicago-Columbia framework, and the demand for contraception to induced or derived demand arising from such a conception. The lack of qualification in Pritchett's statements is worthy of note.[56] It needed someone to answer those who would say that "to achieve fertility reductions, one must change desires and improve contraceptive access", Pritchett drums home what for him is the clear punch line.

> It is fertility desires and *not* contraceptive access that matters. A low level of desired fertility appears to be both a necessary and sufficient condition for low fertility. In contrast, an improvement in contraceptive access (as distinguished from contraceptive use) is neither sufficient nor necessary for large fertility reductions. The best (and perhaps the only palatable) way to reduce fertility is to change the economic and social conditions that make large families desirable (Pritchett 1994a, 39-41).[57]

Pritchett is answering a position that is exemplified by Kennedy's views:

A detailed proposal for dealing with the demographic explosion in developing countries would simply repeat what numerous studies by international agencies have pointed out: that the *only practical way* to ensure a decrease in fertility rates, and thus in population growth, is to introduce cheap and reliable forms of birth control (Kennedy 1993, 338).[58]

It is interesting how the two versions of the theory of demographic transition form a backdrop to the debate sparked by Pritchett's (1994a) contribution.

Bongaarts (1994) reply is in terms of unwanted fertility[59], a concept that we met in the discussion of Easterlin's four phases. He concedes Pritchett's finding that unwanted fertility is not related to overall fertility, but, rather than seeing this as a consequence of the ineffectiveness of family planning programs, he interprets it as precisely a result of their effectiveness. The basic argument reverts to the categories of the canonical theory of demographic transition.

> Early in the transition, women want large families, and they bear wanted children most of their reproductive lives, thus leaving little room for unwanted births. But near the end of the transition, they face one or two decades of fecund married life during which they have to try to avoid getting pregnant. It is not surprising that unwanted pregnancies can then occur unless effective programs are in place (Bongaarts 1994, 617).

This distending of the last phase of incipient decline in the canonical theory deserves to be noted. Modernization has an impact on preferences, but this impact cannot be exercised unless cheap family planning programs are in place. There is a "commodification" of contraception knowledge and use in the form of contraceptive services (Bongaarts 1994, 619), and it is entirely understandable that Pritchett, operating as he does within the categories of the Chicago-Columbia approach, goes into undergraduate detail of the difference between shifts along the curve versus shifts of the curve (Pritchett 1994a). Contraception is a proximate determinant of fertility because "in a mechanical sense, the probability of birth in any given period is the product of coital frequency, natural fecundity, and contraceptive efficiency" (Pritchett 1994a, 21). However, this "is at times taken as evidence that expanding the 'supply' of contraception is an important condition for reducing fertility."

The point is that a shift along the curve in one framework may possibly be a shift of the curve in another framework. We have already seen how Easterlin classifies the individual optimization problems by social criteria depending on natural, desired, and optimal fertility. In addition, the orthodox position that I discussed in the context of the theory of demographic transition can also be reformulated beyond the purely contraceptive dimension to broaden the effect of family planning programs.[60] Bongaarts (1994) and Knowles et al. (1994) emphasize the implications that family planning and affiliated programs have for information, education, and communication.[61] There is another interesting twist in that "family planning programs are highly effective in saving governments money: expenditures (for example on education and health services) saved by averting unwanted births."[62]

There are technical issues in the debate between Pritchett and his critics,[63] but the bottom line is clear. "The primary issue, then, should be *what factors are related to the reduction in desired fertility?*" (see Bhushan and Kincaid 1994, 5) and Bongaarts's answer draws attention to the "central, and often dominant, role of social, educational, cultural, and economic changes in reducing fertility in most developing countries. Nevertheless, governments in the developing world would be well advised to increase investments in human resources and in family planning programs" (Bongaarts 1994, 619).

Thus, irrespective of the extent to which we are still rehashing the basic 1950 debate unleashed by the two versions of the theory of demographic transition, and whatever the interpretation of the underlying relationships, the evidence of son preference is persuasive, and has been corroborated by various demographic studies innocent of economic theory (see Arnold and Kuo 1984, De Tray 1984, Johansson and Nygreen 1993, Knodel and Prachuabmoh 1976, Mahmood 1992, Prachuabmoh et al. 1974, Repetto 1972, Rukanuddin 1982, Westoff and Rindfuss 1974, Williamson 1973). It is also clear that this evidence, and the preferences to which it points, will have to be contended by policy makers in several less developed countries."[64] However, I now turn to an implication of "commodification" of children that is absent in Becker's work.

Welfare Economics with or without Nonconvexities

Demeny (1986) begins his article "Population and the invisible hand" by framing the issues in a way that makes his position explicit:

> The essence of the population problem, if there is a problem, is that individual decisions with respect to demographic acts do not add up to recognized common good—that choices at the individual level are not congruent with the collective in-

terest. A disjunction between the aggregate outcome of individual demographic decisions and what members of the society, if well informed about their own interests, would find
to their liking is of course not a logical necessity, [but] the
disjunction is indeed pervasive and important, both as a description of contemporary reality and as a continuing prospect.

Demeny is denying the applicability of the first fundamental theorem of
modern welfare economics,[65] and in so doing, rejecting what he terms the
revisionist position,[66] and identifying himself with the proactive orthodox
view, one within which he includes Malthus, the more orthodox views of
Davis and Notestein,[67] and the practitioners of the new home economics.[68]
Indeed, given that a third of Birdsall's (1988) survey is devoted to externalities, fertility control and market failure, and to specific policies such
as family planning information and services, entitlements, taxes, and
disincentives, and quotas,[69] it is important to examine the intellectual basis behind the application of welfare economics to questions of population
policy. I turn to this in this section.

The departing point of such an application is the "commodification" both of children and of contraceptive services. The theory stipulates
a finite number of commodities, each of whose characteristics is universally known and proxied by a price system at which utility and profit-
maximizing decisions by economically negligible agents are consistent in
the aggregate. In the words of Demeny (1986, 481), "choices come with
price tags attached to them, determined in a competitive market, prices
over which the consumers have no control. [A] couple has to answer
questions like this: Shall we have steak tonight, or fly to the Bahamas on
a package tour tomorrow, or have a baby nine months hence?" The point
is that once this commodification and the accompanying universality of
markets is subscribed to, one can invoke all of the many desirable properties competitive outcomes possess. They are technologically efficient in
that one cannot obtain more of one commodity, say contraceptive services, without a corresponding diminution in another. They are Pareto optimal in the sense that the welfare of any decision maker cannot be improved without decreasing that of another. They are in the core, group-
rational in the sense that no coalition has an incentive to opt out of the
economy and do better for themselves with their resources and technologies. They satisfy the equal treatment property in the sense that identical
households obtain identical resources; in the case at hand, an identical
number of children. The outcomes are fair in the sense of being in the
value; which is to say that each couple is contributing to the society at
the margin precisely what it is taking out of the society. It seems that the

pursuit of individual self-interest leads to coherence however one formalizes the term (see Khan 1991, 1993).

All this is guaranteed by the first fundamental theorem of welfare economics and its relatives. If agents are "small" relative to the market, and if all the relevant commodities are "priced-out" in the sense that there are no missing markets, the best the government can do is not to do anything at all. The problem, of course, is that there are no explicit markets for children as well as for all those variables that introduce interdependence between tastes and technologies. As Demeny puts it,

> The issue is how each of us would like *others* to behave with respect to demographic choices for our own good, however we choose to define it. But where do we go to barter or purchase from our fellow men demographic behavior that pleases us? (Demeny 1986, 476).

We now have to rely more crucially on the Muelbauer-Pollak-Wachter theorem, and guarantee that prices are independent of individual actions. We also have to fend off second-best considerations whereby introduction of one market in a world of many missing markets is no longer guaranteed to improve welfare. It is this focus on markets and property rights that leads Birdsall (1988, 522) to say that "If parents do not fully internalize the costs of children, they are likely to have higher fertility than is optimal from society's point of view. In a world in which they have no property rights in children (as they once did through arranged marriages), Pareto optimality cannot be obtained." There is market failure in the provision of information in that less than the optimal amount is supplied. "The result of poor markets, for information and services, can be 'unmet need' for family planning" (Birdsall 1988, 525).[70]

However, the theory is now being led away from its original positivistic motivation. The primary purpose of such a theory is prediction in the sense of precise testable hypotheses. Becker's concerns have to do more with positive economics that with normative economics.

> Unlike Marxian analysis, the economic approach I refer to does not assume that individuals are motivated solely by selfishness or material gain. It is a *method* of analysis, not an assumption about particular motivations. The analysis assumes that individuals maximize welfare *as they conceive it*, whether they be selfish, altruistic, loyal, spiteful, or masochistic. Their behavior is forward-looking, and it is also assumed to be consistent over time (Becker 1993, 385-386).[71]

It is one thing to treat children and contraceptive services as commodities
(see Khan 1993), but quite another to attempt to "commodify" consumer
interdependence with personalized prices, especially in large societies
where each agent is economically negligible. How is one to handle Nash
considerations, as emphasized for example by Easterlin's endogenous
preferences, through competitive markets? How does one tinker with the
price system so that it may reflect the altruism that parents bear toward
their children or the hatred of groups they perceive as not their own?

The second and deeper half of the fundamental theorems of welfare economics guarantees the possibility of such markets. Corresponding
to any technologically efficient outcome, there exist prices at which profit-
maximizing decisions can sustain that outcome. Even from a more general equilibrium point of view, corresponding to any Pareto optimal outcome, or one in the core, or in the value, there exist prices such that
competitive behavior at those prices sustains that outcome. Thus Birdsall
(1988, 526) writes:

> Assuming public subsidies are financed appropriately ... and
> programs are fully voluntary, public investment in family
> planning as a means to reduce fertility is generally endorsed
> in the economics literature.

Birdsall distinguishes between incentives to contraception from those to
children. After making it clear that "entitlements and incentives are
specified rewards for specific fertility-related behavior," she discusses two
particular forms of entitlement: "payments designed to compensate for
time and travel costs of ... sterilization,[72] [and] payments to individuals
(immediate or deferred) associated with maintaining a limit on their children."[73] Optimal interferences in the price system simply require the balancing of the costs and benefits of an additional child—"the number of
births averted is irrelevant."[74] She is also unequivocal on quotas, and
finds them "far less efficient than incentives. In short, quotas eliminate
any use of the market, with the typical associated losses in consumer
welfare" (Birdsall 1988, 529). The point is that there are missing markets
as a consequence of externalities and imperfect information, and they
have to be supplemented by modifications in the existing price system.
Indeed population policy is simply one element in a larger policy package,
and the question can be raised whether population policy can also attend
to other ills. "The question in any event is whether or not it is more technically feasible and culturally acceptable to introduce property rights or

population limitation, and whether population limitation, in and of itself, could compensate fully for lack of property rights" (Birdsall 1988, 523).

It is one of the achievements of the first set of fundamental theorems of welfare economics that they require no convexity assumptions on the economic environments. However, this is no longer true of the second set of theorems being invoked above. Indeed, in a world of decreasing average costs, the very concept of a profit-maximizing production plan, and· therefore of a competitive equilibrium, makes no sense. We have to turn to other kinds of equilibria, ones in which a societal agency is ready to subsidize losses. There has been some progress in understanding such environments (see Khan 1991), but, rather than go into details, I shall simply point out that marginal or average cost-pricing equilibria, or Lindahl-Hotelling equilibria in a world of public goods, may no longer even be technologically efficient (see Khan [1991], particularly the section on *Some disturbing examples*). This has profound consequences for an activist orthodox position based on the second fundamental theorem. Some distributions of initial aggregate resources lead to equilibria which are efficient while others do not—the separation of equity and efficiency, and the resulting silence on distributional issues, can no longer be sustained. It is far from clear that average costs are nondecreasing in the provision of children and of contraceptive services; at any rate it is interesting that there has been no discussion of the twin issues of increasing returns to scale and indivisibilities, in the application of welfare of economics to population policies.

> The exact formulation of assumptions and of conclusions turned out moreover, to be an effective safeguard against the ever-present temptation to apply an economic theory beyond its domain of validity. And by the exactness of that formulation, economic analysis was sometimes brought closer to its ideology-free ideal. Foes of state intervention read in these two theorems a mathematical demonstration of the unqualified superiority of market economies, while advocates of state intervention welcome the same theorems because the explicitness of their assumptions emphasizes discrepancies between the theoretical model and the economies that they observe (Debreu 1986).

Birdsall (1988, 493) reads Demeny as "emphasizing market (and institutional failures)". This is true to the extent that the activist orthodox position can be identified with activism propelled by the second set of fundamental theorems of welfare economics. When Demeny (1988, 477) asserts that "In population change, 'goods' and 'bads' tend to exist to-gether in a tightly wrapped bundle", and tends to rely on the market to unwrap them, he is identifying with Birdsall's own position. In the context of payments for the limitation of family size, she does raise cautionary flags: "if the desperately poor have difficulty borrowing, as they often do, such payments may be coercive. [They] also raise the problem of 'entrapment' of the myopic, who may be induced to forego long-term benefits of additional children to capture a short-term monetary payment" (Birdsall 1988, 526-527).

> The line between disincentives and coercion then becomes merely one of degree. Incentive payments in poor societies pose a "tragic choice"—a morally unacceptable choice, for example, between food for the desperately poor, and child-bearing. The framing of such choices raises ethical issues beyond the scope of welfare economics (Birdsall 1988, 528).

However, Demeny's objections go much deeper and he is less willing to be limited by the frontiers of welfare economics. "What the great society ... needs ... is a constitution: an explicit agreement embodied in law, on what the rules of the game are, including an explicit agreement on how the rules can be changed, if so desired. To prescribe what it ought to say is outright inadmissible: that is up to the islanders themselves" (Demeny 1987, 481). The real problems of missing markets have to do as much with time and uncertainty as they have to do with agent interde-pendence.

> What we are confronting is a generalized prisoner's dilemma. We should ask and try to answer more daring questions than neoclassical economics inspires us to. What kind of society would we like to be part of? What kind of arrangements should that society have concerning demographic matters? (Demeny 1988, 476, 486).[75]

As we shall have occasion to see below, these considerations are devel-oped more fully by Sen in his polar collaborate/override choice.

The Design of Optimum Population

Demeny's emphasis on constitutional rules and on institutions tends to take the debate into the very heart of politics.[76] "The point is that distributional considerations cannot be set aside from those of efficiency.

It is not only that pervasive nonconvexities and existing distortions make this problematic; with endogenous fertility, even the concept of intergenerational Pareto optimality is incoherent—the Pareto criterion is not well suited for welfare comparisons of equilibria with different numbers of people" (Srinivasan 1987, 4). The disjunction between the social and the individual becomes particularly sharpened in matters of population policy, and it is far from clear how one is to proceed with purely economic or demographic arguments if paternalistic solutions are to be avoided. [77] In this section, I shall discuss an analysis of optimal population which takes as given the existence of a well-defined social welfare function for a particular society as a whole.

> If it is granted that family-size decisions are, to some extent, based on economic calculation, it will also be granted, perhaps, that the government may have good reason to differ from the family on the criterion employed. I shall argue... that there are... particularly good reasons why the State should follow a preference ordering inconsistent with the preferences of those who decide about family size (Mirrlees 1972, 171).

In his analysis of the design of an optimum population policy, Mirrlees (1972) focuses on two characteristics, fecundity s and tastes t, and takes as a primitive the distribution of these characteristics in a "large" society. There are two basic ingredients defined on this space of characteristics: (i) a couple's objective function, depending on consumption per head c, existing family size n, and attempts to have children N; and (ii) the probability p of attaining a particular family size, again depending on existing family size n and attempts to have children N. A couple's individuality is captured by u being a function of t, and its fecundity by p being a function of s. The point is that an individual couple does not solve for completed family size. Mirrlees attaches importance to uncertainty in matters of procreation, even in a timeless setting, and therefore his couples are only allowed to determine the number of attempts to have children. Once the optimal number of attempts are determined by an individual couple on the basis of the maximization of von Neumann-Morgenstern expected utilities, which is to say $N(s,t)$, the expected average size of the population as well as the expected average level of consumption can be determined. This determination is based simply on aggregating the functions $\Sigma_n np$ and $\Sigma_n ncp$ with respect to the distributions of s and t.

It is interesting to compare Mirrlees's conception with the Chicago-Columbia framework as well as with that of Easterlin. Mirrlees takes the "commodification" of children as given, but assumes a patriarchal household right from the beginning.[78] There is no discussion of the allocation of fixed resources within the household, or of any questions of interspousal disagreement. There is some affinity with Easterlin's emphasis on supply, and it is used to bring uncertainty considerations to the fore. Indeed, Mirrlees has a framework that allows discussion of the problem of population policy when there are no differences in tastes, as in the Chicago-Columbia framework, or in fertility, as emphasized by Easterlin.

Mirrlees's analysis explores the disjunction between the individual and the social. There are no markets for commodities, consumption per head c depends on family size n, and this schedule $c(\cdot)$ is taken as given by the individual family in its attempts to have children. Thus, $N(s,t)$ is more fully expressed by $N(c(\cdot),s,t)$, and individual couples decide on the number of attempts to have children by taking into account the incentives provided by society as a whole. On the other hand, the societal agent (government, state, or whatever) determines the optimal consumption schedule $c(\cdot)$ on the basis of individual actions. All that needs further specification are the production possibilities available to society as a whole. Mirrlees puts these also in the hands of the societal agent, and relies on the assumption of a "large" society to invoke the law of large numbers, and thereby to equate expected and actual population and consumption levels. The social welfare function is simply a measure of expected utilities aggregated over the distribution of characteristics t and s.

We are thus in a principal-agent world, for which Mirrlees proposes three optima. The naive optimum is one where the societal agent is oblivious of the fact that individual families are being influenced by their economic prospects, and determines $c(\cdot)$ by taking N as a given parameter depending only on s and t. Under the utopian optimum, individual couples do whatever is required of them by the societal agent, and it determines both $c(\cdot)$ as well as N, again as functions of s and t. The free optimum is the most interesting of the three. Here "c is chosen by the state, as a function of n, and families are free to choose N, knowing perfectly what function $c(\cdot)$ will determine their consumption (Mirrlees 1972)." The state is constrained by the production possibilities as well as by the fact that there is individual incentive compatibility.

Mirrlees's problem in its full generality remains unsolved.[79] He offers solutions for special cases where (i) only one of the two variables s and t vary and there is no uncertainty, and (ii) neither varies and there is uncertainty. In the second case, Mirrlees's focus is on the 'optimum propaganda' problem: in the utopian optimum, would families tend to wish for a larger or smaller choice of N; or alternatively, ... would the State (if it knew the true circumstances) wish that families had chosen a smaller or larger *N*?" However, even for these special cases, "the results are striking and indeed quite surprising".

> On simplifying but not absurd assumptions, the criterion as to whether large families should be rewarded or penalized prove[s] to be quite simple: namely whether or not the marginal product of labor exceed[s] the average product (Mirrlees 1972, 194).

It is interesting how Mirrlees's consideration of a simple second-best world takes him to the question of nonconvexities and of increasing returns to scale. In opposition to the Coale-Hoover capital-widening argument, whereby "rapid population growth dilutes the amount of physical as well as human capital per worker", (Birdsall 1988, 524), Mirrlees (1972, 196) lists the sources of increasing returns in the "provision of collective goods, represented in part by government expenditure on administration, defence and protection, social overhead capital, and so on, and in part by the diffusion of information. There are also economies of distribution and transportation that may accrue to larger populations."

In summary, Mirrlees's pioneering analysis presents a novel and nuanced attempt at understanding the notion of "optimum" population levels. He emphasized uncertainty, but also notes the dilemma that this poses.[80] He is sensitive to what Easterlin terms questions of supply.[81] He broaches the genetic argument, and registers its implications.[82] He is well aware of the importance of dynamics.[83] Finally, he does not ignore questions of rational expectations equilibria in which individual couples rationalize existing family size, and are influenced by the preference of the previous generation.

> The extent to which this argument is plausible depends on the likelihood that economies will shift course in ways that individuals projecting the more obvious of past trends might fail to predict.[84] Since there are no convincing models of long-run economic development, economists are not in a position to decide these issues, and doubt whether anyone else is. Much work remains to be done between simple models and realistic policies for developing countries (Mirrlees 1972, 223-224, 195).

A Recasting of the Debate

In his recent overview of the population "problem", [85] Sen classifies the literature along two lines: apocalyptic pessimism versus dismissive smugness (Sen 1994).[86] The former relies on conceptual imagery of a
population bomb, too many people, a dying planet, too little food,[87] while
the latter invokes the fact that we did well enough in the past, despite
Malthus's gloomy predictions, and therefore ought to do well enough in
the future. The pessimists "believe that overpopulation is *the* cause of
much of the poverty and misery that exist" (Mirrlees 1972, 169) and tend
"to treat the people involved not as reasonable beings, allies facing a
common problem, but as impulsive and uncontrolled sources of great social harm, needing strong discipline" (p. 62). The dismissive and optimistic viewpoint is concerned neither with the stock nor with the speed with
which the stock is growing. It is interesting to see how far a debate along
these lines has progressed beyond that of the 1950s.

One clear observation is that the anticolonial tint of previous
writing on the demographic transitions is no longer there 50 years later.
However, the concern and preoccupation with the less developing countries, now referred to as the South, remains at the forefront. It has both
selfish and altruistic dimensions, and the former is expressed in the following terms.

> How great a threat of intolerable immigration pressure does
> the North face from the South, and second, is that pressure
> closely related to population growth in the South, rather
> than to other social and economic factors? (p. 62)

A related issue is the distribution of the stock of the world population
given its rates of increase;[88] what Sen refers to as the "psychologically
tense issue of racial balance in the world and the fear for being engulfed"
(p. 63).[89] Thus, in this context, the population problem translates into a
North-South issue, with Northern income levels, the price of food, the
emergence of slums and threats to the environment emerging as points of
principal concern. One cannot locate these concerns in the earlier debates; what is interesting is the lifting of the argument from the conceptual categories of society versus individual to those explicitly involving two
different societies and two larger regional groupings, North versus South.
The literature and the conceptual apparatus that I have reviewed so far is
obviously not designed to handle these issues, and new conceptualiza-
tions are wanting.

When one turns to the institution of policies that are in the best interest of the countries of the less developed world—the North's altruistic concern for the welfare of the South—we are back in Davis's world of direct versus indirect methods, Pritchett's family planning versus desired fertility views, and Mirrlees's three optima. Sen phrases the debate under the dichotomy of collaboration versus override, and his definitions are useful as benchmarks for the discussion, both for the continuity they emphasize, as well as for the break that they introduce.

> One involves voluntary choice and a collaborative solution, and the other overrides voluntarism through legal and economic coercion.

The override view takes its name from the fact that personal decisions are overridden. This is the utopian optimum of Mirrlees—"In matters of procreation, families do what is desired of them, whether they desire it themselves or not" (Mirrlees 1972, 174). However, the use of economic as an adjective to coercion is a fundamental move from a conceptual point of view, and, by it, Sen not only incorporates Davis's direct method and Pritchett's family planning view into the override camp, but also questions the voluntary nature of the whole conceptual structure of welfare economics, especially as it rests on the second theorem.[90]

> Force can also take an indirect form, as when economic opportunities are changed so radically by government regulations that people have little choice except to behave in ways that the government would approve.[91]

Family planning efforts may be coercive, not because they necessarily and directly force households to take one action as opposed to another, but because of their opportunity costs in terms of the provision of health and education services. They skew consumer choice, and frustrate voluntary approaches based on informed and educated demand for these services. We thus see Bongaarts's argument turned on its head.

> [A shift] from development in general to family planning in particular .. [has] exactly the opposite effect on family planning than the one intended, since education and health care have a significant part in the *voluntary* reduction of the birth rate (Sen 1994, 64).

Such policies fit into the general approach of "override" as
well, since they try to rely on manipulating people's choices
through offering them only some opportunities (the means of
family planning) while denying others, no matter what they
themselves would have preferred (Sen 1994, 64).

By putting radical changes in economic policy under the coercive
heading, Sen emphasizes "reasoned human action" under the voluntary
collaborative view—"governments and citizens, through informed discussion of the kind of life we have reason to value, would together produce
economic and social conditions favoring slower population growth. The
approach relies ... not on legal and economic restrictions but on rational
decisions of men and women, based on expanded choices and enhanced
security, and encouraged by open dialogue and extensive public discussions (pp. 64, 68)." Sen goes back to the Malthus-Codorcet debate on
population policy and identifies Malthus as the overridder[92] and Condor-
cet as the collaborator. The collaborative view has as much to do with pri-
orities, with institution building, and by the avoidance of quick paternalistic solutions, as it has to do with the noninterference of governments in
the daily lives of its citizens.

In summary, through these dual pairs of categories, apocalyptic
pessimism versus dismissive smugness and override versus collaboration, Sen crystallizes and returns the debate to my starting point without
an explicit mention of it. He is well aware of the Davis-Notestein orthodox
view whereby family efforts are advocated not by disregarding the theoretical schema of the canonical theory but by focusing on the question of
speed. "In the long run, [economic and social development] may indeed be
exactly the right approach ... but may not act fast enough to meet the
present threat (p. 65)." The punchline is that,

the distinction between the two approaches... thus tends to
correspond closely to the contrast between, on the one hand,
treating economic and social development as the way to solve
the population problem, and on the other, expecting little
from development and using, instead, legal and economic
pressures to reduce birth rates (p. 64).

In this essay, I read recent literature on population and economic development in the light of a discontinuity identified in the theory of demographic transition. The canonical 1940s version of the theory emphasized
long-run social, economic, and cultural changes as the primary determi-

nants of population, whereas the proactive orthodox version of the 1950s stressed short-run control and design, based principally on the provision of contraceptive services. I track this theoretical turn along several methodological indices: a shift in categorization from the social to the individual, in epistemological stance from understanding to quantitative prediction, and in research objectives from social science to policy science.[93] My basic interpretive thesis is that this turnabout, and the consequent shifts that it incorporates and entails, has not yet been resolved in the "scientific" literature. I locate it, in one form or another, in subsequent work on the relationship between population and economic development: the interpretation of the negative effects of income on fertility, the tension between the Chicago-Columbia approach and that of Easterlin, the differing importance given to son preference and interspousal communication, the recent vigorous reemphasis on desired fertility as the principal determinant of fertility, the diverging viewpoints on the relevance and importance of welfare economics, the varying emphases that are given to North-South perspectives, and the "collaborative versus override" approaches to population policy.

My reading is rounded off by other aspects not usually emphasized in the literature. I note a parallel between the canonical theory of demographic transition and Rostow's stages of economic growth. I use the Heckscher-Ohlin-Samuelson theory of international trade as a description of the Chicago-Columbia approach to fertility, and thereby single out the importance of the Muellbauer-Pollak-Wachter theorem. This result offers conditions for the independence of shadow prices of nonmarketed inputs from the actions of the individual agents, and I show that it attains its primary importance in the context of welfare economics. I base the case for government interference in population policy on the fundamental theorems of welfare economics, and underscore the importance of increasing returns to scale and decreasing average costs of production in the applicability of these theorems. I argue that these theorems offer us an important conceptual framework within which we can evaluate the opportunity costs of family planning programs and other public goods, and can deal with questions of agent interdependence and endogenous preferences. I reduce the question of externalities to that between Nash and competitive equilibria. Moving beyond standard welfare economics, I discuss a framework that explicitly faces the issue of interpersonal comparisons in the formulation of population policy, and under the assumption of an omniscient and a paternalistic government, reduces the question of incentives to fertility as hinging on the relationship between average and marginal productivities of labor. Finally, I refer to alternative interdisciplinary treatments if these paternalistic, and inevitably coercive, assumptions are to be avoided. An undercurrent running through my entire essay is the importance of conditionalities that define relevant theorems, and of the way conceptual categories are empirically implemented and interpreted.

The question is whether my reading of this selected literature offers clear and unambiguous guides to policy. Even within a limited well-delineated literature, as the one I consider, one obtains insight by putting Davis and Notestein with Becker and Easterlin, and by examining their work in the context of the Arrow-Debreu model or the one proposed by Mirrlees. In the context of research policy, this suggests a plural approach, and a grounding of mathematical and statistical analyses by institutional and historical studies. In a preparatory lecture for the Cairo Conference, Demeny refers to the "unsettled state of scientific judgment concerning the economics consequences of population change" and makes an argument for research that is local and specific. And just as there are no quick and easy solutions in the research domain, it is too much to expect universal laws that apply to culturally diverse societies with a variety of political and social structures. There are inevitable trade-offs—no single win-win tale for the guidance of governments and international organizations interested in population planning and policy. Problems of population and economic development come wrapped together; the solutions need balance and judgment, and, for maximal efficacy and sustainability, ought to emerge from within the societies for which they are prescribed.

Acknowledgment

The author would like to thank Indu Bhushan, Malcolm Dowling, Dick Flathman, Nadeem-ul-Haque, Alejandro N. Herrin, Nurul Islam, Basant Kapur, C.S. Liu, Sohail Malik, Ernesto M. Pernia, M. G. Quibria, Salim Rashid, Ismail Sirageldin, and T.N. Srinivasan for discussion, references, and encouragement. However, errors of emphasis and/or of interpretation are solely his.

Notes

1. For discussion of this danger, see the essays in Tully (1988).

2. In his critical intellectual history of the study of fertility change, Szereter (1991, 659) cuts his material along orthodox/heterodox lines, with the "orthodox" position characterized by "one dominant line of thought, [namely] the extent to which relatively rapid population growth can obstruct the potential for economic growth in less developed countries." Szereter also refers to the position counter to the orthodox one as "revisionist". The orthodox-revisionist polarity is also adduced and utilized by Hodgson (1988).

3. See van de Walle (1992) for the transition of the theory of the demographic transition from "a dominant paradigm in demography" to one of progressive abandonment. See also Figure 1 in Van de Walle (1992), Birdsall (1988, 479), and Hodgson (1983, 7). The latter gives further references to articles in the 1950s that viewed the demographic transition theory as an "integrated theory of high order" and a "binder" for demography's diverse and particularized findings." Birdsall (1988, Footnote 4) references Notestein (1945) only once "for a statement by a demographic of the theory".

4. Hodgson (1983) discusses the theoretical antecedents of the work of these two authors and gave prominence to the work of W. Thompson (1929) in particular. Szereter (1991) discusses Thompson's claim to priority. I shall not be concerned with this substory in what follows.

5. Szereter (1991, Footnote 14) quotes T. W. Schultz's approval of this typology, "These types are much needed building blocks for social analysis."

6. Notestein (1945, 39-40) writes, "Any society having to face the heavy mortality characteristic of the premodern era must have high fertility to survive. Religious doctrines, moral codes, laws, education, community customs, marriage habits, and family organizations are all focussed towards maintaining high fertility."

7. This statement is particularly interesting in the light of current developments in the 1994 Cairo Meeting.

8. Statements such as these cry for precise, and empirically measurable, definitions of the term modernization.

9. It is worthy of note that education is adduced as an explanatory variable under both stages; this ambivalence presumably reflects a change in the type of education.

10. Notestein (1945, 41) continues in terms of an empirical instantiation, "However, during that period the population of European extraction had increased nearly seven fold throughout the world."

11. Notestein also singles out the fact that in this stage "the family lost many of its functions to the factory, the school, and commercial enterprises."

12. Szereter (1995) remarks that the second half of Notestein's 1945 paper "comprises a pocket political manifesto against the demographic dangers and shortcomings of the colonial past."

13. Hodgson (1983, 8-9) remarks that the founders of the theory, Thompson and Kirk, in addition to Notestein and Davis, had virtually identical contentions in this regard.

14. The modernization of India under British rule is also referred to as one-sided modernization by Davis in 1944; it was one in which "changes conducive to mortality decline were all characterized by "their alien origin and their non-interference with daily life"; the "texture of Indian life" had undergone no substantial alteration" (Hodgson 1983, 14).

15. Szereter (1991, 666) quotes Kirk's 1943 statement that "In regard to demographic matters the different countries of the world may be considered as on a single continuum of development."

16. Hodgson (1983), for example, introduces his article with the statement, "The change in demographic thinking in the United States from 1945 to 1955 is the central phenomenon being examined." See also Szereter (1991).

17. In a 1944 paper, Notestein was to write, "There is no quick demographic solution to the problem of population pressure." In a 1944 piece, Notestein writes, "The dissemination of contraceptive knowledge as the sole solution to the problems of population pressure is of little importance"; see Szereter (1991, 668). Demeny (1986, 473) put the matter thus: "From the 1960s onwards, improved methods of contraception gave some promise of a technological fix."

18. The reader is also referred to this article for a precise reference to Davis's question.

19. See also Szereter (1991, Footnote 50).

20. See Hodgson (1988, 183) and Szereter (1991) for the importance of People's Republic of China and India in the thinking of the period, and particularly that of Davis and Notestein. It is interesting that this emphasis on People's Republic of China and India continues even in current debates; see, for example, Sen's (1994) piece.

21. There is an interesting ambiguity in the relevant literature, and even in my discussion of it in the section above, as to whether it was describing the past or predicting the future.

22. In a 1954 paper, Davis asks, "Can the various phases of social economic modernization be deliberately transposed and foreshortened, or must they be viewed as a rigidly fixed sequence of necessary steps?" (quoted by Hodgson 1983, 19).

23. Hodgson (1983, 12-13) quotes Notestein from a 1953 paper, "It is within the bounds of possibility that the wise use of modern methods of communication and training to promote higher marriage age and the practice of birth control would bring a considerable reduction of the birth rate even in peasant societies."

24. This would involve "changing conditions of life and thus forcing people in their private capacity to seek the means of family limitation"; see Davis (1951, 230).

25. Ricoeur invokes Husserl to refer to these historical communities as "personalities of the highest order".

26. See Hodgson (1983, 18-19, 13) who also quotes Notestein from a 1954 paper, "Most people, however uneducated, are far from stupid."

27. See the forthcoming Handbook of Population and Family Economics and the references therein.

28. Becker (1993, 386) writes, "Different   constraints are decisive for different situations, but the most fundamental constraint is limited time."

29. For references to surveys and other expository accounts, see Khan (1979) and Birdsall (1988).

30. For the precise statements, see Muellbauer (1974); Pollak and Wachter (1975); and Khan (1979, Theorems 1 and 2, 9) for an exposition.

31. Hodgson mentions that by the end of the 1960s, 400 such surveys had been carried out.

32. Birdsall devotes a subsection within her treatment of the macroeconomic approaches to Malthus and successor pessimists.

33. For a treatment of the literature in terms of this "puzzle", see Liebenstein (1974, 1975) and Keeley (1975).

34. Birdsall (1988, Section 4.3.4) references Kelley's work on the relationship.

35. For an extended discussion of education as a commodity, see Khan (1993).

36. In terms of space, Birdsall mentions the "poorest countries of Asia and South Africa", and in terms of time, the short run versus the long instantiated by the "United States in the 1950s".

37. In his Nobel lecture, Becker alludes to the emotional commitment and sustained intellectual effort that was involved in developing the economics of the family; see Becker (1993, 395; paragraphs 4 and 5).

38. The structure of Becker's Nobel Lecture is as follows: leaving concluding remarks aside, a short introduction to the economic approach is followed by sections on *Discrimination against minorities*, on *Crime and punishment*, on *Human capital*, and on *Formation, dissolution and structure of families*. Becker (p. 395) refers to the last section as dealing with topics that are "still quite controversial", and devotes only four paragraphs to fertility.

39. The terminology is also due to Easterlin himself; see, for example, Easterlin (1978) and Easterlin and Crimmons (1982).

40. For more details, see Easterlin (1978) and Easterlin et al. (1980) in particular.

41. This denotes "the number (or usually proportion) of eligible (of reproductive age, not pregnant etc.) women in a sample who say they want no more children or want to delay childbirth, but are not using contraception. It is not equivalent to the economic concept of unmet demand, as it does not take into account any cost constraint, monetary or otherwise, to the use of contraception"; see Birdsall (1988, 525).

42. See Birdsall (1988, 509) for a discussion of the work of Wolfe and Behrman.

43. My emphasis.

44. My emphasis.

45. For more details, see the entire section titled *Archives, documents, traces* on pages 116-126.

46. Birdsall seems unwilling to "commodify" religion, as in the work of Ehrenberg and others on the "economics of church attendance". However, she is well aware of the importance of the variable. "If the Moslem religion causes high fertility, for example, and is negatively correlated with school enrollment (as it is), then the coefficient of enrollment will be upwardly biased in a specification excluding religion"; see Birdsall (1988, 512). Of course this statement, particularly in its assertion of "as it is", raises fascinating epistemological and ontological questions.

47. Birdsall qualifies this by leaving open the possibility of reinterpretation whereby "price and income changes are very broadly conceived to include institutional and historical factors (political change, the decline of religion, the rise and fall of communities)"; see Birdsall (1988, 512). It is precisely this possibility of interpretation and reinterpretation of diverse factors in terms of those of a particular metaphoric framework that is one of the primary motivations behind this essay.

48. Pritchett (1994a) writes, "The two most potent objections to the use of desired fertility as an explanatory variable can be overcome by using both retrospective (was a previous birth wanted?) and prospective (is another birth wanted?) data on desired fertility. Neither ex post rationalization of prior births nor the influence of contraceptive costs on reported fertility desires determines the empirical results.

49. The Bangladeshi and the first Pakistani analysis is based on the *National Impact Survey* conducted in undivided Pakistan in 1968/1969. The second Pakistani analysis is based on the *Demographic and Health Survey* conducted in 1990/1991. The Egyptian analysis is based on the *Egyptian Fertility Survey* conducted in 1980. For details, see Sirageldin et al. (1976), Khan and Sirageldin (1981), Cochrane et al. (1990), and Khan and Malik (1994).

50. For an earlier model, see Cochrane and Bean (1976) and Mason and Taj (1987).

51. See Khan and Sirageldin (1981) and Khan and Malik (1994). The former with simultaneous probit analysis, and the latter also presents estimates obtained through a bivariate probit model.

52. See Khan and Sirageldin (1983) for an estimation of simultaneous probit equations.

53. Such a model would directly respond to Birdsall's interest in religious questions; see Footnote 46. Also see Jenson (1985) and Riley et al. (1993).

54. I have in mind recent reports in the popular press as to the increased demand for abortion services based on the gender of the fetus.

55. Pritchett (1994b, 621) adds "Desired fertility plus a constant is an excellent prediction of actual fertility."

56. As was to be expected, epistemological questions were bound to surface. Knowles et al. (1994) write in their response to Pritchett, "As we have all been taught with respect to empirical research, no set of results ever proves or disproves a theory (e.g., that family planning programs have, or do not have, a significant impact on fertility). I find the inclusion of the word "disprove" interesting indeed.

57. Pritchett continues, "It is tempting to hope that something relatively cheap and easy, like subsidizing contraceptive services, could solve the problem. Reducing fertility is best seen as a broad problem of improving economic and social conditions, especially for women: raising their levels of education, their economic position, their (and their children's) health, and their role and status in society. This is a task altogether more difficult, but with more promise than manipulating contraceptive supply."

58. My emphasis.

59. Bongaarts notes, "About one in four births in the developing world (excluding People's Republic of China) is unwanted—a total of some 25 million per year. In addition, approximately 25 million abortions are performed annually in developing countries, often under unsafe conditions."

60. Also see the last section on *The larger issue* in Pritchett (1994b).

61. "The much broader and powerful influence programs can have by reducing noneconomic costs of contraceptive use such as lack of knowledge,

fear of side effects and social and familial disapproval," see Bongaarts (1994, 619) and Knowles et al. (1994, 614).

62. See Bongaarts (1994, 619) who involves Cassen. I shall have more to say on this below in the context of Sen's work.

63. The use of incremental R^2, Pritchett's Tables 6 and 7 on the costs of children versus contraceptive costs, definition of variables, biases in data and questions of rationalization. Knowles et al. (1994, 611, 613-614) write, "The dramatic result ... is an artifact of the model. The empirical analysis is seriously flawed by his use of an essentially tautological statistical model." Bongaarts goes into what I earlier referred to as first order of discourse—rationalization in desired fertility rates is "largest in the WFS Surveys of the 1970s".

64. In a recent report, for example, one reads: "Normally, women of all races give birth to about 105 or 106 boys for every 100 girls. People's Republic of China's ratio in 1992 was about 13 points off this international norm, meaning that more than 12 percent of all female fetuses were aborted or otherwise unaccounted for." See, for example, the article by N. D. Kristof in *The New York Times*, July 21, 1993, titled "Peasants of China discover new way to weed out girls"; also Sen (1990) and related references for India.

65. See, for example, the canonical works of Samuelson (1947, Chapter 7), Graaff (1957), and Debreu (1959).

66. Note that the use of the revisionist label differs from that of Szereter (1994) where it is used synonymously for the orthodox view. Demeny dates official revisionism to the United Nations International Conference on Population held in Mexico City in 1984. Referring to the statement of the American delegation, he writes that it "caused enormous irritation in and outside the Conference chamber and was widely condemned as a diversionary tactic. Yet no one tried to refute the argument. History's testimony suggests that there is a great deal of truth to it"; see Demeny (1986, 475, 479).

67. Referring to the 200-item bibliography of the 1986 National Council Report, Demeny (1988, 485) writes, "As is the case in much of the economic literature, memory falls off sharply beyond the last five years. One looks in vain ... for names like Frank Notestein, Kinsley Davis, Joseph Spengler or Judith Blake. Or names like Kenneth Boulding, Garett Hardin, James Meade, and Jan Tinbergen."

68. "In this, [Malthus's] approach is somewhat like that of the average practitioner of the new home economics"; see Demeny (1986, 481).

69. Birdsall divides the substance of her survey into three parts: macroeconomic analyses, microeconomic foundations, and the welfare economics of public policies. "The issue is whether individual or household fertility decisions will bring about a socially optimal size and growth rate of population (in the absence of any purposeful intervention" (Birdsall 1988, 522).

70. There has been some discussion in the literature on pecuniary externalities; see Srinivasan (1987). Birdsall (1988, 524) refers to the depression of wages as a consequence of population growth as a pecuniary externality: "Only if one views a reduction in poverty incidence as a public good can the effect of population growth be construed as a true (non-pecuniary) externality."

71. In the same paragraph, Becker writes, "Along with others, I have tried to pry economists away from narrow assumptions about self-interest. Behavior is driven by a much richer set of values and preferences." In the same article (p. 400), he writes "Economic theory, especially game theory, needs to incorporate guilt, affection, and related attitudes into preferences in order to have a deeper understanding of when commitments are credible."

72. Birdsall (1988, 526) observes that such payments take up "20 percent of total public spending on family planning programs in India and Sri Lanka".

73. Birdsall (1988, 527) has the Chinese one-child policy in mind; also Singapore.

74. See Birdsall (1988, 527). Mirrlees (1972, 169-170) also questions the necessary implication that a response to incomplete and imperfect information about contraceptive technology necessarily implies that policies should be taken to reduce the birth rate.

75. Demeny also identifies an early collaborator writing in the 1830s, a mathematician and economist W.F. Lloyd. "The simple fact of a country being overly populous ... is not, of itself, sufficient evidence that the fault lies in the people themselves, or the proof of the absence of a prudential disposition. The fault may rest, not with them as individuals but with the constitution of the society of which they are a part."

76. Thus, Birdsall (1988, 522) is led to Bentham and Mill while Demeny (1986, 487) ends his essays by invoking Rawls.

77. Demeny (1986, 476) takes it as "axiomatic that [couples] will choose what is best for them, given their circumstances. There is no escape from this assumption if we are to avoid crass paternalism."

78. "Think of an economy in which the typical family consists of a husband, who earns income in the labor market, wife who works in the home, and children." Mirrlees (1972, 193) is of course aware of the restrictiveness of this conception, "It will be recognized that this picture ignores the considerable number of households that contain less than, or more than, the nuclear family, but these raise quite different questions which are not at issue here."

79. "I shall not attempt to solve this problem in its full generality, since it seems to be hard." It is also interesting that Mirrlees begins his article with the statement, "Population is a difficult subject."

80. "I believe that uncertainty is not inconsiderable, particularly in developing countries. It may be argued ... that where uncertainty is greatest, deliberation in the choice of family size is least. This possibility, although it can hardly be so completely true as to render the following analysis inapplicable, should be borne in mind when we come to conclusions" (Mirrlees 1972, 172). Elsewhere (p. 194), "Models in which there is uncertainty about family size are not very satisfactory."

81. "Much of the uncertainty that certainly exists should be regarded as variations in fertility, since actual decisions can be taken sequentially. Nevertheless, ... the relevant level of inclination, effort, discipline, and education in developing countries will be influenced by the relation between economic prospects and family size; and that uncertainty about family size is a reason for not recommending grave penalties for those who exceed whatever is taught to be the ideal size" (Mirrlees 1972, 194-195).

82. "We have sufficient evidence to distinguish, with imperfect but adequate accuracy, between families likely to produce children with high social productivity and those whose children will have low social marginal productivity. It is clear what implications this proposition has, in conjunction with the above analysis: the State would wish to subsidize production of people who are likely to contribute substantially to its tax revenues." See also Hodgson (1991) for the eugenic movement and its consequence for population and US immigration polices in the 1920s.

83. "One is inclined to think that population is essentially a dynamic topic, but the points that I have already suggested need analysis all arise in a timeless context. [Nevertheless,] we should not be unaware of the essentially temporal structure of those problems. In any case, the dynamic formulations I have looked at seem too difficult for me." See Mirrlees (1972, 171, 197).

84. This is exactly the topic of Keynes' Galton Lecture.

85. Mirrlees (1972, 169) writes, "I suspect, however, that people generally jump to the conclusion that population is a great problem. and that they would be hard pressed to give a precise statement of the 'problem' and a detailed argument for massive state intervention in this area."

86. Mirrlees (1972) also begins his article by addressing the position that "current birth rates will lead to indescribable disasters. Exact consequences are left obscure and the counterargument of equilibration is not met."

87. Thus Pritchett (1994a, 1) writes "Even those skeptical about the destructive power of the population bomb should be convinced that the political, economic, and environmental landscape of the next century will be greatly affected by the speed of the demographic transition in developing countries."

88. The fact is that 90 percent of the population growth is taking place in the developing world, and of the worldwide increase of 923 million people in the 1980s, well over half occurred in Asia: 517 million, including 146 million in the People's Republic of China and 166 million in India; for all of these figures, see Sen (1994, 62).

89. "Many Northerners fear being engulfed by people from Asia and Africa, whose share of the world population increased from 63.7 percent in 1950 to 71.2 percent by 1990, and is expected according to UN estimates to rise to 78.5 percent by 2050 (p. 63)."

90. Demeny (1986, 473) writes, referring to the early 1960s onward, "Policy measures to shape fertility behavior were increasingly applied. They included measures to deliberately change peoples' values, manipulation of relevant economic and social incentives, and in some instances a direct command mandating conformity to standards set by the political process." All of these measures would come under my reading, at any rate, as overriding.

91. Sen gives examples of Mrs. Gandhi's policy of compulsory birth control, but also of the PRC government's forfeiture of housing from couples with too many children.

92. One can read a mild dissent in Demeny (1986, 480), "[Engels] estimate of the ability of a communist state to regulate population was no doubt correct. Malthus's would have been: "Prudence cannot be enforced by laws without a great violation of natural liberty and a great risk of producing more evil than good." This is a good enough answer ... but it also reveals a fundamental weakness in the Malthusian conception."

93. This point of view is emphasized in Demeny (1988) and Hodgson (1991).

References

Arnold, F., and E. C. Y. Kuo, 1984. "The Value of Daughters and Sons: A Comparative Study of the Gender Preferences of Parents." *Journal of Comparative Family Studies* 15:299-318.

Balfour, M. C., et al., 1949. *Public Health and Demography in the Far East: Report of a Survey Trip.* New York: The Rockefeller Foundation.

Becker, G. S., 1960. "An Economic Analysis of Fertility." In Universities-National Bureau Committee for Economics Research, ed., *Demographic and Economic Change in Developed Countries.* Princeton: Princeton University Press.

———, 1965. "A Theory of the Allocation of Time." *Economics Journal* 76:493-517.

———, 1981. *A Treatise on the Family.* Cambridge: Harvard University Press. Enlarged ed., 1991.

———, 1993. Nobel Lecture: "The Economic Way of Looking at Behavior." *Journal of Political Economy* 101:385-409.

Bhushan, I., and D. L. Kincaid, 1994. "Do Family Planning Programs Matter?" The Johns Hopkins University. Mimeo.

Birdsall, N., 1988. "Economic Approaches to Population Growth." In H. Chenery and T. N. Srinivasan, eds., *Handbook of Development Economics,* Vol. 1. New York: Elsevier Science Publishers.

Bongaarts, J., 1994. "The Impact of Population Policies: Comments." *Population and Development Review* 20:616-20.

Cochrane, S. H., and F. D. Bean, 1976. "Husband-Wife Differences in the Demand for Children." *Journal of Marriage and Family* 38,2(May): 297-307.

Cochrane, S. H., M. Ali Khan, and I. K. T. Osheba, 1988. "The Determinants of the Demand for Children among Husbands and Wives." In A. M. Hallouda, S. M. Farid, and S. H. Cochrane, eds., *Egypt: Demographic Responses to Modernization.* Cairo: CAPMAS.

———, 1990. "Education, Income, and Desired Fertility in Egypt: A Revised Perspective." *Economic Development and Cultural Change* 38:313-39.

Davis, K., 1945. "The World Demographic Transition." *Annals of the American Academy of Political and Social Science* 237:1-11.

———, 1950. "Population and the Further Spread of Industrial Society." *Proceedings of the American Philosophical Society* 95:8-19.

———, 1951. *The Population of India and Pakistan.* Princeton: Princeton University Press.

Debreu, G., 1959. *Theory of Value.* New Haven: Yale University Press.

———, 1986. "Theoretic Models: Mathematical Form and Economic Content." *Econometrica* 54:1259-70.

Demeny, P., 1965. "Investment Allocation and Population Growth." *Demography* 2:203-32.

———, 1986. "Population and the Invisible Hand." *Demography* 23:473-88.

———, 1988. "Social Science and Population Policy." *Population and Development Review* 14:451-79.

———, 1994. "Population and Development." IUSSP Distinguished Lecture. International Union for the Scientific Study of Population, Belgium.

DeTray, D., 1984. "Son Preference in Pakistan." *Research in Population Economics* 5:185-200.

Easterlin, R. A., 1975. "An Economic Framework for Fertility Analysis." *Studies in Family Planning* 6:54-63.

———, 1978. "The Economics and Sociology of Fertility: A Synthesis." In C. Tilly, ed., *Historical Studies of Changing Fertility.* Princeton: Princeton University Press.

Easterlin, R. A., and E. M. Crimmons, 1982. "An Exploratory Study of the Synthesis Framework of Fertility Determination with World Fertility Survey Data." World Fertility Survey Scientific Report No. 40. London.

———, 1985. *Fertility Revolution: A Supply-Demand Analysis.* Chicago: University of Chicago Press.

Easterlin, R. A., R. A. Pollak, and M. L. Wachter, 1980. "Towards a More General Economic Model of Fertility Determination: Endogenous Preferences and Natural Fertility." In R. A. Easterlin, ed., *Population and Economic Change in Developing Countries.* Chicago: University of Chicago Press.

Graaff, J. de V., 1957. *Theoretical Welfare Economics.* Cambridge: Cambridge University Press.

Hauser, P., 1967. "Family Planning and Population Programs: A Book Review Article." *Demography* 4:397-414.

Hodgson, D., 1983. "Demography as Social Science and as Population Science." *Population and Development Review* 9:1-34.

———, 1988. "Orthodoxy and Revisionism in American Demography." *Population and Development Review* 14:541-69.

———, 1991. "The Ideological Origins of the Population Association of America." *Population and Development Review* 17:1-34.

Jenson, E., 1985. "Desired Fertility, the 'Up to God' Response, and Sample Selection Bias." *Demography* 22:445-54.

Johansson, S., and O. Nygren, 1993. "The Missing Girls of China: A New Demographic Account." *Population and Development Review* 17:35-42.

Keeley, M. S., 1975. "An Interpretation of the Economic Theory of Fertility." *Journal of Economic Literature* 113:461-68.

Kennedy, P., 1993. *Preparing for the 21st Century.* New York: Random House.

Keynes, J. M., 1937. "Some Economic Consequences of Declining Population." *Eugenics Review* 29:13-17. Reprinted in *Population and Development Review* 4:517-23.

Khan, M. Ali, 1979. "Relevance of Human Capital Theory to Fertility Research: Comparative Findings for Bangladesh and Pakistan." In I. Sirageldin, ed., *Research in Human Capital and Development.* Greenwich: JAI Press.

———, 1990. "In Praise of Development Economics." *Pakistan Development Review* 28:337-84.

———, 1991. "On the Languages of Markets." *Pakistan Development Review* 30:503-49.

———, 1993. "On Education as a Commodity." *Pakistan Development Review* 32:541-79.

Khan, M. Ali, and I Sirageldin, 1977. "Son Preference and the Demand for Additional Children." *Demography* 14:481-95.

———, 1979. "Education, Income and Fertility in Pakistan." *Economic Development and Cultural Change* 27(3):519-47.

———, 1981. "Intra-family Interaction and Desired Additional Fertility in Pakistan: A Simultaneous-Equation Model with Dichotomous Dependent Variables." *Pakistan Development Review* 20:7-60.

———, 1983. "How Meaningful are Statements about the Desired Number of Children? An Analysis of 1968 Pakistani Data." *Pakistan Development Review* 22:1-22.

Khan, M. Ali, and S. J. Malik, 1993. "Son Preference and Interspousal Communication in Desired Fertility in Pakistan." *International Food Policy Research Institute*. Mimeo.

Knodel, J., and V. Prachuabmoh, 1976. "Preference for Sex of Children in Thailand: A Comparison of Husbands' and Wives' Attitudes." *Studies in Family Planning* 7:137-43.

Knowles, J. C., J. S. Akin, and D. K. Guilkey, 1994. "The Impact of Population Policies: Comments." *Population Development Review* 20: 611-15.

Lancaster, K. J., 1966. "A New Approach to Consumer Theory." *Journal of Political Economy* 74:132-57.

Leibenstein, H., 1974. "An Interpretation of Economic Theory of Fertility: Promising Path of Blind Alley." *Journal of Economic Literature* 12:457-79.

———, 1975. "On Economic Theory of Fertility Decline: A Reply to Keeley." *Journal of Economic Literature* 13:469-71.

Mahmood N., 1992. "The Desire for Additional Children among Pakistani Women: The Determinants." *Pakistan Development Review* 31:1-30.

Marino A., 1971. "KAP Surveys and the Politics of Family Planning." *Concerned Demography* 3:36-75.

Mason, K. O., and A. M. Taj, 1987. "Women and Men's Reproductive Goals." *Population and Development Review* 13:611-38.

Mirrlees, J., 1972. "Population Policy and the Taxation of Family Size." *Journal of Public Economics* 1:169-98.

Muellbauer, J., 1974. "Household Production Theory: Quality and the Hedonic Technique." *American Economic Review* 64:977-94.

Muth, R. F., 1966. "Household Production and Consumer Demand Function." *Econometrica* 34:699-708.

Nerlove, M., 1974. "Household and Economy: Toward a New Theory of Population and Economic Growth." *Journal of Political Economy* 82: S200-18.

Notestein, F. W., 1945. "Population — The Long View." In T. W. Schultz, ed., *Food for the World*. Chicago: Chicago University Press.

Prachuabmoh, V., J. Knodel, and J. Alers, 1974. "Preference for Sons, Desire for Additional Children and Family Planning in Thailand." *Journal of Marriage and the Family* 36:601-14.

Pollak, R. A., and M. L. Wachter, 1975. "The Relevance of the Household Production Function and Its Implication for the Allocation of Time." *Journal of Political Economy* 83:255-78.

Pritchett, L. H., 1994a. "Desired Fertility and the Impact of Population Policies." *Population and Development Review* 20:1-55.

——, 1994b. "The Impact of Population Policies: Reply." *Population and Development Review* 20:621-30.

Repetto, R., 1972. "Son Preference and Fertility Behavior in Developing Countries." *Demography* 12:665-68.

Ricoeur, P. 1984. *Time and Narrative*, Vol. 1. Chicago: Chicago University Press.

——, 1988. *Time and Narrative*, Vol. 3. Chicago: Chicago University Press.

Riley, A. P., A. I. Hermalin, and L. Rosero-Bixby, 1993. "A New Look at the Determinant of Nonnumeric Response to Desired Family Size: The Case of Costa Rica." *Demography* 30:150-74.

Rostow, W. W., ed., 1963. *The Economics of Take-Off into Sustained Growth*. London: The MacMillan Press.

——, 1990. *Theorists of Economic Growth from David Hume to the Present*. New York: Oxford University Press, Inc.

——, 1991. *The Stages of Economic Growth*. Cambridge: Cambridge University Press [1960].

Rukanuddin, A. R., 1982. "Infant-Child Mortality and Son Preference as Factors in Influencing Fertility in Pakistan." *Pakistam Development Review* 21:297-328.

Samuelson, P. A., 1947. *Foundations of Economic Analysis*. Cambridge: Harvard University Press.

——, various years. *The Collected Scientific Papers*, Vols. 1-5. Cambridge: MIT Press.

Sen, A. K., 1983. "Economics and the Family." *Asian Development Review* 1:14-26.

——, 1990. "More Than 100 Million Women are Missing." *The New York Review of Books* 57(December 20).

——, 1994. "The Population Delusion." *The New York Review of Books* 61 (September 22).

Sirageldin, I., M. Ali Khan, A. Ariturk, and F. Shah, 1976. "Fertility Decisions and Desires in Bangladesh: An Econometric Investigation." *Bangladesh Development Studies* 4:329-50.

Solow, R. M., 1994. "Perspectives on Growth Theory." *Journal of Economic Perspectives* 8(1):45-54.

Srinivasan, T. N., 1987. "Population Growth and Economic Development." *Journal of Policy Modelling* 10(1):7-28.

Stigler, G. J., and G. S. Becker, 1977. "De gustibus non est disputandum." *American Economic Review* 67:76-90.

Szereter, S., 1993. "The Idea of Demographic Transition and the Study of Fertility Change: A Critical Intellectual History." *Population and Development Review* 19:659-701.

Thompson, W. S., 1929. "Population." *American Journal of Sociology* 34:959-75.

Tully, J., 1988. *Meaning and Context: Quentin Skinner and His Critics.* Princeton: Princeton University Press.

Van de Walle, E., 1992. "Fertility Transition, Conscious Choice and Numeracy." *Demography* 29(4):487-502.

Westoff, C. F., and R. R. Rindfuss, 1974. "Sex Preference in the United States: Some Implications." *Science* 184:633-36.

Williamson, N. E., 1983. "Parental Sex Preferences and Sex Selection." In N. G. Benett, ed., *Sex Selection of Children.* New York: Academic Press.

Author Index

Subject Index